Limi, the Land In-Between

Inner Asia Book Series

Edited by

David Sneath
Caroline Humphrey
Uradyn E. Bulag

VOLUME 17

The titles published in this series are listed at *brill.com/ias*

Limi, the Land In-Between

The Art of Governing a Buddhist Frontier Community in the Himalaya

By

Astrid Hovden

BRILL

LEIDEN | BOSTON

Cover illustration: Waltse village with Rinchen Ling monastery

Library of Congress Cataloging-in-Publication Data

Names: Hovden, Astrid, author.
Title: Limi, the Land in-between : the art of governing a Buddhist frontier community in the Himalaya / Astrid Hovden.
Description: Leiden ; Boston : Brill, 2025. | Series: Inner asia book series; vol.17 | Includes bibliographical references and index.
Identifiers: LCCN 2024037690 (print) | LCCN 2024037691 (ebook) | ISBN 9789004713666 (hardback) | ISBN 9789004714571 (ebook)
Subjects: LCSH: Customary law–Nepal. | Local government–Law and legislation–Nepal. | Villages–Law and legislation–Nepal. | Nepal–Boundaries–Tibet region. | Tibet region–Boundaries–Nepal. | Indigenous peoples–Legal status, laws, etc.–Nepal.
Classification: LCC KPK230 .H68 2025 (print) | LCC KPK230 (ebook) | DDC 954.96–dc23/eng/20240823
LC record available at https://lccn.loc.gov/2024037690
LC ebook record available at https://lccn.loc.gov/2024037691

Typeface for the Latin, Greek, and Cyrillic scripts: "Brill". See and download: brill.com/brill-typeface.

ISBN 978-90-04-71366-6 (hardback)
ISBN 978-90-04-71457-1 (e-book)
DOI 10.1163/9789004714571

This book is printed on acid-free paper and produced in a sustainable manner.

Contents

Note on Transliteration

Throughout the book I have employed an extended version (THL) of the common romanisation system developed by Turrel Wylie.[1] In order to facilitate comparison, all technical terms are presented in italics and rendered in Wylie transliteration. The pronunciation of Tibetan words differs significantly from their spelling. No standard system for phonetic rendering of Tibetan terms exists, and many different versions occur in the literature.[2] Standardisation is difficult because of the great variety of dialects, some of which, despite using the same written language, are mutually unintelligible. The Western Tibetan dialect spoken in Limi, sometimes referred to as Humli Tibetan, is classified as belonging to the south-western Tibetic languages.[3] Because of uncertain etymology and spelling I have chosen to render local place names and other proper nouns using a phonetic approximation. The term that indicates the inhabitants of the Limi valley is Limigya (Sle mi rgya) in the Limi dialect and Limiwa (Sle mi ba) in Central Tibetan.[4] I am using Limigya in the book, as the inhabitants of the Limi valley prefer to distinguish themselves from Central Tibetan.

As far as possible, the correct spelling of identifiable Tibetan terms is given in Wylie transliteration in parentheses after the first occurrence of the term. Capitalisation has been used only for the root letter in the first syllable of each name. The acronyms s.u. ('spelling uncertain') and d.u. ('date uncertain') are used when necessary. In my edited transliterations of historical and administrative documents from Limi, I have used the following system: cases of uncertain orthography are followed by question marks or commented in the footnotes, misspellings have been corrected and the original non-emended forms are given in square brackets afterwards, whereas necessary additions have been inserted in brackets. The most common Sanskrit, Nepali, and Tibetan terms that have become incorporated into the English language—such as stupa, lama, and rinpoche—have been treated as English terms. For titles of texts, names of people, places and technical terms in Sanskrit and Nepali, diacritics are given. A list of Tibetan technical terms and proper names has been provided in the glossary in the appendix.

---

1 Wylie 1959. The extended version has been made by the Tibetan and Himalayan Library (THL).

2 Attempts to establish a standard system for phonetic rendering of Tibetan have been made by THL.

3 See Tournadre 2014: 122 and 2015: 26–29.

4 In the Limi dialect, *rgya* is generally used as a plural marker for living beings, much in the same way as *rnams* is used in Central Tibetan.

Acknowledgements

Firstly, I owe my deepest gratitude to the people in Limi for sharing their knowledge with me, and for generously inviting me to partake in their lives—during hard times, as well as for rituals and feasts—both inside and outside the monastery walls. The fifteen months I spent in the valley will stay with me for the rest of my life. This book arises from those experiences and the invaluable support I have received from numerous people—too many to name individually. Many of the villagers spent significant amounts of time teaching me about both historical events and contemporary practices. While I am endlessly grateful for their patient help, I have chosen to anonymise them here to maintain confidentiality.

Hanna Havnevik, my main PhD supervisor, and later PI of the HimalConnect[1] research project, has given me unswerving support from the outset. I thank her for her encouragement, attentive reading of my drafts, numerous stimulating discussions, and, for always being there. Similarly, my co-supervisor, Charles Ramble, has provided generous guidance and inspiration throughout the PhD process, and especially in helping me decipher obscure handwriting in poorly spelled documents from remote Himalayan villages. Hildegard Diemberger, Co-I on the HimalConnect project has provided invaluable advice and support in turning the PhD into a book.

I thank Per Kværne for his careful reading of my thesis chapters and for his valuable suggestions on translations of difficult passages. I am also grateful to Mariette Wiebenga for commenting on a draft chapter and, most importantly, for opening the door to Limi for me. I would never have found my way there had it not been for her. Libby Peachey has provided invaluable assistance in the final phase of the work, offering editorial advice and meticulously proofreading the text. I am deeply grateful to Geoff Childs for his detailed comments and critical suggestions that significantly enhanced the quality of this manuscript and also to Patricia Radder and Peter Buschman at Brill, who have skilfully guided me through the publishing process with great patience and compassion. I thank Jacqueline Pitchford for her expertise and dedication in creating the book's index.

Phuntsok Dorje and Rinchen Loden were my field assistants during my first and the last four research stays respectively, and their contribution to this work

1 "Himalayan connections: melting glaciers, sacred landscape and new technology in a changing climate" (HimalConnect) is a Research Council of Norway (RCN) funded research collaboration between the University of Oslo, The University of Cambridge and UiT The Arctic University of Norway lasting from 2018–2023.

has been invaluable. Even post-fieldwork, we had numerous discussions, and they helped me tackle the poor communication infrastructure in Humla and Kathmandu to enable me to stay in contact with my Limi friends. Rinchen Loden supported me with unfailing positivity through the coldest winter months in Limi when temperatures crept down to minus twenty degrees Celsius and has continued to work with me until present. Dawa Tsering worked as translator for my two research trips to Limi in 2018 and 2019 and a number of other young Limigya including Tashi Lhazom, Tenzin Norbu, and Konchog were engaged for shorter stints. Yonten Gyatso, Tenzing, and Thobden Tsering contributed as field assistants for the HimalConnect team during joint fieldwork in 2018.

Thanks go to all the institutions that have supported the academic journey leading towards this book:

- The Department for Culture Studies and Oriental Languages (IKOS), the Faculty of Humanities at the University of Oslo (UiO) for funding my PhD project and for generous scholarships, which enabled me to conduct long term ethnographic fieldwork from 2010–2012.
- The Institute for Comparative Research in Human Culture for co-funding the PhD fieldwork from 2010–2012.
- The Network for University Cooperation Tibet-Norway for providing support on many levels: by employing me as teaching assistant and consultant and through grants.
- The Research Council of Norway for funding the HimalConnect research project through the NORGLOBAL-2 programme and for the Overseas Research Grant that enabled my fieldwork in 2018.
- The Department of Archaeology, History, Religious Studies and Theology at UiT The Arctic University of Norway for co-funding my research since 2019.
- The Williamson Fund for supporting the most recent fieldwork in 2019.

I am grateful to Melvyn Goldstein for his kind support from the very beginning of this project, and for sharing photos from his fieldwork in the 1970s with me. I thank Riamsara Kuyakanon for the many enlightening exhanges during years of work with the HimalConnect research project. In addition, I would like to give special mention of those with whom I have had valuable discussions at UiO: Heidi Fjeld, Inger Vasstveit, Axel Strøm, Theresia Hofer, Thea Vidnes, my fellow PhD candidates, and not least, all the Tibetan and Bhutanese scholars and students that I have been fortunate to get to know throughout my years at IKOS. Similarly, I would like to express my gratitude to Charles Ramble, Peter Schwieger, Jeannine Bischoff, Alice Travers, Berthe Jansen, Kalsang Norbu, Nanda Pirie and other affiliates of the research project Social History of Tibetan Societies for inspiring conversations and for inviting me to join their conferences. Their passion for social history in general and Tibetan documents in particular proved to be infectious.

In Kathmandu, my thanks go to the International Centre for Integrated Mountain Development (ICIMOD), which hosted me as a research associate between 2018 and 2023. I learned so much from cooperating with Janita Gurung at the Kailash Sacred Landscape Conservation and Development Initiative (KSLCDI) programme and her knowledgeable colleagues. I am also very grateful to Tshewang Lama, also known as Chhakka Bahadur, and the generosity with which he shared his knowledge about Humli culture and history through hours of conversations in Kathmandu and Simikot. I thank Professor Ramesh Dunghel and Centre for Nepal and Asian Studies for hosting me as research affiliate at Tribhuvan University from 2010–12. I am grateful for all that I learned from the teachers and fellow language students at Rangjung Yeshe Institute at Kathmandu University in 2009. Furthermore, I want to thank Ian and Lois Alsop and Mary Shaffer, who I was fortunate to have as travel companions from Kathmandu to Limi during late autumn 2011, for their support.

Olav Myrholt and The Norwegian Development Fund, the Norway Nepal association, Brian Peniston and Meeta Pradhan at The Mountain Institute, Mimi Church, as well as the Kathmandu and Simikot staff of The Nepal Trust all gave me valuable advice and assistance. Moreover, it has been inspiring to collaborate with Jan Kropáček across very different academic disciplines.

But my final and warmest thanks go to my dear family: my partner Hans Olav and our twin daughters, Frida and Live, who were born just as I was about to draft the conclusion. An especially heartfelt thanks to my parents, Arvid and Liv, who have been of immense support in so many ways.

Illustrations

All photos are made by the author, unless otherwise mentioned.

Charts

Figures

Maps

Tables

Maps

MAP 1 Nepal and Tibet

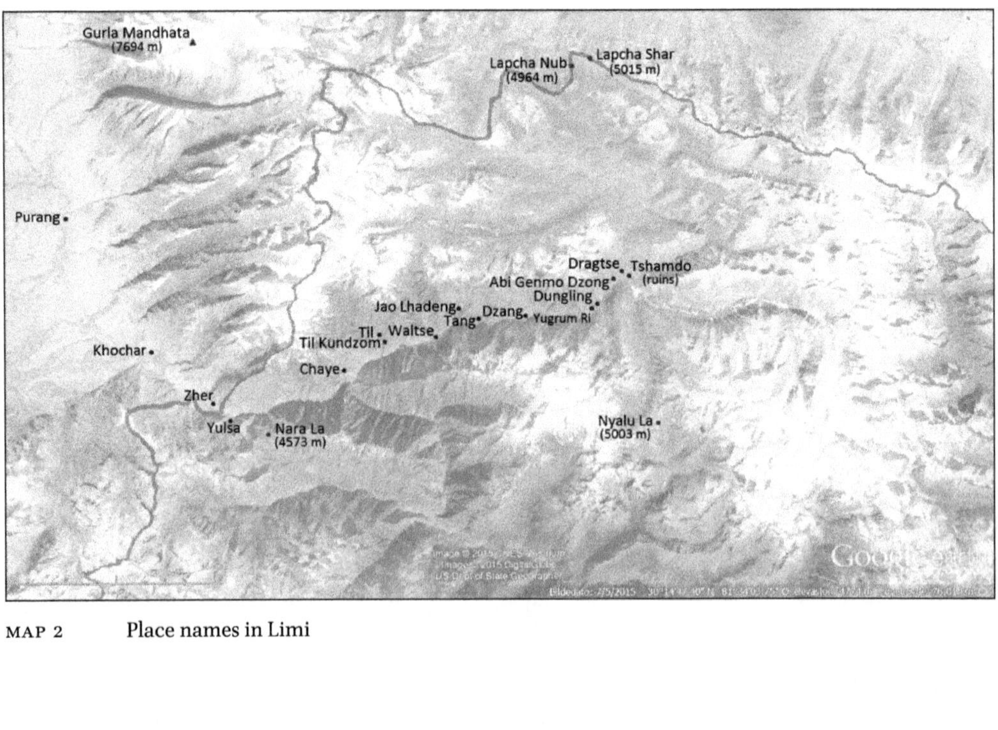

MAP 2 Place names in Limi

CHAPTER 1

Locating Limi

> In June 2015, during the annual assembly meeting in Dzang, one of the villages in Limi, a group of young men presented a request to the representatives. They wanted to end the monk levy, erase the divisions between household categories, and abolish the rule that forces young men back to the village to take over household responsibilities on the retirement of their fathers. The meeting lasted for many days. People from Waltse and Til, fearing repercussions in their own villages, came to persuade the youth to withdraw the request, but they were turned down. The young men argued that the monk levy was an outdated rule instigated according to old Tibetan Buddhist management principles; they wanted to follow the current Nepali system instead. After a long and heated debate, the representatives decided to abolish the levy and agreed that the Nepali laws should be fully implemented. The monks withdrew, handed over the responsibility of the monastery to the village assembly and a new monastic management committee was formed. However, the change did not last for long. Unable to make the Nepali system fit the local conditions and needs, the villagers returned to their old ways of governing after only a few months.

∴

When the villagers first told me about this meeting, I was just about to submit my PhD thesis and had already spent years studying the local system of governance in this Buddhist frontier community. But learning about the generational revolt and the reactions prompted me to think more deeply about both the strengths of the local management system as well as the tensions and challenges that it provoked. Located at the outer margins of the state, Limi has a history of governing its internal affairs that dates back as far as both oral and written memory goes. How the villagers have navigated between shifting Tibetan and Nepali secular and religious administrative cultures and how they have been impacted by larger regional and global processes are central themes in this book. The aim is to provide an understanding of the art of governance

 | DOI:10.1163/9789004714571_002

in a situation of transition and 'in-betweenness' in this remote high-mountain community. But what does 'the art of governing' Limi involve? In this book I use the term art evocatively, in order to show how governing a community such as Limi requires mastery, creativity and navigating complex loyalties and senses of belonging. As a working definition of the 'governing' I adapt Brown et al.'s understanding of governance as 'The process of collective decision-making and policy implementation, used distinctly from government to reflect broader concern with norms and processes relating to the delivery of public goods' to the local context.[1] Given the limited role of the state in Limi and the community's adherence to its own customary laws, I find such a broader approach helpful to understand local governance.[2]

1.1 The Many Meanings of the Name

The name Limi (Sle mi) can be translated as 'the Land in-between'. The villagers explain that the meaning of the name comes from the first settlement in the valley, located on a piece of land between two rivers (Fig. 1.2). Now, Limi refers to a community[3] of three Tibetan speaking villages, Til (Til), Waltse (dBal rtse) and Dzang ('Dzang), located in north-western Nepal, just south of the border with Tibet Autonomous Region, China. While the 'betweenness' in the name refers to its geographical location, it is suggestive also of a number of other socio-cultural, religious, political, environmental and economic relations and processes, which will be discussed throughout the book.

Locating Limi is not as straightforward as one might think. The Limigya (Sle mi rgya)[4] have a strong sense of belonging to the villages and environment, at the same time as they are highly mobile. Although seasonal mobility has been an important part of Limi life throughout history, migration has intensified and

1 Brown et al. 2018.

2 While governance is theorised in multiple ways in scholarly literature in general, and in literature on Tibet and the Himalaya in particular, I adopt a flexible approach to the term to reflect collective decision-making mechanisms in this local context. This working definition is intentionally broad to accommodate local structures and practices without being limited by theoretical debates. My goal is to align as closely as possible with the vernacular, using English terms that elucidate local specificities, which can sometimes diverge from theoretical models. The exploration of how this study can contribute to broader theoretical debates on governance will be addressed in a separate article.

3 The second syllable in Limi, *mi*, can be translated either as people or as short for *mi sde* meaning community.

4 As mentioned in the note on transliteration, I have chosen to refer to the inhabitants in the local dialect as Limigya (Sle mi rgya) rather than in Central Tibetan (Sle mi ba). Similarly, I prefer the local Tibetan village name Waltse over the Nepali name Halji.

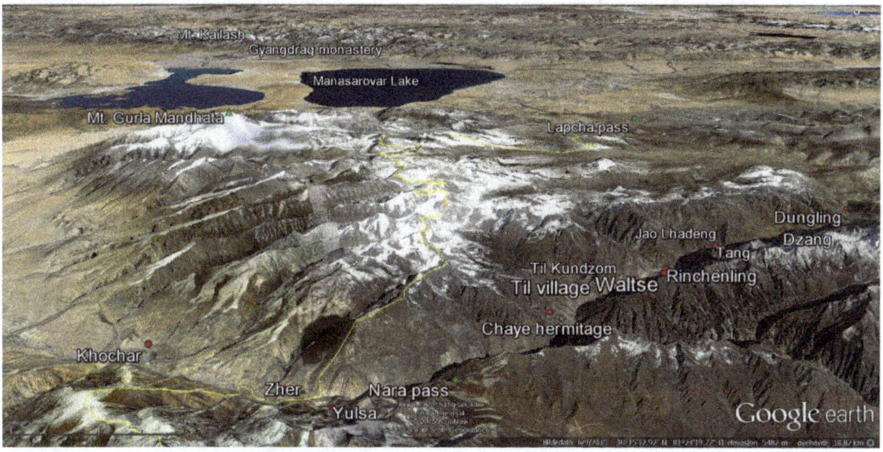

FIGURE 1.1 The Gurla Mandhata Massif with the Limi valley to the south (Google Earth)

FIGURE 1.2 Land at the confluence of the two rivers giving name to Limi

shifted in character the last two decades, as in so many other high Himalayan communities.[5] Most outmigrated villagers live in Kathmandu, many children and youth go to school in India, but some have also migrated and settled in

5 See Childs and Choedup (2019) for the most updated study of migration from high mountain communities in Nepal. See also Craig's (2020) study of outmigrated Nepali residents in New York.

several countries throughout the world, with a sizeable group currently living in New York. Whilst acknowledging the impact of these broader networks, this book will take the villages as its focal point.[6]

Each of the three villages has its own village assembly (*'du ma* or *yul gyi 'du ma*)[7] and monastery belonging to the Drigung Kagyu ('Bri gung bKa' rgyud) school of Tibetan Buddhism. The villagers have historically governed their community and environment through a comprehensive set of laws and customary practices, partly administered by the village assembly, partly by the monastic institution and partly by the two in collaboration. Such a combined wordly and religious model of governance (*chos srid zung 'brel*) has a long history throughout the Tibetan Buddhist world, with significant variation across time and space and depending on the communities' relations to shifting state formations as well as school of Buddhism and type of institution.[8]

The village assembly is a traditional management system that is not formally recognised in Nepal. However, in high mountain communities where the state presence has been weak, such institutions have effectively functioned as local governments. Yet, studies of comparable communities, such as Mustang and Nubri, show that the forms this has taken, and the degree of autonomy has varied.[9] The many changes in the Nepali government system since the overthrow of the Rana dynasty in the middle of the twentieth century have also affected these local governance practices. While adapting to a minimum of the requirements of the Nepali state, local village assemblies are still where most of the local decision-making takes place in Limi and other high mountain communities in the country. However, the New Constitution in 2015 and the subsequent federalisation of Nepal in 2017, with the restructuring of the government at all levels, have created new challenges, which are being addressed in a variety of ways, and is necessitating a stronger integration with the Nepali state.

6 Rather than looking at the villages as bounded entities, I find Sara Shneiderman's (2015: 319) approach, arguing for an understanding of '… the village as a flexible set of social relations within which the villagers 'orient themselves subjectively regardless of their physical location' useful. See also Childs and Choedup 2019: 5.

7 Yeh (2021: 936) writes that they use the word *zhung* [*gzhung*], but this might be based on a misunderstanding or translation issue. In Limi the word *gzhung* is used for 'government' when talking about national governments such as the Nepali government or the past Tibetan government (*sde ba gzhung*), but not for the internal village assembly, which is referred to by the term *'du ma* or *yul gyi 'du ma*.

8 See for instance the volume edited by Cüppers (2000), which provides analyses of the *chos srid* model at various locations throughout history.

9 See for instance Ramble 2008a, Childs and Choedup 2019.

FIGURE 1.3 Waltse village

FIGURE 1.4 Rinchen Ling monastery

FIGURE 1.5 Dzang village and Phelgye Ling monastery

FIGURE 1.6 Til village

FIGURE 1.7 Til Kundzom monastery

1.1.1 *Objectives*

Taking a longitudinal perspective, this book seeks to understand how people in Limi have managed their community and environment through local institutions and customary law, and how this local government system has variously been maintained, adapted and changed in the context of socio-economic and political transformations in Nepal and the broader region as well as global development. Understanding governance in a community like Limi requires attention not only to the secular village administration,[10] but also to the central role of the Buddhist monastery in managing the local community and the cooperation between them. This interplay is complicated, and the book explores the monastery's involvement as ritual provider for the villagers, collector of taxes, its impact on the village economy and its role in local

10 A cautionary note needs to be made when using the word 'secular' in this context. While Tibetan culture operates with a distinction between the dharma and the worldly (as in the compound *chos srid*) this distinction does not map perfectly onto the western distinction of sacred and secular. For instance, what I refer to in the book as secular institutions, like the village assembly, are significantly involved in religious activities. See e.g., Cüppers (2000).

governance and environmental management through monks' participation in decision-making and conflict resolution bodies.

I have chosen to couple a predominantly empirical ethnographic approach[11] with a historical perspective to document and analyse how the local systems of governing the village and environment have developed and changed over time and to gain a deeper understanding of recent and ongoing practices, processes and problems. While I have traced events back to the foundation of the first temple at the dawn of the eleventh century, most of the historical material concerns events from the end of the nineteenth century onwards. This period is covered in local administrative documents and is still part of the collective memory in the villages. The main focus, however, will be on the more recent decades and especially from the 1990s onwards. My last fieldwork ended in 2019, and I have with very few exceptions decided not to include any updates after that.

The historical material consists mainly of chronicles and religious biographies from the broader region, as well as local administrative documents which have been crucial for the understanding of the local legal system. Partly because of their inaccessibility, such documents have often been ignored in ethnographic studies of Himalayan communities, with the works of Charles Ramble, Christian Jahoda and Geoff Childs and Namgyal Choedup among the most notable exceptions.[12] Whilst a comprehensive study of the local archives falls beyond the scope of this book, I found this coupling of ethnographic material with the study of historical and administrative documents invaluable, not only in grasping the details of social organisation and government practices, but also in acquiring a better understanding of local agency in the processes of change. Moreover, while keeping the main focus on local agency and structures, I have tried to pay attention to the socio-economic, religious and political context at regional, national and international levels in order to understand the dynamics influencing processes of continuity and change in Limi. I will argue that much of the development in Limi can only be understood against the background of these larger processes. Moreover, comparison with relevant cases from the broader region has, I hope, helped me to avoid some of the insularity for which traditional village ethnographies have been criticised, and to understand the trans-local aspects of the local transformation processes.

---

11 Fieldwork was conducted in 2010–2012 and in 2018–19. See Chapter Two for details on method.

12 See for instance Ramble 2008a, b and c and 2012a and b, Jahoda 2015 and Childs and Choedup 2019.

When I first arrived in Waltse in 2010, after six days on foot from the district capital Simikot, the community had just got its first telephone.[13] Until then, the nearest phone had been located across the border, in Purang (sPu hreng),[14] two days' walk from Limi. When I returned to the village in 2018, I was able to hitch a ride half the way with trucks and jeeps and the first thing one of the monks asked me was how he could add me on Facebook. The old phone house had been moved, and a brand-new Rural Municipality ward office with a computer, printer and a Nepali national flag at the desk had been constructed next to it. The changes were striking, and indicative of the opening-up that had taken place, though they also brought a new set of complexities that will be explored throughout the book.

1.2 Two Systems of Governance

The villages in Limi have traditionally been governed by a set of village headmen, who preside over the village assembly and manage the community according to a detailed set of customary laws, many of which are recorded in Tibetan language in the local archive. The village assemblies (*'du ma, yul gyi 'du ma*) consist of the male head of each of the households (*kha rgan*) and serve as the main decision-making body in the villages. In the past, the position of headman was hereditary. However, in recent decades, all the village management posts as well as the officials and the responsibility to act as watchmen have been rotating, with the decision-making taking place through a type of direct democracy. Whilst only laymen participate in the assembly, there is a strong cooperation with the monastic institution in areas such as economy, welfare, environmental management, and in certain decision-making and higher-level conflict resolution processes.

Throughout history, the Nepali system of governance has been through a number of changes, to which Limi has had to adapt: from 1962, Limi was made a panchayat,[15] and from the 1990s, Limi became a Village Development Committee (VDC). Yet, Limi constituted a separate administrative unit and

13 The phone, which was a Nepal Telecom satellite phone, had been installed just a few weeks prior to my arrival in July 2010.

14 Purang is also spelled sPu hrengs, Pu hrang, and Pu rang in historical documents. The spelling Burang is used on Chinese maps.

15 The panchayat system, which was implemented in 1962 and prevailed until 1990, was a system of elected councils, introduced after a brief experiment with multi-party democracy after the fall of the Ranas in 1951. During the panchayat period, political parties were forbidden.

integrated only an absolute minimum of Nepali state regulations, governing the community according to their own customary laws. In 2017, with the introduction of the three-tiered government structure in Nepal, however, the former Limi VDC was merged with three other VDCs to form Namkha (Nam bkha') Rural Municipality (RM).[16] One of the main purposes of the restructuring of the state was to decentralise power and the new large municipalities in Humla do indeed have more power and higher budgets than the former VDCs. However, the new municipalities are ruled according to Nepali policies and practices, and this forces the local Tibetan speaking communities to integrate and implement the Nepali management system to a much larger degree than in the past. Recently, the management system has bifurcated: one set of local leaders govern the village according to customary law in cooperation with the monastery, and the other set of leaders have Nepali administrative titles and deal with affairs related to the Nepali government.

1.2.1 *Environment, Economy, and Infrastructure*

The Limi territory is cut off from the Western Tibetan plateau by the Gurla Mandhata Massif (7694 m), which towers above the border (Fig. 1.1). Gurla Mandhata is regarded as the abode of Drabli Gyalmo (sGra bla'i rGyal mo), 'Queen of the warrior deities.' Tshewang Lama writes that in Humla the deity is also sometimes referred to as Gangkar Lhamo (Gangs dkar lHa mo), 'Goddess of the white snow'. Another Tibetan name of the mountain is Memo Nagnyil (sMan mo Nag snyil); the *sman mo* are a wrathful type of spirit forming the female retinue of the goddess, and Nagnyil refers to the 'black fringes'[17] or dark eroded valleys that have been carved out by streams of meltwater from the glacier. In recent years, Waltse village has suffered at least six floods from a glacial lake in the Gurla Mandhata Massif, which destroyed houses, watermills, important infrastructure as well as a large number of fields and pastureland. The most recent flood, which occurred 30 June 2011 during my second period of fieldwork, washed away two houses and approximately one hundred fields, and covered another hundred with debris and silt. The recurring floods have been a matter of great concern in the village and much effort has been put into flood mitigation and adaptation both by the monks and the laity.[18] Other

16 Limi was merged with Hepka, Khagalgaun and Muchu VDC to form Namkha Rural Municipality in 2017.

17 To the Bonpos the mountain is known as Tagri Trawo (sTag ri Khra bo, 'the Striped Tiger mountain'). See Lama 2012: 108.

18 I published a brief eyewitness report in Nepali Times (Hovden 2011) just after the event. Further accounts of the flood and an analysis of local risk perceptions and adaptation strategies are provided in Diemberger, Hovden and Yeh (2015: 262–68), and Hovden

FIGURE 1.8 Houses destroyed by the flood in 2011

FIGURE 1.9 Rescuing the beams after the flood

consequences of a changing climate, such as a changing precipitation pattern, are also being felt in Limi, although they are not necessarily understood as such.[19]

Limi's location in a harsh mountain climate, has made it difficult to make a living out of agricultural and pastoralist activities alone. One of Melvyn Goldstein's findings in his research in the valley in the 1970s was that the population adapted to this vulnerability by economic triangulation between agro-pastoralism, trade, manual labour and craft production.[20] Agricultural output has been meagre and the Limigya have historically been completely dependent on supplementing their diet with grain from further south in Humla. The Humli trade network had branches down to the Indian sub-continent, but the Limi traders' position in this trans-Himalayan trade was mainly in the northern part.[21] Even today, the Limigya still use many of the same economic strategies as in the past, but there have also been considerable changes. Agriculture, pastoralism and crafts are on the decline whereas seasonal manual labour, which used to be a low-paid last resort for poor households, has become a lucrative alternative in Purang since the early 2000s, so much so that it has completely altered the balance in the local economy.[22] The trade has changed from barter to monetary, and a number of educated out-migrated youths are taking more specialised jobs in cities elsewhere and will probably never return. Finally, there have been many initiatives to develop and promote tourism in Limi, most prominently through the International Centre of Integrated Mountain Development (ICIMOD) in cooperation with Namkha Rural Municipality.

Although Humla is the second largest district in Nepal, it has long been the only one in the country with no road connectivity. However, this is gradually changing as the district is experiencing the same road building fever as the rest of Nepal.[23] The first two roads follow the old pilgrimage and trade paths that used to be trodden by caravans, herders and pilgrims on their way to Mount

---

and Havnevik (2021). The causes of the flood have been studied by Kropáček et al. (2015: 6937–71). Local perceptions of a changing climate are also a central theme of the HimalConnect research project.

19 See Hovden and Havnevik 2021.

20 See e.g., Goldstein 1974.

21 See Fürer-Haimendorf (1988), Rauber (1982) and Goldstein (1975) for a description of the Humli part of the trans-Himalayan trade.

22 See also Havnevik, Hovden and Rinchen Loden (forthcoming) for a discussion of recent changes in livelihood strategies.

23 See for example Himalayan News Service 2020 and Shahi 2021.

Kailash. While not yet completed, they have connected the district with Purang on the Tibetan side of the border and have increased access to cheap Chinese consumer goods.[24] The connection with the national road network in Nepal is even more recent. The Karnali Corridor, a road project to link Humla district with Mugu opened as late as spring 2021, but at the time of writing, the final stretch of road towards the district headquarters in Simikot is still not completed and road construction is a major concern also in Limi. At the time of my first research trip in 2010, the community was only reachable after several days' walk across high passes, whereas by 2018, the road had reached two out of three villages, and the population had already invested in several trucks, jeeps, motorcycles and bikes. Together with other recent developments, most notably the setting up of the internet and mobile network, this constitutes a connectivity leap that has significant impact on both secular and religious management in Limi.

FIGURE 1.10 The village phone house in Waltse, 2010

24 See Saxer (2013) and (2017) for an analysis of these road projects.

FIGURE 1.11 Mobile phones have become ubiquitous, Waltse 2018

1.2.2 *A History of Shifting Political Configurations*

Historical documents show that from at least the thirteenth century onwards Limi has been regarded as being located on Mon territory,[25] whereas the inhabitants have been regarded as Tibetans. The political history of this frontier region is complex and this has, among other things, resulted in complex and sometimes overlapping authority and taxation systems.[26] Limi, being a small community, has had little influence in the wider geopolitics of the area and generally would have to comply when powerful rulers of the neighbouring

25 The term Mon has been used in Tibetan sources to designate the lands on the southern border of the Tibetan plateau. In this particular case, it refers to the territory in contemporary north-western Nepal that was ruled by the Khas Malla kings and later the Kalyal kings, as detailed in Chapter Three. While place names suggest that the extent of the core Limi territory as described in *Rinchen Ling monastery inventory* (fol. 50a) is roughly equivalent to the size of today's Ward, Limi used to have pastures on the southern bank of Manasarovar Lake, and these were gradually lost after the delineation of the Sino-Nepali border in 1962. However, the stone pillars that were erected following the demarcation were few and far between and recently disagreements have surfaced regarding the exact location of the northern border.

26 The secular and monastic taxation is discussed in Chapters Six and Nine respectively.

kingdoms demanded taxes and tributes to both secular administrations and monastic institutions. But local documents and oral tradition also recount acts of resistance and avoidance, and the villagers in Limi have carefully protected their internal governance.

The people in Limi trace their origins to the Tibetan plateau, and throughout history they have had a strong affiliation with Western Tibet. This northward orientation has been underscored by the geographical location of Limi. It takes only one to two days to walk to Purang, the nearest town in Tibet, whereas the villagers must walk four to five days over high passes in order to reach Simikot, the district headquarters in Humla. Moreover, the community's winter pastures were originally located south of Lake Manasarovar on the Tibetan side of the border. Although Limi fared better than many other border communities, the villages were seriously affected by the gradual closure of the border from the 1960s onwards. The Limigya's access to their pastures was incrementally reduced until they were eventually lost in the 1980s. Without sufficient winter pastures, the Limi agro-pastoralists had to make drastic cuts in the size of their herds. This period enforced changes in patterns of movement and income strategies and resulted in a shift of orientation towards Nepal. The last two decades, however, have seen both an economic reorientation towards Tibet and stronger political integration with Nepal. Moreover, an increasing exposure to the globalised world—through increased migration, development projects, improved infrastructure and technology and pilgrimage tourism—has likewise contributed to change. Although the full consequences can only be observed from a temporal distance, this recent development is already having a significant impact on the ways the community is governed.

1.3 A Changing Religious Landscape

Religiously, Limi has had strong ties to Western Tibet, and the early history of the community can only be understood against the background of the second dissemination of Buddhism (*bstan pa phyi dar*) in Tibet and the activities of Rinchen Zangpo (Rin chen bZang po, 958–1055), a native of Rongchung (Rong chung) in Guge (Gu ge). He was a prolific translator of religious texts from Sanskrit and is believed to have constructed 108 monasteries and temples in the region.[27] The Rinchen Ling monastery in Waltse received its name from the translator, and in Limi it is commonly held not only that the Vairocana

27 108 is an ideal number not to be taken literally. The translator's biography and historical texts operate with lists of twenty-one named temples and monasteries. See Vitali (1996)

temple was constructed by him, but also that he passed away in the valley. The historicity of these claims will be assessed in Chapter Three.

Located just south of Kailash (Gangs dkar Ti se or Gangs Rin po che) and Manasarovar (Ma pham g.Yu mtsho),[28] great importance is placed on this sacred mountain and lake. For most of the Tibetan Buddhist pilgrims, the mountain is believed to be the abode of Demchog (bDe mchog, Skt. Cakrasaṃvara) and it is regarded as one of the most important pilgrimage destinations in the Buddhist world. This is reflected in texts, oral literature, local imagery, religious practice as well as in new media. A number of the elderly villagers in Limi report that they have completed numerous circumambulations of the mountain (*gangs skor*), and a colophon from a private copy of the *Bhadrakalpikasūtra* (*bSkal pa bzang po'i mdo*) in Til inscribes features of the local landscape of Limi as part of the mandala of Cakrasaṃvara with its centre at Kailash.[29] But those among the villagers whose ancestral deity is Gangri Lhabtsen (Gangs ri lHa btsan) have an extra affiliation with the mountain. Gangri Lhabtsen is the guardian deity (*gnas bdag*, lit. 'lord of the place') of Mount Kailash and is believed to reside on a peak next to the mountain.[30] The two pilgrimage paths to Kailash which cross through Limi territory, on the eastern and western sides of the valley respectively, are also old trade routes and have been important lifelines for the people of Humla.[31] Several hermits and high lamas who undertook the long pilgrimage journey from Eastern and Central Tibet to Kailash spent the winter in the many retreat huts in the slightly warmer Limi valley. These hermits brought ideas, goods, and influences from outside and contributed to forging religious links and networks. As the following chapters will show, some of them had a strong impact not only on the religious life in Limi, but also on how the community has been governed. The multi-layered religious symbolism of Mount Kailash as pilgrimage place has been attested in religious texts and scholarly works.[32] However, for the people living within its orbit, the

---

and his introduction to the *Catalogue of the three silver brothers* (1996) for a discussion of these lists.

28 In historical and religious texts, the lake is also referred to as Ma dros mtsho (lit. 'The ever-cool lake', Skt. Anavatapta).

29 *bSkal pa bzang po'i mdo*: vol. ka, f. 517f.

30 See Bellezza 2005: 249–61.

31 The annual mart at Darchen (Dar chen), the starting point for the circumambulation of the mountain, was until 1960 frequented by traders from Limi and Humla.

32 Scholarly works on the pilgrimage to Mount Kailash include among others Buffetrille (2003), Huber and Rigzin (1999), and the articles edited by McKay (1998). See also the recent ICIMOD publication on the Kailash Yatra by Bubriski and Pandey (2018).

mountain has additional significance in terms of religion, politics, trade relations, and recently also tourism.

1.3.1 *An Everyday Religious Approach to Monasticism*

It is impossible to understand local governance in Limi without a thorough appraisal of the roles of the monastic institutions in the valley as well as their broader networks. My approach to Tibetan Buddhist monasticism is inspired by the perspective of 'lived religion' as formulated by David Hall and Robert Orsi[33] and the closely related 'everyday religion' as discussed by Nancy Ammerman.[34] Since Gabriel Le Bras coined the term 'lived religion' (*la religion veçue*) in the 1960s, the perspective has been advocated by a number of religious studies scholars; first in France and subsequently in the anglophone world.[35] Whereas anthropologists have been concerned with aspects of 'lived religion' for a long time, 'everyday religion' has recently received a renewed focus among scholars working on Tibet and the Himalaya.[36] Studies of 'everyday' or 'lived' religion, part of what Thomas Tweed has labelled 'the quotidian turn' in the humanities, arts and social sciences, grew out of a concern to correct the skewed representation of religion caused by the prevalent elitist bias.[37] The perspective, which has its roots in the French Annales School and in New Social History, seeks to locate the religious in people's lived experiences, in the everyday activities of ordinary people, rather than only in '… the organized religious rites and the systematised theological beliefs of elites in dominant religious institutions'.[38] Since the 'lived' or 'everyday' perspective on religion grew out of a wish to move beyond institutions, it might seem self-contradictory to apply the perspective to a monastic institution. However, I find a shift in scholarly attention from 'religion as prescribed' to 'religion as practised' in the study of a religious institution helpful in avoiding an essentialised image and to broaden our understanding of monasticism. Moreover, since Tibetan Buddhist monasteries have tended to be studied too literally as set apart from the rest of

33 Hall 1997 and Orsi 1997, 2002. See also Tweed's (2015) comments on the limitations of the approach.

34 Ammerman 2007.

35 See Tweed 2015: 365, Hall 1997: 1 and Hervieu-Léger 1997: 22.

36 Everyday religion was for instance one of the main topics discussed at the conference 'Everyday religion and sustainable environments in the Himalaya', arranged 7–8 March 2013 at the New School, and the subsequent conference 'Himalayan connections: disciplines, geographies, trajectories', 9–10 March at Yale University.

37 Tweed 2015.

38 Tweed 2015: 369.

society,[39] an analytical 're-location' of the monasteries into the everyday life of monks—and laity—will produce a more nuanced understanding of the interrelated religious, socio-economic, and political roles of the institution.

1.3.2 *Village Monasteries and Village Monks*

To understand the relationship between the monastery and lay society it is crucial to be familiar with the main categories and terminology that shape their interactions. Tibetan Buddhist monasteries vary greatly in size, scope, and organisation.[40] The Tibetan term *dgon pa* (lit. 'secluded place'), which is normally translated as 'monastery', is used to denote a wide range of institutions ranging from the great monastic universities like Drepung ('Bras spungs), Sera (Se ra) and Ganden (dGa' ldan) near Lhasa, to small household temples tended by non-celibate Nyingmapa (rNying ma pa) monks or solitary hermitages perched high up on mountainsides. There are other terms as well, like *lha khang* (lit. 'god house', but usually translated 'temple' or 'shrine'), *ri khrod* ('hermitage'), and *mtshams khang* ('retreat hut' or 'hermitage'). In Limi, as in many other Tibetan communities, the term *dgon pa* tends to be used for all. However, in the case of Rinchen Ling, the terms *lha khang* and *gtsug lag khang* are also sometimes used,[41] while small, private meditation huts are referred to as *mtshams khang*. In this study, the term 'monastery' will be used in a wide sense to refer to all institutions with a community of monks, whereas 'temple' will mainly be used to denote householder *dgon pa* or shrine rooms.

Per Kværne has distinguished between three main types of monasteries: national monasteries, hermitages, and local monasteries.[42] The first category, which he calls 'national monasteries', refers to large institutions functioning as monastic universities with hundreds, sometimes thousands of monks.[43] These monasteries recruited from all over the Tibetan cultural area and the 'colleges' (*grwa tshang*) were often organised according to the monks' place of origin. The hermitages, the second type of monastery, were solitary retreats often located in the mountains and attracted adepts specialising in meditation. The final category, 'local monasteries,' is defined by Kværne as:

---

39 Mills (2003) and Gutschow (2004) are important exceptions.

40 See for instance Goldstein 2010, Strøm 2001, Kværne 1977 and Mills 2003.

41 The use of the term *lha khang* to refer to the whole monastery probably stems from the time of the founding of the first temple in the village. See Chapter Three.

42 Kværne 1977: 87–8.

43 In his study of Drepung Monastery, Goldstein (1998) points out that these large central institutions had many more functions than monastic universities and that only a limited number of the resident monks pursued higher studies.

> … the many thousand small and medium-sized monasteries whose basis of recruitment was the local area in which each monastery was situated. (…) On the whole, these monasteries did not aim at training doctores theologiae, but rather aimed at meeting the needs of the local community for religious ceremonies of all kinds (…). A characteristic trait of these monasteries—in contrast, at least to some extent, to the two preceding types—is the high degree of contact between the monks and the lay people of the local community.[44]

Strøm, elaborating on Kværne's list, suggests the term 'central monastery' rather than 'national monastery' and argues that, '… "central" and "local" should be seen as two ends of a scale or continuum, along which monasteries may be differentiated according to their internal organisation, functions in society, recruitment of monks, and their position within the structure of the monastic order'.[45] These types are, however, only 'ideal types' and a single monastery might show features of other types. What Kværne terms 'national monasteries', for instance, have often shown features of local monasteries in the services they provide to nearby towns or communities. Another type of institution, which warrants a separate category, is the 'religious encampment' (*chos sgar*). These can have up to ten thousand monastic and lay residents and are common especially in eastern Tibetan areas.[46] More relevant to Limi are the Dharma centres that have been established throughout Asia and the western world, which similarly cater for both monastics and the laity. The current Limi *sprul sku* Senge Tenzin Rinpoche has brought a few Limi monks with him and resides in such a Dharma centre in Taiwan.

The three monasteries in Limi fall clearly into the category of 'local monastery', but I will also use the term 'village monastery' to emphasise the strong bonds between the village and monastery in Limi. The term is also appropriate because of the monastery's physical location in the centre of the village—as in Waltse and Dzang—and very near the village as in Til. In addition, there are at least twenty hermitages and meditation huts in Limi, the most important of which have served as retreats for religious masters from various parts of Tibet. Whereas the monasteries in Limi used to be 'branch monasteries'

44 Kværne 1977: 87–8.

45 Strøm 2001: 85–8.

46 Larung Gar (Bla rung sGar), the largest of these, had as many as ten thousand monks, nuns, and lay devotees in 2000. Antonio Terrone (2009) refers to the religious encampments as quasi-monastic, in the sense that they are not run and administered like traditional monasteries, but instead are loose organisations consisting of a broad pool of devotees revolving around charismatic leaders.

(*dgon lag*) of Gyangdrag (rGyang grags) monastery, the Drigung stronghold at the foot of Mount Kailash, today they are self-sufficient monasteries in terms of funding and organisation. Local monasteries have been by far the most prevalent type of monastery in Tibetan areas, and even though the individual institutions are small, together they must have comprised the majority of monks.[47] A study of these monasteries is therefore important if we are to understand how Tibetan Buddhism is lived and negotiated in Tibetan and Himalayan societies.

Tibetan societies have a rich variety of lay and monastic religious experts, and the boundaries between them are sometimes fluid.[48] When discussing male monastics, some scholars have advocated a strict use of the term 'monk', reserving it for celibate, religious practitioners who are ordained. For the present study, I have chosen a slightly broader and more inclusive approach in line with an everyday religious perspective. I do not intend to use the term 'monk' for all religious experts, neither for all men clad in monks' robes, but I find the term applicable to men ordained in a monastic institution, and who by their peers and the local population are referred to as *grwa pa* (monk, student), regardless of their status in the renunciation hierarchy[49] and the degree to which they maintain the Vinaya vows.

In Limi, *grwa pa* is the general term used to refer to all boys and men enrolled in the local monasteries. In addition to *grwa pa*, the villagers distinguish between novices (*grwa chung*, lit. 'small monk'),[50] regular monks, and fully ordained monks, who are referred to by the respectful title *dge slong* (Skt. *bhikṣu*).[51] When enrolling in the monastery the young boys take the refuge precepts (*skyabs 'gro'i sdom pa*), and after some years they take the renunciate vows (*rab byung gi sdom pa*). But it is only a few of the monks who eventually take the full set of vows (*dge slong gi sdom pa*) to become fully ordained *dge slong*, and this typically takes place long into adulthood. There are a few nuns from Limi, but except for one single nun (*a ni*)[52] in Til Kundzom monastery, they all live outside the valley. There is no preceptor (*mkhan po*) in Limi, and no opportunity for scholastic training. The monks are primarily ritual specialists attending to the various ritual needs of the villagers, though there

47 See for instance Kværne 1977: 87.

48 See the discussion of the different types of religious specialists in Ramble 1984.

49 Mills 2003: 79f. For a discussion of renunciation in Limi, see Chapter Eight.

50 Here the term 'novice' is used in a broad sense to refer to young and inexperienced monks and not limited to those who have received the *dge tshul* vows.

51 The local terminology is explained in more detail in the paragraph about training of monks in Chapter Eight. See also the paragraph about monastic offices in Chapter Seven.

52 For a discussion of female monastic terminology, see Havnevik 1989: 44–45.

are a few monks from the community who have pursued higher religious studies elsewhere. As I shall show, the limited opportunity for scholastic training is partly a result of the implementation of the monk levy as system for recruitment.

1.3.3 *Recruitment and Patronage*

Monastic recruitment has taken a variety of forms throughout time and space in the Tibetan and Himalayan region. Although there have of course been many cases in which the decision to enter monastic life has been made by the individual him- or herself, recruitment has usually taken place at young age, and has hence been the decision of the parents—or it has been part of the household's obligations towards the monastery, and thus enforced by law.[53] Whereas all these forms are to some extent practised in Limi, the latter is the default system for monastic recruitment. Virtually all monks in the three village monasteries are levied on the basis of household size and category.[54] This is not a locally invented system; recruitment by conscription or monk levy, normally referred to as 'monk tax' (*grwa khral, btsun khral, ban khral*), has been listed as one of the 'traditional' ways of monastic recruitment in Tibetan societies. There is a widespread notion that every family in Tibet and the Himalaya with three sons had to make the second son a monk, but the degree to which this norm reflects actual practice needs further investigation. Little is known about the historical roots of the levy, why it has been enforced, how widespread this form of recruitment has been, how it has been implemented or resisted, and what its consequences have been for social organisation in the communities where the rule has been found. In her study of historical instances of the monk tax, Berthe Jansen suggests that there has been significant variation in interpretation and enforcement.[55] The references found in the scholarly literature[56] are rarely, if ever, based on observations of the system in practice, but on documents or interviews with exile Tibetans or with monks and laypeople in places where the rule has now been abandoned. Although the notion that the second son should be sent to the monastery is still widespread in Tibetan communities, recruitment by conscription has been forbidden in monasteries in China and is largely abandoned elsewhere. Limi therefore offers a rare opportunity to study the monk levy in practice.

53 See for instance Childs and Choedup 2019: 75–80 for a discussion of childhood recruitment of monks and nuns.

54 Although conscription has also been used for the recruitment of nuns (e.g., Ramble 2008a: 182f), it is only monks who are recruited in this way in Limi.

55 Jansen 2023.

56 References and discussions of relevant literature are provided in Chapter Eight.

The monk levy is closely connected to the patronage system. The question of how to organise patronage to secure the sustenance of the monk community and the continuation of the monastic institution is as old as Buddhist monasticism itself. The solutions have varied considerably throughout history and in different socio-economic contexts. The rules that were established in Limi, at least from the end of the nineteenth century onwards, comprised a complex mixture of taxes and obligations and various types of voluntary commitments. As exemplified in the opening vignette of the chapter and revisited throughout the book, this practice is both persistently defended and subject to painful opposition in Limi. It can be argued that the whole patronage and recruitment practice has become one of the core dilemmas of the villagers, with significant consequences not only for the monastery and local governance, but as the recent demographic development suggests, potentially even for the survival of the villages.

1.3.4 *Literature on Limi and Humla*

Whilst the Himalaya have been locus for many ethnographies, most of these studies have focused on a limited number of communities. Partly due to its geographical remoteness, lack of infrastructure, and previous status as a restricted area, Humla district used to be among the least studied areas of the Nepal Himalaya,[57] but this situation is rapidly changing with a range of new scholarship on the area arising since my first fieldwork in 2010.[58] After the end of the civil war in 2006, a bewildering number of NGOs have established themselves in Humla.[59] Scholars have followed in the wake of the NGOs with critical analyses of development and other current issues.[60] Of particular relevance is the work of Martin Saxer, who draws on a number of cases from Limi in his analysis of misunderstood development work, trade, and border dynamics in Humla.[61] Emily Yeh's recent analysis of overlapping sovereignties in Limi is

57 Levine 1987: 76.

58 Due to logistical reasons and a twin pregnancy during the preparations of this volume I have not been able to include literature published after 2021, except for works of which I have read earlier drafts.

59 By 2019 (BS 2076) in total 193 NGOs were registered with the Social Welfare Council as operating in Humla, but the actual number is likely to be considerably higher. See the Social Welfare Council website 2018.

60 See for instance Rabindra Roy's (2010) analysis of non-timber forest products' contribution to livelihoods, Sigrid Nagoda and Siri Eriksen's (2015) study of food security, David Citrin's (2010, 2012) sharp critique of ephemeral health care, and Kimber Haddix MacKay's (2003) study of health care access in the maoist period.

61 Saxer 2013 and 2017.

another important contribution.[62] Tara Bate's PhD research will yield further valuable knowledge about environmental management and pastoralism in Limi. ICIMOD has also initiated a number of policy and development-related research projects in the region. The most relevant project for my own work is the Kailash Sacred Landscape Conservation and Development Initiative (KSLCDI), which has published several working papers and reports.[63]

Christoph von Fürer-Haimendorf was the first anthropologist to conduct research in Humla. The findings from his research expedition to the district in 1972, which were subsequently published in the penultimate chapter of *Himalayan Traders*, provide a valuable contribution to our knowledge about settlement pattern, livelihoods, and trade connections in Humla.[64] Encouraged by Fürer-Haimendorf's recommendations, Nancy Levine followed up with field research among the Nyinbas from 1973 to 1975 and in seven anonymised communities in the district between 1982 and 1983. Her monograph and articles provide insights into the mechanisms of polyandry, kinship relations, social organisation, and livelihoods, and together with Hanna Rauber's study of the Humli Khyampas from 1976–77, serve as valuable material for comparison and understanding of the historical and regional context.

The first and only scholar to have conducted long-term fieldwork in Limi before I started my work there in 2010, however, was Melvyn Goldstein. He made three research trips to Dzang village in the summers of 1974, 1976, and 1977, which resulted in a series of articles on ecological adaptation, polyandry, and demography.[65] Goldstein's articles also explored the processes of change instigated by the gradual closing of the border with Tibet, most of which have greatly intensified since the seventies. The other early anthropological studies in the region revolved around similar topics.[66] The complex history and the cultural, socio-political and religious diversity of Humla, however, have received little scholarly attention.[67] Mariette Wiebenga and Mimi Church

62 Yeh 2021.

63 See for instance ICIMOD 2011 and 2013.

64 Fürer-Haimendorf 1988: 223–85.

65 See Goldstein 1974, 1975, 1976, 1977, 1978, 1981a, 1981b, 1981c and Beall and Goldstein 1981.

66 Some references to Limi are found also in Levine (1988a) in her work on polyandry in Humla and Fürer-Haimendorf in his *Himalayan Traders* (1988). See also Ross 1983, Levine 1987, Bishop 1990, and Haddix and Gurung (1999).

67 The coffee table book *The Hidden Himalayas*, with photos by Thomas Kelly accompanied by texts by Carroll Dunham (1987), the brief article by Niels Gutschow (1990) about the *mchod rten* in Humla, Church and Wiebenga's (2008) study on iconography, the architectural survey by Bidari (2004), and the pilgrimage guide to Kailash by Lama (2012) as well as Kevin Bubriski and Abhimanyu Pandey's *Kailash Yatra. A Long Walk to Mt Kailash through Humla* (2018) are the only publications so far.

published an article on the iconography of the Vairocana statue in the Rinchen Ling monastery in Waltse,[68] and the architect Keshav Bidari wrote a short architectural survey of the same monastic complex.[69] Building on this earlier literature, the contribution of this book is to fill some of the gaps in our knowledge of the local governance and Buddhist institutions during times of rapidly changing socio-political, economic and environmental conditions.

1.3.5 *Structure of the Book*

The book consists of three parts: The first part (Chapters One–Three) locates the society between state formations, religious institutions and systems of governance, providing a brief presentation of material and methodological approaches, and traces the history of the monastery and the local consequences of the shifting political configurations in the region. The second part (Chapters Four–Six) starts with an outline of the mechanisms of social organisation, changing demography, education and livelihood strategies. Then, it examines the leadership structure, decision-making process, legal system and taxation policies in the local government in Limi, and discusses how they are adapted to meet changing needs and demands. The last part (Chapters Seven–Nine) investigates the role of the local monasteries in the ritual and administrative management of the community, their organisation as well as the specific mechanisms for monastic recruitment and patronage, and discusses some of their implications. Finally, the concluding chapter addresses how the villagers navigate the Buddhist, national and local laws and institutions in the governance of the local community and environment. It reflects on how internal factors—such as increasingly felt generational tensions, requirements from the Nepali state and influences from the outside world—affect experiences and practices of belonging as well as the art of governing Limi.

68 Church and Wiebenga 2008.

69 Bidari 2004: 1–5.

CHAPTER 2

The Long Way to Limi

On a bumpy bus ride in Kathmandu in 2009, Mariette Wiebenga, in the seat next to me, asked about the topic of my PhD thesis. I explained my interest in the history and religious traditions of Western Tibet and my initial plan to do research in the area where the tenth-century translator Rinchen Zangpo was born. However, the difficult situation in the Tibet Autonomous Region (TAR) had made it impossible to carry out my original project. After many attempts at relocation, I finally realised that I would have to move over the border to Nepal. She needed some time to think about it, but eventually Mariette said, 'Why don't you go to Limi?'. She then suggested that I study the old monastery in Waltse, which, according to local tradition was founded by Rinchen Zangpo. What she then told me about her own anthropological research in Humla and her visit to Limi kindled my curiosity about this mountain community, its monastery and its tradition of self-governance, far from national authorities.[1] In this way, the seeds for this study were sown.

∵

Limi is a geographically remote community—even by Nepali standards. Simikot, the district headquarter, does not have road connection with the rest of the country, and is reachable only by foot or by plane from Nepalgunj in the Terai, or from Surkhet Airport in the neighbouring district. Flights are frequently cancelled because of difficult weather conditions and when I embarked on my first fieldwork in 2010, there were no flights for two months. Fortunately, after a few weather-bound days in Nepalgunj, I and my research assistant Phuntsok Dorje were able to get a reasonably priced seat on a transport helicopter (Fig. 2.1). We stayed a couple of days in Simikot hiring pack animals and buying provisions, and from there it took us six days on foot via the narrow Tshongsa Valley and across the Nyalu pass to reach Limi (Fig. 2.2).

1 Church and Wiebenga 2008 and Wiebenga and Lama (in press).

 | DOI:10.1163/9789004714571_003

Between 2010 and 2012 I spent in total twelve months in the Limi Valley doing ethnographic fieldwork for my PhD, and most of the material on which the book is based was collected during this period. Before and between my visits to Humla, I spent months in Kathmandu speaking with outmigrated Limi villagers, NGOs, civil society and representatives of various government bodies. Because of the strong seasonal variations in the villagers' activities, I timed the fieldtrips to Limi so that I could cover the whole year. At first, I was hesitant to stay over the winter as the only pathways to the valley wind across passes that are sealed off by snow for several months. But it is during late autumn and winter that the vast majority of monastic rituals, all weddings, the tax collection and most of the village assembly meetings take place and I eventually decided to embark on a winter stay. Those six freezing months from 2011–12 did indeed turn out to be the most productive and important for my understanding of Limi society. As part of the research project HimalConnect I was able to make another two field visits to Limi in 2018 and 2019, lasting in total three months.[2] In addition, I carried out research in the district headquarters in Simikot and the seat of the new Namkha municipality in Yalbang. At that time, infrastructure had improved, and for large parts of the journey to Limi we were able to catch rides on trucks and jeeps (Fig. 2.3). These last two field visits enabled me to observe some of the tremendous changes that were taking place and to study the local adaptation of the administrative reform in Nepal since the 2015 constitution.

The villagers in Limi speak *Sle mi skad*, a Humli Tibetan dialect[3] that is quite different from Central Tibetan, though most monks and laymen in the villages, as well as women who have spent time working in Purang or Kathmandu are familiar with Central Tibetan. Some elderly villagers of both sexes can also communicate in the Nyinba (Nyin pa) variety of Humli Tibetan. People from the Nyinba villages, located to the east of the district headquarters in Simikot, have had close relations to people in Limi for generations, and many elderly people from Limi have worked there.[4] In addition, an increasing number of the men are conversant in Nepali and the local teachers know basic English.

---

2 These two latter fieldtrips were conducted as part of the research project "Himalayan connections: Melting glaciers, sacred landscapes and changing technologies in a changing climate" (HimalConnect), funded by the Research Council of Norway. In 2018, I was joined by Riamsara Kuyakanon, Hanna Havnevik and Hildegard Diemberger for parts of the fieldwork.

3 The Humli Tibetan dialects, most of which closely resemble the dialect spoken in Purang, can be further sub-divided into Limi, Upper, Lower and Eastern Humli groups (De Vries 2014: 26). Apart from this socio-lingustic report on the Humli Tibetan dialects by De Vries (2014) and a phonological study of the Limi dialect for an M.A. in linguistics by Wilde (2001), these dialects have never been studied. Although valuable as preliminary reports, both studies suffer from the fact that the authors were not conversant in Central Tibetan, Humli Tibetan, or Nepali.

4 See Levine 1988a, Havnevik, Hovden and Rinchen Loden (forthcoming) and Chapter Four.

FIGURE 2.1 The still unpaved airstrip in Simikot, 2010

FIGURE 2.2 Walking up the Tshongsa Valley towards Limi, 2010

FIGURE 2.3 On the way to Limi by truck, 2018

Goldstein had warned me that the Limi dialect was difficult, and when I arrived in Kathmandu in June 2010, I therefore started studying *Sle mi skad* with two young men from Limi while preparing for my fieldwork. Realising that it would take me a long time to gain sufficient fluency, I decided to work with an interpreter. I was lucky to be introduced to Phuntsok Dorje, a young Nyinba with good English skills and a strong interest in Humli cultural and religious traditions. Although there are some differences between the Nyinba and Limi variants of Humli Tibetan, he had a flair for languages, and his family had close relations (*ngo shes*)[5] with several households in Limi. Phuntsok Dorje accompanied me on my first research trip in 2010 and recommended one of his friends, Rinchen Loden, to accompany me for my following fieldwork stays. Rinchen Loden turned out to be a very sociable young man, with an unfailingly positive attitude and good *ngo shes* connections with local households. The importance of the contributions of these two young Nyinbas for my work cannot be overstated. Both had grown up in Humla but had also spent years in Kathmandu and India for their education, which enabled them to see

5 The term *ngo shes* is normally translated as 'acquaintance', but in this context it means 'ritual friendship' (N. *mit*). See Chapter Four for a more detailed explanation.

the culture from both viewpoints. Moreover, during our many discussions, they helped me distinguish between the local customs that were particular to Limi and those that were common in Nyin and other parts of the district. Since the Nyinba community is the only other community in Humla which has been subject to detailed anthropological study, comparisons will be made where relevant.[6] Rinchen Loden also joined me during parts of my fieldwork in 2018 and 2019, but most of the time I was skilfully assisted by Dawa Tsering, a young talented man from Waltse, who had been called back to the village to take over the responsibility as head of his household after completing high school in India.

No matter how professional the interpreter, speaking through a third person can potentially obscure communications. I therefore worked systematically on my own language skills, but it was not until my second and third periods of fieldwork that I started to be able to hold independent conversations with the villagers in a hybrid between the Limi dialect and Central Tibetan. Reading local documents was another linguistic challenge. These primary written sources were of diverse kinds, each with its own genre conventions, composed in different languages, occasionally in a mix of classical Tibetan and a phonetic rendering of the local vernacular. Moreover, whereas a few of the monastic documents were written in beautiful calligraphy (often variants of *'bru tsha*), the majority were written in an often hard-to-decipher cursive script (*'khyug yig*). Initially, I did not intend to spend much time on the documents, but I soon discovered that they contained a wealth of information which I would not have been able to access simply through interviews.

Written culture has traditionally been strong in Tibetan areas, and in some places, such as Limi, it seems to be given particular importance.[7] There are multiple reasons for keeping written records; but the presence of the monasteries as well as the ambiguous position of the community vis-à-vis the regional powers, have been important. I was intrigued by trying to understand the status of these documents, how they were kept and by whom, how they were used by the community, and the degree to which they were actually followed. The local documents proved to be invaluable sources for my understanding of the local management system.

6 See for instance Levine 1976, 1987, 1988a, 1988b and Wiebenga and Lama (in press).

7 There are a number of other Tibetan speaking communities with a similarly strong emphasis on written culture. See for instance Ramble 1984, 2002, 2008a, 2008b, 2008c, 2012a and 2012b, Jahoda 2015 and Childs and Choedup 2019.

2.1 Arrival, Negotiations and Positionality

Prior to my first fieldwork, I had been told that people in Limi were somewhat mistrustful of outsiders. Thus, in planning my trip, one of my main concerns was whether I would be accepted by the community and whether they would find my proposed research useful. A former politician and intellectual from further south in Humla district, who knew many people from this community was very concerned about preserving knowledge about the cultural and religious heritage of the region and immediately supported my research. He generously shared his knowledge and introduced me to some of the village leaders who happened to be in Kathmandu and helped me with many of the practical arrangements. Upon my arrival in Limi, the leaders summoned a village assembly so that I could introduce my proposed research project and ask for permission and advice. One representative from each of the large and small households attended the assembly meeting, and to my great relief, approval for the project was granted.[8] During the same meeting, the leaders asked me to help them gain support for protection against the recurrent floods threatening the monastery and village. Whilst environmental and climatic change was not originally intended as part of my research, their initiative highlighted to me their vulnerability in the face of rapid climate change and prompted me to document the situation and changes that were affecting the community.[9]

2.1.1 *Spreading the Blessings and Burdens*

The youth club in Waltse was given the responsibility to arrange my stay.[10] When I arrived in Limi in 2010, they had already prepared a small house for me, a short distance outside the village itself (Fig. 2.4). It was conveniently located next to the phone house with the only phone in the valley that had been set up there a few weeks earlier (Fig. 1.10).[11] Many villagers visited me while waiting for their turn to make phone calls, and I used the opportunity to get to know them, pick up news from the village, and make appointments for meetings. Initially this unobtrusive arrangement worked quite well, people could choose when they wanted to come and talk with me, and I slowly learned the local

8 Although the initial project idea was mine, it was continuously reshaped throughout my stays; the local community's feedback made me adjust the project and informed what I wrote about, as well as what I left out.

9 See for instance Hovden 2011, Diemberger, Hovden and Yeh 2015 and Kropáček et al. 2015.

10 The role of the youth club in local decision-making processes is discussed in Chapter Five.

11 The phone, which was a Nepal Telecom satellite phone, had been installed just a few weeks prior to my arrival in July 2010. Until then, the nearest phone had been located across the border, in Purang, two days' walk from Limi.

dialect and increased my knowledge about how the community was organised. Soon I was invited to participate in major events in the village, but I felt somewhat removed from daily life so for my subsequent field trips I asked if I could live in private houses in the village. The leaders of the Youth Club accepted my request but were concerned that the blessings and burdens of catering for a foreign researcher should be equally distributed among its members. We therefore agreed on a system of rotation, with one or two weeks' stay in each house. The Youth Club selected the households by lottery, a system that goes well with the methodological research ideal of random selection, and this arrangement gave me the opportunity to live in houses belonging to all social strata. During my five research stays, I have either lived in or had my meals in about fifty percent of the households in the three villages. One problem with the arrangement, however, was that the majority of the families I stayed with belonged to the two upper social strata. This was partly due to the fact that the villagers belonging to the lower social strata were underrepresented among the youth club members, and partly by chance, but I tried to counter this imbalance by making visits to many of these households. The rotational system had the obvious advantage that I gained inside knowledge of so many of the households in the three villages, but it also had drawbacks. Besides being tiring to keep moving it made it difficult for me to establish close relations with individual villagers or families.

FIGURE 2.4 The Youth Club house in Waltse where I lived in 2010

2.1.2 *Positionality and Gender*

While positionality and gender may have significant impact on the outcome of the research, I did not give my own gender much thought until I approached the Village Assembly to make a formal request. Since this was the first time, I asked for advice on how I should proceed. The men told me that I should wear a hat, take it off, and bow in front of the assembly. Then, I should present my request and place a silk scarf with a symbolic sum of money on the table in front of the village leader. I borrowed Phuntsok Dorje's hat and did accordingly, but as I took off the hat and bowed, I realised that through this act I had symbolically transformed into a man. Whereas the local women occasionally place requests in front of the assembly, women never wear hats, and women never bow in this way. I had been given the role of what is sometimes referred to as a 'pseudo male' or 'honorary male' in literature on ethnographic research methods.[12] This position was also reflected in seating arrangements. I would almost always be placed among the men.

I felt very uneasy about the low position that was invariably given to local women, which was most visible at celebrations, where women were given the lowest seats. Moreover, especially during my first stay, I found it much more difficult to get close to the local women than I had expected, it seemed that I had marginalised myself from the women's sphere, not only through my research topic but also by my behaviour. Another main reason that it was difficult to get close to the women was my poor mastery of the local dialect. With most of the men I could speak Central Tibetan and communicate more easily, whereas with women who only spoke the local Humli dialect it was more difficult. I therefore decided to work harder on my language skills and on building better rapport with them to gain a deeper understanding of their situations and perspectives.[13]

2.2 Research Methods and Material

2.2.1 *Interviews*

I conducted numerous formal and informal interviews with members from most of the households in Waltse, and a number of people from Dzang and Til as well as Limi residents in Kathmandu. For confidentiality, all interlocutors

12 Warren 1988: 26 and 2001: 214ff.

13 See Havnevik, Hovden and Rinchen Loden (forthcoming) for a study of gender norms and division of labour in Limi.

from Limi are anonymised in the text.[14] I also had some long discussions with Tshewang Lama, who provided valuable historical and contextual information about Humla. In addition, I conducted interviews with the district secretary and the former Nepali government-appointed 'chief' (N. *mukhiyā*) of Limi in Simikot, as well as several officials in the current administrative system. Limi is a highly stratified society where age, gender, family background, and work have a strong impact on people's understanding of society and their own roles in it. To reflect this diversity, I chose my respondents so that all social groups were represented, but I spent more time with former village leaders and senior monks in the monastery as these were regarded as the most knowledgeable in matters of local history, the administrative systems and local religious traditions. The interviews ranged from semi-structured sessions centred on specific topics to open-ended interviews and more informal conversations. I also conducted a few life-story interviews, collected oral history, legends, and songs, mainly wedding songs, but also other genres. Songs are sung during social gatherings and festivities in Limi, and analysis of these traditions provide valuable insights into local culture.[15] Finally, I conducted household surveys, which became important for my understanding of social organisation in the three villages and their respective monasteries.[16] For most of the interviews, I took notes by hand as many villagers were uncomfortable about being recorded on tape. I tried to type the interviews into my computer as soon as possible, but this was more challenging during the coldest months. Because of the limited capacity of the grid, the only place where I could charge my computer was in the powerhouse when electricity was available between six and nine o'clock at night. It was a risky business, however. During winter, the computer would freeze at night, and I therefore had to slowly defrost it next to the kitchen stove in the morning.

2.2.2 *Observations*

James Fernandez argues that participant observation is essentially a method aimed at the experience of place. It enables us to get closer to what our respondents may feel in the spaces they occupy and in which they act.[17]

14 In a few cases where the narrative requires a name, I have used pseudonyms.

15 A thorough analysis of the songs falls beyond the scope of this book, but I am planning to publish some of the material in an article.

16 Due to methodological challenges, such as the high mobility of the population, these surveys are not one hundred per cent precise; this is particularly the case for the surveys of Dzang and Til. However, the data should be reliable enough to describe the population trends.

17 Fernandez 2003: 187.

Moreover, participant observation can also be a method aimed at the experience of practice—to try to appropriate and understand with our own bodies the various practices of our respondents. However, the load of assumptions and different cultural luggage we carry with us is an important constraint.

Some ethnographers advocate that the researcher partake in everyday tasks in the society or social group under study;[18] Anna Grimshaw's study of a community of nuns in Ladakh is a rather extreme example. During her five months with the nuns in Jomo Ling (Jo mo Gling), she lived there as one of them, sharing all their hard physical work.[19] Mainly because of my research topic, but also because of the way my stay was arranged, I choose to keep a more distant researcher role. My observations during fieldwork were of many different kinds: In order to study social organisation and the local decision-making processes, I attended a number of village meetings together with the men. I joined the monks in the monastery and observed their daily work as well as a large number of rituals and religious festivals. Occasionally I joined the women doing agricultural work, roasting barley grain to make barley flour (*rtsam pa*), and weaving. Similarly, I joined the villagers on trips to buy provisions and walked with the animals in the autumn when it was time to change from autumn to winter pastures. Moreover, in my study of the religious history and contemporary practices, I arranged excursions to the sacred places in the valley, I collected toponyms, and was invited to participate in most of the rituals and festivities in Waltse and the other two villages. But arguably the most valuable approach was just to take part in daily life inside people's homes, the everyday routine in the monastery, environmental management, and the collection and measurement of offerings and taxes—all yielding important insights into the local governance system. The only major restriction I experienced was that people did not want me to be present at conflict resolution meetings.[20]

2.2.3 *Textual Sources*

Access to documents from the local monastery and village archives could only be granted by the assembly of monks and lay villagers respectively, and it was only after I had stayed for several months that I got the opportunity to ask for permission to read the relevant texts. While I was not able to study them

18 For a discussion of the various roles the ethnographer may take in the field, and some of the consequences of these choices, see for instance Hammersley and Atkinson (1995: 104ff).

19 Grimshaw 1994. The nunnery is referred to as Julichang (s.u.) in her thesis.

20 This shortcoming was partly remedied by the villagers agreeing to explain the conflict resolution system to me. See Chapter Five.

thoroughly until after my return to Norway, senior villagers helped me with an initial perusal. Their patient explanations were invaluable for my understanding as local documents that are meant for internal use tend to leave much information unspecified. The written source material is discussed in the respective chapters. Below is a list of the Limi documents I drew on for this book, with short English titles and full Tibetan titles in brackets, arranged in alphabetical order.

- The *Biography of Serta Rinpoche*, alias Pema Lungtog Gyatso (Padma Lung rtogs rGya mtsho, 1891–1964). (Full title: *The biography of the siddha Padma Lungtog Gyatso, called the teaching on the path to enlightenment*, T. *Grub dbang padma lung rtogs rgya mtsho mchog gi rnam thar byang chub lam bstan zhes bya ba.*)
- The *Biography of Tshogkhang Rinpoche*, known as Etaradza (E ta rā dza) or Pema Dewa Gyalpo (Pad ma bDe ba'i rGyal po, 1873–1933). (Full title: *Biography of the extraordinary life of Pema Dewa Gyalpo, called the ornament of the ocean of wisdom*, T. *mKhas sgrub rgya mtsho'i gtsug rgyan padma bde ba'i rgyal po'i rnam thar ngo mtshar mchog ldan zhes bya ba.*)
- *Contract by the assembly of laity and monks* (T. *lHa thog gnyis skya ser gnyis nas 'grig khrims kyi* [*khrim gi*] *gan rgya yin*). The document is a copy of a 'legal contract' (*'grig khrims kyi gan rgya*) detailing a new set of laws and disciplinary rules from the '[council of] the fifteen', mainly regulating the relationship between monks and laity. The laws were made during a large joint meeting between monks and laity (*skya ser*) in the summer of 2009. The copy I was allowed to photograph was written in cursive (*'khyug yig*) on a scroll of paper consisting of thirty-one lines in 2011.
- The *Drigung dance manual* (date unspecified). (Full title: *An introductory compendium to the 'cham dance called the lion's play*, T. *'Bri gung bka' brgyud kyi gar 'cham ngo sprod snying bsdus seng ge'i rnam rol zhes bya ba*).
- The *Drigung history of Kailash*. (Full title: *The crystal mirror: an analysis which briefly explains the chronicle of past events at the great snow mountain Kailash together with the great lake Manasarovar*, T. *Gangs ri chen po ti se dang mtsho chen ma dros pa bcas kyi sngon byung gi lo rgyus mdor bsdus su brjod pa'i rab byed shel dkar me long.*) The text has been studied by several scholars,[21] and is frequently referred to as *Ti se gnas bshad*, the short title written on the folios. The text was composed in 1896 by the thirty-third Drigung throne holder Tenzin Chökyi Lodrö (bsTan 'dzin Chos kyi Blo gros).

21 See for instance Huber and Rigzin 1999.

- The *Limi monastery regulations* (*Sle mi dgon gyi bca' yig*) are based on the monastic regulations (*bca' yig*) from Yangrigar (Yang ri sgar), one of the main Drigung monasteries in Central Tibet.[22] The document was written in 1806 at the order of the twenty-ninth Drigung throne-holder, Tenzin Pema Gyaltsen (bsTan 'dzin Pad ma rGyal mtshan). The text is of a general kind, perhaps because it was modelled on the Yangrigar regulations, and does not include much local information.[23]
- The *Monastic recruitment contract*. (Full title: *Contract [regarding] the obligation for each [household] with two sons in the three villages to [make] one son enter the monastery …* T. *Yul tsho gsum na bu gnyis byung phyin bu re chos sgor zhugs rgyu gan rgya …*)[24] The document was written by Tenzin Chökyi Lodrö during his visit to Limi in 1896.
- The *Record of the resident lama's belongings*. (Full title: *Record of objects donated to the lama's residence in Limi Rinchen Ling, the treasury of jewels*, T. *Sle mi rin chen gling gi bla brang sprod deb nor bu'i bang mdzod*). Some of the names occurring in the list stem from the sixteenth *rab byung* and the Earth Ox year, which is mentioned twice, therefore probably refers to 1949.
- The *Rinchen Ling dance manual*. The untitled dance manual (*'cham yig*) is used during the Rimchö festival. It was composed in 1895 during the visit of Tenzin Chökyi Lodrö and consists of 48 lines written on cloth mounted on silk brocade.
- The *Rinchen Ling list of ritual expenses*. (Full title: *Handbook of Rinchen Ling's offering expenses, the clear lamp*. T. *Rin chen gling gi mchod rgyun gtong gzhi'i [bzhi'i] len sprod [krod] lag khyer gsal ba'i sgron me*). The list exists in two versions: the older more detailed list was composed in an unspecified year of the Wood Pig (probably 1935) and is kept in the monastery archive, whereas the more recent version (1995) is an updated summary kept by the steward (*gnyer pa*).

22 The monastery, founded in 1681 by Drigung Trinle Zangpo ('Bri gung 'Phrin las bZang po) and Dondrup Chögyal (Don grub Chos rgyal), was under the control of the Drigung *bla brang*.

23 The text consists of thirty-four lines written in *tshugs thung* script on a scroll of Tibetan paper and is authorised by the seal of the throne holder. The text, which normally is simply referred to as 'the old laws' (*khrims rnying pa*) belongs to the *bca' yig* genre. The term *bca' yig* was translated as 'monastic constitution' by Ter Ellingson (1990) in his pioneering study of the genre. However, Berthe Jansen (2015) persuasively argues that the vaguer 'monastic regulations' is a better translation.

24 The last two syllables are illegible. See Chapter Eight.

- The *Rinchen Ling monastery inventory*. (Full title: *A summary of the great inventory of permanent [possessions of] the sacred Waltse Thubten Rinchen Ling temple, as an immaculate string of white lotuses*. T. *Chos 'khor dbal rtse'i gtsug lag khang thub bstan rin chen gling gi [gis] gtan deb [debs] chen mo don bsdus dri med padma dkar po'i 'phreng ba tshar du mngar ba*). The document, which was first composed in 1690, contains historical information about the monastery and an inventory of the monastery's objects. The text notes that it was copied from an older original in 1870, but contains numerous updates, and I suspect the current version to be more recent, perhaps from the first part of the twentieth century.[25]
- The *Rinchen Ling tax register*. (Full title: *List of grain due as lease fee in the eighth month of the Water Dragon year*. T. *Chu 'brug zla 8 nang gi [kyi] bca' [ca] yong 'bab [bab] zhal 'bru [brus] tho bkod [bskod] pa la*). The sixty-year (*rab byung*) cycle is not specified, but judging from the names in the list it was most likely composed in 1952.
- The *Til Kundzom list of ritual expenses*. (Full title: *List of offerings to [Til Kundzom] Dongak Monastery*, T. *mDo sngags dgon [rgon] gyi mchod deb [debs]*). The text is dated the Earth Monkey year, probably 1968, and lists the expenses for the Rimchö (Rim mchod) and Saga Dawa (Sa ga zla ba) festivals.[26] There is also an updated register from Til, which was adapted from the Waltse register written after the split of the monasteries in the 1990s.[27]
- *Waltse tax register*. (This unnamed booklet consists of two main documents referred to locally as *bCa' yig* and *Ban yig*).[28]

The above-mentioned texts belong to different genres, and most were handwritten by different scribes. Some contain a mix of Central and Humli Tibetan with inconsistent spelling. The Village Assembly assigned a senior villager to help dechipher the village tax documents, and he spent hours and numerous cups of butter tea going through relevant texts with me and Rinchen Loden. Similarly, a senior monk was given permission by the monk assembly to be absent from some of the monastic rituals so that he could patiently help us read through the monastery inventory, the list of ritual expenses, the monastery regulations, and the tax register. Phuntsok Dorje helped me to study the relevant sections of *grub thob* Senge Yeshe's (Seng ge Ye shes, 1181–1255) biography

25 More information about the monastery inventory is provided in Chapter Three.

26 As detailed in Chapter Seven, Rimchö (Rim mchod) is the most important festival in Limi, celebrated with monastic dances. The Saga Dawa (Sa ga zla ba) festival celebrates the Buddha's birth, enlightenment and *parinirvāṇa*.

27 More information about the texts is provided in Chapter Nine.

28 The spelling and meaning of *ban* in *ban yig* are uncertain. See Chapter Six for a brief discussion.

(part of the thirteenth century *bKa' brgyud kyi rnam thar chen mo rin po che'i gter mdzod dgos 'dod 'byung gnas*) as well as the biographies of Serta (gSer thar) Rinpoche and Tshogkhang (Tshogs khang) Rinpoche, two Nyingma masters who visited Limi. Rinchen Loden similarly helped me to study most of the other texts. For my translation of the monastic recruitment document, which I only obtained after I had returned to Norway, I received invaluable help from Charles Ramble, Nyima Drandul, and Per Kværne.[29]

---

29 The recruitment document is translated and discussed in Chapter Eight.

CHAPTER 3

Limi's Frontier History

> Whether in the sunny inner courtyard of their houses, whilst sipping tea in the kitchen or chatting at the gathering place in front of the monastery, it was mainly the grandfathers who used to sit and teach me about the old Limi history. They so generously shared their knowledge and memories of what their grandparents had told them, helping me piece together the origins of their community, the history of monasteries and hermitages, pilgrimage, trade and the various interconnections with neighbouring administrations and communities. Their recollections were filled with stories of distant ancestors, abandoned settlements, the meaning of place names, remarkable events, occasionally interspersed with descriptions of colourful characters and religious miracles. We had a mutual interest in bringing together the living memories of the historical and mythological past and connect these with the ancient historic documents, enigmatic enough to require a lot of interpretation.

∴

Stitching together the history of a small Himalayan frontier community like Limi is a difficult and time-consuming task. The nature of individual recollections of events in ancient times is necessarily messy and mentions of Limi in historical documents and biographies are rare. Although a few historical accounts can be found in the village archives, they are fragmented and no attempt has been made to (re)construct more comprehensive narratives. This chapter explores what local and regional source material tells us about the history of the Limi settlements, the temples and monasteries, and about the community's relationship to regional powers, all compounded by the frequently changing political configurations.

Throughout the centuries, Limi has been under varying degrees of control by kingdoms on both sides of the border. Several times throughout history, these kingdoms were at war, and it is not always clear which kingdom exercised control over which territory. Documents show that Limi has been regarded as

 | DOI:10.1163/9789004714571_004

located on Mon[1] territory from at least the thirteenth century onwards, and this has been reflected in the practice of paying land tax (*sa khral*) to the various kingdoms ruling in Western Nepal. Yet, the people have been regarded as Tibetan and have paid a poll tax (*mi khral*) to the administration in Purang as well as taxes to three of the monasteries in the Ngari (mNga' ris) region. As Nancy Levine has pointed out, much of the early history of the westernmost part of Nepal remains unwritten.[2] A proper study of the history of Limi would have required meticulous scrutiny of numerous Tibetan, Nepali, and Sanskrit documents and inscriptions, and falls beyond the scope of this book but I will provide a brief historical outline to aid our understanding of the system of local governance and the role that temples and monasteries came to play in the community.

Firstly, I give an account of the migration stories and the establishment of the first settlements in Limi, but because of the inconsistencies and legendary nature of the sources, this section will be kept brief. The second part will be devoted to a discussion of the foundation of the first temple in Waltse and how it relates to the broader history of the second dissemination of Buddhism (*bstan pa phyi dar*) in Tibet and the activities of the translator Rinchen Zangpo (Lo tswa ba Rin chen bZang po, 958–1055), a figure that has been subject to considerable mythologisation. The next part of the chapter will detail how Limi came to be included in the Drigung fold, and how the system of monastic patronage was established. Following a rough chronology, I will then piece together an account of Limi under the Jumla kingdom, Limi's relations with Tibet in the seventeenth century and the newly formed state of Nepal in the eighteenth. Finally, I will summarise some key historical events in the nineteenth and twentieth centuries, which provide important reference points for the current relationship between monastery and community in Limi, culminating with the split of the monasteries in the 1980s.

My brief re-construction of Limi's history is based on a combination of historical documents, oral history, toponyms, and observations, supplemented

1 The term Mon has been used in Tibetan sources as a general term to designate the lands on the southern border of the Tibetan plateau. In this case Mon refers to the territory in contemporary north-western Nepal that was ruled by the Khas Malla kings and later the Kalyal kings of Jumla. See for instance Tucci 1956.

2 Levine 1988a: 24. Tucci's preliminary report from 1956, which is mainly a genealogical study, is still one of the most important sources. Other important contributions include those of Petech (1984), Adhikary (1997) and articles by Pandey (1970a–c, 1971). See also Bishop 1990.

by secondary sources.[3] The main textual source is the *Rinchen Ling monastery inventory*, but relevant passages from the *Drigung history of Kailash* (*Ti se gnas bshad*) will be frequently quoted.[4] Other historical documents consulted include the *Middle length biography of Rinchen Zangpo* (*Lo tswa ba'i rnam thar 'bring po*),[5] the *Catalogue of the three silver brothers* (*Jo bo dngul sku mched gsum dkar chag*), the *Catalogue of Khochar Monastery* (*Kho char dkar chag*), the *Great Biography of the Kagyu masters* (*bKa' brgyud rnam thar chen mo*) and the *Biography of Chenga Drigung Lingpa* (*sPyan snga 'bri gung gling pa'i rnam thar*).[6]

The *Rinchen Ling monastery inventory* contains historical information about the monastery and an inventory of the monastery's objects and consists of 54 folios stitched together to form a booklet. The inventory was first compiled in 1690 at the order of the Drigung vajraholder of Kailash, but the current version of the text contains several updates and was probably copied in the first part of the twentieth century. Although the *Rinchen Ling monastery inventory* is a *gtan deb* (lit. 'permanent inventory') manuscript,[7] the overall structure and most of the contents are consistent with with the *dkar chag* ('list of contents') genre.[8] After an opening eulogy of the Buddhas, Bodhisattvas, and protectors, the inventory provides an outline of the monastery's history, followed by a catalogue of the monastery's belongings, and a number of administrative records. The book is a handwritten manuscript consulted mainly for administrative purposes. The scribe reports that the inventory had to be reconstructed as the older original had become 'tattered' (*hrul skyon*) and 'fragmented' (*'thor ba*)

3 Vitali's (1996) translation and analysis of the *Ngari Chronicles* (*mNga' ris rgyal rabs*) in *The Kingdoms of Gu.ge Pu.hrang* has been particularly useful.

4 This text is also referred to as *Ti se gnas bshad*, the short title written on the folios, and has been studied by a number of other scholars. See for instance Huber and Rigzin 1999.

5 I have consulted two versions of Rinchen Zangpo's biography included in the *Collected biographical material* (1977) from Kyil (dKyil) monastery in Spiti. Snellgrove and Skorupski (1980) made their edited version and translation mainly based on the biographies in this collection, and to facilitate comparison I have adopted their system and refer to the texts as A and C respectively. Snellgrove and Skorupski (1980: 83f) regard A as the earliest text and C as an edited version of A. The nineteen-folio manuscript reprinted at the end of Tucci's (1988) book about Rinchen Zangpo is very similar to, but not identical with, C.

6 The Tibetan titles in parentheses are only abbreviated versions. Full titles are provided in the bibliography.

7 The *gtan deb* is a type of document that has not been discussed in studies of Tibetan historical genres. The only reference I have found is Dan Martin's brief comment in the THL online dictionary: 'Vitali, Tho-ling 5, corrects to *rten deb* "register of icons". However, it may not require correction, and would mean "permanent inventory' or "inventory of permanent [possessions of the temple].'"

8 See Martin 1996: 500–14 and Venturi 2013: 141–71.

after several years' usage but claims that an effort has been made to ensure that the text is correct.[9] Nevertheless, there are several lacunae in the historical outline and important historical events which are supposed to have taken place in Limi receive no more than cursory mention. Although the book is an important source of local historical knowledge, the text must be read with caution and compared with other sources.

3.1 Before and Beyond Buddhism

3.1.1 *Migration Stories*

People in Limi say that a long time ago, during 'the early dissemination of the teachings' (*bstan pa snga dar*), their ancestors migrated southwards from the plateau and settled in the Limi valley. Exact knowledge of their origins seems to be lost, but some of the elderly people say that the first settlers came from the area surrounding Hor Kongyu Tsho (Hor Gung rgyud mTsho), a large lake in Hor Chu, a nomadic area about two days' walk to the east of Lake Manasarovar. Other people believed that their ancestors came from elsewhere in Ngari and, as will be discussed below, a number of local names suggest origins from Purang (sPu hreng),[10] the Kailash area, and the upper Sutlej River valley.

There have been several waves of migration from the Tibetan plateau to Humla.[11] The ancestors of the current Nyinbas,[12] for instance, who have traditionally had close relations with people in Limi, seem to have migrated as late as the seventeenth century,[13] whereas Limi was settled before the eleventh century and may be among the earliest Tibetan communities in the district. Tracing old clan names[14] could have helped shed light on the obscure

9 The scribe assures the reader that when they wrote the new version of the inventory, they investigated (unspecified) 'written documents' (*yig cha*) as well as the elders' 'authentic' (*tshad thub*) oral tradition. *Rinchen Ling monastery inventory* f. 2b, l. 3–5.

10 Purang is also spelled sPu hrengs, Pu hrang, and Pu rang in historical documents.

11 Humla is normally spelled 'Om lo in Tibetan. However, spellings like 'Um lo, 'Om blo, and Wom lo also occur in historical documents. In daily speech Humla is referred to either as 'Om lo or 'Om bu lung pa.

12 The Nyinba villages form a community near Humla's district headquarters Simikot. See for instance Levine 1976, 1987, 1988, Wiebenga and Lama (in press) and Lama 2012.

13 According to the legend quoted in Levine (1988a: 27f and 1976).

14 The term 'clan' has been subject to considerable discussion (see for instance Fjeld 2022: 14ff and 49ff). In Tibetological literature it has been used to translate *rus pa* ('bone [line]') or the more general *rgyud pa* ('lineage' or 'succession'). The term can be interpreted in different ways according to context. I use it according to Tibetological convention to refer to the ideology of patrilineage, but (as several scholars have pointed out) the Tibetan

origin of the community, but the old lineages in Limi no longer have any corporate identity and knowledge about the clans has been largely forgotten. Initially I thought that the names of the three main 'groups' (*tsho*)[15] for social organisation in Waltse, Khyungdruwa (Khyung bru ba?),[16] Serwa (gSer ba?),[17] and Drablasungwa (sGra bla srung ba?), could provide clues about the origins of the villagers' ancestors. The former two consist of old Tibetan clan names, whereas the latter refers to the cult of warrior deities (*dgra lha*).[18] However, the villagers did not recognise them as clan names; instead, they pointed out that Khyungdruwa, Serwa and Drablasungwa are names of pastures formerly belonging to each of the groups (*tsho*) used to organise communal activities. Some of the villagers thought that the names attributed to the group of people belonging to the three 'ancestral deities' (*pho lha*)[19] had originally been clan names: the adherents of the deity Gangri Lhabtsen (Gangs ri lHa btsan) are called Chogrowa (Cog ro ba),[20] the adherents of Takhyung Karpo/Namse (rTa khyung dKar po/rNam sras)[21] are referred to as Miluwa (Mi lus pa?), and finally, the adherents of the deity Gyalpo (rGyal po) are called Rimdzöwa

terms *rus pa* or *rgyud pa* do not necessarily imply kinship relations. In Limi they say that whereas clan membership may still hold significancy in certain contexts, the patrilineage has since long been watered down. See also the discussion of the term *pha'i spun* in Chapter Four, footnote 18.

15 *Tsho* simply means 'group' and is used to denote many different types of social organisation. Here it refers to the groups through which obligatory labour and other communal activities are organised in Limi. For more details, see Chapter Six.

16 According to Tshewang Lama (personal communication) Khyungpa (Khyung pa) and Druwa (Bru ba) are common clan names in the Nyinba villages. The Khyungpa name has its origin from the Sutlej river valley, whereas Druwa stems from from Drusha (Bru sha), contemporary Gilgit-Baltistan, and is one of the six first clan names in Tibet. See also Lama 2012: 43.

17 According to Tshewang Lama (personal communication), Serwa is a common clan name in the Drugchu Lung (Drug bcu lung) villages further south in Humla. See also Childs' (1997a) article on Serwa clan membership among the Sherpas.

18 According to Snellgrove (1967: 258, n. 20), the prevalent spelling in Bon literature is *sgra bla*, whereas in Buddhist literature, this type of deity is often spelled *dgra lha*. For a brief account of the performance of *dgra lha* rituals in Limi, see Chapter Seven.

19 Although *pho lha* is normally translated as 'ancestral deity' or 'god of the males', Ramble (2008a: 138f) argues that in the case of Te, in Nepal's Mustang District, the *pho lha* is more appropriately described as 'household god'. A similar argument could be made in the case of Limi. Adherence to *pho lha* normally follows patrilineal descent, but in the case of uxorilocal *mag pa* weddings the groom has to change his *pho lha* to that of his wife.

20 Cog ro is also spelled lCog ro.

21 Takhyung Karpo is a local territorial deity (both a *pho lha* and a *yul lha*), who has been partly merged with the deity Namse. The deity is believed to reside in a pointed mountain in Limi and is also worshipped by other communities in Humla. See Chapter Seven.

(Ri mdzod pa?). The fact that Gangri Lhabtsen is one of the three ancestral deities in Limi suggests an origin from the Kailash area as the deity is also the territorial protector deity (*zhing skyong*) of Mount Kailash.[22] Chogrowa, the name of his followers in Limi, strengthens the connection as Chogro (Cog ro) is both the name of a village in Purang and an ancient clan from Western Tibet.[23] However, even if these were names of old Limi clans, a direct relation between patrilineal descent and adherence to ancestral deity, if it ever existed in Limi, has been forgotten. Given the limited evidence it seems safest to assume that the ancestors of the current inhabitants were migrants (*khyams pa*) moving to Limi from different places. This would explain the villagers' diverging accounts and is also what people further south in Humla say about them.[24]

3.1.2 *Nettle Eaters from 'the Land In-Between'*

Whereas their exact origin is uncertain, the Limigya agree that their ancestors migrated from the Tibetan plateau and first settled in Tshamdo (mTshams mdo?),[25] the ruined hamlet at the eastern end of the valley. This settlement was built at the confluence of the two rivers from Hrakya (Sra skya?) and Nying (sNying) and subsequently gave its name to the community. Sle means 'the land in-between [the rivers]'[26] and Sle mi can therefore be translated as 'the people from the Land in-between' (Fig. 1.2). A fortress, which was initially named Chödzong Nyinda Khabjor (Chos rdzong Nyi zla Kha sbyor, 'The religious fortress where the sun and the moon unite'), was built on top of a high hill overlooking the area. According to local lore, the fortress was once attacked. A storyteller from Waltse provided this version:

> At one time, a Mon[27] king set out to conquer the settlement in order to incorporate Chödzong Nyinda Khabjor into his kingdom. He sent an

22 Buffetrille 2003: 239.

23 Dotson 2012: 185.

24 Fürer-Haimendorf 1988: 271.

25 In the local documents, the place name is variously spelled mTshan rto (*Rinchen Ling monastery inventory* f. 50a) and mTshams tho (*Waltse tax register*, pp. 79 and 81). To further complicate the matter, the place name is occasionally pronounced mTshams mtsho/tsho. I have chosen to use the spelling mTshams mdo, as the meaning of *mdo* is akin to that of *sle*, the first syllable in Limi. I am grateful to Per Kværne for pointing out the connection.

26 In this context Sle and Gle seem to have the same meaning. *Bod rgya tshig mdzod chen mo* (p. 427) defines *gle* as 'a plain between two rivers' (*chu gnyis bar gyi gram thang*).

27 The term Mon has been variously used in Tibetan sources to designate the lands to the south of the Tibetan plateau, from Sikkim in the east to Nepal in the west. In this case it refers to the territory in contemporary north-western Nepal that was ruled by the Khas

> army, but when the commander saw the large fortress, he realised that they had to make a clever plan. He decided to besiege the fortress; the strategy was to wait until the inhabitants ran out of water. However, one of the grandmothers was very clever; on the seventh day of the siege, she melted a large amount of butter and from the top of the fortress, she pretended to wash her hair with the oil. From a distance the oil looked like water, and in this way she deceived the army. The Mon commander thought that there would have to be an internal water source in the fortress and gave up the siege. Since this time, the fortress has been given the name Abi Genmo Dzong (A phyi rGan mo rDzong), 'The old grandmother's fortress'.[28]

Four remaining stone pillars indicate that there has indeed been a fortress on the hill, strategically located at the conjunction between the Limi valley and one of the main paths from Humla to the Tibetan plateau.[29] It is likely that the fortress has been attacked, as control of this area would entail control of an important trans-Himalayan trade and pilgrimage route. One of the oldest men in Dzang related that in the middle period Tshamdo was captured by Tibet and established as an administrative unit (*rdzong*),[30] but later the fortress was destroyed by the Jumla king.[31] The remaining ruins below the fortress show that the hamlet originally consisted of two settlements, which are the subject of another local legend:

> Originally, there were two settlements in Tshamdo. One of the settlements, which was inhabited by wealthy people, was called Chugpo Zhangzhung [Phyug po Zhang zhung][32] and the other, which was inhabited by poor people, was called Mepo Changthang [Med po Byang

---

Malla kings and later the Kalyal kings. For a pioneering study of these kingdoms, see Tucci 1956.

28 This legend is apparently a Limi adaptation of a general motif to the community's 'mythical' past. Bellezza (2010: 29 and 82) recounts legends with relatively similar plots connected with two different western Tibetan archaeological sites.

29 Bellezza (2011: 93, n.97) speculates that Rgan mo rdzong may be one of the surviving pre-Buddhist sites in this region.

30 The *rdzong* as an administrative unit was established in Central Tibet by Ta'i Si tu Byang chub rGyal mtshan in the fourteenth century.

31 Interview with an elderly man from Dzang, 19.04.12. This detail is of little help in dating the event as the Jumla king could refer to any king from the Yatse kingdom (twelfth–fourteenth centuries) or the Jumli Kalyal principality (fifteenth–eighteenth centuries).

32 Some people used the name Chugpo Zhanang (Phyug po Zhwa nang).

> thang].[33] The wealthy inhabitants of Chugpo Zhangzhung owned large herds of animals, whereas the people from Mepo Changthang worked as their servants. However, Mepo Changthang had a lot of nettles and once, during the third month, as the nettles were growing, the villagers told their rich masters: "We have plenty of food, we don't need to be your servants, we can sustain ourselves on nettle soup," and so they resigned.

The story was told in many variants, but the above version was the most common. Whether the legend is a reminiscence of a history of dependency and poverty is difficult to assess, but it is suggestive of the self-sufficient mentality of the people from Limi, and nettle soup is still one of the most important local staples. After some time, so the story goes, the population in Tshamdo increased, but there were problems with irrigation. One lama made the villagers construct irrigation canals to bring water down from Lhadzin Gompa (lHa 'dzin/rdzing dGon pa?),[34] an old hermitage just below Rakarwu (Ra dkar dbu?).[35] But eventually, some of the households migrated into the Limi valley: seven households settled in Waltse, four in Til, and seven in Dzang.[36] Tshamdo village seems to have continued to thrive until it was suddenly abandoned, possibly in the first half of the nineteenth century.[37]

The first settlement in Waltse was located at Lehong,[38] the ridge to the west of the current village. Several ruins can still be seen and one of the villagers, commented that the ruins showed that the houses must have been quite simple with only one floor and two rooms: one for people and one for animals.[39] He had found a number of clay (*rdza*) pots among the ruins, which had been used for boiling food and water, and there are still threshing stones on the site, which would be used to hull the grain during harvest. He explained that after some time the population at the Lehong ridge increased, and the first

33 In alternative versions of the legend, the names Mepo Zhaphug (Med po Zha? phug) or Mepo Thaljor (Med po Thal 'byor?) are used. Zhaphug is still used as toponym.

34 This may be another candidate for 'Lhi mi lHa rdzing' mentioned in Rinchen Zangpo's biography. See the discussion in Chapter Three.

35 Rakarwu is the name of a high valley to the east of Tshamdo used as pastureland. The villagers were uncertain about the meaning of the place name, which may also be spelled Ra dkar rus.

36 Lists of these households were provided by senior men and women in the three villages.

37 A brief discussion of how the settlement may have become abandoned is provided at the end of the chapter.

38 Uncertain spelling.

39 In the past, such a division was common also in small Norwegian mountain farms.

three families, the Dzardziwa (rDza rtsibs ba),[40] Kurgyab (sKu rgyab?),[41] and Zurkhang (Zur khang) moved over to the current location of the village and sought refuge around the temple.[42]

Very little is known about the history of the Zhangzhung kingdom,[43] but recent Bonpo works like *A study of the early history of Tibet according to Bon* (*sNga rabs bod kyi byung ba brjod pa'i 'bel gtam lung gi snying po*) by Tenzin Namdak list Limi and Humla among the Zhangzhung communities.[44] However, we do not know if Limi was populated that early and even if it was, connections with Zhangzhung are now forgotten.[45] Be that as it may, the conversion to Buddhism is likely to have been a gradual process, and there are some remnants of what may be perceived as pre-Buddhist cults in Limi.[46] Moreover, as Church and Wiebenga point out, the name of Waltse village, at least in its spelling dBal rtse,[47] may suggest a link to the Bonpo deity Welse (dBal gsas)[48] or Welchen Gekhö (dBal chen Ge khod). Welchen Gekhö is believed to reside at Mount Kailash[49] and his consort Drabli Gyalmo (sGra bla'i rGyal mo, 'Queen of the warrior deities')[50] is believed to reside in Mount Memo Nagnyil (sMan mo Nag snyil),[51] the massif that forms the border between Limi and Manasarovar. But spellings of toponyms vary considerably and cannot be taken as evidence,

40 rDza rtsibs, which means 'to the side of the rocks', refers to the location of the house near a field of scree and large boulders. The variant spellings rDzar rdzib pa/rtsib pa/tsib pa can be found in the *Rinchen Ling monastery inventory*.

41 The spelling is most likely sKu rgyab, which means 'behind the statues' referring to the location of the house just behind the monastery.

42 I was given many different explanations for the moving of settlement. Some people suggested that the inhabitants were haunted by spirits and therefore sought refuge around the temple.

43 Kværne 2001: 13.

44 Tenzin Namdak 1997: 24.

45 Zhanzhung imagery is comparatively much more prevalent in oral and ritual traditions further south in Humla.

46 See Chapter Seven.

47 The spelling dBal rtse occurs more frequently in the monastic documents, whereas Wal rtse is the most common spelling in village documents. The spelling on the village stamp is the phonetically simple Wa tse. In English, the spelling Halji is normally used.

48 Church and Wiebenga 2008.

49 Kværne 2001: 80.

50 Also known as Logbar Tsame (Glog 'bar Tsa med). See Kværne 2001: 81. For an account of Drabli Gyalmo traditions in Humla, see Lama 2012: 108.

51 The *sman mo* are female wrathful spirits constituting the retinue of the goddess Drabli Gyalmo, whereas *nag snyil* means 'black fringes' (Lama 2012: 108), referring to the many dark eroded valleys carved out by melt water streams from the glacier. On western maps this mountain is more commonly known as Mount Gurla Mandhata (7694 metres). See also Diemberger, Hovden and Yeh 2015. The name Gurla suggests that the mountain

and even if the spelling dBal rtse were correct, knowledge of such a link is lost in Waltse today. In the following account, I will concentrate on the period from the second dissemination of Buddhism (*bstan pa phyi dar*)[52] onwards, which is better documented.

3.2 *The Second Dissemination of Buddhism as Experienced from the Frontier*

The territory of Zhangzhung, which had been conquered by Tibet in the middle of the seventh century, had been largely left to itself after the collapse of the Tibetan monarchy.[53] During the period from the middle of the ninth century, which later Tibetan historiography has characterised as a dark age,[54] the monasteries in Central Tibet lost their royal support and many were abandoned. Traditional accounts of religious persecution seem to be exaggerated; instead, research suggests that Buddhist traditions continued to thrive at the local level outside institutional control.[55]

In the beginning of the tenth century, Kyide Nyimagön (sKyid lde Nyi ma mgon), a descendant of the royal family, fled from the turmoil in Central Tibet and decided to establish himself in the West.[56] Through marital affiliation he first gained control of Purang, then he conquered Guge,[57] and after a bloody campaign against Ladakh (La dwags)[58] he founded a new kingdom in the 'Three districts of Ngari' (mNga' ris skor gsum).[59] His heirs subsequently divided the districts into three separate kingdoms.[60] Tashigön (bKra

has also been associated with the *mgur/'gur lha* class of deities. See Nebesky-Wojkowitz 1996: 223.

52 See Dalton (2011: 97–109) for an interesting analysis and van Schaik (2011: 54ff) for a very readable summary of the events. More details are provided in Snellgrove (2004), Petech (2003), and Vitali (1996, 2003).

53 Petech 2003: 33.

54 This period is also referred to in Tibetan sources as 'the age of fragmentation in Tibet' (*bod sil bu'i dus*) (Stoddard 2004: 55). For an analysis of the causes of the political fragmentation of Tibet, see van Schaik (2011: 41–47).

55 See for instance Dalton 2011: 45–47 and 49–57.

56 Stoddard 2004: 89.

57 Purang and Guge were originally separate kingdoms, but throughout much of its history Purang was part of Guge.

58 Ladakh is referred to as Maryul (Mar yul) in early texts, sometimes confused with Mangyul (Mang yul), the district to the east of Guge and Purang.

59 Vitali (2003: 54f) suggests 912 as the earliest possible date for the establishment of the kingdom.

60 See Petech 2003: 33 and Vitali 2003: 55.

shis mgon) inherited Guge and Purang,[61] and his son, the devout King Songe (Srong nge), more commonly known by his ordination name Yeshe Ö (Ye shes 'Od, 947–1024),[62] initiated a religious campaign which marked the onset of the second dissemination of Buddhism in Western Tibet.[63] In 986 he issued 'the great edict' (*bka' shog chen mo*), in which he proclaimed Buddhism to be the state religion, followed in 988 by a 'decree' (*chos rtsigs*) which introduced a new legal system that detailed both 'religious law' (*chos khrims*) and 'civil law' (*rgyal khrims*)[64] and introduced the rule that except for the heir to the throne, all other male members of the royal family should become monks, thus avoiding previous violent throne succession strategies.[65] Only if the throne was vacant should a monk member of the family leave the monastery to take up the royal seat. Snellgrove characterises this rule as '... remarkable because for the first time in Tibetan history an aristocratic family appears in the dual rôle of head of state and religious head, sharing these functions between them'.[66] This would later become one of the most distinctive characteristics of the Tibetan governments.[67] This 'division of labour' within the royal household may perhaps also be seen as a precursor to later monastic recruitment rules in Tibet.[68] The decree also stated that Buddhism should be 'reintroduced' to the three districts of Ngari.[69] Shortly after, a 'pronouncement' (*bka' stsal*) was delivered in front of an assembly of headmen in the kingdom, encouraging them to follow the laws of religion and the state detailed in the decree. Finally, troubled by what he saw as degenerate tantric practices, Yeshe Ö subsequently wrote an 'ordinance' (*bka' shog*) in the form of an open letter in which he criticised the

---

61 According to the twelfth century *Nyang ral chos 'byung* (quoted in Vitali 2003: 55), the kingdom of Tashigön included also Yatse. If so, Limi may also have been included, but this might have been a later interpretation.

62 According to Vitali's (2003: 57) chronology, King Songe gave the throne to his younger brother Khorre (Khor re) and was ordained as a monk in 988. In some sources Yeshe Ö has been identified with Khorre rather than Songe, whereas in other sources Khorre is identified as the elder brother rather than the younger. I have chosen to follow Karmay (2003: 134f) and Vitali (2003 and 1996: 171–78), who have provided the most thorough discussions of the topic.

63 Vitali 2003: 54. The other major centre for the second dissemination of Buddhism was Eastern Tibet. See for instance van Schaik 2011: 50ff.

64 Dalton 2011: 103.

65 See for instance van Schaik 2011: 275, n. 28.

66 Snellgrove 2004: 472.

67 Ibid. 472.

68 The monastic recruitment rules are discussed in Chapter Eight.

69 Vitali 2003: 57.

tantric practitioners for too literal interpretations of the tantric teachings and encouraged a stricter adherence to conventional Mahāyāna tradition.[70]

Yeshe Ö and his descendants advocated a monastic form of Buddhism and sponsored the construction of a number of temples and monasteries in the region. In order to avoid further spread of what he saw as deviating interpretations of the tantric teachings, the king also sponsored a large number of new translations of what were regarded as authentic Buddhist texts from India.[71] The translator Rinchen Zangpo, a native of Räni (Rad nis) in Guge, who had spent years studying with Sanskrit masters in Kashmir, proved ideal for the task of leading the translation work and overseeing the temple construction. In 1037 Changchub Ö (Byang chub 'Od), the king's nephew who had now taken over the throne, sent the translator Nagtsho Tshultrim Gyelwa (Nag mtsho Tshul khrims rGyal ba) to Vikramaśīla in India in order to invite the religious master Atiśa Dīpaṃkara Śrījñāna (Jo bo rje dPal ldan A ti sha, or rJe A ti sha, 982?–1054).[72] Nagtsho eventually succeeded and returned with the religious master to Ngari in 1042.[73] The latter became, together with Yeshe Ö and Rinchen Zangpo, emblematic for the second dissemination of Buddhism. Rinchen Zangpo is reported to have been involved in the translation and revision of more than 170 Buddhist scriptures.[74] He is also credited with the foundation of 108 temples and monasteries throughout the region,[75] the most renowned of which is the temple of Tholing (Tho ling gtsug lag khang),[76] founded in 996.[77] This extensive building of temples and monasteries was a conscious imitation of the first dissemination of Buddhism in Tibet.[78] Major temples were built at

70 The ordinance has been most thoroughly studied by Karmay 2003: 134ff.

71 For an account of Yeshe Ö's efforts to purge the contemporary religious practices, see Dalton (2011: 95ff).

72 According to later Tibetan historiography, the pretext for inviting Atiśa was that King Yeshe Ö had been captured by the Turks, who demanded his body weight in gold as ransom. However, as van Schaik (based on Vitali's 1990 study of the *Ngari Chronicles*) points out, the captive is more likely to have been Changchub Ö's brother, as Yeshe Ö is reported to have died of old age in the *Middle length biography of Rinchen Zangpo*. Van Schaik 2011 (e-book): 57, 275 n. 29.

73 Davidson 2005: 109.

74 Rigzin (1984: 32–36) provides a list of 174 works, whereas Gangngegi (1998) provides a list of 178.

75 108 is an auspicious number, not to be taken literally.

76 The name Tholing occurs also with the spellings mTho lding, mTho ling, mTho gling, and Tho gling, but Vitali (1999: 4) points out that the earliest texts used the phonetically simple spelling Tho ling, whereas the spelling mTho lding originated with the dGe lugs pa in the fifteenth century. I have chosen to follow Vitali's approach and will use the spelling Tho ling, which is also the one used in the *Rinchen Ling monastery inventory*.

77 For a detailed study of Tholing Monastery, see Vitali 1999.

78 van Shaik 2011: 56.

the centre of the Western Tibetan kingdoms, but smaller temples were also constructed in the periphery as support for the dissemination of Buddhism.

3.2.1 *The Foundation of the First Temple in Waltse*

At the height of the Western Tibetan kings' temple-building fervour around the turn of the eleventh century, a temple was built in Waltse to house a four-fold Vairocana (rNam par snang mdzad) statue (Fig.3.1).[79] The Vairocana ensemble is placed on a richly ornamented four-sided throne, one statue facing each of the cardinal directions. The complex measures 5x3.5 metres from the floor to the top of the spire and is located in the centre of a temple at the western side of the present-day monastery compound.[80] As described in the *Rinchen Ling monastery inventory*, life-size statues of the Buddhas of the four other Buddha families[81] and their retinues are placed on a ledge along the walls surrounding the four-fold Vairocana.[82] Today only twenty-five statues remain (Fig. 3.2), but according to the senior monks a total of thirty-two statues surrounded the Vairocana in the past. Moreover, the *Rinchen Ling monastery inventory* records that the walls were covered by murals of the inner and outer circle of deities of the celestial palace of the Vairocana mandala.[83] Elder villagers confirm that there were indeed murals in the past, but that they were destroyed during restoration of the crumbling temple walls approximately forty years ago. Today the walls are painted in a stark blue colour. The statues too have recently been repainted, but according to Church and Wiebenga's iconographic analysis, the style and overall proportions of the statues bear resemblance to the tenth century Kashmiri style.[84] The artists, however, may have been local; the inventory simply records that '... the artists crafted the statues according to the excellent Indian style.'[85] Vitali writes that the appropriation of the Kashmiri style by local workshops was in fact explicitly encouraged by Yeshe Ö in his decree

79 The Vairocana statue has been studied by Church and Wiebenga (2008). The dating of the statue will be discussed below.

80 Church and Wiebenga 2008.

81 The five Buddha families (*rigs lnga*) consist of Vairocana (rNam par snang mdzad) in the centre, Akṣobhya (Mi 'khrugs pa) to the east, Ratnasaṃbhava (Rin chen 'byung gnas) to the south, Amitābha ('Od dpag med) to the west, and Amoghasiddhi (Don yod grub pa) to the north.

82 *Rinchen Ling monastery inventory*, f. 11a, l. 2–3: *phyogs bzhir rigs bzhi bcos tam* (difficult *bsdus yig*) *sku tshad gtso bo dang mtshungs sa 'khor sems dpa' dang sems ma mchod lha bcas kyi pad sgrags tho lnga pa kha shas dang.*

83 *Rinchen Ling monastery inventory*, f. 11a, l. 3f: *gzhal yas khang phyi nang gi lha tshogs bris 'bur sna tshogs kyi kun rig gi lha mgron yong rdzogs yod 'dug.*

84 Church and Wiebenga 2008.

85 *Rinchen Ling monastery inventory*, f. 11a, l. 4f: *gzo ris rnams kyang rgya gar gyi lugs ltar khyad du 'phags pa sha stag yod snang yang.*

(*chos rtsigs*).[86] Nevertheless, the construction of the statues must have been a costly affair and required highly skilled craftsmen.

Who could have erected such statues, who could have been the sponsor, and what could have been the reasons for establishing them in a place like Limi? The first place to start looking for an answer is the monastery's own records. Curiously, nothing is mentioned about the foundation of the temple in the historical section of the *Rinchen Ling monastery inventory*. But on folio 11a, in the section describing the monastery's statues, we find the following passage:

> In the centre of the lower part of the temple, which was originally constructed by the translator Rinchen Zangpo, the main religious object is a four-fold[87] statue of Vairocana. Each of the four (statues) measures five 'face lengths'[88] and is placed on a throne upheld by six lions, behind a wall-sized curtain.[89]

This states clearly that the Vairocana temple was founded by the translator Rinchen Zangpo himself. However, the presence of the Vairocana statue and the corresponding passage in the *Rinchen Ling monastery inventory* do not suffice as proof; similar claims of association with Rinchen Zangpo made about other temples in Western Tibet, for instance Alchi (A lci) in Ladakh, have been shown to be unfounded.[90] There is therefore good reason to be suspicious about the claim.

The extant biographies of Rinchen Zangpo contain lists of temples supposed to have been built by the translator, but Waltse does not figure in any of these lists.[91] If the *Rinchen Ling monastery inventory* had been the only source, the claim could therefore have been dismissed as unlikely. However, the lists of temples in the different versions of Rinchen Zangpo's biographies are not

86 Vitali (1996: 271): 'This legal act [*chos rtsigs*] promoted the creation of local workshops to produce images for the temples, which integrated the foreign output and assured a local supply'.

87 Literally *kun tu*—'in all directions'.

88 See Luczanits 2004: 15.

89 *lha khang shod kyi lte* [*lde*] *bar sngon du lo tsha+tsa ba rin chen bzang pos bzhengs pa'i rten gyis gtso bor rnam par snang mdzad kun tu zhal mtho* [*tho*] *lnga re yod pa bzhi la seng khri deng drug 'degs kyi rgyab yol bcas thog tshad ma. Rinchen Ling monastery inventory*, f. 11a, l. 1–2, my tentative translation.

90 See for instance Snellgrove and Skorupski 1980: 84.

91 The middle length biography is attributed to Rinchen Zangpo's direct disciple Pel Yeshe (dPal Ye shes) of Khyithang (Khyi thang) in Guge. Unfortunately, the extant versions of the manuscript are not dated, and mistakes could have been made over centuries of copying.

FIGURE 3.1 The fourfold Vairocana statue

consistent, and probably not complete.[92] Moreover, as Vitali points out, Limi is included among the twenty-one temples connected with Rinchen Zangpo

92 See for instance Snellgrove and Skorupski (1980: 91ff), Tucci (1988: 71–73), and Vitali (1996: 249–79) for a discussion of the conflicting lists of temples attributed to the translator.

FIGURE 3.2 Statues in the Vairocana temple

from the 996 period in two texts from the neighbouring Khochar (Kho char)[93] monastery (the sixteenth century *Jo bo dngul sku mched gsum dkar chag*[94] and the nineteenth century *Kho char dkar chag*[95]). Despite this, Vitali warns us that the inclusion of Limi in these two lists from Khochar may be due to regional bias.[96]

93 The name of Khochar (Kho char) is also frequently spelled 'Khor chags. For a discussion of the meaning of the name of the monastery, see Tsering Gyalpo (2006: 119). In Nepal, the monastery and village are frequently referred to as Khojarnath.

94 *Jo bo ngul sku mched gsum dkar chag* 1996: 22: *gzhan yang gu ger mtho lding lha khang / mar yul nyar ma'i lha khang / pi ti rong chung / ti yag kha se/ zher/ gling /pu rangs / sle mi sogs mu ku chos 'khor gyi jo bo mi skyod rdo rje dang mtshungs gtsug lag khang yul chung nyi shu rtsa gcig tu lha khang brgya rtsa brgyad bzhengs pa sogs bstan pa bya ba lhag par che bar mdzad/*

95 The *Catalogue of Khochar Monastery* 1988: 54f: *lo chen 'di dang / mnga' bdag kho re dang/ de'i sras lha lde te mchod yon 'di rnams kyi sku dus su gu ge mtho ling lha khang / mang yul du nyar med lha khang / spi ti rong chung / ti yag kha zang / pu rang bzher/ sle mi sogs yul chung nyi shu rtsa gcig tu lha khang brgya dang brgyad bzhengs pa sogs la/ rgyal po'i sras kyis bdag rkyen* [*skyen*] *mdzad/.*

96 Vitali 1996: 268, n. 405.

Yet, there are a few other indicators suggesting that Rinchen Zangpo might have been involved in the building of the temple in Waltse. Many of the early temples had Vairocana statues as their central images.[97] According to Matthew Kapstein, the Vairocana cult constituted '… a clear reference to the symbolic codes of the old empire'.[98] Today, there are only two other remaining four-fold Vairocana statues from this period in the region. The two statues, which are in temples associated with Rinchen Zangpo in Spiti, show some similarities with the Vairocana in Waltse, but are more clearly crafted in Kashmiri style.[99] There also used to be a central Vairocana ensemble in Tholing, which was destroyed during the Cultural Revolution.[100] Hence, the Vairocana temple in Waltse fits well into a broader pattern. Folio 9a in the catalogue of the statues in the *Rinchen Ling monastery inventory* shows that there are also other statues suggesting a link with the translator:

> Moreover, (there is) one blessing-emanating statue of Lotsawa Rinchen Zangpo (containing) the lord's bodily remains erected on a lotus (throne) measuring 1 cubit and 3 finger-widths in height. Another statue of the Lotsawa is made of medicinal clay measuring 1 cubit and 4 finger-widths.[101]

Not only does the inventory identify two clay statues of Rinchen Zangpo in the monastery, but it also claims that one of the statues contains the remains of his dead body (Figs. 3.3 and 3.4). The monks in the monastery were not aware of the identity and importance of these statues until they were identified during the visit of the head lama of the Drigung Kagyu school, Drigung Kyabgön Chetsang Rinpoche ('Bri gung sKyab mgon Che tshang Rin po che, b. 1946)[102] in 2008. It was most likely the above passage in the inventory that prompted the hierarch to search for the rare statues. The statue, which is supposed to contain the relics of the translator, is covered in cobwebs and dust and is placed high up on a shelf in the corner of the assembly hall in the monastery.

97 See Snellgrove 2004: 209ff.

98 Kapstein 2006: 91.

99 Church and Wiebenga 2008.

100 See Tucci 1989 and Church and Wiebenga 2008. For a detailed study of Tholing, see Vitali 1999.

101 *yang lo tsa+tsha ba rin chen bzang po'i 'dra sku rje de nyid kyi sku gdung gi cha las bzhengs [gzhengs] pa pad sgrags kyi dpangs [dpang] su khru gang sor gsum yod pa byin ldan gcig/_yang sman 'jim las grub pa'i lo tsa+tsha ba'i 'dra sku khru gang sor bzhi pa gcig.* Rinchen *Ling monastery inventory*, f. 9a, l. 2–3.

102 Hereafter referred to as Kyabgön Rinpoche.

FIGURE 3.3 Rinchen Zangpo statue, supposedly containing his relics

It has lost both its hands but is otherwise intact. After its discovery by Kyabgön Rinpoche, the other statue was placed in a newly built shrine at the back wall of the Vairocana temple. If the inventory's claim is correct, the first statue may have been constructed a relatively short time after the translator's death but since they have not been dated it is impossible to verify this claim.[103] The statues are nevertheless quite interesting as the only other known statues of the translator are to be found in Khochar monastery[104] and in a temple in Katse[105] in Rongchung (Rong chung), the birthplace of Rinchen Zangpo's father.[106] The Katse statue is made of bronze, but the iconographic resemblance to the two clay statues in Waltse is striking.

When assessing the likelihood of Rinchen Zangpo's involvement in the foundation of the first temple in Waltse, the geographical location of the village should also be taken into account.[107] Waltse is located only one long day's

103 I will return to the discussion about the location of Rinchen Zangpo's place of death below.

104 The bronze statue in Khochar was built in the sixteenth century. See Tsering Gyalpo et al. 2012: 60.

105 Katse is variously spelled Kā rtse or Kha rtse.

106 I was made aware of the statue by David Pritzker, who kindly shared his photos and translation of the inscription with me. See also Pritzker 2000: 131ff.

107 Kurt Tropper (personal communication) points out that like Khochar, Tholing, and some other temples from this period, Rinchen Ling is constructed on flat ground, whereas most of the later monasteries were located at hilltops or on hillsides.

FIGURE 3.4 Rinchen Zangpo statue made of medicinal clay

walk from Zher (Zher), where Rinchen Zangpo owned an estate[108] and only a few hours' walk from Chaye (sPya ye),[109] which, according to the thirteenth

108 Snellgrove and Skorupski 1980: 95.

109 The name of the cave is occasionally also spelled Ca se and lCags ye.

FIGURE 3.5 Entrance to Rinchen Zangpo's meditation cave at Chaye

century *Great biography of the Kagyu masters,* was the meditation cave of Rinchen Zangpo (Figs. 3.5 and 3.6).[110]

The Rinchen Ling temple in Waltse appears to have acquired its name from Rinchen Zangpo, but none of the three written sources which include Limi on the list of the translator's temples specify their names.[111] The fifteenth century *Ngari Chronicles* (*mNga' ris rgyal rabs*), however, does indeed mention a temple with the name Rinchen Ling, but this temple is associated with a different founder.[112] The chronicle records that King Sönam Tse (bSod nams rTse) of Guge[113] and his wife Lhadrön (lHa sgron), built a three-storey temple called Rinchen Ling on the model of the Golden temple of Tholing around 1095.[114]

110 See the discussion below. See also the *Collected biographical material* (1977: 121f and 274), Snellgrove and Skorupski (1980: 97 f. 45) and Tucci (1988: 120).

111 Apart from the temple in Tholing, the temples listed in Rinchen Zangpo's biographies are identified only by place name.

112 This is the only reference apart from local Limi documents I have found that specifies Rinchen Ling as the name of a temple in the region.

113 King Sönam Tse was the nephew of King Wangde (dBang lde).

114 Vitali 2003: 67; Vitali 1996: 126, 346f; the *Ngari Chronicles*, 75: '... *tho gling 'dra* [*dgra*] *bor rin chen gling gsum thon ba bzhengs*.'

FIGURE 3.6 Stupas and inscriptions by Rinchen Zangpo's meditation cave

The location is not specified, however, and the vague possibility of this temple being identical with the temple in Waltse remains unresolved. Be that as it may, the indicators discussed above combine to make a strong case for the inventory's claim that the temple in Waltse was indeed founded either by Rinchen Zangpo or by some of his contemporaries. This theory is further corroborated by the carbon dating of a sliver from the base of the Vairocana statue. The radiometric dating of the sample confirms that the material from which the statue is made dates back to the eleventh century.[115] Hence, whilst it may never be possible to settle the case once and for all, it seems safe to conclude whoever the actual founder was, the Vairocana temple certainly conforms to the translator's heritage in religious, stylistic, and historical terms.

3.2.2 *The Birth, Death, and 'Revival' of Lotsawa Rinchen Zangpo*

Although the *Middle length biography of Rinchen Zangpo*, which is attributed to one of his direct disciples, provides an authoritative account of the famous translator's life, there are sufficient uncertainties and inconsistencies in the

115 Thomas Pritzker, personal communication 2011.

different versions to make room for speculations and competing claims. The *Rinchen Ling monastery inventory* adds to these speculations in its brief summary of the life of Rinchen Zangpo:

> The famous translator known as Lotsawa Rinchen Zangpo, who was born in Upper Guge Zhangzhung, erected 108 temples as the basis for the [Buddhist] teaching, the foremost being the Golden temple of Tholing in Guge.[116] Thereafter, at the end of his life, at the hermitage of Lhadeng, near this very seat that he had established, his physical manifestation dissolved into the pure land [of the Buddhas].[117]

The text claims that the translator meditated and passed away at a place called Lhadeng (lHa sdengs), but where could this place Lhadeng be? This question was also raised by Kyabgön Rinpoche after he had visited Limi in 2008. Having studied the local manuscripts, he asked the villagers if they knew a place called Lhadeng. One of the men from Waltse came to think of Jao Lhadeng (Bya'u lHa gting/lding?), an old hermitage underneath a large triangular boulder resembling a bird's beak (Fig. 3.7).[118] Kyabgön Rinpoche subsequently visited the Jao Lhadeng hermitage and added it to the list of possible locations for the translator's final departure.[119] The suggestion that the translator went to Limi at the end of his life can also be found in at least two versions of the *Middle length biography of Rinchen Zangpo*:[120]

116 The first temple in Tholing was the *gtsug lag khang*. The *gser khang* was built between 1067 and 1071 by Zhiwa Ö (Zhi ba 'Od) and his nephew king Tsede (rTse lde), but the two temples are often confused in Tibetan historical sources. Vitali (1996: 311f) and (1999: 29f).

117 *gu ge zhang zhung gi yul stod du sku 'khrungs pa'i/ lo tswa ba [bas] rin chen bzang po zhes mtshan yongs su grags pa de nyid kyis [kyi] gu ger tho ling gser khang gi gtsos pa'i bstan gzhi gtsug lag khang brgya rtsa brgyad bzhengs [bzheng] pa'i phyi mtha' sku tshe'i smad la grub par bskrun pa'i gnas gzhi 'di nyid dang nye ba'i sgrub gnas lha sdengs su sku'i bkod pa dag zhing du bsdus pa/. Rinchen Ling monastery inventory*. 2b–3a, my translation.

118 The first syllable in the name Jaolhadeng might come from *bya'u*, 'small bird', and the second syllable *deng* might be *gting*, as in 'below'. Conversation with one of the villagers during an excursion to the cave, summer 2010.

119 Konchok Pasang 2008: 15. There are at least six possible candidates for the site of Rinchen Zangpo's death. In addition to three places in Limi which will be discussed below, there are claims that the translator passed away in Ladakh, in Tholing, and in Katse.

120 The version published by Tucci (1988) and text C in the *Collected biographical material*. Text B in the same collection can perhaps be read as misspelling for Limi, whereas A refers more vaguely to Omlo/Humla ('Om lo).

> It is said that he passed away from the mouth of a rock [cave][121] in Limi Chumig Lhadzing,[122] not leaving any trace of his physical body behind. Regarding that place, he stayed there meditating for one year …[123]

So far (if lHa sdengs and lHa rdzing refer to the same place), the accounts in the inventory and biography seem to concur, but then the author of the biography goes on to refute the claim:

> [However,] regarding [the location of the place where he] passed away, it is not correct. So, from where did [he] depart? He died at Mount Wergo in Khache,[124] in the year of the sheep, at the age of ninety-eight, in the evening of the seventeenth day of the last winter month in the Aśvinī constellation.[125]

This quotation from Rinchen Zangpo's biography shows that the controversy surrounding the location of the site where the translator passed away goes far back in history. In fact, the biography states that Rinchen Zangpo manifested his passing away in three different places: from the Limi Chaye (lHi mi Ca se) cave in Purang, from the Yangkur (gYang skur) cave in Shiwar (Shi war) and from the Wergo (Wer go) mountain in Katse Gokhar (Kha che Go khar).[126] Text A in the *Collected biographical material* provides a similar list of sites, but instead of the Limi Chaye cave in Purang, it refers to the Omlo ('Om lo) cave in Purang, and the third candidate is identified as Rewingo (Re wing go) in

---

121 The phrase 'mouth of a rock' (*rdo yi kha*) presumably refers to the opening of a cave. One of the locations in Limi which might be identified with Limi Chumig Lhadzing is a hermitage built under a boulder with the shape of a bird's beak (see Fig. 3.7).

122 Text A in the *Collected biographical material* (p. 121, l. 4f) writes: *'om lo'i chu mig lha rdzing*. This may refer to the same place, since Limi (lHi mi) is located in 'Om lo.

123 *lhi ma'i chu mig lha rdzing na rdo yi kha nas phung po lhag med du gshegs so zer te/_der ni lo gcig sgrub pa mdzad pa yin*. Text C in the *Collected biographical material*, p. 273, l. 4f

124 Text A in the *Collected biographical material* (p. 121f) writes: *kha tse'i re wing go*.

125 *mKha' spyod du gshegs pa ni ma yin no/ /'o na gang nas phebs pa yin na/ kha che'i ri wer go ru lug gi lo/ dgung lo dgu bcu go brgyad dgongs tsam na/ /dgun zla tha chung gi tshes bcu bdun la/ /skar ma ta pa la phebs pa'o*. Text C in the *Collected biographical material*, p. 274, l. 1f. Text A (p. 121, l. 5f.) reads: *mkha' spyod du gsheg pa ma yin ste/ mkha' spyod du ni kha tse'i re wing go ru lug gi lo la dgong lo dgu bcu go brgyad 'don tsa na dgun zla tha chung gi tshes bcu bdun la skar ma rta pa la gzhan don du mkha' spyod du gshegs so/*.

126 Spellings according to text C in the *Collected biographical material*, p. 274, l. 3f: *pu hrangs kyi lhi mi yi ca se brag phug dang / shi war g.yang skur phug dang / kha che go khar gyi ri wer go nas mkha' spyod du gshegs pa'i tshul bstan pa ste/*

Katse Gokhar (Kha tse Go khar).[127] Omlo surely means Humla. Elderly people in Humla explain that the name Humla is a Nepali version of Ombu Lungpa ('Om bu Lung pa, lit. 'Valley of the tamarisk') and that the district got its name from the *'om bu* plant (*Myricaria dahurica*, a type of tamarisk used as horse medicine), which is abundant near its rivers and streams. While the text places the Humla cave in Purang, I find it likely that both place names refer to the Chaye cave in Limi (see Figs. 3.5 and 3.6). At certain points in history, Limi and neighbouring Purang have been under the same rule.[128] The Chaye cave is mentioned in the thirteenth century *Great biography of the Kagyu masters* as the meditation place of both Rinchen Zangpo and important Drigung masters in the westernmost part of the Limi valley, located only a few hours' walk from Zher in Purang. Moreover, the *Great biography of the Kagyu masters* also describes the cave in Limi as the site of Rinchen Zangpo's tantric meditation (*lo tswa ba rin chen bzang pos bsgrubs pa mdzad pa'i sa*).[129] The place Lhadzing, as quoted from the biography above, could, if taken literally as 'sacred spring', refer to the *grub chu* (spring) in the Chaye cave. However, if Lhadzing is a misspelling of lHa gting/lding (lHa sdengs in the inventory) it could refer to the meditation cave identified by Kyabgön Rinpoche mentioned above.[130] A final possibility that I did not get the chance to discuss with people in Limi is that Lhadzing could refer to the ruined Lhadzin hermitage near Tshamdo, the abandoned settlement at the eastern end of the Limi valley. In their work on the translation of the *Middle length biography of Rinchen Zangpo*, Snellgrove and Skorupski lamented '… the utter impossibility of fixing

127 Spellings according to text A in the *Collected biographical material*, p. 122, l. 2f: *pu hrangs kyi 'om lo'i brag phug dang / shing wang gi g.yang sgur kyi phug dang / kha tse go khar gyi re wing go nas mkha' spyod du gshegs pa'i tshul tha dad ba bstan no//* Gokhar is the name of the temple built by Rinchen Zangpo in Katse and Tsering Gyalpo argues that the variants Kha che and Kha tse in the biography both refer to Katse Okar (Kā rtse O dkar). Katse is the birthplace of Rinchen Zangpo's father, whereas Okar refers to the Okar cave (O dkar phug, 'cave of the wild cat'). There is reportedly a reliquary (*gdung rten*) in the village (the middle of three *mchod rten*), which, according to local people, is the burial *mchod rten* of Rinchen Zangpo. (Tsering Gyalpo, personal communication, July 2013.)

128 Limi is located in Humla, but borders Purang. The communities have historically had very close relations and have occasionally been under the same ruler, but the exact affiliation of 10th–11th century Limi is not known.

129 The *Great biography of the Kagyu masters*, p. 472 l. 5 (f. 236b).

130 When Kyabgön Rinpoche visited Limi in 1993 and 2008, he specifically collected information about the local sacred geography in order to investigate a possible match between the names provided in the old texts and the places in Limi.

names without precise local knowledge of the area ...'[131] Whereas fieldwork has helped identify some of these places, the problem is not yet solved.

If an extended version of the biography is ever found, it might help us to identify the sites of the translator's activities with some more certainty. Whereas it seems most likely that Rinchen Zangpo passed away in Katse,[132] the biography suggests that he meditated in Limi before his death. Moreover, judging from the evidence presented above, he either constructed, or at least inspired the construction of a temple in the valley. Despite all these references, prior to Kyabgön Rinpoche's visit, many of the Rinchen Zangpo traditions had been forgotten. However, as a result of his work, people in Limi have become reacquainted with their heritage and its significance which they are actively using in the promotion of their monastery and village.[133] This case gives us an example of how stories about such religious masters are forged, forgotten, and remembered or (re-)created in a local community.

FIGURE 3.7 The Jao Lhadeng hermitage, one of the possible sites of Rinchen Zangpo's death

131 Snellgrove and Skorupski 1980: 97, n. 45.

132 David Pritzker and Tsering Gyalpo (personal communication, July 2013) both support the theory that Rinchen Zangpo passed away at his father's birthplace Katse in Rongchung.

133 See Chapter Seven.

3.3 The Arrival of Hermits and Diplomats from Drigung

The period from the second dissemination of Buddhism until the middle of the thirteenth century can be described as a time of cultural and religious florescence in Ngari. From the end of the twelfth century, the newly formed Buddhist schools sent large numbers of hermits to Kailash. The Buddhist schools needed political and economic support from the regional kings and competed for patronage. The Drigung history in the region started in 1191 when Kyobpa Jigten Sumgön (sKyob pa 'Jig rten gSum mgon, 1143–1217), the founder of the order, dispatched the first group of hermits (*ri pa, mtshams pa*) to Kailash. The first mission failed to establish the pilgrimage, but the two subsequent expeditions, which arrived in 1208 and 1215, were reportedly more successful.[134] *The Drigung history of Kailash* writes that 55,525 hermits were sent towards the sacred mountain in this period, a number which is certainly exaggerated.[135] Nevertheless, the area is likely to have been swarming with hermits. Vajraholder Ghuya Gangpa (rDo rje 'dzin pa G+hu ya sGang pa)[136] arrived in Ngari in 1215 and founded Gyangdrag (rGyang grags) Monastery[137] at the foot of Mount Kailash, which became the Drigung stronghold in the region. Limi's location in a sheltered valley close to the sacred mountain attracted a number of recluses to its many hermitages and meditation caves. As will be detailed in the following passage, the visits of two of these masters, Drigung Chenga Lingpa ('Bri gung sPyan snga Gling pa, 1187–1241)[138] and *grub thob* Senge Yeshe (Seng ge Ye shes, 1181–1255) in the first half of the thirteenth century were to have important religious, economic, and political consequences for Limi.

3.3.1 *The Foundation of the Monasteries in Dzang and Til and the Establishment of the Monastic Patronage System*

The stories of the visits of the two Drigung lamas are recorded in various sources. Here I will mainly quote the *Drigung history of Kailash*, the *Rinchen Ling monastery inventory*, and the lamas' respective biographies. Drigung

134 The first Drigung mission which departed for Kailash in 1191 was not able to 'open the pilgrimage' (*gnas sgo 'byed pa*) because of war, but relations with the rulers were established (Vitali 2003: 70). According to Buffetrille (2003: 234) the pilgrimage was opened by the Drukpa master Götshangpa (rGod tshang pa), who visited Kailash in 1214–16. Alex McKay (1998: 11) in his introduction to *Pilgrimage in Tibet*, points out 'the close association between religious topography and taxable areas'.

135 *Drigung history of Kailash*: f. 27b.

136 *Drigung history of Kailash*: f. 27b.

137 Ghuya Gangpa became the first vajraholder of Kailash.

138 Also referred to as dBon Shes rab 'Byung gnas or sPyan snga Shes rab 'Byung gnas.

Chenga Lingpa was a close disciple of Kyobpa Jigten Sumgön. After the Drigung founder passed away, Chenga Lingpa went on a pilgrimage to Kailash where he stayed for seven years (1219–25).[139] The *Drigung history of Kailash* tells us that during his pilgrimage, Chenga Lingpa met Krācalla (Grags pa lde), king of Jumla (T. 'Dzum lang), at the shore of Lake Manasarovar.[140] After having spoken with Chenga Lingpa, the king was so impressed that he took him as his 'root lama' (*rtsa ba'i bla ma*). Krācalla subsequently invited the religious master to Yatse (Ya rtse)[141] in a golden palanquin (*gser gi mdo li*) and showered precious gifts upon him.[142] Yatse was the capital of the Khas Malla kingdom of Jumla, which at its peak controlled much of Western Nepal, Ngari, Kumaon, and Garhwal.[143] King Krācalla became a great patron of the Drigung school and was, according to the *Drigung history of Kailash*, instrumental in disseminating the teaching to the southern lands of Mon.[144] Chenga Lingpa must have been a skilled diplomat because during this period he also managed to secure support for the Drigung Kagyu order from all the other regional kings as well as the Mongols of Southern Turkestan.[145] A number of monasteries and hermitages, including two in Limi, were consequently incorporated into the Drigung fold.[146]

According to Drigung tradition, it was Chenga Lingpa who founded the Tilchen (Til chen) monastery in Dzang (Fig. 3.8). During his seven-year pilgrimage to Kailash, Drigung Chenga Lingpa spent some time meditating in a cave in the mountains above Dzang and the monastery was reportedly founded near his retreat.[147] The story is not mentioned in Chenga Lingpa's biography, but the written sources do confirm that there was a Drigung temple or hermitage in the village in the thirteenth century. The ruins of the original two-room structure can still be seen on a little plateau on the mountainside, about half an hour's walk above the village.

---

139 The seven years' stay is recorded in the *Biography of Chenga Lingpa* (22–29), the *Drigung history of Kailash*, f. 30a, and a shorter version is provided in the *Rinchen Ling monastery inventory*, f. 3b.

140 The *Biography of Chenga Lingpa*: f. 23f and *Drigung history of Kailash*: f. 29b f. See also Petech (2003: 35) and Vitali (2003: 74).

141 Tucci (1956: 116) identified Yatse with Sinja/Seṃjā in the present-day Jumla District of Nepal.

142 Summary from *Drigung history of Kailash*: f. 30a.

143 Kumaon and Garhwal currently belong to the Indian state of Uttarakhand.

144 *Drigung history of Kailash*: f. 30a.

145 Vitali (2003: 73f) reports that Chenga Lingpa succeeded in establishing relationships with Guge, Purang, Ladakh, Upper Hor, Garlog, and Yatse.

146 *Drigung history of Kailash*: f. 30a.

147 Drikung website n.d. d)

FIGURE 3.8 Ruins of the 13th c. Dzang Tilchen monastery, founded by Chenga Lingpa

In the same period, a small hermitage (*mtshams khang*) was founded high up the mountain on the sunny side of the Til valley by a certain Lama Kundzom (Bla ma Kun 'dzom) (Fig. 3.9).[148] A few years later, *grub thob* Senge Yeshe, who had been part of Chenga Lingpa's group of pilgrims, arrived at Kailash for the second time. The *Great biography of the Kagyu masters* records that Lama Kundzom offered his hermitage in Til to Senge Yeshe during his visit in the year of the Wood Dragon (1244).[149] The hermitage was extended and given the name Til Kundzom Dongak Chöling (Til Kun 'dzom mDo sngags Chos gling), or Til Kundzom for short. Just as in Dzang, the original structure consisted of two rooms, which today form a sealed basement in Til Kundzom monastery (Fig. 3.9).[150]

Senge Yeshe spent more than three years in Limi and built a hermitage in Chaye called Chaye Yeshe Dzong (sPya ye Ye shes rDzong, currently referred to as sPya ye Nam mkha' rDzong), spectacularly located on a cliff in a vertical rock face, about one thousand metres above the confluence between the Limi and Karnali rivers where Rinchen Zangpo was said to have meditated two and

148 His full name was Lodrö Rinchen (Blo gros Rin chen).

149 The *Great biography of the Kagyu masters*: 472, l. 1.

150 The rooms were opened during the visit of Kyabgön Rinpoche in 2008, and then re-sealed.

FIGURE 3.9 Til Kundzom, given to *sgrub thob* Senge Yeshe in the 13th century

a half centuries earlier (Figs. 3.5 and 3.6).[151] The *Great biography of the Kagyu masters* was written during the retreat in Chaye, based on the dictation of *grub thob* Senge Yeshe. Seven hundred years later, a rare copy of this biography was found in Limi and eventually published by Tsondu Senghe in 1985. Because of the strong influence of Humli Tibetan dialect in the biography, one may assume that the scribe was a native of the region.[152]

The construction and upkeep of all the temples and monasteries founded during this period must have required substantial resources and organisational effort, and it was therefore vital for the religious schools to secure support from the regional kings and to establish a system of monastic patronage. The *Rinchen Ling monastery inventory* records that:

> Out of reverence to [Chenga Lingpa's] prophecy, [King Krācalla and his two sons] bestowed the Tilchen[153] estate in Dzang, the Kundzom

151 The *Great biography of the Kagyu masters*: 472, l. 5. See also the discussion above.

152 The *Great biography of the Kagyu masters*: 472. The biography mentions two names: Don mo ri pa and rDo rje mdzes 'od. Mathes (1999: 62) proposes that the names belong to two different scribes; whereas Vitali (personal communication, 2013) argues that the two names must refer to the same person.

153 Til chung in the original, but this must be a slip of the pen.

> monastery in Til, and a lama's estate, with individual property rights, and lay sponsors in the Limi valley. Whatever resources[154] the individual [sponsors] would provide could be collected unhindered for however long. By obtaining these orders and regulations[155] from the king and his two sons, [Tilchen and Kundzom] were united with Tise Gyangdrag as branch monasteries.[156]

King Krācalla reigned from ca. 1225–55, and the endowment must have taken place around the middle of the thirteenth century. For the villagers in Limi, the donation of land and the establishment of a lama's estate, with lay sponsors and the authority to collect taxes, would have important religious and economic consequences.[157] We do not know how patronage was organised within the community and how monks were recruited at the time, but with the establishment of these two monasteries, the Drigungpas gained a strong presence in the valley that has continued to the present day. Rinchen Ling monastery in Waltse was reportedly affiliated to the Sakyapa (Sa skya pa) school at the time, but as we will see below, that was to change a few centuries later. This quotation from the inventory further suggests that since Krācalla had the authority to donate the monasteries in Dzang and Til to the Drigungpas, Limi must have been regarded as part of the Jumla kingdom.

3.4 Changing Religious Affiliations

3.4.1 *The Drigungpas' Loss of Power to the Sakyapas and the Drukpa Kagyupas*

Throughout much of the order's history, the Drigungpas were involved in power struggles in Central Tibet,[158] and the ebb and flow of their successes and failures had a strong impact on the resources they were able to spend on their

154 *rnyed skur* can be translated as 'riches and honour', but here I have opted for a simpler version.

155 The word *bcad* can also be translated as 'taxes' or 'interest' and this is most likely what the king's donation of land to the monasteries meant for the villages.

156 *lung bstan pa dang bcas [cas] kyi gus 'dud du _sle mi yul 'dzang du gnas gzhi til chen [chung]/_til [stil] du kun 'dzom dgon dang_bla brang [grang] sa yul bdag thob dang mchod gzhis yon bdag so so'i rnyed bkur [skur] gang bgyis sdud [sdu] len sogs ji srid bar 'gog med du/_rgyal po yab sras gsum gyi bka'i gnang ba rgyas bcad du thob pas _ti se rgyang grags dgon gyi ya gyal dang khongs su 'thus pa.* My tentative translation of *Rinchen Ling monastery inventory* f. 3b–4a.

157 Some of the most important religious consequences will be detailed in Chapters Seven and Eight, whereas the economic aspects will be discussed in Chapter Nine.

158 See for instance Petech 1978.

monasteries in Western Tibet. The fifteenth century was a period of decline for the Drigungpas in Central Tibet and few Drigung monks went on pilgrimage to Kailash during this period. The monks who remained in Guge and Purang suffered hardship and were unable to sustain the monasteries and hermitages,[159] and this must also have been felt in Limi. According to the *Drigung history of Kailash*, a number of monasteries in Ngari were lent (*g.yar*) to the Drukpa Kagyu ('Brug pa bKa' brgyud) order in this period and remained with them.[160] The situation for the Drigungpas improved somewhat in the sixteenth century. During the reign of the sixteenth and seventeenth Drigung throne holders[161] three hundred hermits were sent to Mount Kailash, and Denma Kunga Drakpa (lDan ma Kun dga' Grags pa), who was central in the spread of the Drigung order to Ladakh, was installed as Vajraholder at Gyangdrag monastery.[162]

The fifteenth century was also a difficult period for the kingdoms of Guge and Purang, which were severely weakened by war and a series of droughts.[163] In the last half of the century there were a number of interventions by Lo Monthang (Glo sMon thang)[164] in Purang and Khochar.[165] The *Drigung history of Kailash* relates that Amgon Zangpo (A mgon bZang po, 1419/20–82?), the King of Lo, offered the Khochar temple, which had been affiliated with Drigung since the thirteenth century, to Ngorchen Kunga Zangpo (Ngor chen Kun dga' bZang po, 1382–1456). Vitali regards this claim as doubtful, as it is not mentioned in other sources, but the temple which used to belong to the Drigungpas seems nevertheless to have been taken over by the Sakyapas during this period.[166] From 1496–97, there was a war between Lo and Purang/Guge.[167] Lo appears to have exercised authority over Limi and Humla as well at the time, because the governor (*sde pa*) wrote a fifteen-line authorisation letter (*bka' shog bco lnga*) allowing the collection of wood from Humla. The governor of Lo also ordered the villagers in Limi to build wooden carts (*shing rta 'khor lo*) for the construction of embankments in Khochar to protect the

159 Petech (1978: 319) based on *Drigung history of Kailash*.

160 *Drigung history of Kailash* f. 32b and Petech 1997: 319. See also the discussion about the Drukpa presence in Ngari in Chapter Six.

161 Gyalwang Kunga Rinchen (rGyal dbang Kun dga' Rin chen, r. 1484–1527) and Gyalwang Rinchen Phuntsok (rGyal dbang Rin chen Phun tshogs, r. 1527–34).

162 Petech 1997: 321f.

163 The relation between severe droughts and social and political changes in Western Tibet during the last millennium has been discussed by Mark Aldenderfer in Sinha et al. (2011: 49).

164 Lo Monthang is also spelled Glo sMos thang.

165 Vitali 2012 and the *Catalogue of the three silver brothers*, p. 27ff.

166 Vitali 2012: 163. See also Petech (2003: 45), and Tsering Gyalpo et al. (2012: 60).

167 *Catalogue of the three silver brothers*, p. 29.

monastery from recurring floods.[168] Purang must have been returned to the Guge kingdom shortly after, but Khochar monastery remained Sakya.[169]

3.4.2 *Transition from Sakya to Drigung*

The Sakyapas seem to have been strong contenders for power in Ngari, especially after their alliance with the Mongols from the late thirteenth century onwards. The Sakyapas had a number of temples in Humla,[170] and *Rinchen Ling monastery inventory* records that during the early period, the religious schools (*chos grwa*) in Purang belonged to the Sakyapas.[171] According to the same inventory, the temple in Waltse was also Sakya, but the text was composed by a Drigung monk, and unfortunately gave no details of the temple's Sakya past.[172] It seems likely that Khochar monastery, which became Sakya in the fifteenth century, and the temple in Waltse must have belonged to the same school for some time. However, Waltse temple was later handed over from the Sakyapas to the Drigungpas. The dramatic story is described in *Rinchen Ling monastery inventory*:

> The Sakyapa shrine keeper in the Waltse temple killed some Drigungpa monk over sectarian issues regarding tenets. After having been banished from the temple, [the monk] then fled [in haste, leaving only] a cloud of dust. Because [there] was no possibility to fetch [him], [according to] the kings' laws, it was decided for perpetuity that the Waltse temple and its estate, together with a small fine, should be taken as blood money for the Drigung monk. Thus, the central temple's interior and exterior, as well as its shrine objects, were thereafter owned by the Drigungpa.[173]

The identity of the king is unfortunately not specified, and the episode is therefore difficult to date. Various Drigung publications place the event around the

168 *Catalogue of the three silver brothers*, p. 29. See also Diemberger, Hovden, and Yeh 2015.

169 Purang seems to have belonged to Guge most of the time, but according to Petech (2003: 45) Purang had its own king in the middle of the sixteenth century.

170 Tshewang Lama, personal communication. Today, the temple in Tumkot is the only remaining Sakya temple in Humla.

171 *Rinchen Ling monastery inventory*, f. 3a.

172 A thorough reading of Sakya historical documents might provide an answer.

173 *dbal rtse lha khang du sa skya pa'i sku gnyer ba de khas _'bri gung pa'i grwa [gra] rigs zhig grub mtha'i phyogs 'dzin gyi rkyen lam du btang nas lha khang rgyang skyur gyis bros bud du song bar rtsa 'dzin thabs bral du song gshis bcas kyis _rgyal po gtso phal rnams kyi bka' khrims las _dbal rtse lha khang mchod gzhis bcas pa 'bri gung pa'i grwa pa'i stong bcal du rtsa len ji srid bar 'jags gnas su bcad brtsal du byung ba _de kha'i lha khang lte ba mdo sbug rten mchod. Rinchen Ling monastery inventory*, f. 4a. My tentative translation.

fifteenth century.[174] The chronology of the inventory suggests that it took place during the reign of the Kalyal kings, who ruled from the fifteenth century until the end of the eighteenth.[175] The passage preceding the description of the murder mentions the names of three kings: Karandza, Meuradza and Bheuradza, which may help us date the event.[176] The *Drigung History of Kailash* records that Karandza reigned after Narasiṃha (seventeenth century), 'the last religious king' (*chos rgyal gyi tha mar*).[177] The biography of the Fifth Dalai Lama records that King Narasiṃha of Jumla sent a mission to Lhasa in 1679 and confirms both his dates and support for Buddhism.[178] Hence, if the chronology in the *Rinchen Ling monastery inventory* is to be trusted, the event may have taken place as late as the seventeenth century. After the seventeenth century, the monasteries in the region seem to have lost royal support.

3.4.3 *Merging of the Monasteries and the Rule of the Five Mon Brothers*

Whereas the Yatse kings have been portrayed as staunch supporters of Buddhism in Tibetan sources, the Kalyal rulers initially gave their support both to Buddhists and Hindus before they gradually turned away from Buddhism. Karandza, the king mentioned in the excerpt above, was characterised as worshipping Hindu deities and criticised for treating his subjects badly in *Drigung history of Kailash*.[179] The harsh rule and heavy taxation are also confirmed in oral accounts in Limi and Nyin.[180] In Limi the oppression became so bad that, at one point, the villagers could not bear it any longer and took a drastic step

174 In The bilingual magazine written by Konchok Pasang (2008: 16) notes that the monastery was given to the Drigungpas by the Yatse Jumla king (which would mean either the thirteenth or the fourteenth century), whereas the presentation of Rinchen Ling monastery at the official Drigung Kagyu website places the event in the fifteenth century. However, no references are provided.

175 The Kalyal were regional kings who ruled in Jumla from the dissolution of the Yatse kingdom in the fifteenth century until the unification of Nepal in the late eighteenth. More details are provided below.

176 *Rinchen Ling monastery inventory*, f. 4a: *phyis rgyal po spun lngar lhags shing spu hreng rdzong kyang mon rgyal spun lnga nas 'dzin bzhin pa'i rgyal po ka ran dza dang sme'u ra dza b+he'u ra dza bcas kyi snga phyir …*

177 *Drigung History of Kailash*, f. 35b.

178 Tucci 1956: 128.

179 *Drigung History of Kailash*, f. 35b: *de'i rjes su rgyal po ka ranyadza dang/ bhishnu ra dza zhes pa la sogs pa byung ba de dag gis lha mo dbu ma dang/ ma ha de wa / khyab 'jug sogs lhar bsten nas mu stegs byed kyi chos lugs bzungs/ chab 'bangs rnams la'ang mnar spyod cher byas/ dkon mchog gsum la dad gus byed pa las phyi rol du gyur bas/ bsod nams kyang dgun gyi chu bran bzhin skad cig res zad nas mnga' thang je chung du song/*

180 See Levine (1988a: 21f, 91) and (1987: 78f). For the Tibetan communities in Humla the rule of the Kalyal kings seemed to have been 'marked by great instability and oppression'.

to escape the taxes. The story is briefly described in the *Rinchen Ling monastery inventory*:

> Because of the severe oppression caused by the five Mon brothers'[181] heavy taxation[182] the villagers supporting the Drigung Dzang Tilchen monastery abandoned their houses and dispersed. They were hardly able to survive (*'khra tshugs*) because they [also] had to provide extensive provisions to support[183] the monastery, lama, and monks. [They] therefore moved the shrine objects[184] [and] all the monastic property [of Dzang Tilchen] to the Waltse temple [for protection].[185]

According to this account, the villagers left their houses and became tax refugees.[186] Since the descendants of the first settlers still live in Dzang, the villagers must have left their houses only temporarily. The inventory does not give us much information, but the strategy presumably worked. It is worth noting that the villagers decided not to let their monastic tradition be discontinued, but instead secured its future survival by merging with the monastery in Waltse.[187] The transfer of property to Waltse must have relieved the economic burden of the sponsoring villagers. The merging of the monasteries is not dated but probably occurred after the temple in Waltse was given over to the Drigungpas. If my theory, that the conversion took place as late as the seventeenth century, is correct, the merger must have taken place shortly after. The following passage in the *Rinchen Ling monastery inventory* states that all objects were recorded in the inventory in the year of the Iron Horse. The sixty-year cycle (*rab byung*) is not mentioned here, but it probably refers to the twelfth *rab byung* (1690) when the inventory was first composed. It seems quite likely that the monks

181 The Five Mon brothers refer to the Kalyal kings.

182 *khral khrims* can also mean 'taxation laws' or refer to both taxation and laws, but in this context I found the simpler translation 'taxation' more probable.

183 *'khra* literally means 'to prop oneself up on the elbows'

184 *rten* [*brten*] *gsum* literally means 'the three supports', representatives of Buddha's body, speech, and mind.

185 *de rjes rang re 'bri gung pa'i 'dzin bdag 'dzang gi til chen dgon pa'i mi sde zhabs 'degs pa rnams mon rong spun lnga pa'i khral khrims* [*mkhrim*] *gyi mnar spyod che bas* [*ba'i*] *bud stongs thor zhig du song shis _ dgon gnas bla grwa* [*gra*] *rnams la gzan rgyag* [*zan gyag*] *ches pas* [*pa'i*] *'khra tshugs* [*'khra' tshugs*] *ma thub nas/_rten* [*brten*] *gsum mchod cha rnams dbal rtse'i lha khang du gdan drangs pa bcas.* My tentative translation of *Rinchen Ling monastery inventory*, f. 4a.

186 Hovden 2013: 215f. See also Chapter Five.

187 Rinchen Ling served all three villages until the 1980s, when the monasteries again split after a bitter strife about the monastic economy.

found it necessary to write an inventory after bringing all the objects from the monasteries in Til and Dzang over to Waltse.[188]

3.5 Changing Political Configurations

The changing religious affiliations discussed above were strongly linked to political reconfigurations in Ngari and Jumla. As we will see below, the kingdoms in Ngari changed hands from local kings via Ladakhi sovereigns, to Tibetan and eventually Chinese rule, whereas the Yatse kingdom of Jumla was subsequently taken over by Kalyal kings before it was incorporated into Nepal.

3.5.1 *The Fall of the Yatse Kingdom*

After King Krācalla, the power of the Yatse kings declined until the reign of Ripumalla[189] and Pṛthvīmalla (r. 1338–58) in the first half of the fourteenth century when the kingdom again flourished.[190] Both kings expanded their territory through a series of wars and both donated golden roof ornaments (*gser thog*) to the Jokhang in Lhasa.[191] The kings of Yatse reportedly continued to support the Drigung hermitages in the Kailash area until the end of the fourteenth century, and Petech interprets this to mean that after this date their support ended.[192] At the turn of the fifteenth century, the Yatse kingdom crumbled and was replaced by a fragmented confederation. Baliraj, the ruler who took over the principality centred at Jumla and established the Kalyal dynasty in 1404, was probably a descendant of the Khas Mallas, but Rajput immigrants from the south took control over other parts of the former Yatse kingdom.[193] The principalities of Purang and Guge, which had been part of the Yatse kingdom under Pṛthvīmalla, regained their independence. The *Drigung history of Kailash* writes that the Kalyal, or 'five Mon brother kings' (*mon rgyal spun lnga*) as they were called in Tibetan sources, ruled over petty kingdoms centred at

188 *Rinchen Ling monastery inventory*, f. 2b. Details about Til's merger are not provided.

189 The exact dates of Ripumalla's reign are uncertain, but inscriptions are found from 1312 and 1314. According to Petech (2003: 37), Ripumalla must have been one of the greatest kings of the Yatse dynasty. See also Alsop 2005.

190 Pṛthvīmalla ruled for more than twenty years and the famous pillar inscription at Dullu, studied by Tucci (1956) was written in 1354 according to Petech 2003. Adhikary (1997: 63f) provides the date 1357.

191 Petech 2003: 37–39.

192 According to Petech (2003: 39), the patronage continued until the reign of the eleventh abbot of Drigung, Dzamling Chökyi Gyalpo ('Dzam gling Chos kyi rGyal po, r. 1351–1400).

193 Bishop 1990: 112ff.

Jumla, Narlang, Khale, Doram and Phuya.[194] These petty kingdoms, part of the polities referred to as the Baisi (lit. 'twenty-two') states in Nepali,[195] retained control over the region until they were conquered by the Gorkha army of King Pṛthvī Nārāyaṇ Shah at the end of the eighteenth century.

3.5.2 *Incorporation of Guge into Central Tibet and Nepal*

In 1630, sixty years before *Rinchen Ling monastery inventory* was written, the kingdoms of Guge and Purang had been conquered by Ladakh. Upper Ngari's position in general was weakened, partly due to changing climatic conditions,[196] exhaustion of the gold mines, and war. In the years from 1679 to 1684 the kingdoms were caught in the middle of the war between Tibet, Ladakh and the Mughal empire. The army sent by the Fifth Dalai Lama, led by the Mongol general Ganden Tshewang (dGa' ldan Tshe dbang),[197] won the war in 1684, and thereafter the former principalities of Ngari were incorporated into Central Tibet.[198] According to oral tradition in Humla, there was also a conflict with the Kalyal kings over the border with Humla, which ended with a treaty. The Kalyal king brought a *khukuri* knife, the Tibetan general a golden sword, and the weapons were buried at Lapcha Shar (La rtse Shar) at the northern end of Limi. A border treaty was subsequently inscribed on a copper plate (*zangs yig*) which reads: 'the black ravens obtained the north; the yellow geese obtained the south' (*pho rog nag po byang thob, ngang pa ser po lho thob*).[199] It is difficult to assess to what extent Limi, which was located in Mon territory controlled by the Kalyal kings, was also incorporated into Tibet,

194 *Drigung history of Kailash*, f. 35a: *dzum li ra dza/ nar lang ra dza/ kha las ra dza/ rdo ram ra dza/ phu ye ra dza te rgyal po spun lnga las rgyal phran lngar gyes pa de thams cad.*

195 According to Pandey (1971: 52), the Baisi states included as many as thirty-seven principalities, but the number is likely to have varied throughout the centuries.

196 Sinha et al. 2011: 49.

197 Ganden Tshewang was one of the grandsons of Gushri Khan and a Dzungar Mongol prince. He served as lama in Tashi Lhunpo (bKra shis Lhun po) monastery before he was appointed as warlord by the Fifth Dalai Lama. His dates are uncertain; Emmer (2007: 83f) proposes that he was born towards the middle of the seventeenth century and passed away before 1689.

198 See for instance McKay 2003: 3. A translation of the 1684 treaty between Ladakh and Tibet is reprinted in McKay (2003: 785f).

199 It was also at this time the market (*tshong ra*) in the Tshongsa valley south of Limi was established. In the treaty it was specified that the people from the southern valleys (*rong pa*) would be allowed to trade grain and flour, whereas the nomads (*'brog pa*) from the plateau would trade salt, wool and animals. Conversation with an elderly man from Til, March 2012.

but the following account in the *Rinchen Ling monastery inventory*, composed only six years after the war, seems to hint that the political transitions have had implications for Limi too:

> [From the time of] the lineage kings, the three lords (*mgon*),[200] the successive kings [in power] were, in order: the Mon kings, the Ladakh kings, and the Tibetan king [sic] Ganden Tshewang.[201] Whichever [borders there were] in the past have remained the same until now, as everybody knows. Regarding the specific borders between the villages in Limi, they have been settled by the previous kings and are clearly documented in the [villages'] respective main records.[202]

Little is known about the last part of his life, but according to some traditions, Ganden Tshewang settled in Ngari after the war.[203] This is also in accord with oral history in Humla. The Nyinbas recount that Ganden Tshewang's three sons fled south to Humla, and one of them became the first settler in the Nyinba village Todpa (sTod pa).[204] A few decades later, in the last half of the eighteenth century, the Gorkha king Pṛthvī Nārāyaṇ Shah (1722–75) set out on a series of conquests which would subsequently earn him the credit for having unified Nepal. He conquered Kathmandu in 1769,[205] followed by a number of principalities to the east and west of the valley, and later he succeeded in expanding his kingdom to comprise much of contemporary Nepal. His son, the regent Bahadur Shah, continued his father's expansion westwards, but the last king of

200 The *mgon gsum* presumably refers to dPal gyi mGon, bKra shis mGon and lDe gtsug mGon—the three sons of sKyid lde Nyi ma mGon, who established the kingdom of mNga' ris skor gsum. I am grateful to Charles Ramble for this suggestion.

201 Ganden Tshewang is often referred to as a 'king' (*rgyal po*) or 'war time king' (*dmag dus kyi rgyal po*) in regional sources.

202 *Rinchen Ling monastery inventory*, f. 50a, l. 3ff. *gdung brgyud rgyal po mgon gsum nas rim par mon rgyal po/_la dwags rgyal po/_bod rgyal po dga' ldan tshe dbang gis* [*gi*] *mnga' dbang bsgyur nas da lta yan chod la sngar bdag snyon med dang_snga khyun 'jags gnas yin pa kun shes ltar la_bye brag sle mi nang mtshan yul mtsho so so'i sa mtshams rnams/_so so'i ma yig ban khrar gsal ltar la.*

203 Emmer 2007: 84.

204 Levine (1976) uses the spelling dGa' ldan Tshe dbyang, but it is clear that the legend refers to the Mongol general.

205 Whelpton 2005: 35.

Jumla, encouraged by the Tibetan government, did not give up his land without a fight and reportedly summoned an army of 22,000 men.[206] The *Drigung history of Kailash* records that in the Iron Bird year of the thirteenth *rab byung* (1801), the Gorkha king Rana Bahadur[207] of 'the hot Nepal valley' destroyed the Jumla kingdom with his army, confiscated all property, and made the people his subjects.[208] The year does not agree with the dates provided in other sources, which state that Jumla fell in 1789. Be that as it may, Bahadur Shah conquered the Jumla kingdom and the other Baisi states[209] and waged war with Tibet (1788–92). Limi was also incorporated into Nepal together with the Baisi states at the end of the eighteenth century.[210] What consequences did the inclusion into Nepal have for Limi? Mahesh Regmi pointed out that the Nepali rulers were mainly interested in revenue and the impact of the new regime was most likely felt through the tax bill.[211] As mentioned above, the heavy taxation by the Kalyal kings prompted the villagers to merge the three monasteries. When the Nepali state took control over the western region, the Thakuri descendants of the Kalyal kings were able to preserve many of their privileges, including the prerogative to collect taxes.[212] These Thakuri leaders, as we will see in Chapter Six about taxation below, did not make the burden any easier for the villagers.[213]

3.5.3 *The Abandonment of Tshamdo and Lama Pale's Revenge*

The Nepali incorporation of Limi presumably also meant the incorporation of Tshamdo. As mentioned earlier, the villagers in Limi trace the name of their community from this settlement. Yet, the relationship between Limi and Tshamdo is not entirely clear as the two territories were separated by a border, and oral tradition suggests that at least for the period after the settlement

206 Bishop 1990: 128. The number sounds exaggerated.

207 It should be noted that king Rana Bahadur Shah, the grandson of Pṛthvī Nārāyaṇ Shah, was in his minority, and the military expansion was led by his regent, uncle, and namesake, Bahadur Shah.

208 *Drigung history of Kailash*, f. 35b–36a: *rab byung bcu gsum pa'i lcags bya lor/_bal yul tsha ba tsha shod kyi rgyal po gor Sha ra dza ra Na ba dur zhes bya ba'i dmag gis 'dzum lang rgyal sa bcom zhing mnga' thang thams cad 'phrog nas 'bangs su bcug pas de phyin la rgyal po'i bya ba byed pa'i dbang thang ni med mod/_rgyal brgyud tsam ni da lta'ang snang ngo/*

209 See Pandey 1971: 54.

210 Nepali jurisdiction in Limi in the nineteenth century is confirmed by documents kept in Limi as well as the Nepali government archive. See *Regmi research papers*, vols. 3 and 20.

211 Regmi 1999. See Chapter Six for more details about taxation.

212 Levine 1987: 78f.

213 A number of complaints about heavy taxation throughout Humla and Jumla are recorded in Nepali archives. See for instance *Regmi research papers*, vols. 3 and 20.

of Til, Waltse, and Dzang, Limi and Tshamdo formed two distinct communities. The border between Limi and Tshamdo is marked by a red swastika (L. *yugrum*, T. *yung drung*) painted under a large boulder at Yugrum Ri ('the Swastika Hill'), which can still be seen.[214] Nevertheless, at the end of the seventeenth century, when the *Rinchen Ling monastery inventory* was composed, Tshamdo was regarded as one of 'the four hamlets in Limi'. The following statement from the inventory is explicit about the four villages existing at the same time: 'Regarding the borders and the protecting mountains, in general, the four hamlets belonging to Limi from Tshamdo to Til are (surrounded by) powerful protective borders.'[215] But at some point, probably in the nineteenth century, Tshamdo was suddenly abandoned. According to local legend, the settlement's miseries were caused by the vengeful spirit of a lama:

> Some generations ago, a powerful lama named Pale (s.u.) lived in Tshamdo village. He owned large flocks of sheep and had accumulated considerable wealth. The other villagers were therefore quite jealous at him. As he approached the end of his life, he entered a state of deep contemplation preparing to pass away while meditating (*thugs dam*). But even before he passed away, the villagers started to take his property. His only relative shouted out in frustration: look, they are stealing all our belongings, you cannot pass away right now! By hearing this, the lama was shaken out of meditation and turned into an angry spirit (*'dre*).[216]

The villagers in Limi say that the lama's spirit sought revenge through a destructive spell (*mthu*).[217] He reportedly made a poisoned cake offering (*gtor ma*) which he threw at people who got sick and died. It is commonly held that death from sorcery causes the victims to turn into wandering spirits (*'dre*). The villagers also relate that Lama Pale killed the birch forest that used to cover the area and generally made life so difficult for the few who survived that they eventually abandoned the settlement. Such stories need to be treated with caution, but it is possible to look beyond spiritual causalities to also detect

---

214 I was shown the swastika by one of the villagers. Whereas the location of the border between Tshamdo and Limi is common knowledge, most of the stories about the villages' relationship seem to be forgotten.

215 *Rinchen Ling monastery inventory*, f. 50a, l. 1–3: *sa mtshams bsrung ri'i skor la /_spyir gyi sle ma'i yul mtshams mdo* [*mtshan rto*] *nas til* [*stil*] *tshun gyi yul tsho bzhi'i khongs su mthus pa'i bsrung mtshams.*

216 I was told different versions of the story, but this was the most common.

217 See Ramble (2008a: 49) for a similar explanation of the abandon of the settlement of Tsele, in Mustang district, caused by *mthu*.

traces of historical events such as severe illness and death, that can be read as indications of epidemic disease. In a similar way, the withering away of the birch forest could have been the result of environmental stress, as birch trees require a lot of water to thrive. This would be corroborated by observations of dried irrigation canals, suggesting that drought may have been one of the reasons why the villagers left. Even after abandoning the settlement, the wrathful spirit is believed to have continued to haunt the remaining three villages in Limi and all the way up to Purang. In Waltse, the lama's spirit is blamed for a number of problems, and the 'two legged' entrance stupa (*rkang gnyis* or *ka ni*)[218] at Choprang Ganga (s.u.), the ridge to the east of the village, was reportedly built to stop the spirit from coming too close. According to local tradition, a number of lamas have tried to pacify the spirit of Lama Pale. A Sakya lama from Khochar is believed to have performed a fire ritual (*sbyin sreg*) to kill the spirit, but supposedly only partially succeeded. But the thirty-fourth Drigung hierarch, Tenzin Zhiwe Lodrö (bsTan 'dzin Zhi ba'i Blo gros, r. 1906–43) is believed to have finally relieved the villagers of its threat. When the Drigung Rinpoche arrived at Phulgong Lhä,[219] north of Tshamdo, he is reported to have seen the roaming spirits of Lama Pale and all the people who had succumbed to his sorcery. Villagers recount that Zhiwe Lodrö Rinpoche threw his rosary at them, and thus killed (and liberated) all the spirits. Whatever the historicity of the story, it suggests that Tshamdo, the first settlement in the Limi valley, must have been abandoned before the 1919–20 visit of Zhiwe Lodrö Rinpoche, probably sometime in the nineteenth century.[220]

3.6 Demarcation of Borders and Split of the Monasteries

Whereas only fragments of Limi's early history are preserved in local documents, the more recent history from the last part of the nineteenth and through the twentieth century is better covered. Religious biographies tell of the visits of important masters, most notably Drigungpas, who had the authority to impose new rules and regulations on the community of monks and lay people

218 Nils Martin (personal communication) suggests that *kangnyi* is actually a reference to a mantra that is painted on the interior of this category of stupas. Entrance-way stupas are frequently sacred to Akṣobhya (Mi 'khrug pa), whose mandala normally features in the ceiling. The mantra of Akṣobhya, which is usually written somewhere inside, contains the words *kaṃkani kaṃkani*. I find Martin's suggestion that '*ka ni mchod rten*' is the origin of the *kangnyi* entrance stupas quite convincing.

219 Probably 'Phul sgang Lhas.

220 See Ramble's (2007: 45ff) discussion of 'living and dead' settlements in Mustang.

in the three villages.[221] The visit which turned out to have the most far-reaching consequences was the 1894–96 pilgrimage by the thirty-third Drigung throne holder Tenzin Chökyi Lodrö (bsTan 'dzin Chos kyi Blo gros, 1868–1906). As will be detailed in Chapters Seven and Eight below, he 'corrected' the rituals[222] and instituted a system of monk levy that has formed a critical part of local legislation until today.[223] During his stay in the region, he also composed the *Drigung history of Kailash*, an important source for our knowledge of the religious history of Limi as well as the broader region. A number of historical events from this period will be discussed in subsequent chapters. However, accounts of the border settlement with China, which took place at the beginning of the 1960s, and the split of the monasteries in the 1980s will be discussed here because of the social, political, economic, and religious ramifications for the community.

3.6.1 *Apchi's Decision*

After the Chinese had annexed Central Tibet, they gradually expanded towards Western Tibet at the end of the 1950s. In order to try to gain the allegiance of the local leaders, they reportedly made rich gifts of silver coins. At one point the leaders in Limi were summoned to Purang and were presented with a 'box with 1000 [coins]' (*stong sgam*) together with an invitation to become part of China. The local leaders were uncertain about how to handle the case, and since the matter was so important, they sent a message to Waltse instructing the villagers to ask the Drigung protector deity Apchi Chökyi Droma (A phyi Chos kyi sGrol ma). A 'prediction ritual' (*rtags pa*)[224] was subsequently performed in front of the statue of the deity in the Rinchen Ling monastery, and the answer was a clear 'no', Limi should not join the PRC. The box was returned unopened to the Chinese representatives, and the leaders hastily left. The border between China and Nepal was demarcated in the treaty of 1961 and Limi unambiguously belonged to Nepal.[225] Whilst this ended the fiscal relations between Limi and Western Tibet, the border closed only gradually and partially. As Goldstein noted during his fieldwork in the 1970s, the villagers in Limi were still able to use

221 A number of Dzogchen (rDzogs chen) masters of Nyingma affiliation also made their marks on the local traditions. See Chapter Nine.

222 His successor Tenzin Zhiwe Lodrö is also remembered to have 'corrected' the performance of many of the rituals in the monastery. Because of the similarity of names and close temporal distance between their visits, the two hierarches are sometimes confused.

223 Tenzin Chökyi Lodrö is the last Drigung lineage holder depicted on the murals in Rinchen Ling's assembly hall, suggesting that the murals were re-painted during or just after his visit.

224 For more details about the use of prediction rituals in village decisions, see Chapter Five.

225 Goldstein 1974: 261.

one of their two former pasture areas south of Manasarovar.[226] Furthermore, the cross-border trade, which has been so important for the communities in the whole region, never ceased, although the premises, content, and volume were radically altered.[227] Even after the demarcation of the border, the villages continued to have connections with Purang, but with the onset of the Cultural Revolution, Gyangdrag and the other monasteries with which Limi had been affiliated had to close, and Rinchen Ling monastery was left on its own.

3.6.2 *The Split of the Monasteries*

Although Rinchen Ling had not been dependent on the Tibetan monasteries either for its management or for its ritual services, the closure of the monasteries was nevertheless felt in a number of ways. When Limi's reincarnated lama (*sprul sku*) Kushog Ramjor (sKu zhabs Rab 'byor) passed away at the end of the 1970s, Rinchen Ling was without a religious leader. The lineage of the Limi *sprul sku* had originated in Purang,[228] but at this time it was not possible to launch any search for a reincarnation. Instead, the monks in Limi took turns serving as lama. In the late 1970s, a bitter conflict broke out, which would last for more than a decade.[229] The conflict was started by monks, who wanted to claim a larger share of the monastery's donations for their village.[230] There were repeated attempts at reconciliation, but all failed and the Dzangbas therefore decided to split from the monastery in Waltse and rather rebuild their own monastery in 1985. The monks from Til initially decided to remain in Waltse, but in the early 1990s they followed the example of Dzang and re-established their own monastic community in Til Kundzom. During the three centuries that had passed since the merger, the temples in Dzang[231] and Til had been staffed only by shrine keepers (*sku gnyer*). The buildings were small and did not have capacity to house a community of monks, and therefore had to be extended. The re-establishment process took

226 See Goldstein 1974: 264. According to Saxer (2013: 49), access was finally lost in 1991.

227 Fürer-Haimendorf (1988: 251ff) noted during his field trip to Humla in 1972 that there was still a considerable amount of cross-border trade. See Chapter Four.

228 According to a prophecy, the Limi *sprul sku* would always be born in either Gezhing or Tösa village in Purang.

229 The villagers requested me to avoid getting into details as the long-lasting conflict is still fresh.

230 The sponsorship system will be detailed in Chapters Six and Seven.

231 Dzang Tilchen, the thirteenth century monastery in Dzang had been in ruins for generations. When re-establishing a monastic community, the villagers therefore decided to extend the Phelgye Ling ('Phel rgyas Gling) temple instead, which had been looked after by a shrine keeper. The dates and origin of Phelgye Ling are uncertain.

several years, and the villagers report that they had to spend a lot of time and effort on fund raising missions. The monks in Til, for instance, related how they had sent monks to beg for donations from their 'fictive kin' (*ngo shes*)[232] in Tibet and further south in Humla. The donations, which were generally given in kind, were subsequently sold and converted into money which was spent on the extension of the building complex, the painting of murals, and the purchases and construction of new statues. The consecration (*rab gnas*) ritual for Til Kundzom monastery was performed in 1993 during the first visit of the current Drigung hierarch, Kyabgön Rinpoche. Whilst the split of the monasteries can be seen as an example of the many intra-village conflicts that have troubled the community throughout history, it is also likely to have been influenced by the broader context of socio-political changes that marked the last decades of the twentieth century. This influence can probably be seen most clearly in the changes in village management which will be discussed in the following chapters.

As much of the community's way of governance can only be understood within the context of the larger historical picture, this chapter has provided a rough sketch of the religious and political history of Limi from the establishment of the first settlements until the end of the twentieth century. The first temple in Waltse was founded during the missionary fervour of the second dissemination of Buddhism in Western Tibet, and throughout the centuries, Limi's location within the gravitational field of Mount Kailash attracted a number of religious masters. The history of the region has been characterised by shifting political and religious transformations, and the chapter has showed how interventions from kings and religious masters from both sides of the border influenced the development of the monastic institutions in Limi. But we know little about how these transformations were felt on the ground. For more recent times, the availability of administrative documents and ethnographic data allows the agency of the villagers to come into clearer view. The remaining part of the book will focus on the various ways the local people have negotiated their systems of social organisation, village government and monastic patronage in the face of major socio-economic, religious, environmental and political transformations in the region.

232 Lit. 'acquaintance'. See Chapters Four and Nine.

CHAPTER 4

Social Organisation and Economy in Transition

> Tenzin (bsTan 'dzin) lives a nomadic life in a black yak-hair tent moving with the family's herd all year round, but he often has to step in for village or monastery work when his elder brother is away trading, as the third brother is a monk in Rinchen Ling and the fourth brother studies abroad. Formally, all brothers are married to the same wife, who together with her mother-in-law, sister-in-law, and one of her daughters takes care of the family's fields, the domestic chores and spends parts of the year with the animals in the pasture. The remaining four children go to school: three of them in India and one in the village.

•••

> Nyima Putri (Nyi ma bu 'khrid) is the female head of a single woman household. She is unmarried and has two children with the monk in a polyandrously married household. She does not have enough fields and animals to sustain her family, so she has established a new field on the outskirts of the village; a strenuous task because of lack of irrigation system, long walking distance, and all the hours needed to clear stones from the moraine soil. In addition, she spends as much time as possible doing manual labour in Purang, a job that is largely incompatible with agriculture in a household consisting of only one adult.

These examples from my field notes demonstrate how two different types of households in Limi divided labour in 2011. Similar to Tenzin's family, most households belonging to the two upper social strata have traditionally depended on a combination of income sources, including agriculture, pastoralism, trade, crafts, and manual labour. In contrast, Nyima Putri's single-woman household presents a very different reality. Heads of single-woman households often juggle agricultural work with lucrative but demanding manual labour

 | DOI:10.1163/9789004714571_005

in Purang, while also managing the household's compulsory communal work (L. *biri*).[1] In my notes from 2011, I wrote that agro-pastoralism (*sa ma 'brog*, lit. 'neither [fully] farmer, nor nomad') still formed the basis of local livelihood strategies, with money playing an increasingly important role. A few years later, Nyima Putri found the manual labour in Purang so profitable that she had left her fields fallow and sold her animals. By 2018, the money economy appeared to be firmly established and had largely taken over, although the continued importance of agriculture and animal husbandry should not be underestimated. Additionally, road construction and climatic events have posed further challenges to pastoralism. Following the severe snowstorm in the winter of 2014–15, which took a great toll on his herds, Tenzin's family decided to sell all their animals.

The two examples above also illustrate how livelihood options and assets in Limi are dependent on household category and the individual's position within it. Goldstein noted that, 'A great deal of the difficulty in understanding the overall adaptation of areas such as Limi stems from the fact that there are major internal social divisions which have different access to resources and productive output and consequently different adaptive strategies.'[2] Four decades later, household category, gender, age, and position within the family are still decisive for the villagers' access to assets, but as we will see below, the economic differences between the social strata have become greatly reduced. This development has wide-ranging consequences not only for social organisation, migration pattern and livelihood strategies, which will be explored in this chapter, but also for local decision-making, and monastic patronage and recruitment, to be discussed in the remaining part of the book.

4.1 Household Categories and Social Stratification

At the heart of social stratification and differential adaptive strategies is the household (*grong pa*). This forms the basic corporate and administrative unit in Limi, and most of the social, religious, economic, and political rights and duties in the community are dependent on household category and the person's position within it.[3] The term *grong pa* is both used as generic term for

1 Uncertain spelling. The various types of compulsory communal labour for the village and monastery are detailed in Chapters Six and Nine respectively.

2 Goldstein 1975: 92.

3 The household categories in Limi share a number of similarities with those of the Nyinba villages studied by Levine (1988a: 100f), but there are also important differences both in

household as well as a synonym for large household, pointing to the continued symbolic privilege placed on the original households. There are three main social strata: the 'large household' (*grong chen* or *grong pa*), whose members claim to be descendants[4] of the original settlers and own the largest estates; the 'small household' (*grong chung* or *mi re*, 'individual [household]'),[5] formed after a brother has split off from the *grong chen* and has inherited a part of an estate; and finally the 'single woman household' (*bom btang* or *mo rang*, lit. 'woman self').[6] These households are normally established by unmarried women who have split off from their brothers' estates and own little or no land. Some of these women, like Nyima Putri in the example from the vignette above, live together with their monk partners and/or children. While the names of household categories in Limi are similar to those of other Tibetan speaking communities,[7] the ways in which they are used in Limi are context specific. For this reason, I have chosen to present an emic perspective on the household like Childs and Choedup.[8] In Waltse there were eighty households in 2019: thirty *grong chen* families, thirty-one *grong chung* families, and nineteen *bom btang* families. In addition to these, there were fourteen predominantly elderly women or men living alone, who were categorised as *khral med* ('without tax obligations').[9] Although the rights and duties vary across the social strata,

terminology and organisation. The Nyinba estates seem (at least in the 1970s and 1980s) to have an even stronger corporate identity, and house names are more important than in Limi. Levine also describes a larger difference between *trongba* and *khangchung* than I found between *grong chen* and *grong chung* in Limi, but I think much of the relative equality in the latter is of recent date. Furthermore, Limi has never had slaves like in Nyin, and the class of freedmen does therefore not exist there.

4 This is the expressed norm, but there are some recent exceptions, and we must assume that there have been exceptions also in the past.

5 The *grong chung* households are also called *mi re* in daily speech and local administrative documents. I have not found the term *mi re* in dictionaries, but it can probably be translated as 'man by himself'. In order to avoid confusion, I will use only the term *grong chung*.

6 The villagers prefer to refer to the single woman category as *bom btang* rather than *mo rang*, as the former is regarded as more respectful. I have not found the term *bom btang* in dictionaries, but the villagers opined that the term is derived from the phrase *bu mo btang* (lit. 'to send a daughter'). I have chosen the spelling *bom btang*, rendering the first syllable as a contraction of *bu mo* ('girl', 'female'), as this is most frequently used in the *Waltse tax register*.

7 A brief comparison with for example Ramble's (2008: 126) description of *grong pa, rgan tshang* and *pho rang mo rang* in Te in Mustang, and Childs and Choedup's (2019: 43ff) study of the *grong chen, po rang mo rang* and *po mchod* in Trok in Nubri show that names, composition, rights and obligations of the dependencies vary.

8 Childs and Choedup 2019: 43.

9 This was the number of households when I left Limi in 2019. Figures here are to be taken as an indication, as the village communities are in flux.

all household categories, except the *khral med*, are considered 'taxpayers' (*khral pa*).[10]

In Limi, the 'male head of the household' (*kha rgan*) and his wife, the 'matron' (*ma rgan*), have the formal responsibility for the household. In the two upper strata, the position as head of household is always held by a male between the ages of fifteen, the age of majority, and sixty-five, the retirement age. Elderly family members normally continue to live in the house after retirement, and it is therefore common to find up to three generations under the same roof. The *kha rgan* has the right and duty to meet in the village assembly (*'du ma*), carries the responsibility for the household's taxes including the communal work (see Chapters 6 and 9), is the household's representative in conflict resolution meetings and, on a happier note, in celebrations. If the male household head is not present, he will send a 'replacement' (*tshab*). However, in the case of compulsory events this is not accepted as sufficient, and he will be fined for not attending. While the *kha rgan* has the highest status (except for monks) in the household and enjoys a lot of rights, he also bears formal responsibility for the household's duties. As illustrated in the vignette about the generational protest in the opening chapter of the book, this has led to challenges for the young men who are sent out of the village to obtain an education. Many of them have been forced back to the village to take up these responsibilities against their will. If their father is nearing the retirement age, they may have to leave school before they have completed their education, and this is part of a larger dilemma that will be further explored throughout the book. The responsibilities of the *ma rgan* wives in the two upper social strata include management of domestic work as well as most agricultural activities. It is also normally the *ma rgan* or another female member of the family who takes care of the household's rotational duties towards the monastery, such as carrying water, fetching firewood and other services, and it is normally a female task to prepare and facilitate most of the household's rituals. The *ma rgan* generally does not have the formal right to participate in village meetings. However, as will be discussed in Chapter Five, the possibilities for women to influence local decision-making processes in general, and village politics in particular, are gradually increasing. The lower stratum households (*bom btang*) are generally headed by a single woman who either lives alone, with children born out of wedlock, parents and/

10 I suspect this to be a relatively recent development, possibly the result of socio-political influence from Nepal. See the discussion in Ramble (1984: 186ff). The *grong pa* was probably also regarded as an 'indissoluble' unit in Limi in the past, and it may have been only recently that the *grong chung* and *bom btang* families were included in the tax registers.

or possible monk partners.[11] These women bear the main responsibility for ensuring that all their household's duties are met, and this is often particularly challenging if they have children. The *bom btang* families have no representation in the village assembly, as this is a prerogative for non-monastic male *kha rgan* above the age of fifteen. While the roles of the male and female heads of the households are relatively clearly defined, there is considerable difference between other members of the households. Grandparents may in some cases have significant power over decisions and contribute with work. If the young couple is working in Purang, it is often the grandparents who take care of the household and even small children. However, when they get old and sick and need care themselves, the task often falls to their daughter-in-law and/or unmarried daughters. Most children are sent to boarding schools in India or Kathmandu or study in the local community school, while a few are kept home to help with the work. Siblings of grandparents, female siblings of the *kha rgan*, and children born out of wedlock contribute with much of the work but tend to inhabit the lowest positions in the household hierarchy. They generally have less influence over decisions but are also freer to leave the village if they wish and have the means. The position of family members who are monks often complicates the picture and is dealt with in Chapters Eight and Nine.

4.1.1 *Household Size*

An examination and comparison of the households in the three villages presented in Table 4.1 below shows, as expected, that the *grong chen* households are the largest in all three villages. However, it also shows a significant difference in household size between the three villages: the average household (including the *khral med*) in Dzang counts 7.5 members, in Waltse the average is 5 and in Til it is 5.5. How can these differences be explained?

TABLE 4.1 Household size in the three villages, 2011

Waltse	Inhabitants	Households	Average size
Large household	194	31	6.3
Small household	157	29	5.4
Single woman	70	22	3.2
Tax exemption	3	3	1
Total	424	85	5

11 See also Havnevik, Hovden and Rinchen Loden (forthcoming).

TABLE 4.1 Household size in the three villages, 2011 (*cont.*)

Dzang	Inhabitants	Households	Average size
Large household	144	15	9.6
Small household	238	30	7.9
Single woman	36	10	3.6
Tax exemption	1	1	1
Total	419	56	7.5

Til	Inhabitants	Households	Average size
Large household	123	13	9.5
Small household	58	11	5.3
Single woman	43	15	2.9
Tax exemption	3	2	1.5
Total	227	41	5.5

The large size of the families, especially the *grong chen* households in Dzang and Til, indicates that there have been fewer formal partitions in these villages than in Waltse.[12] There may be several reasons for that. Many of the larger households from these two villages have two houses: one in the village and the other in Kathmandu.[13] Moreover, members of several households from Dzang have migrated abroad. In many cases, the *kha rgan* and the *ma rgan* have their principal residence in the village, while siblings in Kathmandu and/or abroad may have their own spouses. These migrants tend to have little interest in the fields and in village property, but have chosen not to make any formal partition from the household. Since the main bulk of the household's taxes and obligations to the village and monastery are calculated per household rather than per capita,[14] this hardly increases the tax burden. As will be discussed

12 An additional possibility is that there are differences in fertility rate or higher childhood mortality rates in Waltse, but although I suspect that the latter may be the case, I do not have reliable data to support such speculations.

13 In Waltse there is only one household with property in Kathmandu, and most of the adult population is still registered as living in the village.

14 As will be explained in Chapter Six, the taxes calculated per capita in Limi are of insignificant size.

in Chapter Eight, this also has consequences for monastic recruitment since monks are levied on a household basis.

4.1.2 *Social Mobility and Changes in the Household Structure*

Membership of a household is hereditary, but there is a certain latitude for social mobility. Change of household status can take place in different ways. The villagers related some cases of *grong chung* households being elevated to the status of *grong chen*, either because they were economically successful or because the *kha rgan* was a talented speaker. There are also examples of *grong chung* households merging, and *grong chung* taking over vacant *grong chen* households.[15] Social mobility has reportedly increased during the last decades, a development closely related to broader social, economic, and political transformations.

In the past, being part of a *grong chen* household yielded significantly more prestige and rights than membership of a *grong chung* household. The *grong chen* households were the largest landowners, and to the degree that they were dependent on their own agricultural produce for sustenance, this provided a relatively secure economic base. But there were also significant differences in political rights between the two household categories and, until the change in leadership system from the 1990s onwards, the *grong chung* had little influence in local decision-making processes.

With the democratisation of the village government and the recent economic changes, however, the differences between the two categories have been greatly reduced. Some villagers find the *grong chung* status desirable, since the tax burden for this category is lower and landownership is much less important for sustenance than in the past. But a certain number of households are needed to fulfil the *grong chen* duties towards the village and monastery. During a village meeting in Til at the beginning of the 2000s the *grong chen* representatives complained about heavy taxes and seeing the increasing number of economically successful *grong chung* families they requested that some of them should be converted to *grong chen* to share the tax burden. The villagers agreed to elevate one family, chosen by lottery, to *grong chen* status.

The most significant change the last two decades, however, is the situation for the *bom btang* households. Elderly single women report that their lives in the past were tough and many of them would therefore remain part of the households of their brothers. If a single woman chose to, or was forced to, separate from her brother(s)' household, she would have to feed herself by working

15 The villagers told me that in the past, the main reason for abandoning a *grong chen* household would be debt.

for other families either in the Limi valley or in other communities. Whereas this type of labour would provide food and lodging she would receive hardly any payment and it would be very difficult to raise any children. With the opening of new work opportunities in Purang since the beginning of the 2000s,[16] the economic situation of single women has improved dramatically, and the number of single women households has increased. Another recent change, which reflects the improved economic situation for this category, is that *bom btang* families with a son above fifteen are automatically transferred to the *grong chung* category. Taking on the increased tax burden and other responsibilities that such an upward mobility requires, would have been impossible for most single mothers in the past.

4.2 Marriage Pattern and Inheritance Rights

The household is the basic corporate unit on which the governance system is based, and the continuation of a household through marriage is key for the maintenance of the community. This is still the case, despite the fact that marriage patterns in the community seem to be changing, a development that is indicative of a number of other major transformations. The importance of marriage is reflected in elaborate wedding ceremonies, lasting up to three days. The first I was able to observe took place on a crisp, cold November morning in 2011:

> Early in the morning, eight men dressed in maroon woollen gowns lined up at the Lhazhing (lHa zhing) field in front of the monastery in Waltse.[17] The men constituted the bride's party (*pha'i spun*, kinsmen of the [bride's] father).[18] The groom's party (*gnya' bo*),[19] a group of thirty-five men,

16 Livelihood strategies are discussed at the end of the chapter.

17 The exchange of songs is supposed to take place in the courtyard of the bride's house, but normally the ritual takes place in a field, to make room for all the guests and spectators.

18 There has been a debate in the scholarly literature on Ladakh regarding whether the term *pha'i spun* refers to a form of kinship organisation. Brauen (1980: 24) understands the kinship reference to be largely symbolic, whereas other scholars, such as Crook (1994: 501ff) and Dargay and Lobsang (1980, quoted in Crook 1994: 503) have found a more explicit kinship link. After providing a summary of the discussion, Crook (1994: 502) argues that the original emphasis of the term stresses the patrinileal kinship association, but in some areas the focus on kinship has been reduced. This seems to be the case also in Limi. The villagers maintained that *pha'i spun* (or *pha ming*, as they are referred to in Dzang) should always adhere to the same ancestral deity (*pho lha*). In theory the *pha'i spun* in Limi are agnates, but they can also be affines since inmarried *mag pa* and adoptees will have to

> women, and musicians clad in blue, red, white, and black gowns according to gender, function, and how closely they were affiliated with the groom, arrived shortly after (Fig. 4.1). This was the start of a three-day wedding between a young girl from Waltse and a man from Dzang. Special wedding songs were sung from morning until evening, symbolising the negotiations between the two households and the sealing of the marriage contract. The monks performed rituals throughout the day in order to appease the territorial deities and enhance the families' well-being and prosperity, as change of households is considered a risky affair (Fig. 4.2).

During the wedding, the bride[20] leaves her 'old paternal [home]' (*pha rnying*) to become a member of her husband's family. When the groom's father retires, the young couple will take over as the heads of the household with all the rights and responsibilities that entails. It is household membership that determines the villagers' access to land and other communal resources, participation in decision-making, level of taxation, and various types of responsibilities to the monastery. A proper understanding of these basic categories of belonging is therefore vital for my analysis of the local governance system.[21]

The three villages in Limi used to constitute a largely endogamous society, but as noted by Fürer-Haimendorf in 1972, the Limigya would occasionally intermarry with the Purangbas in the past.[22] There are also cases in which a spouse has been received from other neighbouring communities, but until recently these were rare. Among those who live in the Limi Valley, the marriages are still predominantly endogamous, but among those who have migrated to Kathmandu, India, and other countries abroad, another pattern is emerging as many choose cohabitation or marriage with a partner from outside the community. It should be noted that these alliances are not regarded as relevant

---

change their *pho lha* (and hence *pha'i spun*) affiliation to that of their respective wives. Occasionally, the situation demands pragmatic adaptation and in the case of this particular wedding, only seven out of eight men in the *pha'i spun* group belonged to the *pho lha* Gangri Lhabtsan.

19 The term *gnya' bo* means both 'witness' and 'one who welcomes the bride and groom' (*mag pa dang mna' ma skyel bsu byed mkhan*). *Bod rgya tshig mdzod chen mo* 2006: 977.

20 Or the groom in case of uxorilocal *mag pa* weddings. Here, the term *mag pa* refers specifically to 'matrilocal groom'. In Limi, men who have married into their wife's household are generally addressed with the prefix *mag* before their name.

21 The economic responsibilities of the households will be discussed in detail in Chapter Six, while the religious responsibilities will be detailed in Chapters Eight and Nine.

22 Fürer-Haimendorf 1988: 270. However, the only case of intermarriage with Purangbas that I know of is the family of the former hereditary headman (*spyi khyab*) in Til.

FIGURE 4.1 The bride's party challenges the groom's party during a wedding in Waltse, 2011

FIGURE 4.2 Monk performing ritual to appease the local deities during a wedding, 2011

for administrative purposes in Limi, unless the couple decides to move back to the village and claim some of the village property. Yet, they are frequently still regarded as part of the households.[23] For most individual villagers living in Kathmandu or abroad, splitting off from the original household makes little sense as that would force them to formally renounce their ties to the village. In Dzang and Til, the villages with the highest percentage of outmigrated family members, this inclusion has resulted in nominally very large households.

Marriage patterns in Limi were studied in some detail by Goldstein, who observed that most marriages were monogamous, but in cases of two or more male siblings, virilocal fraternal polyandry was the norm.[24] In Limi there is no particular term for polyandry, it has simply been the default mode of marriage whenever there is more than one brother in a household.[25] There have been variations to this polyandric practice, either where a brother splits off from his paternal home to establish a *grong chung* household or marries as *mag pa* into his wife's household. Since polyandry has been abandoned in surrounding communities, one would expect the same development in Limi. The practice, however, seems to have continued until quite recently, at least nominally. During my first stays in Limi, virilocal fraternal polyandry was still practised when there were two or more brothers in a family. This meant that when the elder brother married, the younger brothers were automatically included, but in many cases these polyandrous marriages would end in partitions a few years later.[26] During the autumn of 2011, I observed three weddings: the first, described above, was monogamous as the brothers of the groom had passed away, while the other two weddings were regarded as polyandrous. It was not visible in the ceremony that these marriages were polyandrous, however, as only one of the brothers participated in the ritual. When I enquired about the absence of the brothers, the villagers still insisted that the marriage was polyandrous and explained that in Limi it is not common practice for the brothers to accompany the main groom in polyandrous wedding ceremonies.[27] When I returned in the autumn of 2018, I observed another three weddings, all of which were monogamous, and reportedly, there have been no polyandric

23 A similar practice has been observed by Childs and Choedup (2019) in Nubri.

24 See for instance Goldstein 1976, 1977, and 1978.

25 This has been the case also in Nyin, see Levine (1988a) and Wiebenga and Lama (in press).

26 Goldstein (1977: 48) noted that there were several partitions in Dzang in the seventies, but only two of twenty-five took place before the marriage of the elder brother.

27 Interview with a young man from Waltse, 29.04.12. Whereas this is reportedly common in other Tibetan societies, the situation is different in Nyin, where younger brothers join the elder also in the ceremony.

marriages since. Rather than villagers taking pride in continuing the tradition, as Fjeld reported in Tsang,[28] the young generation in Limi is giving it up. Goldstein already noted a decline in polyandric marriages in the 1970s, so the practice has been decreasing for some time.[29] The more recent decline is likely for several reasons. Firstly, most of the young Limigya are sent to school far away from the village where they find a completely different set of norms and expectations. Secondly, the practice of polyandry has also ceased in neighbouring communities on both sides of the border. Moreover, while the polyandrous form of marriage used to be well suited to the traditional division of labour within a Limi household, the outmigration and changing livelihood priorities make it easier to manage without it.[30] Finally, it seems that the practice has been kept artificially alive due to the monk levy and the affiliated taxes. This last point may require some explanation. As mentioned in Chapter One, the rules for monk levy oblige large households with two sons and small households with three sons to provide one monk to the local monastery.[31] But the monks continue to live in their paternal home for most of the year and many of them have not practised celibacy and have participated in the polyandrous union. The fact that the monks' households have to finance a number of costly rituals over a period of fifteen years[32] makes it difficult for a monk brother to split from his natal household even if he wanted to, and one may argue that this has contributed to maintaining an artificially high number of (nominally) polyandrous unions. Some of the non-celibate monks have girlfriends, but largely for the above-mentioned fiscal and inheritance reasons they have normally remained in their paternal households. The girlfriends are typically unmarried women who either reside in their paternal homes or, if financially viable, have established their own single woman household; a few of them together with their monk partner. Nowadays, there may still be a monk brother in the household of a newlywed couple, but they no longer conceive of themselves as polyandrously married.[33] Another recent sentiment that I noted, especially amongst the lay people in Til, was a reluctance to get married. Some of the young people I spoke with said that if they got married,

28 Fjeld 2022.

29 Goldstein 1977: 58.

30 This list of observations is by no means meant to be exhaustive. A proper discussion of the reasons for the decline of polyandry would require a separate paper.

31 The monk levy will be explained in more detail in Chapter Eight.

32 This obligation is detailed in Chapter Nine.

33 To an outsider at least, this seems to be an example of blurred categories as it is not entirely clear what distinguishes a polyandrous marriage from a monogamous marriage with one or more cohabiting brothers (apart from their own understanding of their status).

they would have to take over the household responsibilities, and remaining single was a strategy to avoid that. In Waltse, they more commonly complained that young women moving out for educational purposes make it harder for the men in the village to find a spouse.

Inheritance rights are largely determined by household and the individual's position within it. The older brother automatically inherits the household's property, rights and obligations, and traditionally other male siblings were expected to remain part of the household. In case a younger brother seeks to establish a new *grong chung* household, he will normally not receive more than a quarter of the family property. Occasionally, it is also possible for younger brothers to be married as *mag pa* to a family without a male heir, but in most such cases he will not receive any share from his paternal home as he will take over the household of his new parents-in-law. Finally, there are cases of adoption (*bu tshab*), in which a couple without children adopt a son who will then inherit the property and become the head of the household, but this is rare. In his description of inheritance rules in Limi, Goldstein wrote that all brothers are in theory entitled to a share on demand.[34] However, this right has normally not been exercised in the case of levied monks. The saying in Limi, that the only property the monks inherit is the shrine room, illustrates this well.[35]

The situation for women is different and depends significantly on their marital status. Being married is a way to secure access to key resources such as fields, which in Limi are registered in the name of the male head of the household. A high number of unmarried women is a side effect of fraternal polyandry, and those who split from their natal household to form a single woman household, do not automatically have the right to inherit fields. Hence, in the past, unmarried women often had little option but to remain in their brothers' households. Single women may obtain user rights to fields for temporary periods, but the fields are still registered in the name of her father or brother, though the taxes are paid by the single woman. When she passes away, she is not entitled to pass the fields on to any children and must return the fields to her natal household. Such non-transmissibility of dependent households is a feature that is recorded in most relevant ethnographic literature.[36] Single women who continue to live in their paternal household have to participate in the household's work, and if a woman has children out of wedlock

34 Goldstein 1977: 55.

35 As mentioned above, this rule may together with the heavy taxation on monks' household have the side effect of limiting the number of partitions.

36 See for instance the analysis of the relation between households and subsidiary units in Ramble (1984: 194–202).

her situation may become particularly difficult. As mentioned above, levied monks who have not taken *dge slong* vows occasionally split from their elder brother's household and join their partner's *bom btang* household.[37] Normally neither the monks nor the women can claim much of a share of their respective household's property, and there are special limitations to their legal rights and duties. The roles of monk and *kha rgan* are regarded as incompatible, and it is the women who are in charge of these households. Overall, the household is seen as the pivotal element in administrative arrangements that allow for a wide range of practical arrangements and in providing that duties in terms of taxation and services are maintained.

4.3 Population and Residence Pattern

In 1974, Goldstein recorded that the total population of Limi was 791. In subsequent articles, he predicted a population increase that he connected to the dissolution of the polyandrous system and a resultant increased fertility.[38] Table 4.1, which compares the available figures from 1974 to 2011, shows that during the thirty-seven years between Goldstein's fieldwork and my own, the number of Limigya has increased by 35.3%.

TABLE 4.2 De jure population increase from 1974–2011[a]

	1974	1991	2004	2011	% Increase
Waltse	320	n.a.	411	424	32.5
Dzang	288	n.a.	405	419	45.5
Til	183	n.a.	229	227	24
Total	791	988	1045	1070	35.3

a The population statistics for 1974 are quoted from Goldstein (1974: 261), the figure from 1991 is quoted from the national census, the figures for 2004 are quoted from Bradley et al. (2004: 5), and the numbers for 2011 are based on my own survey. See Chart 4.3 below for population trends and residence patterns from 1974 to 2019.

37 As mentioned in Chapter One, only a few of the monks have taken the full set of vows, and many do not observe celibacy.

38 Based on vital statistics collected from Dzang from 1973–77, Goldstein (1981c: 725) estimated that if the current trend continued, the population of the village would double over the course of thirty-one years.

However, because these figures are based on domicile, i.e., a person's registered home for legal purposes, rather than actual residence, they do not reveal the whole truth. Seasonal migration for the purpose of trade, labour, pilgrimage, and religious education has been common for centuries, but recent decades have seen a significant increase in mobility which will be discussed in the paragraphs about outmigration and livelihoods below. The number of seasonal migrants varies from year to year. In 2011, I wrote that many people from Limi, especially men, tended to spend the winter months away from the village. These seasonal migrants are referred to as *phyi ba* (lit. 'outside [travellers]'). Many men used to spend this winter migration on travelling to India to fetch wood for the wooden drinking bowls (L. *phurru*, T *phor ba*) that Limi has been so famous for, but also other types of trade. Since the early 2000s and especially between my initial research stay in 2010 and 2019, summer migration to earn an income in Purang has become increasingly widespread. This development has had a great transformative effect on the society which will be discussed below. Moreover, there are a significant number of Limigya with a permanent *de facto* residence outside the village. Determining the exact size of the population is therefore not a straightforward matter. The difficulty can be illustrated by comparing my household survey from 2011 with the national census conducted by the Central Bureau of Statistics the same year. My own survey recorded a total of 1070 people, whereas the national census counted a population of only 904.[39] How can this divergence be explained? Most of the 18% discrepancy appears to be caused by different criteria used to determine the villagers' domicile. The Central Bureau of Statistics chose the following approach for the census that they term 'modified *de jure*':

> A person was counted at his/her usual place of residence. Usual place of residence is defined as a place where a person had been living or intends to live for at least six months. A person absent from usual place for short period for the purpose of treatment or pilgrimage or similar causes is treated as present in the usual place. Persons away or absent from birth place or usual place for employment or study or business purpose is [*sic*] considered absent population and thus, not counted as present population. However, homeless or mobile population was counted at the place where they were traced on the last day of enumeration or 27 June 2011.[40]

39 Central Bureau of Statistics 2014.

40 Central Bureau of Statistics 2014.

The modified *de jure* approach chosen by the Central Bureau of Statistics could in theory have been useful for my book, but it turned out that the selection criteria were not always consistent between the three villages, making the figures in the census difficult to use for demographic analysis. Moreover, as pointed out by Aase, Chapagain and Dangal, 'Squeezing a complex and fuzzy reality into narrow analytic categories gives a simplified picture of reality that hardly reflects actual events and processes on the micro level.' They argue for a definition of Himalayan households in rural areas as 'multisited economic units'.[41] This approach aligns well with the way the Limi community operates, using a broad definition of domicile for the purpose of local village governance. To conform with the local system I have therefore chosen to include all Limigya in the total figure of my 2011 survey, except those who had permanently renounced what I will refer to as their 'local citizenship'.[42]

4.3.1 *Local Citizenship*

The village assemblies in Limi operate with specific criteria that determine membership of the community and the rights and duties such 'local citizenship' entails. This includes the *kha rgan*'s duty to participate in the village assembly meetings (described in Chapter Five), taxes to the village (discussed in Chapter Six), the monk levy obliging the second or third brother in *grong chen* and *grong chung* households to serve in the local monastery (elaborated in chapter Eight) and the taxes to the monastery (studied in Chapter Nine), a number of rotating positions, as well as rights to use the villages' communal resources.

Local citizenship appears to be counted at the household level, and normally all members of a Limi household are included almost regardless of actual residence. Limigya who have temporarily settled elsewhere are still counted as local citizens. Even if an individual decides to leave the village permanently, unless he or she marries into another household (which in practice means that claims to local resources have been renounced), the paternal household will still have to fulfil the migrant's duties towards the community and the monastery. This principle becomes clearly demonstrated during the annual tax calculation meetings, when taxes and fines for absent family members are due.[43] Before outmigration began in the 1990s, compensating for the temporary

---

41 Aase, Chapagain and Dangal 2018: 1.

42 To gain an overview of the *de facto* residence pattern, I also distinguished between permanent village residents, the outmigrated population (who theoretically may return), and members of the population who have permanently renounced their local citizenship.

43 See Chapters Six, Eight, and Nine for more details.

absence of individual villagers was straightforward. However, by 2011, with as many as 381 Limigya living in Kathmandu, India, or other countries abroad still counted as local Limi citizens, this had become more challenging as the community's temporal and monastic duties apply also to these migrants.

The village assemblies in all three villages have imposed rules designed to prevent individuals and especially households from abandoning the villages, but there are significant differences in implementation. There is pressure on the *kha rgan* to spend at least some time in the village to participate in the assembly meetings, and on the household's women to do agricultural work, but as will be discussed in more detail, the highest pressure is caused by the monk levy. While many individuals have left the villages permanently, they will normally still be counted as local citizens unless all members of the household decide to formally abandon the village. The term used for taking leave from the village is *khral gcog*, lit. 'to break the taxes' and refers to the fact that a household leaving the village implies cutting the tax responsibilities, as well as the rights to communal village resources.[44] Households who have permanently left the village after a formal application to the village assembly (or after rare cases of expulsion) are referred to as 'migrants' or 'wanderers' (*khyams pa*), while individual migrants without tax responsibilities are referred to as *yul thon ba* (lit. '[person who has] departed from the village'). People from this latter group are not expected to come back but do have the right to return. Applications for permission to leave the village must be presented at one of the two main village assembly meetings, and significant pressure is put on the household to persuade them to stay. In addition to these formal negotiations, relatives will visit the household and try to convince them to remain in the village. In Waltse, abandoning the village means that the household must relinquish all its claims to immovable property such as land and other collective village resources,[45] whereas in the other villages, especially in Dzang, they have agreed on more flexible solutions.

4.3.2 *Outmigration*

The outmigration from Limi seems part of a larger trend in the country's mountain districts. In an article analysing the demographic patterns in three communities in Gorkha and Mustang districts, Childs et al. show that despite a general population increase in Nepal, the size of the Tibetan speaking communities

44 *Khral gcog* is different from *khral dgongs pa*, the term used for temporary tax reduction or tax exemption applications. See Chapter Six,

45 The rules discussed by Ramble (2008a: 284f) for dissuading the inhabitants from abandoning the village of Te appear quite similar.

TABLE 4.3 The increasing number of outmigrated Limigya from 1974 to 2011

	1974 Village residence	1974 Other residence	1991	2004 Village residence	2004 Other residence	2011 Village residence	2011 Other residence
Waltse	320	n.a.	n.a.	371	40	330	94
Dzang	288	n.a.	n.a.	306	99	230	189
Til	183	n.a.	n.a.	160	69	129	98
Total	791	n.a.	988	837	208	689	381

in the highlands of Nepal is rapidly declining because of outmigration.[46] The authors argue that the main driving force for the outmigration from these highland valleys is education, with parents deciding to send their children either to monasteries or boarding schools outside the village—a phenomenon that is analysed in more detail in Childs and Choedup's book on the transformative effect of migration in Nubri.[47] Limi largely conforms to this pattern, but as we will see below, features some interesting particularities.

Goldstein reported that there was virtually no outmigration from Limi in the 1970s.[48] According to my respondents, it was not until the 1990s that the first households started to send their children away from the villages for education and a few wealthy villagers bought property in Kathmandu. Assuming that the figure from the national census in 1991 refers to *de facto* residents, the size of the resident population appears to have reached its peak in the early 1990s.

As illustrated by Table 4.3, the villagers then started to move out of the valley, and the outmigration escalated. In 2004, the number of outmigrated Limigya amounted to 19.9% of the total population; in 2011 the number had reached 35.6%. Hence, although Goldstein was right in his predicted general population increase, the number of people actually living in the villages in Limi was 12.9% lower in 2011 than in 1974. However, this figure conceals significant intra-village differences: the resident population in Dzang was reduced by 20.1% between 1974 and 2011, whereas the population in Waltse increased by 3.1%. The reasons for this difference in population pattern are complex, but compared to the other two villages, Waltse has imposed stricter rules that make it difficult for people to leave. Moreover, hardly any people from Waltse own property in

46 Childs et al. 2014.

47 Childs et al. 2014: 89. Childs and Choedup 2019.

48 Goldstein 1981c: 730.

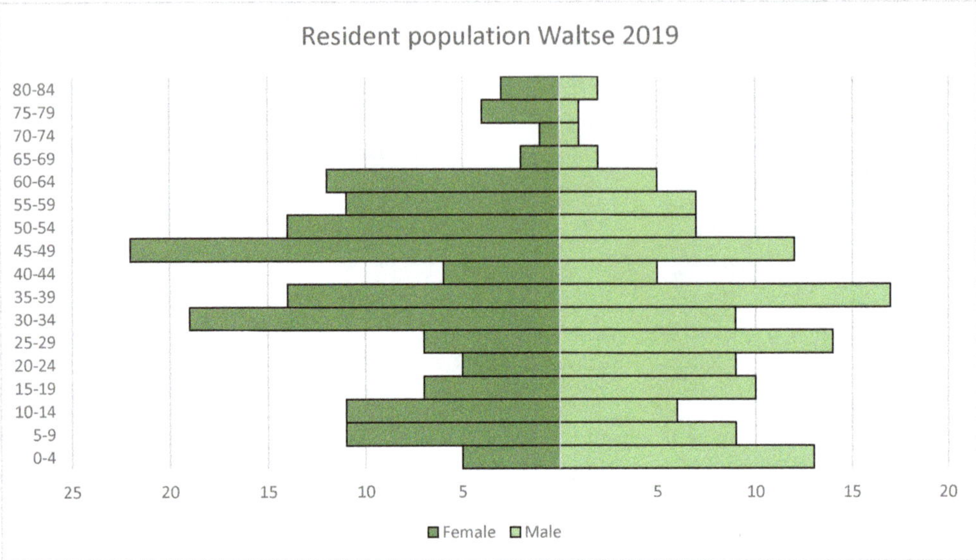

CHART 4.1 Resident population, Waltse 2019

Kathmandu. These factors help explain the intra-village differences.[49] But who is leaving, and who is staying? A closer look at the sex/age composition of resident and outmigrated villagers from Waltse in 2019, yields a bit more nuance.

Chart 4.1 shows the total number of villagers residing in Waltse at least part of the year and reveals that there is an imbalance between the sexes and generations. If we look at the figures for people above the age of 30, we see that there is a higher number of women than men. In the younger segment below 30, there is a higher number of males. This figure confirms the young men's complaint mentioned above that there are too few potential spouses in the village.

If we look at Chart 4.5, showing which sex and age groups have left the village 'temporarily', we see another imbalance. There are slightly more women outmigrating than men, and 67% of those women are currently undergoing education.[50] Many villagers expressed concern about the future of the village, if these young people do not return.

Examining the total population figures from all three villages in 2019, as shown in Chart 4.3 below, reveals that individual outmigration had not only escalated further; many households were now renouncing their local citizenship. There was a significant decline in the population registered with Limi

49 Differences in economic strategies between the three villages are also likely to have an impact on the migration pattern.

50 See also Havnevik Hovden and Rinchen Loden (forthcoming).

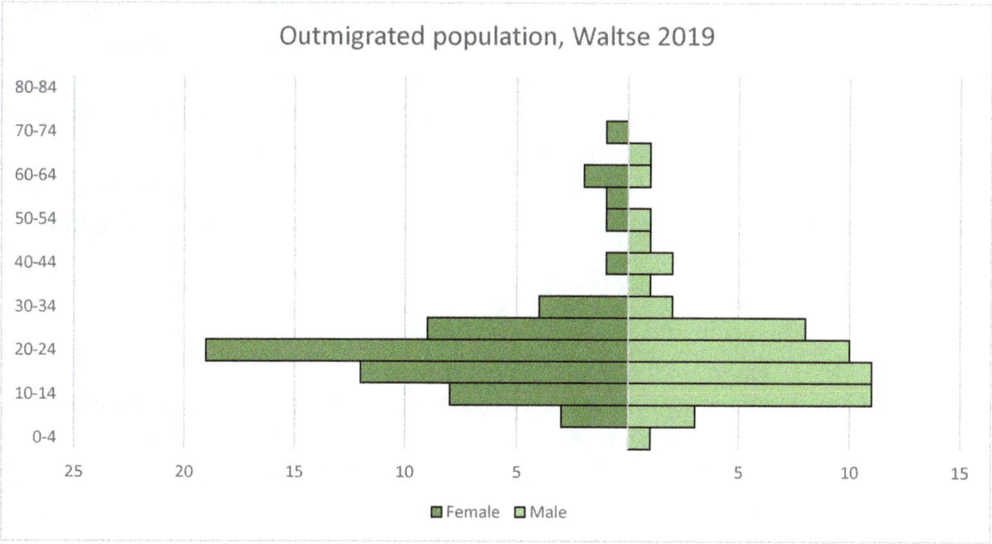

CHART 4.2 Outmigrated population, Waltse 2019

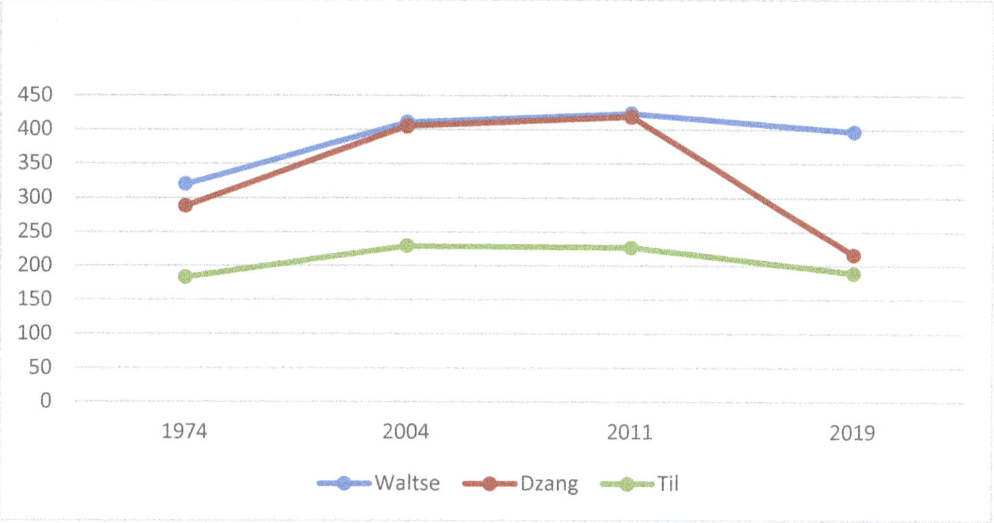

CHART 4.3 Population trend from 1974 to 2019, showing the renunciation of local citizenship from 2011

as their domicile; as many as twenty-four households with almost half of the population had abandoned Dzang, and this was reportedly just the beginning (see Chart 4.3). What was happening?

Although the reasons were complex, villagers in Dzang explained that the massive renunciation of local citizenship and abandonment of their village was closely related to the dilemma described in the opening vignette of the book: the pressure on young outmigrated men to return to the villages to take over as household heads and the pressure on levied monks to remain in the local monastery.[51] Several of these men were undergoing secular or religious education and were reluctant to abandon their studies. Many households in Dzang also own property in Kathmandu, providing them with the material means to leave. However, as expressed in multiple ways, the decision to leave was a difficult one, affecting both those who left and those who stayed behind.

4.4 Education and Some of Its Side Effects

The first rudimentary education in Limi was introduced by Nepali authorities in the mid-1970s.[52] Villagers report that in that early period, the education consisted of a teacher visiting the valley for a few weeks in the summer to teach the Nepali and English alphabets as well as some basic mathematics. The men and women who had attended the summer school told me that the outcome was very limited; they learned how to write their names and had to memorise some words but were not taught how to form full sentences. Most of them admitted that their interest in education was generally low, partly because of the poor quality of the teaching, and partly because they did not see the relevance of the school for their own livelihoods.[53] The fact that some of the teachers knew only Nepali and were hardly able to communicate with the Tibetan speaking villagers contributed to the lack of interest. In some periods there were also teachers from Humli-Tibetan communities further south in the district and these were in general more popular, but the main change in attitude to education did not take place until about 2000. At that time, more of the parents sent their children to schools in Kathmandu and to schools run by the Central Tibetan Administration (CTA) at various locations in India.[54] The education at

51 This dilemma and the multiple push and pull factors will be discussed further throughout the book.

52 Goldstein (1975: 92) wrote that in 1974, a two- to three-week teaching programme in Nepali language was arranged every summer in Limi.

53 According to the survey conducted by Bradley et al. (2004: 8–10) for Nepal Trust, this attitude was still prevalent in 2004. When I did my first fieldwork in 2010, my overall impression was that the parents were quite positive to sending their children to school, but apart from the positions as teachers, there were no jobs in the villages where they could use their education.

54 The children at the CTA schools in India are generally recruited among Tibetan refugees, but also an increasing number of Tibetan speaking communities in Nepal send their children there. See Childs and Choedup (2019) for an analysis of this trend. The first Limigya

these schools was regarded to be of much better quality than that offered in Humla's district headquarters, Simikot. Nevertheless, sending children so far away was expensive and possible only for families of sufficient means. In 2008, the Antahkarana Society, an American organisation, established local schools in the Nepali state school buildings in Limi to provide at least a minimum education to the children. To ensure that the teachers would stay and teach, the organisation opted to employ young men from the villages as teachers in addition to those appointed by the government. Even though most of these local teachers only had primary or secondary school education, it was considered a much better alternative than the largely absent government-funded teachers. However, the lack of formal teachers' training meant that the village schools, which were serving mainly children from the poorer families, were only able to provide very basic education. A few years later, another American organisation called Citta took over the village schools through its Nepali branch Aatmiya. By that time more of the young villagers with an SLC (School Leaving Certificate) had been called back to Limi, and with some additional support from other organisations the schools in Waltse and Dzang have expanded (Figs. 4.3 and 4.4). This process has been assisted by the rapid increase in connectivity linking Limi to the rest of Nepal and the world.

Before summer 2010, there was no telephone in Limi, infrastructure in Humla was poor, and sending children to far-away places meant that they would be out of touch with their families for a number of years. Indeed, some children who had enrolled at the CTA schools in India lost contact with their family members and a few of them even forgot their native dialect.[55] After a few years in school, several families recalled their children to the village. While girls were taken back to work in the fields, boys were called back to take over as head of the household. Although the children had missed their families while attending school, many of them told me that it had been very challenging for them to return to the village. The boys who were to become heads of their respective households experienced the strongest pressure to return home. According to the village law described above, the eldest son must assume responsibility as head of the household when his father retires at sixty-five. A maximum of three years' leave may be granted a son for attending school, but the prospective household head is then required to take on his responsibility. Hence,

were sent to boarding schools already in the 1990s like other Tibetan speaking communities in Nepal, but it took some years before it became common practice.

55 This was mentioned in a number of conversations with young adults who had returned from India to Kathmandu or Limi. Childs and Choedup (2019) similarly report that the loss of native tongue has been a problem also in Nubri.

FIGURE 4.3 Class 3 in Waltse, 2011

FIGURE 4.4 The school in Dzang, 2019

several boys have had to interrupt their education before receiving the SLC, without which the young adults will have difficulties getting a proper job or continue their education elsewhere.[56] With the recent exception of the positions as teachers and health workers, the villages do not have any job opportunities for young, educated adults resulting in few changes in village livelihoods. The returning youngsters are expected to resume the family's traditional ways of income generation including agricultural work, trade, manual labour and crafts. The situation for educated girls is also difficult. I spoke with girls who had attended boarding school since the age of eight who reported that they found it extremely difficult to return since they neither had the experience nor the muscles for the heavy lifting agricultural work in Limi requires. Therefore, unless they are called back to the village for marriage most well-educated girls never return.

In the past, monastic and secular education was largely the prerogative of men, but a closer look at education in Waltse in 2019 reveals important changes to this pattern: The total proportion of women and men with at least a minimum of secular education is virtually the same (43 versus 42%). If we look at secular and monastic education combined, however, the educated men outnumber the women (70.3 versus 45.1%).[57] If we compare the percentage of women *currently* going to school with men, the women outnumber the men with 31.5 versus 18.7%. Moreover, in higher education, there are 17 women, while only 3 men have so far reached this stage. These figures seem surprising in a community with such a clear preference for men but are partly a result of more men than women being summoned to the village to take up household responsibilities. There appear to be twice as many young men in the village with a secular education than there are young women and if we add the calling back of monks, it becomes clear that there is a particular pressure on men to remain and a relatively high portion of female outmigration (see Chart 4.2 above).[58] The women with educational aspirations cherish the fact that they now have opportunities that the older generation never had. But if they do not return, this presents a challenge for the marriage opportunities of those young men who want to—or have to—settle in the village. Thus, in the long run, if the quality of the village school is strengthened, parents can choose to let their children remain in the villages for longer without compromising their educational quality. This improvement may have transformational consequences for

56 According to Nepali law, no public positions can be pursued without the SLC, and there are hardly any further education possibilities without the certificate.

57 The figures are taken from my household survey from 2019.

58 16 of the women and 31 men staying at least part of the time in Waltse (excluding the children currently attending the local school) have at least some education.

the local population.[59] However, this will at least partly depend on what livelihood prospects there are for these educated Limi youth in the valley.

4.5 Local Livelihoods

As was mentioned at the beginning of this chapter, the Limigya have traditionally relied on a combination of various income sources, and this last part of the chapter will explore the different livelihoods options in more detail. I will adopt Carney's definition of livelihoods, which he describes as consisting of 'the capabilities, assets (including both material and social resources), and activities required for a means of living'.[60] Livelihood analyses acknowledge the varied and complex activities people engage in to sustain themselves and explore how different approaches impact their livelihood paths.[61] Another key aspect of livelihood analysis is examining how households' access to assets and activities is shaped by institutions and social factors like gender, class, kin, and belief systems.[62] This is particularly relevant for Limi, with its clear gendered division of labour within the families, and significant variation of possibilities depending largely on household category.[63]

4.5.1 *Agriculture and Pastoralism*

Although not all households in Waltse are landowners, they have various degrees of usufruct rights to land.[64] Barley and radishes constitute the main crops, but some potatoes, oilseed, wheat, peas, and leafy vegetables are also cultivated.[65] In addition, the villagers have traditionally collected quantities of nettles (*zwa*, Lat. *Urtica dioica*), which, as the only green vegetable locally available during the winter months, constitute an important source

59 Possible effects on the local gender pattern are discussed in Havnevik, Hovden and Rinchen Loden (forthcoming).
60 Carney's (1998: 4) frequently quoted definition is based on Chambers and Conway (1992: 7).
61 See for instance Scoones 2009: 172.
62 Ellis 2000a: 291 and 2000b.
63 See also Havnevik, Hovden and Rinchen Loden (forthcoming).
64 See Chapter Six for details about landownership in Limi.
65 The items are listed according to the amount of produce in descending order. See Bradley et al. 2004: 21.

of nutrition. However, this is changing. In 2010, the monks in Rinchen Ling built the first greenhouse in the valley and, shortly thereafter, another was built next to a teahouse in Dungling (s.u.) (Fig. 4.5). Both were constructed on the model of greenhouses in Purang, and already in the first winter season they yielded a supply of fresh green vegetables. By 2018, there were as many as thirteen greenhouses in Waltse, and the monastery and many of the households were experimenting with new types of vegetables (Fig. 4.6). The fields are traditionally fertilised with compost made from a mixture of human and animal manure and pine needles. Recently, chemical fertilizer is also being used, but the traditional fertilizer is regarded as giving a better yield. The soil in Limi is sandy and requires frequent irrigation (Fig. 4.7). Cultivating the fields is labour-intensive work, but apart from ploughing (Fig. 4.8), which requires a man to lead the horse or yak,[66] and the harvest (Fig. 4.9), which requires all available hands, work in the fields is done by the women.

The agricultural activities, which are strictly coordinated to ensure proportionate distribution according to the three household categories and access to resources, are supervised by local constables.[67] For instance, there are rules obliging all households to irrigate the fields at least nine times a year, regardless of the amount of precipitation, but additional irrigation may be organised if needed. The responsibility to manage the irrigation is given to a set of female leaders, referred to by the Nepali term *mailah* ('woman'). The timing of most of the other agricultural activities are collectively decided and there is little room for individual variation.[68] Since the road advanced into the Limi valley, the villagers in all three settlements have purchased a number of agricultural machines, which reportedly saves a lot of time (see Fig. 4.12). The threshing, for instance, which was still done with the help of long wooden sticks in 2010 (Fig. 4.11) was done by machine in 2018. Similarly, the crushing of straw for fodder which was done by horse in 2010 (Fig. 4.10) was done by machine a few years later. While there were some issues related to ownership, operation

66 The first ploughing in the spring is done by yak and the second ploughing after sowing is done by horse.

67 The term 'constable' does not correspond to any specific local position. I have used the term 'constable' for pragmatic reasons, in order to refer to local officials with various supervision tasks in the villages. See Chapter Five about the village management for more details.

68 The decisions are made after consulting the Tibetan calendar for auspicious days and after assessing local conditions. There is little room for individual variation, but in some cases, villagers may be able to postpone an activity by *skar 'dzin* (lit. 'star-catching'), symbolically starting the activity on the chosen auspicious day, but in reality, carrying out most of it at a later time.

FIGURE 4.5 The monastery greenhouse in Waltse, 2019

FIGURE 4.6 New types of seeds at the shop in Dzang, 2019

FIGURE 4.7 Irrigation in Dzang, 2019

FIGURE 4.8 First ploughing in Waltse, May 2011

and maintenance of the machines, most villagers seemed to welcome the new technology making agricultural work a little bit easier.

Another, even more important change is the combination of more money circulating and the availability of cheap barley, wheat, rice, and other supplies in Purang. In 2011, some of the households with fewer working hands and fewer mouths to feed chose to leave some of their fields fallow and instead purchase the necessary grain. By 2018, as many as 31 percent of the *grong chung* and 37 percent of the *bom btang* had left agricultural work completely to focus on earning money from work in Purang.[69] Many villagers told me they were acutely aware that neglecting agriculture for the sake of work on the other side of the border was a risky affair, as the border could suddenly close. But most believed that the short-term benefits outweighed the risk.[70]

The fields have probably never yielded sufficient grain for subsistence. For many of the two upper strata households, animal husbandry has been an important supplement, and for some of them it has constituted the main source of wealth.[71] Pastoral nomadism on a larger scale has mainly been practised among families from the upper social strata, wealthy enough to own sizeable herds, but has declined rapidly in recent years. In 2011, only members from one household in Waltse and two in Dzang retained the nomadic lifestyle following the animals from pasture to pasture all year round, and by 2018 there were none. Animal husbandry has been more important in Til (Fig. 4.13), but because of the accessibility of winter pastures near the village, none of the pastoralists are living as full-time nomads. The severe snowstorm during the winter of 2014–15 mentioned at the beginning of the chapter reduced the herds significantly, and since then most of the villagers in Waltse decided not to reinvest in animals. However, recently, a few households have joined a new yak farming cooperative.[72]

Goldstein reported that in the 1970s, there were approximately 5000 sheep and 1000 yaks in the valley, as well as a smaller number of goats, yak-cow hybrids (*mdzo*), cows, horses and mules.[73] In 2004, the number of sheep had

69 Many of the *grong chen* households had also reduced the number of fields they tilled, but none had left all the fields fallow like the *grong chung* and the *bom btang*.

70 See Chapter Ten for how villagers adapted to the 2020 Covid border closure.

71 Goldstein 1975: 92. The households with large herds were also able to engage in long distance trade and tended to be among the wealthiest in the valley.

72 The yak farming cooperative, initiated by the High Mountain And Livelihood Improvement (HIMALI) Project in 2018, has reportedly been successful but is operating on a small scale. See Havnevik, Hovden and Rinchen Loden (forthcoming) for more details.

73 Limi herds had grown significantly, as Tibetan refugees, unable to move their flocks to lower altitudes, sold animals cheaply (Goldstein 1977: 58). But the harsh winter of 1972–73 had taken its toll (Goldstein 1975: 93).

FIGURE 4.9 Harvest in Waltse, 2010

FIGURE 4.10 Horses crushing straw for fodder in Waltse, 2010

FIGURE 4.11 Threshing in Waltse, 2010

FIGURE 4.12 Inspecting the new agricultural machine in Waltse, 2018

dropped to approximately 800, the number of yaks had dropped to about 600, whereas the number of goats had increased to more than 1100.[74] During my fieldwork six years later, many households had reduced their herds of yak and all the sheep had been sold. One of the nomads I spoke with estimated that the total herds in Limi had been reduced from about 10 000 in his youth to 8–900 in 2010.[75] Compared with the numbers provided during the tax collection meeting in 2011, the nomad's estimate appears quite plausible. Nevertheless, the majority of the households in Limi still own at least a few milking animals. The seasonal movement of herds between the pastures is strictly coordinated between the three villages. Lots are drawn to decide the distribution of campsites for the tents (Fig. 4.15), all animals must be moved on the same day (Fig. 4.14) so that every household can start cutting the grass for winter fodder at the same time and prevent any household gaining an advantage over the others (Fig. 4.16).

Animals have traditionally been kept for several purposes; yaks, hybrids, cows, sheep and goats have been raised for transportation, wool, leather products, meat, and milk products. Some of the milk is churned into butter (*mar*), and the buttermilk is then used to make dried cheese (*phyur ba, L. churpi*). In addition to the butter used for private consumption, large quantities are needed for paying taxes[76] and ritual patronage. However, none of the households can produce enough. Elderly villagers told me that in the past, they made up for the shortage by bartering butter for salt or other goods with trading partners from the southern valleys (*rong pa*).[77] Today, most families simply buy large packages of a manufactured butter-margarine blend for tea, and a type of margarine that Drepung monastery has officially approved for butter lamps from the market in Purang. Nevertheless, the households in Waltse have been encouraged to keep milking goats for butter production, and in 2011, fines were imposed on households without goats.[78] By 2018, however, priorities had changed and all households had sold their goats.

The decline in animal husbandry in general and nomadism in particular is due to several factors, but the main reasons include the decreasing availability

74 Bradley et al. 2004: 23.

75 Interview 08.08.10.

76 The 'great tax of Limi' (*sle mi khral mo che*), which used to be paid to Tibet until 1960 consisted of 50 loads (*khal*) of butter. For details about village and monastery taxes, see Chapter Six and Nine respectively.

77 The term *rong pa* ('person from the valleys') is used by Tibetans in Purang to denote people from the valleys south of the border. Although included in the Purangbas' definition, the Limigya do not use the term about themselves, only about people from the communities further south in Humla.

78 See Chapter Six.

of pastureland, the improved infrastructure, changing trade patterns, and outmigration. The Limi herders used to graze their animals in Tibet, south of Manasarovar, but lost access to the best pasture area in the 1960s, and throughout the 1980s they gradually lost access to the remaining pastures.[79] Villagers told me that they had to pay a 'grazing fee' (*rtswa rin*), payable only in timber and that they had to agree to reduce the size of the herds grazing in Tibet by 1000 each year. Except for the pastoralists in Til, who had access to pastures near the village, most households therefore decided to reduce their herds. The next blow to pastoralism in Limi came with the construction of the two roads from the Chinese border. As I will explain below, the Lapcha and Nara roads have gradually reduced the need for pack animals for transportation. While the villagers still sent yak caravans to Purang to buy provisions in 2010 (Fig. 4.19), they were able to transport foodstuffs, consumer goods and construction material by vehicle only a few years later. What constitutes an even bigger challenge to pastoralism, is the rapid escalation of seasonal and more permanent outmigration. Men's absence during winter as was common in the past was not seen as too big of a hindrance, but the current large-scale absence during summer season due to more lucrative work in Purang has made it impossible for most villagers to continue to keep their herds. Some villagers believed that only a future market with high enough prices for animal products could attract the young adults back and partly reverse this trend.

In addition, the villagers now must also adapt to the challenges of a changing climate, most notably the changing precipitation pattern. So far, the villagers are managing by adapting the timing and amount of irrigation of their fields and they are also performing more extensive rituals to appease the serpent deities (*klu*) believed to control water (Fig. 7.13). Over the last few years, the villages have been struck by several glacial lake outbursts as well as other types of floods, as previously mentioned, which have caused considerable damage. But with some outside support the villagers have made the necessary repairs and have so far managed to protect themselves. If the recent climate models are correct, indicating that the weather will become more erratic in the future, stronger measures may be needed.[80]

---

79 Saxer (2013: 49) writes that the Limi herders finally lost access to the pastureland in Tibet in 1991.

80 See Hovden and Havnevik (2021) for a more detailed discussion of the religious management of the climate and environment.

FIGURE 4.13 Animal husbandry in Til, 2018

FIGURE 4.14 Moving the animals to the winter pasture 2010

FIGURE 4.15 Nomad tent at the campsite in the Nying valley, 2010

FIGURE 4.16 Cutting grass for winter fodder, 2010

4.5.2 *Trade, Crafts, and Manual Labour*

The combination of agriculture and pastoralism has constituted the traditional basis for subsistence, while trade, crafts, and manual labour have been the most important supplementary sources of income throughout history.[81] However, there have always been differences between and within the social strata, and households with little or no land have relied primarily on craft production, trade and/or various types of manual labour. The main trading items have traditionally been salt, sheep's wool, animals, and local handicraft products, such as wooden bowls (T. *phor pa*, *phor bu*; L. *furru*). However, the type of trade has also varied according to the households, and as several authors have pointed out, trade and animal husbandry have been closely connected.[82] Among the Limi families it was mainly those with sizeable herds who were able to engage in the salt-trade. Elderly villagers recalled that during winter, they used to herd their animals on the pastures south of Manasarovar, and in spring they returned to Limi with salt, which they subsequently bartered for grain and butter at the Tsala mart, north of Mt. Saipal.[83] A nomad from one of the families with the largest herds explained that during his father's time they would go to the Tibetan plateau to fetch salt by themselves. The journey to the Nganglag Tshakha (Ngang lag Tshwa kha) salt lake used to take twelve days on foot.[84] His father had told him that the salt-traders travelled in groups and that each group usually brought about 200 sheep. The groups were strictly organised with a leader, a cook, a helper and herders, and special rules applied; after a certain point on the journey to the salt lakes they would only be allowed to communicate in a special language in order to appease the deities.[85] He said that it was hard work, but as illustrated by the saying 'the precious treasure of salt in the northern plains is for the youth's hand [to take], whoever comes first', the trade was very profitable.[86]

81 Although it could have yielded important insights, I do not have systematic data on the content and relative importance of trade compared with the other sources of income. There has been significant variation between households and throughout history.

82 See for instance Fürer-Haimendorf (1988), and Lama (2012).

83 Tsala is the same as Chala, mentioned as an important regional mart by Fürer-Haimendorf (1988: 256).

84 Ngang lag means 'duck feet', whereas Tshwa kha means 'salt field', or 'salt lake'. The name is probably derived from the flocks of shelducks that migrate to the shores of the lake every summer.

85 This secret language spoken by the salt caravaners was also mentioned in the 1997 documentary 'The saltmen of Tibet'.

86 Interview with a nomad, 08.08.10.

After the Chinese annexation of Western Tibet, the Humli traders were denied access to the salt lakes, and all trade was restricted to depots in Purang.[87] Rauber writes that the exchange rates at the Purang depots were initially not too bad, but gradually worsened.[88] However, it was probably Nepal's new development policy of introducing subsidised iodised salt from India, gradually implemented from 1964 that had the most detrimental effect on the salt trade.[89] The traders from Limi operated only the northern section of this long-distance trade. In comparison with the Nyinbas and the Humli-Khyampas,[90] who used to travel all the distance from the markets in Tibet to the Indian border, the barter seems to have been less important for the Limigya.[91] Yet, because of the salt trade's central role in the trans-Himalayan trade network its gradual decline nevertheless had important consequences for the economy in Limi.

Traders who did not have large enough herds to engage in the salt trade would sell craft items instead. Elderly men from Limi told me that in their youth, they sold these goods at the marts at Gyanyima (rGya nyi ma), Darchen (Dar chen) south of Kailash, and a few of the wealthier families used to travel as far as to the great marts in Ngari Gar (mNga' ris sGar). There were also other important seasonal marts on both sides of the border.[92] However, these marts were gradually closed from the sixties onwards, when the Chinese officials decided that the trade should be restricted to Purang.

Nowadays, many Limi traders sell watches[93] and some of the local entrepreneurs make a considerable profit from selling herbs, used as ingredients in Chinese and Tibetan medicine. Other increasingly important trading items include beer and Chinese liquor. When I stayed in the Youth Club house next to

---

87 See for instance Fürer-Haimendorf 1988: 251 and Goldstein 1978.

88 Rauber 1982: 152.

89 Rauber (1982: 147) in her study of the Humli-Khyampas, a group of trading nomads, wrote that the change already started in the 1930s, when Indian salt became available. The Nepali Government started to import salt from India in 1964. This led to decreasing prices, but the salt-trade in Humla still continued for a few more decades.

90 The Humli-Khyampas or Khyampas (Khyam pa, lit. 'the wanderers'), are a group of nomadic traders studied by Rauber (1980, 1982). In Limi the term *khyam pa* is used both to refer to this group of traders and in the more general meaning of pilgrims and other wanderers.

91 Levine (1988a: 205) ranks trade as the second-most important among the Nyinba livelihood strategies, whereas trade was the most important occupation of the Humli-Khyampas studied by Rauber (1982). See also Fürer-Haimendorf (1988: 250ff).

92 See for instance Lama (2012: 66f) and Fürer-Haimendorf (1988: 250ff).

93 Watches bought in Kathmandu are considered to be of higher quality than the Chinese-made watches available in Purang, and the traders report that the former fetch good prices.

the main path through the valley during my first fieldwork in 2010, I observed sheep caravans passing by my doorstep every day. A disturbingly large number of the saddlebags revealed bottle-shaped contents.[94]

People in Limi have for centuries been regarded as skilful craftsmen, and the men's wooden products and leatherwork and the women's weaving skills have been valued throughout the region. Limi has been especially famous for its wooden bowls (T. *phor pa, phor bu*; L. *furru*), the production of which has constituted a significant part of many households' income, especially from the *grong chung* strata (Fig. 4.17).[95] Goldstein reported that the trade in wooden bowls was expanded to a new market in the exile communities in India and that the prices in the 1970s made the trade very profitable for the Limigya.[96] However, the bowls are made out of the burl from a maple tree growing in India, and after the Indian authorities made the search for maple burls semi-illegal, the young men from Limi have suffered serious difficulties. Recently men from other communities in Humla, like Yakba (s.u.), have also started to travel to India to search for this valuable wood, and the number of burls collected has declined from about 3–400 to 100–150 per person in a good year. Young men from Limi still made the journey during the winter season of 2011–12, but most abandoned this activity only a few years later because of the high risk. Recently, Limi traders have acted as middlemen purchasing the bowls from others, getting them decorated with silver and reselling them at higher prices.

Although the production of other types of handicrafts has decreased with the availability of cheap mass-produced goods from China, handmade products are regarded as more valuable, and it is not difficult to find buyers. Skilful men produce beautifully carved tables and other wooden objects sold mainly in Purang. A number of women in Limi earn an extra income by spinning and weaving woollen cloth (*snam bu*) used for robes for trading partners (*ngo shes*)[97] in Purang. The weaving is always done in the winter months, and for the *snam bu*, they use a backstrap loom, which they set up in the fields. The

94 Goldstein (1978) and Saxer (2013) describe also how some Humli families were tempted to participate in the trade in antiques and prohibited animal products. Today, this trade appears to be greatly reduced.

95 For a detailed description of the technicalities of the production of wooden bowls, see Ronge 1984.

96 Goldstein 1975: 95 and 1981b: 16.

97 The term *ngo shes* is normally translated as 'acquaintance', but in Humla and in Ngari, the term is used to denote the 'ritual friendship' (N. *mit*) forged between trading partners. Such relationships, which are inherited from father to son, are are common among the trans-Himalayan traders. In Mustang and Dolpo, for instance, the term *gnas tshang* (lit. 'lodging'or 'dwelling') is used. See Ramble (2008a: 288) and Bauer (2004: 41f).

hardiest of the women stretch a tarpaulin over the loom so that they can weave even when it is snowing (see Fig. 4.18).

The most important source of income for men and women with little land and animals, however, has been manual labour. In the past, many people from Limi used to spend the winters working in the Nyinba villages and other communities further south in Humla.[98] The work included farmwork, housework, crafts, spinning, weaving, and the recitation of religious texts. The latter would be done by monks and literate laymen.[99] The work would be paid for with food and lodging, and a little extra to bring home to the families, but the salary would be minimal. In Limi they used to refer to this low-income seasonal work as *dgun nyal* ('hibernation'), suggesting that this practice was regarded as a last resort to survive, whereas the elderly Nyinbas refer to the same practice as *tshe phyid* ('life sustenance').[100] Nowadays most households, at least in Waltse, earn their extra income through manual labour on construction sites (Fig. 4.20), work in restaurants or other ventures in Purang district in the summer season, and on the two road projects in Humla. The contrast with *dgun nyal* could hardly have been greater, as this work pays very well and has contributed to a significant increase in income. While this work is referred to as a 'side job' (*zhor las*), it has for many households become the main source of income; especially for the *bom btang* households who are now much better off than in the past. Some of the single women spend months in Purang every summer season loading cement trucks. The work is very hard and the days long, but in 2011 was rewarded with a salary of approximately CNY 100 per day and in 2018 the salaries had increased significantly. Considering that it is hard for the women from *bom btang* households to make a living from agriculture alone, it is not surprising to see that this household category tops the statistics of female manual labourers in Purang. In 2019, as many as 66% of the *bom btang* in Waltse sustained their households through work in Purang, whereas only 36% of the female members of *grong chen* households did the same. The availability of this work has had significant

98 Levine (1988a: 228) reports that during her first fieldwork she encountered a number of women from Limi weaving or doing other types of labour for wealthier Nyinba households.

99 Monks would generally only be allowed to work in the summer season, but exceptions were made for monks with special sponsorship responsibilities (*las sne*). See Chapter Nine.

100 Oral communication with Rinchen Loden, January 2020.

FIGURE 4.17 Traditional wooden drinking bowl (*phurru*)
© TENZIN NORBU LAMA

FIGURE 4.18 Woman from Waltse weaving on a cold winter day, 2012

FIGURE 4.19 On the way to Purang to buy provisions for the winter, 2010

FIGURE 4.20 Construction site in Purang
© BRUCE HUETT

consequences for Limi. While many years have now passed since the barter trade was replaced with trade for money, one may argue that Purang has been key in thrusting Limi society into the global market economy. Following the Covid-19 crisis and the tense global political landscape at the time of completing this book, the closing of the border has created new challenges and evidenced the vulnerability of this economic strategy.[101]

4.5.3 *The First Shops*

During the summer of 2011, the youth club in Waltse[102] opened a small shop a few minutes' walk to the south of the village.[103] The shopkeeper was one of the young, educated men, who had been called back to the village to take over as head of his household. The shelves were filled with bags of instant noodles, soft drinks, alcohol, cigarettes, and sweets which had been brought from Purang, and it was felt that the location at the main path through the valley, next to the public phone house and the health post would secure customers. The shop immediately attracted a horde of village children, who begged their parents for money to buy sweets, and some young adults who bought alcohol and cigarettes, but not many others. Although a few trekking groups and traders passed through the village during the summer months, the former brought all their supplies from Kathmandu or Simikot, and the latter did not spend much since they were on their way to or from the market in Purang anyway. Unable to attract customers other than their own family members and relatives, the Youth Club closed the shop after a few weeks. The village was probably not ready for a shop then, but the attempt can be seen as indicative of a broader socio-economic transformation process.[104] When I visited the village again in 2018 and 19, there was a small shop in the local phone house both in Waltse and Dzang, and the presence of consumer goods (mostly bought from Purang) was highly visible throughout the villages (Fig. 4.22).

---

101 See Chapter Ten and Havnevik, Hovden and Rinchen Loden (forthcoming).

102 Youth clubs are a relatively recent phenomenon in Nepal. Inspired by student associations, they have become important forums for adolescents and young adults all over the country for political engagement and strengthening of ethnic identity. The youth clubs in Limi, which were founded from 2008 onwards, are discussed in Chapter Five.

103 This shop in Waltse was the second in Limi. The first shop was established at the roadhead in Dungling shortly after the first stretch of road from the Lapcha pass reached Limi territory in 2010 (Fig. 4.21).

104 Already in the 1970s Goldstein (1981b: 17) wrote that Limi was '... in the throes of a major transformation'; a characteristic that appears just as apt today.

FIGURE 4.21 The first shop in Dungling, 2010

FIGURE 4.22 Quantities of bottled drinks are now compulsory during celebrations

4.5.4 *Tourism Development*

Humla was only opened for tourism in 1994, but since trekking permits were expensive and visits allowed only together with liaison officers, the number of tourists was limited. In 1999, the first year listed in the National Tourism Statistics of Nepal, only 785 tourists visited the district. Limi was not opened for tourism until 2001,[105] and initially Limi received only very few visitors: a total of 39 tourists were registered in 2004, and during my first fieldwork in 2010, only five regular trekking groups walked through the Limi valley (Fig. 4.23). In addition, the village was visited by a travel writer and his team, a group of journalists and staff from development organisations, and finally Joan Halifax, a western Buddhist dignitary, who travelled with about one hundred staff including a group of western medical doctors for her charity 'Nomad's Clinic' and a film crew shooting a documentary about her life. In this early period, there were various initiatives to promote tourism to Limi. The valley was included in the 2001 edition of Lonely Planet's *Trekking in the Nepal Himalaya*.[106] Moreover, Michael Buckley in his creative guidebook *Shangri-La: A travel Guide to the Himalayan Dream*, listed Limi as one of the contenders for the 'real' location of this mythical place.[107] In subsequent years, the number of trekkers increased somewhat, but the total number of tourists visiting Humla was still low. The disastrous earthquake in 2015 caused severe destructions to the other two border crossings, and the tourism entrepreneur managed to reroute the Indian pilgrims heading for Kailash to Simikot. While this initiative created a boost in the number of visitors from 2016 onwards, the majority of the pilgrims have been helicoptered up to the border settlement Hilsa and the profit has largely been concentrated in these two places.

Although the number of tourists is likely to increase, the local people will not automatically benefit. Following a pattern from the more developed parts of Nepal, sustainable tourism development in the form of 'pro-poor tourism', 'eco-tourism', and 'pilgrimage tourism' has therefore become one of the key focus areas of a number of (I)NGOs operating in Humla district.[108] In addition,

---

105 Bradley et al. (2004: 29) writes that until then, Limi had the status of 'restricted area'.

106 Armington 2001: 444ff.

107 Buckley 2008: 136.

108 Organisations like Netherlands Development Organisation (SNV), the Nepal Trust, the Norwegian Development Fund, but also initatives like the Great Himalayan Trail, and the research cum development organisation ICIMOD are all involved in sustainable tourism development in the district. For an assessment of SNV's pro-poor tourism initiative in Humla, see Saville 2001.

many of these organisations engage in various forms of 'voluntourism'.[109] Yet, despite of such well-intended initiatives, much remains to be done before tourism can become a viable livelihood option for people in Limi and other parts of Humla outside the district capital. The special permits that are still needed to go to upper Humla, the very unreliable flight service[110] and the general lack of facilities, combine to keep the numbers of visitors down. Saville points out that the strict regulation of tourism in the region forces trekkers to travel in organised groups, and these groups tend to bring all staff and equipment including tents from Simikot or Kathmandu.[111] Another obstacle is that the monopoly situation in Humla's tourism business has made it difficult to establish new enterprises and to use tourism as a strategy to improve the livelihoods of the poor.[112] As a result, most of the profit tends to end up with the various Kathmandu-based or foreign travel agencies. Finally, the most acute obstacle to tourism is infrastructure; particularly the low availability of flights. None of the airlines operating the routes between Nepalgunj or Surkhet and Simikot want to keep aircrafts in the district in the main tourist season. They prefer to send them to Lukla and other popular tourist destinations, making it almost impossible to get a seat. Wealthy Indian pilgrims can be helicoptered in, but for regular tourists this is not an option. However, many villagers, especially the young generation, regard tourism as a potential source of income and, despite the challenges, have taken more and more initiatives.[113] Initially, the youth clubs collected camping fees from tourists, while individual villagers occasionally sold food or provided horses, and the monasteries received some donations from travellers. Over the last few years, ICIMOD in cooperation with Namkha Rural Municipality as well as groups of Limigya have invested significantly in various promotional activities (Fig. 4.24) and the number of tourists visiting Limi has reportedly increased somewhat. The recent closure of the border to the Tibetan Autonomous Region after the onset of the Covid-pandemic led the Humli tourism entrepreneurs to send Indian pilgrims to the Lapcha pass in Limi to

109 The benefits of such initiatives for the local communities are disputed among development researchers. See for instance Citrin (2010) for a critique of health care voluntourism in Humla.

110 During the summer of 2010, for instance, the airport in Simikot was closed for two consecutive months.

111 See Saville 2001: 13. This is a problem encountered at many of the tourist destinations in Nepal, as most trekking companies are based in the capital. See for instance Spiteri and Nepal 2008.

112 Saville 2001: 11.

113 This interest in tourism was registered already in 2004. See Bradley et al. 2004: 29f. But in that year only 577 trekkers visited Humla District, according to Nepal Tourism Statistics (2012: 49), and of these, only a tiny fraction went through Limi.

FIGURE 4.23 Tourist tents at the campsite in Waltse

FIGURE 4.24 Photos to promote Limi as tourist destination decorate the departure gate at Nepalgunj airport

see Mount Kailash from a distance instead, and at the time of writing, Limigya have built facilities at the viewpoint to cater for the pilgrims. But it is uncertain how the reopening of the border with TAR will affect the profitability for the local community, and the above-mentioned infrastructural bottle neck in Simikot still persist.

4.5.5 *Road Construction*

Humla is ranked as the second lowest of Nepal's seventy-five districts on the Human Development Index (HDI).[114] There are significant differences between and within communities, and the many reasons for the low score are too complex to be discussed here, but changes in the trade pattern and the poor infrastructure in the region are clearly among the more important. Until 2020, there were no roads connecting Humla district with the Nepali road network. All goods had to be either carried in on the backs of porters and pack animals or flown by small aircraft to the airport with only a short gravel runway connecting the district capital, Simikot, with Nepalgunj in south-western Nepal. This has created extremely high prices in Humla, averaging about ten times the prices in Kathmandu for many goods.

During the budget meeting with the Humli district authorities in December 2011 (Fig. 5.2), the district secretary asked the representatives from Limi how they wanted to spend their share of the budget. The answer from the Limi side was clear: They wanted to spend it all on the road. There are currently two roads under construction. Both follow old paths that for centuries have been used by herders, traders and pilgrims on their way to Manasarovar and Kailash. The easternmost of these roads crosses the border at the Lapcha pass south of Manasarovar and cuts through Limi territory, over the 5000 metre Nyalu pass and down to Simikot. When I first arrived in Limi in the summer of 2010, work on the road had just started. However, by August of the same year, Humla's first truck—a brand new Chinese Dongfeng, richly decorated with Buddhist symbols, which had recently been bought by an entrepreneur from Waltse—crossed the border from Tibet.[115] The truck was loaded with 108 volumes of the *Kangyur* that had been bought in Lhasa. This was considered very auspicious both for the road project, the truck owner, and his village.

114 Nepal Human Development Report 2014: 16. Similarly, the most recent version of the Nepal Human Development Report from 2020, which measured the HDI only at province level, gave Karnali the second lowest score.

115 By February 2014, 75 out of 95 km of the Lapcha road were completed. The other competing road project starts from the border at Yulsa and traverses the 4620-metre-high Nara pass and is planned to reach Simikot and finally Dulya.

People in Limi have been working hard for this road project but have expressed mixed feelings about its consequences. Initially, when the road-head was still in Limi territory, people were quite optimistic, and the first entrepreneurs opened small teahouses and shops in a place called Dungling to the east of Dzang (Fig. 4.21). But as the road-head moved further south, they realised that they would not automatically profit from it. In 2015 there were a couple of dozen trucks traversing the rough stretches of road and people from many of the communities further south in Humla had joined the race.[116] Sceptical voices in Limi said that it would be useless to buy more trucks in Limi as they do not have anything to sell, and many people were worried that with shops and easier transportation of goods they will become more dependent on cash. But much more than that, they feared that the roads will bring thieves, and they were especially concerned about the safety of the statues in their monasteries. Yet they were still working for the road with all the possibilities and challenges that it brings (Fig. 4.25). Being unconnected was not an alternative, and on 4 October 2018, an auspicious day according to the Tibetan calendar, the village leaders in Waltse, representatives from the Nepali police station and

FIGURE 4.25 Road construction in Waltse, 2018

116 Some of the challenges and possibilities offered by the road are discussed by Saxer 2017.

FIGURE 4.26 Celebrating the arrival of the road in Waltse, 2018

the truck drivers gathered to celebrate that the road had finally reached the village (Fig. 4.26).

4.6 A Period of Transition

The same infrastructure that makes it easier to bring people and goods to Limi also makes it easier for the villagers to leave the valley. The number of outmigrated Limigya is increasing and thus mirrors the general demographic trend among the other Tibetan speaking communities in Nepal. In most cases there are ways that the households can make up for an individual's absence, such as providing replacements (*tshab*) and paying fines for absence, but in other cases the laws are stricter, and this has resulted in a number of conflicts. In the last three decades the villagers have introduced a number of rules to prevent permanent outmigration, including rules for calling sons and daughters back from school, and for keeping levied monks in the local monasteries.[117] The villagers generally explained the introduction of these rules in terms of fears that the community would collapse, and in Waltse, they have opted for

117 These rules will be discussed in more detail in the relevant chapters below.

a rigid implementation of the rules. In Til and in Dzang, there has been more flexibility, but also higher outmigration. Some of the Limigya in Kathmandu have taken the step of renouncing their village membership (*khral gcog*, lit. 'to break the taxes'). This means that although they are sharing Limi identity and participating in all the activities of the community in Kathmandu, they have cut their formal ties to the village, abandoned their claims on land and other resources. They are therefore free to leave, but not to come back unless they agree to resume all responsibilities towards the village and monastery.[118]

Despite maintaining a seemingly traditional livelihood structure, the local economy in Limi is becoming increasingly interconnected with the global economy and the transnational and multidirectional flows of people, capital and information.[119] The flows include, on the one hand, the mobility and migration of members of the local community: migrants from Limi have settled in Kathmandu, in various cities in India, the PRC, Taiwan, Europe and in the United States. Moreover, a significant percentage of the population, still registered as village residents, move between these places throughout the season for trade, pilgrimage, and family visits. On the other hand, Limi is visited by an increasing number of international tourists and pilgrims, and occasionally also Buddhist dignitaries, on their way to and from Mt. Kailash. The contact zones also extend to cyberspace, through websites and social media, increasingly managed by young Limigya themselves. The various ways in which local agents respond to the challenges and opportunities brought about by these connections and transitions, and their impact on the management of the villages and monasteries in Limi, will be recurrent themes in the following chapters.

118 This is how the rules have been practiced in Waltse, the other two villages have differed in the restrictions placed on permanently outmigrated villagers.

119 See for instance Tambiah 2000, and Hannerz 1997.

CHAPTER 5

From Hybrid to Dual Village Governance

On a chilly December morning in 2011, in a secluded, but sunny courtyard, a group of men sat down in a circle with their drinking bowls for tea and chang. One of the local officials had walked from house to house calling the male head of each large and small household in Waltse to the annual winter meeting of the Village Assembly, which was to last for several days. After the village leaders had recorded attendance and meted out fines for a few absentees, the rest of the day was spent on calculation and payment of the various taxes according to the old registers (Fig. 5.1). The following days were devoted to rotating positions,[1] discussion of administrative issues, payment of debt and conflict resolution. While the debates could be intense, everybody knew their roles and the procedures.

•••

Just a few days earlier, the same leaders had been called to attend a meeting with the district secretary together with representatives from the other two villages (Fig. 5.2). The participants were given badges, and each group was asked to decide the usage of their allotted percentage of the budget. However, the villagers' involvement seemed hesitant, the representatives had not been given information about the figures in the government budget beforehand and their expectations were reportedly low. The meeting was held in Nepali, but since a majority of the attendees did not understand the language, a member of staff from a village further south in Humla translated to Tibetan.[2]

∵

1 It is only a few local positions like the caretaker of the Mani temple (*ma ni lha khang sku gnyer*), the drummer, leaders of the shon dancers (*shon 'go*) and gar dances (*gar dpon*) and guardians for the festival place (*khrom srung ba*) that are rotated during the autumn meeting. Most administrative positions are rotated during the spring assembly meeting.

2 Fieldnotes, December 2011.

 | DOI:10.1163/9789004714571_006

For an external observer these two meetings highlighted some of the differences between the two systems of governance with their distinct sets of laws and regulations. The former purely local, of great detail, and handled with strict precision according to old legal documents and customs, and the latter according to national laws, in Nepali language and with variable relevance to the local specificities. This chapter presents a basic outline of local governance in Limi. I discuss how the villagers have navigated the vernacular and national systems in the context of the political transitions since the middle of the twentieth century, with main emphasis on the period from the introduction of the VDC system in the 1990s onwards. Firstly, I examine the transition from hereditary to rotating leadership and discuss the Limi adaptation of the Nepali administrative structure. The next part presents the local decision-making bodies along with an overview of the legal system and the procedures for conflict resolution. I will then explore how the changes in village management relate to the larger democratisation processes in Nepal, and how the community's increasing integration with the Nepali political administration led to a hybrid village management system. Finally, the chapter explores the most recent changes after the administrative reforms in 2017, which have caused Limi to replace the hybrid with a dual system of governance and considers some of the challenges and opportunities this entails.[3]

FIGURE 5.1 Village assembly meeting in Waltse, 2011

3 This chapter focuses primarily on the management systems until 2015 when I submitted my PhD thesis, with particular focus on the Village Development Committee. But the last

FIGURE 5.2 Meeting with the district secretary in Tang, 2011

5.1 The Historical Development of the Village Government

As discussed earlier, the community's historical relationship with surrounding state formations has had a significant impact on both the administration of the village community and the monastic institution. Whilst Limi has had its own leaders who have governed the community according to a set of detailed local customary laws as far back as people can remember, they were formally headed by a Nepali speaking Thakuri *mukhiyā*[4] from a village further south in Humla, who acted as the representative of the Nepali government. At the same time, the community also had tax relations with Purang, and the Lhasa appointed district commissioner (*rdzong dpon*) in Purang therefore seemed to have had a certain influence.[5] Throughout much of their history and until the demarcation of the border with Tibet in 1961, the villagers in Limi found

paragraphs are newly written based on fieldwork in 2018–19 and covers the Limi adaptation to the new administrative reforms in Nepal after the 2015 constitution and with the introduction of the Rural Municipalities in 2017. The material is based on interviews, observations of village assembly meetings and day-to-day village management, as well as study of administrative documents.

4 *Mukhiyā* is a Nepali term for 'chief' or 'revenue officer', a title which has been given to officials at various administrative levels throughout history. The position of the Limi *mukhiyā* was hereditary.

5 Apart from the payment of taxes, this contact was reportedly largely informal. The Purang administration was occasionally consulted by one of the leading families when in conflict, whereas competing leaders would ally with the Nepali side.

themselves in a particular situation of 'betweenness'.[6] In some cases, they simply had to comply with demands from these external forces, at other times they skilfully played the two sides off against each other.[7] Largely due to this ambiguous situation, the Limigya became suspicious of outsiders and relied on a strong local management system. The Kalyal, and subsequently the Thakuri overlords from Humla, although extracting what taxes they could and occasionally intervening in local conflict settlement, were seldom present in the villages and refrained from interfering in day-to-day management. The last *mukhiyā* told me that he would normally visit Limi only two or three times per year.[8] This is contrary to what Levine reports from the Nyinba villages and other Tibetan speaking communities further south in Humla, where the Kalyal were more continuously present. She writes that the Kalyal manipulated the headmen and undermined the building of effective local political institutions with a divisive effect on village unity.[9] Limi's relative freedom was probably largely due to its geographical location, combined with cultural and linguistic distance.

The Limigya's relations with the Tibetan speaking officials on the other side of the border was reportedly a bit more frequent.[10] The distance to Purang was much shorter, geographically, linguistically, culturally and religiously. Needless to say, the Chinese takeover of Tibet, which largely coincided with the introduction of the panchayat system in Nepal, had a notable impact on local rule. The harsh suppression and breakdown of the traditional institutions on the Tibetan side of the border contributed to the marked conservatism that can be found in Limi. Such external circumstances bolstered the local hereditary leaders' strategy of managing internally as much as possible of the decision-making and conflict resolution, providing an important framework for understanding the mechanisms for internal village management.

5.1.1 *The Past System of Hereditary Leaders*

In the past, the three villages in Limi were governed by hereditary leaders according to a Tibetan model. The 'chief' (*spyi khyab*) from the Trongtö (Grong stod)[11] house in Til village was the main leader of the community as well as

6 Such ambiguous state affiliation appears to have been relatively common along the Nepali-Tibetan frontier. See for instance Childs (2000) for a discussion of the incorporation of Nubri into the state of Nepal.

7 This was expressed both by elderly people in Limi and by Nepali officials.

8 Interview 13.05.12.

9 Levine 1988a: 89–95.

10 Interview with the *mukhiyā*, 13.05.12.

11 The term *grong stod* (lit. 'upper village') is normally used to refer to the households in the upper section of the village. This location has also given name to the houses owned by the *spyi khyab* family in Til and Dzang.

head of his own village. In addition, there were three 'headmen' (*'go ba*) in Waltse and one in Dzang village. These four headmen were subordinate to the chief, but responsible for the internal management of their respective villages. Among the women, the female heads of the families of the chief and headmen had the most prominent position and enjoyed certain privileges. The outline of the past leadership system given below illustrates the logic of the system and highlights some of the most important changes in village management.

Elderly villagers still remember life under the hereditary leaders, and although personal experiences and opinions vary, there is no doubt that the *spyi khyab* and *'go ba* leadership exercised considerable power. Decisions that today require lengthy discussions in the village assembly were simply made by the headmen in the past. Similarly, the headmen settled local disputes, wrote legal documents, and kept the boxes in which the village archives were stored. While this gave them considerable control over the community's legal system, it is important to note that their rule was not arbitrary but bound to follow customary law. The hereditary leaders would also negotiate with external authorities, whether in Nepal or Tibet. The *spyi khyab* family in particular was reportedly very powerful, but its power was occasionally challenged by the *'go ba*, and there are many stories about power struggles between the leading families in the three villages.[12] However, the hereditary leaders did not have the authority to rule over monastic affairs, which were governed by a separate administration according to its own set of regulations.

The hereditary leaders enjoyed a high status in the community which was marked in a number of ways. During the three main days of Rimchö (Rim mchod), the most important festival[13] in the community, the *spyi khyab* and *'go ba* would have separate balconies overlooking the monastery courtyard. Similarly on the first day of New Year (*lo gsar*),[14] representatives from every household in Til village would have to go to the house of the *spyi khyab* with a flask of barley beer and a silk scarf. There they would first prostrate in front of the altar and then to each member of the household. Similarly, the inhabitants of the other two villages had to prostrate in front of their respective *'go ba*. As long as the hereditary leaders were at the height of their authority, the *spyi khyab* and the *'go ba* also enjoyed privileged access to community resources.

12 This was pointed out by many, but most eloquently in my interview with an elderly man from Til, 08.03.12.

13 The Rimchö festival is celebrated with monastic dances ('cham) to pacify the deities and protect people and animals from diseases and other types of harm. See Chapter seven for a brief description.

14 In Limi, New Year is celebrated at the beginning of the eleventh Tibetan month.

They were entitled to choose pasture areas before the pastureland was distributed among the rest of the households by lottery. The *spyi khyab* household had the additional privilege of cutting grass in the mountain meadows one day before everybody else, and they were allowed to graze their animals even in restricted areas. In the summer, the sunny side of the valley where the Til Kundzom monastery is located would be prohibited for animals in order to save the grass for the village's winter reserve, but the *spyi khyab* family had the right to graze its livestock there.[15] The herds were traditionally one of the foremost sources of wealth in Limi, and getting unrestricted access to otherwise limited grazing areas and fodder gave the hereditary leaders a major advantage that enabled them to be counted among the wealthiest households in the community. However, from the middle of the twentieth century, the power and privileges of the hereditary leaders gradually declined until they had to resign in the 1990s. As one of the villagers in Waltse put it, 'In the past, during the time of the four Dzardziwa brothers,[16] the *'go ba* behaved almost like kings, whereas by the time of the panchayat system, they had lost most of their former power.'[17]

5.1.2 *Change of Leadership System*

What led to this significant shift? After the overthrow of the reign of the Ranas in the middle of the twentieth century, and especially with the introduction of the panchayat system in the 1960s, traditional forms of leadership changed throughout the country. Ramble writes that, '… the role of the headman—as well as other categories of local elites—was supplanted in most parts of Nepal by the local representatives of the new state machinery'.[18] However, he explains, some communities retained the local management structures '… as a sort of civil counterpoint to the panchayats and VDCs'.[19] In most of Mustang, internal village affairs would be managed through the old leadership positions, whereas the new leaders would only manage the external affairs.[20]

15 Interview with a man from Til, 08.03.12.

16 The Dzardziwa brothers were members of the main *'go ba* family in Waltse around the turn of the twentieth century, who achieved almost legendary status in Limi. Numerous stories are still told about the bitter power struggle with the equally powerful *spyi khyab* in Til.

17 Interview with a man from Waltse, 10.01.12.

18 Ramble 2008a: 324.

19 Ramble 2008a: 325. Until 2017, the Village Development Committee (VDC) used to be the lowest administrative level in Nepal. Nepal was subdivided into 5 Development Regions, 14 Administrative Zones, 75 Districts, and 3625 VDCs.

20 Ramble 2008a: 325.

Limi initially chose a different, hybrid form of adaptation. The traditional leadership structure and the system imposed by the Nepali government were merged. As one of the villagers pointed out, the changes were initially merely nominal,[21] i.e., the hereditary leadership system continued, but the leaders were given Nepali titles in addition to the local Tibetan titles.[22] Hence, during the rule of the Rana dynasty,[23] the *spyi khyab* would also be called *mukhiyā*, and the *'go ba* called *jimmāwāl*. With the introduction of the panchayat system, the *spyi khyab* received the title *pradhān* (N. leader), whereas the *'go ba* were called *upapradhān* (N. vice leader).[24] Towards the end of the panchayat period, the power of the hereditary leaders was greatly reduced. The main change took place in 1991, with the introduction of the Village Development Committee (VDC) as the new administrative unit at the local level. This was when the hereditary leaders finally lost their positions, and the number of leaders was increased to correspond to the central government directives. The VDC was divided into nine wards, and a ward leader was appointed for each. With the end of the hereditary leadership, the titles *'go ba* and *spyi khyab* were largely replaced by the Nepali leadership terms.[25] However, the main tasks of the new leadership remained broadly the same as those of the hereditary leaders, viz. to govern the community according to the internal village laws. Since the community's engagement with the "external" Nepali state apparatus was fairly limited at the time, they opted for a hybrid system in which the leaders managed both affairs. When I discussed the reasons for the end of the hereditary leadership system with the Limigya, they explained that conflicts had arisen in each of the three villages, which greatly reduced the leaders' legitimacy. One elderly man elaborated:

> The old *'go ba* were in a dilemma. By the time of the election, the leaders had lost virtually all their power, but they still had many responsibilities. The villagers asked them to continue in their duties for at least two to three years because of their experience, but the leaders were reluctant to do so. The villagers reacted by saying that governing the village was a task of the people; they were also people, they could learn how to govern. Then the *'go ba* resigned.[26]

21 See Hangen (2010: 93) for a similar observation in Maidel (pseudonym) village in Ilam.
22 Conversation with senior villager, 17.08.10.
23 The Rana dynasty ruled Nepal from 1846–1951.
24 Conversation with senior villager, 17.08.10.
25 In Dzang, the old terms were used a bit longer.
26 Interview with senior villager, 16.01.12.

However, whereas most of the villagers I spoke with insisted that these were purely local processes, the change of leadership system must be seen as part of a long and complex process influenced by political changes in Nepal. One of the oldest men in Waltse, drew longer historical lines and explained that the *'go ba* had lost their power gradually as a result of Nepali law. 'Was the transition between the two systems difficult, I asked?'. 'No', he said, 'they only received orders from the Nepali officials regarding the kind of positions they should fill'.[27]

When the villagers in Limi abandoned the hereditary leadership system, they had to find a way to select new leaders. According to the Local Self-Governance Act 2055 (1999),[28] the local leaders, who now were to be called *adhyaksha* and *upadhyaksha*, should be elected every five years. However, in Limi the villagers made their own variant and decided to choose the leaders through sortition instead. Sortition, or the 'casting of lots' (*rgyan rgyag*), is a traditional way to distribute rights and duties in Limi and other culturally Tibetan societies.[29] With the gradual democratisation of village management, however, this system has been more frequently used. Another common way of distributing tasks in Limi is by rotation according to household lists. Election, in the sense of selection based on voting, has until recently been used only in very few cases, as will be discussed below.

Because of the unstable political situation in Nepal, local elections have been few and far between. After the re-introduction of democracy in 1990–91, local elections were arranged in 1992 and in 1997. When the term of the VDC and District Development Committee (DDC) leaders ended in 2002, a new election was supposed to have taken place. But the election was called off because of political turmoil, and the village and district government positions throughout most of the country were filled by representatives from multi-party coalitions instead.[30] In Limi, however, the villagers had not engaged in party politics and ruled largely according to their own customary laws. They therefore chose to keep the VDC and ward leaders, even though the system had been abandoned elsewhere. The villagers also chose to continue rotating the positions approximately every four to five years. In this way, the community maintained stable governance compared to other local administrative units in the country.

---

27 Interview with senior villager, 16.01.12.

28 The Local Self-Governance Act replaced four earlier Acts from 1991–1992, including the the Local Bodies Election Act from 1992.

29 For a discussion of the selection of leaders by lottery, see Ramble (1993) and (2008: 329 ff).

30 This was a turbulent period for the country with the royal massacre in 2001, the maoist insurgency ending in 2006 and the subsequent abolition of the monarchy in 2008. After a long period of discussions and disagreements, the parties finally managed to agree on a new Constitution in 2015 turning Nepal into a federal state.

It would take twenty years before Nepal arranged the next local elections in 2017 (Fig. 5.3).

5.1.3 *The Hybrid Village Management during the VDC System*

From the introduction of the VDC system in 1991 and until its abolition in 2017, the village management in Limi could be characterised as a hybrid system, in which the Nepali leadership positions were adapted to fit the local administrative system. The VDC leader, as head of the community, took over some of the responsibilities of the old *spyi khyab*. But whereas the old *spyi khyab* was also the headman of Til, the position as VDC leader rotated between the villages, and involved mainly responsibilities at the community level and in negotiations with Nepali authorities. Moreover, the VDC and ward leaders did not enjoy the privileges and power of the past *spyi khyab* and *'go ba*.[31]

VDCs in Nepal were normally divided into nine wards, regardless of local structures.[32] When Limi VDC was formed in 1991, Waltse was divided into four wards, Dzang into three, and Til into two. Each ward was to be headed by a leader, and the number of local leaders thus increased from five to eleven: the three *'go ba* in Waltse were replaced by four ward leaders, the single *'go ba* in Dzang was replaced by three ward leaders, whereas the *spyi khyab* in Til was replaced by two ward leaders for internal village management and by the VDC leader and vice leader for community management.

As one of the senior villagers pointed out, the transition to the new leadership system went relatively smoothly as '… everybody knew the village laws (*yul gyi khrims*)'.[33] Nevertheless, many were also ambivalent: one middle-aged man, for instance lamented that, 'in the past, the headmen were very powerful and knowledgeable; they did a lot for their village. Nowadays the leaders are chosen by lottery and have few qualifications.'[34] Such complaints are not unique to Limi; lack of qualifications and enthusiasm are often cited among the chief disadvantages of sortition.[35] Villagers frequently pointed out that with the current management system, the leaders do not always know how to read and write and often need help with such tasks.[36] This is indeed visible in the

31 Even though the hereditary leadership system has been abandoned in all three villages, the *'go ba* family in Dzang still enjoys a higher status than the rest of the villagers. This status is reflected, among other ways, in seating arrangements during village gatherings.

32 Exceptions to this rule were made in Kathmandu and some of the larger municipalities.

33 Interview with a senior villager from Waltse, 16.01.12.

34 Interview with a man from Til, 08.03.12.

35 See for instance Engelstad 1989: 32.

36 While most men are able to read Tibetan, writing skills are often poor. Few of the men who remain in the villages have much proficiency in the Nepali language and, as mentioned below, that raises a host of challenges when dealing with the Nepali state apparatus.

administrative documents from the village. The entries added during the last three decades are written by many different scribes and the spelling, handwriting, and style of the text is of markedly lower standard than the older entries written by the hereditary *'go ba*. Moreover, in many of the documents only the names of the forefathers are listed, and inexperienced leaders might not know them.[37] The solution to this problem, as I observed during the tax collection meeting in the autumn of 2011, has been to ask one of the former *'go ba* to help read the village documents and calculate the taxes. One perhaps unforeseen consequence of entrusting management to poorly educated leaders is that the reading of the tax registers and other administrative documents has become a public affair, and the village management has become more transparent.[38]

In day-to-day management, the system of lottery-selected leaders appears to have functioned reasonably well. The villages are so thoroughly regulated by laws that efficient internal management has been relatively independent of leadership skills. The main challenge facing the VDC and ward leaders has been negotiations with the Nepali authorities. In the past there was a general distrust of the Nepali district officials,[39] but especially after the end of the civil war in 2006, an increasing integration with the Nepali district and national government bodies has been taking place. However, lack of Nepali language skills, lack of insight into the power structures and political party system, as well as lack of experience in dealing with highly corrupt officials and contractors have placed the Limigya at a disadvantage. As Jeff Key points out, corrupt officials siphoning off parts of grants and other funds constitutes a serious problem for local governments in Nepal.[40] Humla is no exception and village leaders in Limi reported that the VDC received only a fraction of its allocated budget. In late autumn 2010, during a three-village meeting, the representatives therefore decided to send three men to Simikot to learn about the political processes and to lobby for Limi's interests at district level. One skilful man from each village was chosen, and their accommodation and allowances were paid by their respective village assemblies. They were reportedly successful in securing a small budget for the construction of a bridge and the establishment of village telephones in Dzang and Til.[41] Subsequently, with the growing adaptation to the Nepali administrative system, the local leaders have been engaging in more

37 Conversation with former leader, 27.11.11.

38 Conversation with senior villager, 16.02.12.

39 Such distrust towards Nepali officials has been common in the Tibetan communities in Humla. See for instance Levine 1988a: 94.

40 Key 2003: 101.

41 Interview with man from Waltse, 13.04.12.

frequent negotiations with the district authorities and increasingly also with the national government bureaucracy.

5.1.4 *The* las 'dzin *Officials and Other Management Positions*

In addition to the headmen there are a number of other village management positions. The most important of these are the 'senior officials' (*las 'dzin rgan po*), who used to be second in the local hierarchy, and the 'officials' (*las 'dzin*). I have chosen the broad term 'officials' in my translation because the *las 'dzin rgan po* and *las 'dzin* perform a variety of tasks for the village community: they play an important role in the day-to-day administration of communal village affairs, they have to provide hospitality during visits by Nepali officials, and they function as 'constables' as well as ritual facilitators. Like the hereditary leader positions, the officials and senior officials are traditional management positions in Limi. However, the number of responsibilities of the *las 'dzin* have reportedly increased with the transition from hereditary to elected leaders. The positions are not rewarded with any salary, and the duty to serve is often seen as burdensome, but the assignment is accepted since the position is for no longer than a year.

The *las 'dzin* officials rotate annually according to an old list, the change of position (*las 'dzin rtsis sprod*) taking place during the spring village assembly meeting. The positions are distributed according to household category, and it is only the head of the *grong chen* households who can be chosen as senior officials. In Waltse there are currently two *las 'dzin rgan po* and three *las 'dzin* from the *grong chen* households, two *las 'dzin* from the *grong chung* and two *las 'dzin* from the *bom btang* households. The latter only manage work related to the *bom btang* category and are not always counted among the *las 'dzin*.[42]

The two senior officials in Waltse have taken over the responsibility of keeping the village archives from the old *'go ba*. In order to ensure that they do not secretly access the contents, one of them keeps the box and the other keeps the key and the village seal. Together with the village headmen, the officials supervise the village tax collection in the autumn, and they are responsible for the administration of the 'transportation duty' (*'u lag*).[43] Moreover, if a household has cleared new fields, it is the responsibility of the officials to estimate the seed capacity and hence the size of the taxes. The officials also have to

42 When I asked the villagers about the *las 'dzin* system, many of my interlocutors spoke only about the *grong chen* and *grong chung las 'dzin*, suggesting that the positions among the *bom btang* was a more recent addition with limited responsibilities.

43 A discussion of the translation of the term *'u lag* is provided together with further details about taxes and the transportation duty in Chapter Six.

facilitate and sponsor some of the activities for the annual 'welfare rituals' (*bde rim*) requested by the village community.

The most important of these village rituals include the Rimchö festival, the fire offering rituals (*sbyin sreg*), casting of dough effigies (*gtor rgyag*), and the rain making rituals (*char 'bebs*).[44] In preparation for these, the *las 'dzin rgan po* are responsible for providing some of the ritual items. The *las 'dzin* officials also keep lists of compulsory contributions from the households and have the responsibility to measure and collect these contributions. During the fire offering and rain making rituals, the *las 'dzin* have to cook and serve tea for the officiating monks. For the organisation of large events like the Rimchö festival, the *las 'dzin* officials are assisted by 'stewards' (*gnyer pa*).

For the day-to-day management of the local environment, the *las 'dzin* also act as constables in the village charged with the tasks of supervising the borders between fields and making sure that the regulations for collection of animal fodder are followed. If any of the village rules are broken, it is the *las 'dzin* who are required to make investigations. In addition, there are a number of annually rotating constables with a special mandate to supervise the observance of the local environmental regulations and other village rules. These include the 'watchmen' (*lta rtog pa*) ensuring that the villagers respect the prohibition against the cutting of green wood as well as other rules made by the '[council of] the fifteen' (*bco lnga*), the '[animal] watchmen' (*lo rags*)[45] responsible for hindering livestock from entering the fields, and the 'guardians of the festival place' (T. *khrom srung ba*, L. *khrung khrung ba*), two disciplinarians who maintain order during the Rimchö festival. Then, there are a number of posts for the management of specific tasks in the village, including the coordinator of the 'goat herding' (*ra rdzi*), the 'shrine keeper of the Mani temple' (*ma ni lha khang sku gnyer*), and the various positions for the main festivals like the dance leaders (*shon 'go*, *gar dpon*, and *gar g.yog*) and the drummer.

In addition to the positions considered to be traditional, there are posts initiated by the Nepali government like the female leaders (N. *mailah*), the School Management Committee, the Female Community Health Volunteers (FCHV) and membership of an increasing number of committees.[46] The female leaders provide an interesting example of a Nepali government initiative becoming largely integrated with the local system of environmental management. They are always elected from the single women households, and they have

44 For more details about the rituals, see Chapter Seven.

45 This is the spelling used in *Waltse tax register*. See also Fürer-Haimendorf 1988: 272.

46 The Public procurement act from 2007 allows user committees to manage projects with budgets below ten million rupees. See Government of Nepal 2007.

been given the responsibility for irrigation management. As mentioned in the report from the meeting with the district secretary at the beginning of the chapter, the *mailah* are also called to represent the women in certain meetings although often with limited possibilities to influence the decision-making. Finally, there are some positions in the villages initiated by NGOs, such as the phone operator, the manager and keeper of the micro-hydroelectric power plant, the teachers, and the health worker.

5.2 Village Assembly Meetings, Decision-making and Conflict Resolution

The village assembly (*'du ma*) functions as a village government and is the main decision-making body in each of the three villages. Particularly important cases are decided during joint meetings of the laity and monks (*skya gser*) in the village. Finally, whenever decisions regarding the whole community have to be made, they call a three-village meeting (*yul 'dzin gsum gyi 'du ma*). The latter is arranged on a regular basis at least twice a year. In the past, the hereditary leaders presided over the village assembly, and as mentioned above, a considerable number of decisions were made by them. When the VDC and ward leaders took over, they did so with reduced authority and hence the importance of the assembly in local decision-making processes increased. One male representative from each of the households aged between fifteen and sixty-five years is obliged to be present at these meetings and should ideally be the head of the household (*kha rgan*). Absence from the main village meetings is punished with a fine, whereas for less important meetings, sending a replacement (*tshab*) is acceptable. The *bom btang* households have, by definition, no male member above the age of fifteen, except monks.[47] But monks are not allowed to participate in village politics and these households are therefore not represented in the village assembly. The increasing outmigration, discussed in the previous chapter, also raises challenges for the local village government. The problems are felt most acutely in Til village, which in winter is mainly populated by women, monks, elderly people and a handful of children, none of whom had the right to take part in the assembly in the past. It is understood that concessions have recently been made permitting women to act as the household's representative in the village assembly meetings. A number of

47 As was pointed out in Chapter Four, *bom btang* households are automatically transferred to the *grong chung* category in case of a son reaching the age of fifteen.

other rules have similarly been relaxed in the past decades to ensure the efficiency and continuity of the village management.

There are many meetings in the village assembly throughout the year, but there are two main meetings when all representatives have to be present: the spring meeting (*las 'dzin rtsis sprod*)[48] held just after sowing the fields, normally at the end of May, and the autumn meeting (*khral rtsis*)[49] which takes place just after harvest. As the names suggest, the spring meeting is the time when most of the village management positions rotate, whereas the main activity during the autumn meeting is the payment of taxes. These meetings are also occasions for discussing environmental management and other administrative issues, payment of debt and for conflict resolution. Conflicts are normally presented before the assembly as the final item on the programme. Depending on the number and gravity of the conflicts, the meetings can last for several days.[50]

When all the representatives have convened at the meeting, the village archive will be opened by the village leader. If the village leader is not present, one of the ward leaders will be authorised to open the box, but the leader will have had to check beforehand that the seal is unbroken.[51] The archive contains a number of documents, including the tax registers, name lists, various legal contracts, unsettled conflict reports, and debt letters. Many of the documents contain sensitive information about village and intra-village conflicts; the metal box containing the archive is therefore guarded carefully, and the rules for displaying the documents are strict.

One senior villager explained that the procedures for opening the box and obtaining access to the documents had changed in recent years, and consequently, as mentioned above, village management had become more transparent. The responsibility for the village archive used to be held by the three *'go ba* and the documents were kept as their property. Nowadays, the man commented, the content of the village archives is not secret in the same way as in the past. With the change of political system, the *grong chen* families were allowed access and subsequently also the *grong chung* and the *bom btang* were given this right. The *bom btang* and the monks are still excluded to some

48 The meeting has acquired its name from its most important activity. The term *las 'dzin rtsis sprod* can literally be translated as 'transferring the authority of the officials'.

49 The name comes from 'tax calculation' (*khral rtsis*). The collection of taxes is the main responsibility of the autumn assembly. In Waltse, this meeting is also referred to as the Changcham (lCangs 'cham) meeting after is location in the Changra Cham (lCang ra 'cham) courtyard.

50 The village assembly meeting in the autumn of 2011, for instance, lasted eight days.

51 Conversation with villager, 24.03.11.

extent, since they are not represented during the assembly meetings, but they are entitled to plead their cases in front of the assembly and to request access to relevant documents in the archive. To prevent too many people from prying into the documents, and hence to prevent conflicts from escalating, some restrictions are placed on access. A fee of 5000 NPR must be paid to read an 'obligation contract' (*gan rgya*), and since the archive can only be opened in public, everybody will know.

When decisions have to be made, the procedures are generally as follows: the assembly is divided into three groups, which convene in separate locations to discuss the matter and produce a resolution proposal. In the case of a majority of at least two thirds, the majority wins, but if all three groups propose different solutions, the final decision is arrived at by lottery. Although there are ways of manipulating the system, and only men are represented in the assembly, these procedures are principally democratic. Dieter Schuh and other scholars have pointed out that local level governments in Tibetan speaking communities in Nepal were also often quite democratic in the past.[52]

However, some cases are difficult to resolve. In such cases, the decision is made after performing a 'prediction ritual' (*rtags pa*) in front of the statue of the protector deity, Apchi, in the monastery. The decision with the most grave consequences, as to whether Limi should join the PRC or remain part of Nepal, was presented in Chapter Three. Most of the prediction rituals are performed in the local protector chapels, but Drigung rinpoches and other high lamas are also increasingly consulted. In 2011, for example, a request was sent to a high lama in Dehra Dun asking for advice on which rituals to perform to protect the village and monastery from floods.[53] The frequency of interventions by religious leaders from outside the valley has grown steadily with the increasing improvement of infrastructure and technology. Especially, the establishment of phone connectivity has made it much easier to enquire with external religious authorities before making important decisions in the villages.

5.2.1 *Laws and Regulations*

Laws and regulations are variously referred to as *khrims* ('law'), *sgrig khrims* ('law and order' or 'agreement'),[54] or simply *'gro stangs* ('procedure'); the rules

52 Schuh (2000: 294), for instance, remarks that the government of some of the villages in Mustang resembles the democratic structure of Athens during antiquity.

53 Interview 07.12.11.

54 In Limi, the term *sgrig khrims* (or *'grig khrims*) is frequently used about legally binding 'agreements' or 'collective decisions'.

for taxation and other obligations are referred to as *khral* ('tax', 'obligation') or *khral khrims* ('tax law').[55] However, it is important to bear in mind that although partly overlapping, these Tibetan terms have meanings and are used in contexts that differ from those of English legal terminology. Moreover, their use in different Tibetan communities has varied considerably throughout time and space.[56]

The laws and regulations in Limi are based on the Tibetan legal tradition, but since I was unable to obtain full access to the village archive my material has not allowed a detailed analysis of the degree to which the legal procedures in Limi were related to the traditional Tibetan legal system, as practiced in pre-1960 Purang and the Nepali legal system in Simikot. Yet, it seems safe to conclude that the community's legal system was (and still is) semi-autonomous from the district and national levels. During the reign of the Ranas and until the panchayat era, the Thakuri *mukhiyā* who had the hereditary privilege of acting as the district's revenue officer for Limi also engaged in conflict resolution. But the former *mukhiyā* explained that the villagers were not familiar with the Nepali legislation and had their own system, and that in these cases he had to apply the local laws.[57] This has been common also in other remote communities in Nepal. Lukas Heckendorn Urscheler, for instance, writes that, '... the diversity of the Nepalese society (...) and the inaccessibility of the terrain made it necessary to allow for different customary regimes (...). Still today, many ethnic groups live according to their traditional norms and values, and disputes are often settled within them without having recourse to state authorities.'[58]

The strict organisation of the society can be said to be an important characteristic of Limi, but although there are a considerable number of laws, customs, and norms regulating daily life in the community, only some of them are written down; there is no legal code as for instance in some places in Mustang.[59] The villagers told me that many of the laws were recorded in writing only after the change of the leadership system. This was partly because the new rotating leaders were not as knowledgeable as the hereditary leaders, had less authority to impose their will, and partly due to the need for revisions.

---

55 For a clarification of the term *khral* ('tax' or 'obligation'), see Chapter Six. Taxation is also discussed in Chapters Eight and Nine.

56 Tibetan legal systems have been studied by scholars such as Schuh (1984), Dreyfus (1995), French (2002), and Pirie (2007). See also Frechette (1996), Huber (1998) and van der Kuijp (1999) for a critical reading of French (2002 [1995]).

57 Interview, 13.05.12.

58 Heckendorn Urscheler 2012: 100.

59 Ramble 2008a: 278ff.

The village archive contains a large number of legally binding documents. Among the most important is the *Waltse tax register*, which will be studied in more detail in Chapter Six. But the archive also contains several laws written on scrolls of Tibetan paper after a village assembly (*'du ma*), a joint village and monastery (*skya ser*) meeting, or a three-village (*yul gsum*) meeting. In addition there are numerous 'obligation contracts' (*gan rgya*) written after conflict-settlements, which create precedents for future cases. The documents appear disorganised, and to facilitate easy access, summaries of important regulations have been copied from various obligation contracts and other documents and added towards the end of the *Waltse tax register*.[60] These summaries include regulations of ritual patronage, sponsorship of *dge slong* monks to facilitate their lives in the monk cells, sponsorship of meditating monks, tax reductions, and temporary tax exemptions, an agreement regarding grazing permissions for people from further south in Humla (referred to as *rong pa* in the document), procedures for replacing damaged or missing objects during change of officials, a note regarding the possessions of a *dge slong* monk who passed away, and donation of fields to generate merit for a villager who passed away prematurely. The entries seem somewhat arbitrary as they have been added by different scribes as needed. Since Limi has traditionally been an agro-pastoral society, a considerable portion of the local laws deal with various forms of environmental management.

5.2.2 *Environmental Management*

Although many of the laws and regulations for how to manage the local environment are recorded in various written documents kept in the village and monastery archives, they are also embodied in all the women and men of the community who work the land. A significant portion of the responsibilities of the local village assembly involves the management of these laws, and it is the work of the local leaders, officials, constables and watchmen to make sure they are correctly observed. If we look at the customary laws, which regulate the use of natural resources in Limi, the most important include taxation, lease fees and directives for the use of communal land; coordination of agricultural activities; regulation of forest use and the harvest of non-timber forest products; rules for irrigation; management of pastureland; and protection of wildlife. While a thorough description and analysis of the different

60 See e.g., Ramble's (2008a: 279) comments about what makes villagers compile and fix regulations in writing.

regulations and practices fall out of the scope of this book, a brief investigation of some of the regulations may illuminate some of the core mechanisms at play.[61]

Coordination of the main agricultural activities such as planting and harvesting times are done according to a combination of observances of the sun (*nyin thig*, sun line), weather patterns and conditions in the fields. The activities are timed to match one of the religiously auspicious days according the the Tibetan calendar (*lo tho*). Unlike what Manandhar et al. reported from a village in Mustang, the Limi farmers do not blindly follow the general astrological predictions, but balance these against local ecological knowledge, weather observations and other needs.[62] Decisions are made collectively according to the regular democratic procedures in the village assembly. Moreover, the timing of the main agricultural activities is also coordinated between the villages in order to enable people to help their relatives in the most intensive seasons. The management of pastureland and rangeland are subject to similar regulations at the village level. The harvesting of particular species of nutritious grass as winter fodder for the animals is timed so that none of the villagers get unfair advantages. All eligible households have to participate in the collection and will get their share of the harvest according to household category. There is also pastoral activity in areas collectively owned by the whole community. The management of these areas, for instance the careful timing of the movement of herds to the seasonal pastures to ensure equal access to the grass is decided during annual three village meetings.

Another section of the regulations concerns restrictions on forest use such as a ban on logging and the collection of green firewood in demarcated areas as well as protection of sacred trees. The sacred trees refer to old junipers believed to be the residence of serpent deities (*klu*), which are considered to have the power to influence local environmental and climatic conditions. While there are many reasons for (and consequences of) the introduction of these restrictions, it seems to have been significantly important for the prevention of erosion in this landslide-prone area and contributes to securing wood resources for the future. However, the restrictions also have side effects, as women now must walk a long distance from the village to collect firewood. The restrictions on the harvesting of non-timber forest products (NTFP) like medicinal herbs

61 A more thorough analysis can be found in Hovden and Havnevik 2021. See also Basnet and Chaudhary (2017) and Bhattarai's unpublished report (2021).

62 Manandhar et al. 2014.

are similarly connected with the territorial deities and have contributed to the maintenance of rich biodiversity in the area.[63]

Many of the regulations that are employed have old roots which is reportedly recorded in a 'Mountain Valley Decree' (Ri klung rtswa tshig) type of document, but my interviewees had not seen the actual document themselves. As mentioned for instance by Rebecca French and Toni Huber, such decrees were issued by the old Tibetan government since at least the middle of the seventeenth century and both regulated the use of the local environment and prohibited the killing of wild animals. Multiple copies were distributed throughout the Tibetan plateau, and special decrees were periodically issued for Ngari, the region immediately north of Limi.[64] In addition, there are several customary laws regulating the use of the local environment in Limi. These laws, and the punishment for breaking them, are written down in local obligation contracts and other documents. Finally, there are also more recent documents, such as the rules of the '[council of] the fifteen', a local conflict resolution body consisting of 15 monks and laymen. In an obligation contract (*gan rgya*) made by the council in 2009, for instance, it is written that ...

> if somebody has given dry firewood, timber, or other wooden building material to outsiders they have to pay a fine of NPR 10 000. It is allowed to cut wood for the purpose of monastery use. The villagers are permitted to bring dry firewood to their homes, but it is forbidden to cut any single wet, living tree and bring wet wood to one's home.[65]

The system, while ancient, is dynamic and provisions are made for necessary adaptations. In case of a particular situation such as the occurrence of a natural disaster or the observation of disturbing changes in the local environment, laity or monastics can appeal to the village assembly and make the case for new or updated regulations. The late lama, for instance, appealed to the village assembly to extend the prohibition on cutting wood near Waltse resulting in a new rule that has since been practised. Finally, as will be described in Chapter Seven, an important part of the management of the local environment is through ritual activity.[66]

---

63 See also Hovden and Havnevik 2021.

64 See French 2002 and Huber 2003.

65 *Contract by the assembly of laity and monks* 2011 [2009]. My translation.

66 The ritual management of the local environment is also discussed in Hovden and Havnevik 2021.

To what extent can the traditional environmental management system in Limi be regarded as conflicting or complimentary with the Nepali system? During my first stays in the valley between 2010 and 2012, most of the Limigya I interviewed did not express much concern about this point. They commented that the Nepali rules were more general, whereas the Limi rules were more specific and detailed. For that reason, they felt there would not be significant problems in implementing the Nepali rules, but at the same time, they emphasised that the Nepali rules were insufficient for catering to the local needs. However, as will be discussed at the end of the chapter, after Limi became part of Namkha Rural Municipality a new set of challenges appeared. Villagers from other communities in the same municipality now opine that they have user rights to Limi territory, and this has caused a number of conflicts and attempts at encroachment. The Limigya follow their traditional rules in attempting to handle these cases but suffer from the lack of acknowledgement of customary law at the higher government levels, as the legislation is not yet completed.[67]

5.2.3 *The Local Court and Conflict Resolution System*

Conflicts are perceived as a serious threat to the cohesion of the society, and considerable effort is put into mediation.[68] Settling conflicts frequently starts with informal attempts at reconciliation, but if that fails, the case will be forwarded to what I have chosen to call the 'village court'. It should be noted that the term 'court' (*khrims khang*) is not used by the Limigya themselves, but I find the term applicable in a loose and evocative sense because the way the conflict-resolution procedures are institutionalised resembles a court system and implies a clearly defined legal process. The 'village court' in Waltse consists of three levels of appeal: the village assembly meeting (*'du ma*), the [council of] the fifteen (*bco lnga*), and the three villages' meeting (*yul 'dzin gsum gyi 'du ma*). After the court has reached a conclusion, the decision is recorded in a legal document. Most of these documents are legally binding 'obligation contracts' (*gan rgya*), which are signed by the concerned parties and stored in the village archive. The contracts, which are signed after conflict resolution, establish a precedent for similar cases in the future.

67 Interviews with villagers and local leaders 2018–19. See the unpublished policy report by Bhattarai (2021) and the joint policy brief by ICIMOD and HimalConnect, Gurung et al. (forthcoming). Both the policy report and the policy brief were funded by The Global Challenges Research Fund (GCRF).

68 See e.g. Pirie (2005) about mediation in traditional Tibetan societies.

If the conflicting parties are a married couple, for instance, the first to intervene is a particular group of relatives referred to as 'neighbours' (*khyim mtshes*).[69] If they fail in their mediation, the case is presented in front of the two senior officials (*las 'dzin rgan po*), and if they, too, are unable to resolve the case, it is handed over to the three-tiered 'court'. First, a village assembly meeting will be convened which starts with a hearing of the case. In the past, the *'go ba* (or the *spyi khyab*) would preside over the meeting and function as judges. In recent years it has been the elected leaders who preside over the conflict-resolution meetings, with the representatives of the households (except the ten members from the '[council of] the fifteen') functioning like a jury. In the past, the next step would be to call a three-village (*yul gsum*) meeting. Nowadays, however, if the village assembly is unable to solve the case, it will be forwarded to the '[council of] the fifteen'. The '[council of] the fifteen', which consists of ten laymen and five monks, was established in 2009 and exists only in Waltse. It functions like a court of appeal, with jury members serving for a period of five years. Initially the jury was selected by lottery, but subsequently the villagers decided to appoint the members according to qualifications. The monks appoint the lay members and vice versa. The main reason why the villagers decided to establish the '[council of] the fifteen' was to keep the conflict-resolution processes within the village. Calling a three-village meeting is not only expensive and time-consuming, but such a meeting does also imply that information about the conflict spreads to the two other villages. This is regarded as highly embarrassing and should be avoided if possible.[70] Another important rationale, I was told, was to hinder favouritism. When all villagers were given a vote, the representatives tended to support their relatives, but with a more professional 'court system', the verdicts became more just.[71] If the '[council of] the fifteen' proves unable to resolve the case, the third step in the local conflict-resolution system is the 'three-village' (*yul gsum*) meeting. Finally, if the three-village meeting is unable to solve the case, it may be taken to the district court in Simikot. Prior to 1960, the case could also be taken to Purang Dzong. The *spyi khyab* in Til had stronger connections with Purang and would therefore more often seek Tibetan mediation, whereas the competing *'go ba* in Waltse and Dzang would cultivate stronger ties to the

69 In this case 'neighbour' (*khyim mtshes*) does not refer to whoever is living next door, but in case of a *grong chung* household for instance, the 'neighbours' are members of the *grong chen* household from which they once split off.

70 Interview with a former member of the '[council of] the fifteen' 18.06.11.

71 Interview with a senior villager, 13.04.2015.

district authorities in Simikot and more frequently appeal to Nepali officials for conflict resolution.

Just like the village government and general decision-making processes, the procedures for conflict resolution have changed substantially since the hereditary leadership system was abandoned in the 1990s, as discussed above. The hereditary leaders used to function as judges, kept the archive with legal decisions, and although probably not entirely immune, were to some extent placed above the law. The selected leaders nowadays do not enjoy such privileges, and the legal procedures have been democratised. Moreover, in this transitory phase, the villagers have felt the need to set down more of the legal decisions in writing. The current 'village court' system, in which verdicts and the meting out of punishment are collectively decided by a jury, perhaps does not qualify to be characterised as 'rule of law', but the conflict-resolution procedures have certainly moved in that direction.

5.2.4 *The Role of the Local Youth Clubs*

A relatively recent development in the management of the three villages is the formation of youth clubs. These organisations do not form part of the village leadership as such, but their members have become increasingly important actors in the local decision-making processes and, as we will see below, also in conflict-resolution procedures. Youth clubs are currently established all over Nepal. Whereas the youth clubs may be seen as a form of generational mobilisation, the category 'youth' (N. *yuva*) is frequently stretched to include members well into their forties.[72] The organisations seem initially to have been modelled on student organisations at the Universities in Kathmandu, but have later spread all over the country and many are closely connected with political parties. In ethnic minority areas, however, or at least in Humla, the youth clubs focus on activities intended to strengthen community identity and other local issues. The youth club in Waltse (Halji Youth Club Limi, HYCL) started in 2008 as the first youth club in the Limi valley. In addition, there are at least two youth clubs in Dzang, one in Til, and another among the Limi community in Kathmandu and India. The latter is registered as an NGO under the name Limi Youth Society and is very active. The youth clubs in the villages, while operating largely according to traditional village logics, occasionally challenge the established authorities. The youth club in the city, which consists mainly of educated youth with easy access to resources and technology, also keep some traditional ways, but are more

72 Snellinger 2009.

innovative in terms of management, activities and use of technology such as social media.

The youth club in Waltse has been formally registered with the District Administration Office in Humla and the Social Welfare Council in Kathmandu as an NGO since 2010. The purpose of the organisation, as stated in the registration papers, is to work for the protection of wildlife and natural biodiversity, protect and promote tangible and intangible cultural heritage, contribute to the management of Rinchen Ling monastery, and engage in income generating activities and support of local education.[73] When scrutinising the organisation's work, however, it becomes clear that it differs somewhat from the development jargon and ideology in the registration document. With fifty-four members in 2010, almost thirteen per cent of the total population in the village, the organisation has become quite powerful. Leadership positions are generally held by men, but the seventeen female members of the club have their own leader. The membership rules for men and women are the same, though women have to resign upon marriage. The reason, I was told, is that married women have too many household responsibilities to be able to participate in the compulsory activities of the club. The club engages in various income generating activities, like business and tourism. While many tasks are carried out by the male and female members together, they generally follow the local customary division of labour meaning that the women cook and do most of the agricultural work. The village shop described in Chapter Four was a short-lived experiment, but by summer 2012, the youth club in Waltse had built three houses: a meeting place in the village, a house next to the campsite, and a house in Dungling, which was raised in the hope of establishing a base for business activities in connection with the road. By 2018, the youth club had also invested in other items such as a truck for transporting goods from Purang and a threshing machine that can be used by villagers against a lease fee. The club is also actively engaging in conflict resolution. Although not formally part of the system described below, the members mediate in conflicts, and occasionally they help the parties involved to cover the cost of the case and pay a proportion of the accrued fines.[74]

The youth club in Waltse is strictly organised. Collective decisions are made according to democratic procedures similar to those followed in the village assembly, but the leaders are elected according to qualifications, and written records are kept for all the economic transactions. The club has the authority

73 HYCL Constitution, pp. 5–6.

74 For an example of the youth club's involvement in conflict resolution, see Chapter Seven.

to impose compulsory labour (L. *biri*, s.u.)[75] on its members—sometimes lasting for several days.[76] On a happier note, the youth club also arranges festivities, and occasionally invites the whole village for opera performances (*lha mo*) or for other plays. Waltse youth club is by far the largest organisation in Limi, and it is the club with the strictest management. The youth club in Til, on the other hand, consists solely of women and the twenty-three members are more loosely organised. Although the youth club in Til is less active than the one in Waltse, it organises homestays, cultivates its own fields, and arranges festivities. When I visited Til in January 2012, the youth club invited the whole village for a three-day celebration. This is not unusual in Limi, but the women staged a theatre performance with their own skits. Such performances have traditionally been the domain of men in the community and this event can therefore be read as a sign of gradually changing gender roles.

Limi Youth Society in Kathmandu was registered already in 2005 and operates more as a regular NGO. The organisation works to promote the rights of the Limigya and increase their share of the budget, but much of their effort is also directed towards raising ethnic awareness among its young members. Educated Limigya, who have not been back to Limi since they left for school as children, regard ethnic awareness-building as particularly important. They also actively promote Limi as a tourist destination and search for sponsors; already in 2010 they had an active Facebook page and a website and they had printed a sixty-seven page English language magazine presenting the community and the local customs. The year after the club made a short promotional film.[77] In recent years, they have posted many videos on YouTube, and they have also become active on other social media platforms such as Instagram and Tiktok. Together with Limi Welfare Society, which is a group of more senior Limi residents in Kathmandu, they occasionally involve in lobbying and participate in various meetings with political institutions at the national level. The youth clubs also directly cooperate with religious leaders. When Drigung Kyabgön Rinpoche and the Limi *sprul sku* Senge Tenzin Rinpoche visit Kathmandu, the Limi Youth Society is frequently called to assist. The most salient example took place after the devastating earthquake of 25 April 2015, when Senge Tenzin Rinpoche travelled from his residence in Taiwan to Kathmandu

---

75 See also Chapters Six and Nine.

76 In 2011, for instance, the Waltse youth club arranged *biri* for the cultivation of their fields, in order to build a new club house in Waltse, to extend the gabion walls protecting the village from flood, and in order to help a sponsor in Til with the harvest, totalling almost a month's work. If a youth club member is unable to participate in the work, he or she will have to provide a replacement.

77 Limi Youth Society (n.d.).

to sponsor the distribution of relief material to the worst affected areas of Sindhupalchowk. The Limi Youth Society formed the staff of 'the Senge Tenzin Relief Team', which, as thoroughly documented on the youth club's Facebook site, was led by the Rinpoche himself.[78]

5.3 Gradual Integration with the Nepali Administrative System

After a brief experiment with democracy in the 1950s, it was not until the People's Movement (Jan Āndolan) in 1990, that Nepal restored a multi-party democracy. A democratisation process also took place at the local level, but as some writers have pointed out, this was slowed down by the lack of locally elected government bodies. As noted by Ramble in the case of Mustang, the local democracy in a number of remote communities has been quite different from the national democratic movement, one reason being these communities' lack of 'national political aspirations'.[79] As shown in the description of the village management and the local legal system above, a similar insularity vis-à-vis national and regional political institutions has also been the prevailing attitude in Limi, where local strategies have been characterised by elusiveness and only a nominal adaptation to national requirements. Recent years, however, have seen an increasing integration with Nepali government institutions. This integration has been fuelled by the villagers' engagement in some concrete cases, most notably in the search for funding for road construction and, in the case of Waltse, protection against recurring floods.

The local elections, which were supposed to have taken place in 2002, were called off, and the local councils were dissolved by the Nepali Congress government of Sher Bahadur Deuba in order to prevent the Unified Marxist Leninist (UML) party from dominating the local political scene. Later the same year, King Gyanendra dissolved the parliament and dismissed Prime Minister Deuba.[80] As a result, the local administrative structures broke down and the district management posts were taken over by party coalitions. The villagers in Limi, however, had not been involved in party politics, and during the local and national elections held after 1990, Limi voted uniformly. That is, prior to the elections, the village assemblies convened and decided who to support, and all the eligible villagers subsequently voted for the same candidate. Their choice to stay away from party politics can be seen as a continuation of the

78 Limi Youth Society 2015. Facebook post about the Senge Tenzin Relief Team.

79 Ramble 2008a: 263f.

80 See Kramer 2003.

elusive strategy in their interaction with Nepali authorities throughout history. In June 2011, during the national census, the Nepali officials also registered the villagers as voters for the upcoming Constituent Assembly (CA) election.[81] The district secretary, who visited Limi later that same year, tried to persuade the villagers to change their voting behaviour and invest more interest in the political parties in the district, but with little initial success.

Humla's poor infrastructure has created logistical challenges for all elections, but for the CA election, which was eventually arranged in November 2013, the election committee sent representatives to all the VDCs in Humla (Fig. 5.3). In Limi, one voting centre was set up in each of the three villages. During this election, the villagers reportedly voted independently for the first time.[82] Moreover, this was also the first occasion the women cast their votes, an important landmark as customary practice in Limi had previously barred women from formal participation in political decision-making.

5.3.1 *Claiming Limi's Share of the Nepali Government Budget*

In 1995, during the rule of the then Prime Minister Man Mohan Adhikhari (UML), the government started to provide annual block grants to the VDCs in order to facilitate the improvement of local infrastructure and services.[83] According to villagers in Limi this was when they started to receive a VDC budget from the Nepali Government. However, both villagers and analysts report that substantial portions of the budget disappeared on the way to the villages.[84] In 2011, when the district secretary went to Limi to discuss the VDC's share of the district budget as described in the opening vignette of the chapter, the local leaders had not seen the document detailing the district's budget beforehand. They were not familiar with either the procedures or the various budget posts, and therefore unable to detect whether parts of the budget had ended up in other pockets. When the district secretary asked for their opinions on the budget, they simply stated that they wanted to spend it on road construction. The road from the border with Tibet at Lapcha towards Simikot was already covered, but the villagers wanted to construct a road through the Limi valley and connect it with the main road. They therefore allocated those parts of the budget that were not already earmarked, such as the 10% to the children and 10% to

81 The CA election was originally planned for 2012 but was eventually postponed until November 2013.

82 Interview with a man from Limi in Kathmandu, December 2013.

83 Inlogos 2009: 2f.

84 Interview with men from Waltse, 23.09.10. The widespread corruption at the district government level can, as several analysts have pointed out, to a large extent be read as a consequence of the local democratic vacuum since 2002. See for instance Acharya 2011.

the women, to that purpose. In addition to the male VDC and ward leaders, the local teachers and the leaders of other government appointed committees, the female leaders were also called to participate in the budget meeting. They were not only invited to listen to the discussions but were also asked to decide how they wanted to spend the part of the budget that was earmarked for women. Moreover, at the concluding session at the end of the two-day meeting, the women were asked to give speeches in front of the whole assembly (Fig. 5.5). The women appeared uneasy about it since, except for the teacher, none of them had given speeches before, but all performed well.

5.3.2 *Dual Village Management after the New Constitution*

With the new Constitution in 2015, the Limi adaptation took a new turn. The constitution paved the way for massive administrative reforms implemented from the elections in 2017 onwards; Nepal was made into a federal state with a three-tiered government system. The country was divided into seven provinces, and Limi and Humla district joined the newly formed Karnali Province with Birendranagar as capital. At the local level of government, the reforms were also considerable. The former 3157 VDCs and 58 municipalities were reduced to 753 local government units referred to as Rural Municipalities (N. Gaunpalika). While the Constitution gave these new and larger Rural Municipalities more authority and larger allocations of funds from the Federal Government as part of an effort to decentralise power, the mass merger of former VDCs also had an opposite effect: a centralisation of power from the micro-level of the communities up to larger clusters of communities represented by the rural municipalities. This gives leaders from other communities more direct influence over matters that were previously managed internally. A similar process has taken place in the district administration, which has lost much of its former authority to the newly formed province governments.[85]

Accordingly, while Limi had previously been governing itself as a separate VDC, in 2017, the community was merged with three other VDCs to form Namkha Rural Municipality. This administrative reform put new demands on local village management, and a new structure was developed: the nine former wards in Limi were now counted as one, with only one chairman and three vice-ward leaders (Fig. 5.4). Although all the former VDCs in Namkha Rural Municipality were Tibetan-speaking, they had to adopt the national administrative framework and Nepali as administrative language. The use of Nepali

85 Similar processes of merging local administrative units into larger ones in Norway and several other countries have involved significant friction.

language when discussing local government matters in the meetings in the Namkha municipality headquarters in Yalbang, however, has created difficulties for many of the Limi representatives, especially the women, who have no or very limited Nepali language skills.[86]

Arguably one of the main challenges for the new municipalities has been the task of developing new legislation. This process is still ongoing and is made even more demanding as the laws and policies are not completed at the province and federal level of government.[87] This new administrative structure thus placed much greater demands on the leaders in Limi, making it virtually impossible for them to simultaneously manage the villages according to their own customary laws. Hence, the villagers decided to separate the tasks, and the previously hybrid village government has now bifurcated into a dual system. One set of leaders, elected through a rotational lottery system, referred to as *yul gyi dpon po* ('village leader'), take care of the customary village management. Another set of leaders, elected through voting, represent Limi in the Namkha Rural Municipality and have the responsibility of dealing with secular affairs within the framework of the Nepali state structure.

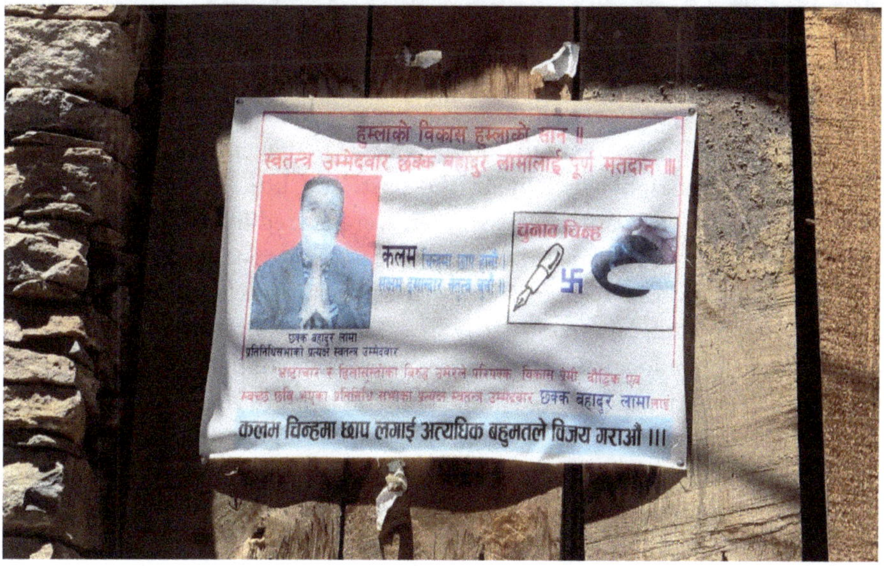

FIGURE 5.3 Election poster in Dzang, 2019

86 See Havnevik, Hovden and Rinchen Loden (forthcoming).

87 See Bhattarai 2021.

FIGURE 5.4 The Ward chairman explaining the new Rural Municipality system, 2018

5.3.3 *Women's Political Rights*

As discussed in the paragraphs about village management above, women had few political rights in Limi in the past, and little direct influence on decision-making processes.[88] The women were barred from attending village assembly meetings and from the right to have a say or give their votes. However, this situation is gradually changing, partly as a result of Nepali legislation and district government practices, partly as a result of initiatives by NGOs and partly as a result of local needs. The women's participation at the meeting with the district secretary mentioned in the paragraph above gave them experience in political management processes (Fig. 5.5). Similarly, membership in the youth clubs gives women organisational training, and, especially in Til, leadership experience too. So far Til is the village where the women have acquired the most political influence, and the villagers explained that this is largely due to the high proportion of male outmigration. As mentioned in Chapter Four, 98 Tilwas, or 43.2% of the population, live permanently outside the village,[89]

88 See also Chapter Four.

89 One fourth of the households in Til own apartments in Kathmandu, and many of those who do not own property themselves, live in relatives' houses.

and many of the villagers spend several months per year travelling. The majority of these migrants are men. Some women have therefore recently started to take over several tasks previously reserved for men, such as participating in village assembly meetings. However, these political rights do not appear to have had much influence on the women's general status in society, however. The women in Til are still carrying out the same hard work as the women in Waltse and Dzang and are still given the lowest seats at public gatherings. Yet, although the status of women in Til is only marginally better than in the other two villages, this development can be seen as a small step towards the political empowerment of women. A further step may be taken when the women become literate.

The administrative reforms following the new 2015 constitution represented further progress in female participation in political work. According to part 18 of the constitution, it became compulsory for all wards in the rural municipalities to have female representatives. In 2017, Limi therefore elected its first female ward member, a woman from Dzang. This was yet another landmark in the political history of Limi. In 2019, I witnessed her presiding over a village assembly meeting in Dzang and participating in a workshop at ICIMOD in Kathmandu. Yet, there are still many challenges barring her and other women from political influence. She reported that one of the main challenges, which she shares with some of the male leaders, was lack of Nepali language skills.[90] While I noted in the previous chapter that more women than men in Waltse are attending higher education, all of these women have outmigrated. At the time of writing, to the best of my knowledge, there is no woman in the villages able to speak Nepali well enough to engage in politics on par with the men, let alone possess sufficient reading and writing skills to engage in budget applications and reading administrative and legal documents in Nepali. With further development of the local school and with educational programmes for adult women, this predicament could be amended. Yet, there are also many other obstacles for women's participation in such work, including the traditional hierarchy, division of labour and constraint in terms of time and workload. This was repeatedly mentioned by all women I spoke with about the topic. For instance, during an interview in Waltse in 2018, I asked a group of women if they would have participated more in the local decision-making processes if they were given the same political rights as men. The answer was a resolute no. That would just add another burden to their shoulders. They emphasised that they hardly have any spare time after all their work obligations, and simply

90 Interview May 2019.

FIGURE 5.5 Woman giving her first public speech, 2011

could not see how it would be possible to engage in local political activities without some serious structural changes.[91] Recent initiatives from the Nepali government, such as the female empowerment meetings arranged in 2018

91 Women's participation in decision-making processes is discussed in more detail in Havnevik, Hovden and Rinchen Loden (forthcoming).

FIGURE 5.6 Women's empowerment meeting in Dzang, 2019

(Fig. 5.6) along with initiatives by a young outmigrated Limi woman on women's health and a female adult education programme, have garnered greater local attention to women's issues and represent steps in that direction.

5.4 A Local Management System in Transition

This chapter has provided an overview of the systems for local government, decision-making, and conflict resolution in Limi, as well as of some of the local consequences of the political changes in Nepal and on the Tibetan side of the border over the last decades. Throughout most of their history, the Limigya have chosen to adopt only a minimum of the Nepali policies, in a way that they felt best harmonised with their traditional legal system. There appears to have been several internal and external reasons for that, including the fact that most of the villagers had no or limited Nepali language skills, poor connectivity, and little experience with the Nepali state apparatus, which for much of the history was experienced as extractive. The villagers felt that their own system served them well and enabled them to carefully manage their environment, and they therefore sought to protect their strong degree of autonomy in the management of internal affairs.[92] However, with the democratisation process and general transformation of district management and politics in Nepal, as well as the increasing number of development initiatives after the end of the insurgency, integration with the Nepali state has gradually become more pronounced and more attractive. Similarly, some major events, such as the split of the monasteries, the road construction, the search for funding of flood mitigation after the glacial outbursts, have led to more intensive involvement. But the main turning point came after the 2015 Constitution with the administrative reforms in Nepal and Limi's inclusion into Namkha municipality. As the examples discussed in the chapter have showed, this entail both benefits and challenges. One of the more pressing issues according to local leaders, is whether there will be room for their local natural resource management system within the new rural municipality.[93]

---

92 A similarly high degree of autonomy has been reported for example by Jahoda (2015: 68), Ramble (2008a: 27, 67–70, 71ff), and Schuh (2000: 294).

93 This concern was pointed out in many conversations. The question of how to secure local control over natural resource management was discussed during a stakeholder workshop at ICIMOD in Kathmandu 2019. See also the report by Bhattarai (2021), Bhattarai et al. (forthcoming) and Gurung et al. (forthcoming).

CHAPTER 6

Village Taxes and Community Obligations

> A long time ago, two men from Limi who visited Purang were arrested by the district commissioner (*rdzong dpon*). One of them managed to escape so the commissioner sent his officers to Limi to fetch him. The officers asked the local chief to hand the fugitive over so they could tie him up and bring him to Purang. The chief, however, cleverly replied that since they were paying half of their taxes to Purang, the officers had the right to arrest him, but since they were paying the other half of their taxes to Nepal, they could only tie up half of his body. Hearing this, the officers left.[1]

∵

Throughout history, many tax collectors, both religious and secular, have found their way to Limi. The community's ambiguous frontier status resulted in a situation of 'double taxation', i.e., the simultaneous payment of taxes to two states.[2] Taxes to Nepal were referred to locally as *mon khral* ('Nepali tax'),[3] and were collected by the district authorities in Simikot until the end of the 1990s. Taxes to the Tibetan administration were referred to as *bod khral* ('Tibetan tax'), and were paid to the Purang district commissioner for distribution to three monasteries in Ngari until the middle of the twentieth century, when the Chinese annexation led to a cut in fiscal relations between Nepali border communities and Tibet. In addition to the taxes paid to external authorities, the people in Limi have also paid a considerable amount of taxes to their own villages and monasteries.

In this chapter I will start with a broad historical perspective and make a sketch of Limi's external tax relations with Tibet and Nepal. After giving an

1 Story told by a senior villager to illustrate how the Limigya navigated their relationship with the northern neighbour, 31.01.12.

2 This phenomenon has been relatively common in Tibetan frontier regions. See for instance Bray (2012), Childs (2000), Jahoda (2007), Levine (1992), Schuh (2000: 294), and Thargyal (2007).

3 As explained in Chapter Three, in Limi the term Mon has been used to signify the successive state formations in what is today Nepal.

 | DOI:10.1163/9789004714571_007

overview of the former external taxes, I shall describe the different types of internal taxes currently paid to the village government and discuss continuity and changes in fiscal practices. I will also briefly analyse how the taxes have been formed and developed from voluntary donations to compulsory contributions. Finally, I will investigate the actual usage of the taxes in contemporary Limi and provide a preliminary assessment of how these taxes influence the relation between secular and religious authorities.[4]

Taxation, even if seemingly static, has varied considerably through time and across space, but has only been given limited attention in scholarly work on Tibetan and Himalayan communities.[5] Only a handful of publications have been devoted to the topic, the most important of which include Pedro Carrasco's *Land and Polity in Tibet* from 1959 and articles by Wangchen Surkhang and Goldstein.[6] The Nepali taxation system has been investigated by Mahesh C. Regmi in his four-volume landmark study *Land Tenure and Taxation in Nepal*.[7] However, there have been great regional differences within Nepal itself, and except for some observations by Levine in her monograph on polyandry in the Nyinba community, little is known about the taxation system in Humla.[8] Comparative material from other parts of the Nepal Himalaya has been provided mainly by Ramble and more recently by Childs and Choedup, but some details can be found also in works by other scholars.[9]

6.1 Terminology and Sources

Before discussing the ethnographic details, it is necessary to clarify the terminology. The English term 'tax' is defined as a compulsory contribution to

4 This question will be dealt with in greater detail in the final part of the book.

5 In an effort to fill this gap in our knowledge of Tibetan taxation systems, a conference on taxation was held in Fontainebleau, 6–7 December 2013. The proceedings volume, edited by Travers, Schwieger and Ramble, was published in 2023.

6 Carrasco's (1959) pioneering study was based mainly on secondary literature and although thorough, it suffers from the lack of primary source material. Surkhang 1984. 1986, Goldstein 1971. See also Cassinelli and Ekvall 1969, Dargyay 1982, Aziz 1974, and Thargyal 2007. The topic is also treated in publications on Tibetan administrative documents by Schuh, e.g., Schuh 1988. Literature on monastic taxation will be reviewed where relevant in Chapter Nine.

7 Regmi 1978.

8 Levine 1988a.

9 Ramble's unpublished PhD thesis from 1984 provides an interesting case for comparison, as does Childs and Choedup's (2019) study from Nubri, which devotes a chapter to the study of the local taxation system. See also Jest's (1975) monograph on Tarap in Dolpo.

a governing authority and should be distinguished from voluntary donations and punitive fees. However, it is not always obvious where to draw the line between taxes and other community obligations, of which there are many in Limi. Moreover, as I will discuss at the end of the chapter, Limi also has a shifting boundary between voluntary donations and tax obligations.

The Tibetan word *khral* has a wide range of meanings and while overlapping with the English term 'tax', there are also important differences.[10] Ramble remarks that although 'tax' does not provide an accurate translation of *khral*, the very fact that the word 'tax' is vague makes it the most appropriate English equivalent.[11] In Lubra, Ramble notes, the term *khral* is mainly used for certain types of payment to the Nepali government.[12] In Limi, however, the term *khral* is used in a looser sense to cover a variety of compulsory contributions formerly paid to the Nepali and Tibetan administrations and monasteries as well as internally in the villages. The obligations covered by the term *khral* also have more specific names which will be translated as they occur in this work and will also be listed in the glossary. Approximate conversion of measurement units will be provided in Appendix III. Many taxation terms have been used across large parts of the Tibetan plateau and the Himalaya, and whereas the specific meanings and actual usage of the terms may vary, the basic understanding is largely the same.

Prior to the 1950s, the Tibetan taxes were divided into 'external tax' (*phyi khral*) and 'internal tax' (*nang khral*). The 'external tax' was paid to the central government in Lhasa, whereas 'internal tax' referred to tax paid to a local lord.[13] In the *History of the three districts of Ngari* (*sTod mnga' ris skor gsum gyi lo rgyus*), for instance, the term *phyi khral* is used for taxes paid to the government via the governor (*sgar dpon*), whereas *nang khral* refers to taxes paid to the district (*rdzong*) or monastery.[14] Limi, however, paid 'external taxes' to Nepal as well as to Tibet, in addition to various taxes on trade and natural resources. Since the taxes on trade are less relevant for the topic of this book, it is sufficient to mention that taxes on trade were collected and paid in money or

10 See for instance Cassinelli and Ekvall 1969: 233. Compare also with Hovden 2013.

11 Ramble 1984: 240f.

12 Ramble 1984: 241.

13 Goldstein 2004: entries at pp. 604 and 689. See also Levine (1992: 349) and Ramble (2008a: 158).

14 *History of the three districts of Ngari* 1996: 187.

kind at the marts on both sides of the border until the 1950s.[15] In Limi, the 'internal taxes' are not paid to a landlord, but to the village community and are used for internal village purposes. The internal taxes can be divided into 'village taxes' (*yul gyi khral*) and 'monastic taxes' (*dgon pa'i khral*). The former will be investigated in this chapter, whereas the latter will be discussed together with the monastic economy in Chapter Nine.

Although taxes are collected separately by each village administration, the tax laws and procedures are largely the same in all three villages in Limi. Most of my data for this chapter were collected from Waltse, but information about the other villages will be included where relevant. I have photographed and read the tax registers of both the village assembly and the monastery in Waltse. In addition, I have studied the monastery's recruitment document, list of ritual expenses and its inventory.[16] These five documents, which are the main administrative documents of the village and monastery, articulate—together with the landownership certificates—the legal basis for the local tax system in Waltse. Other important primary sources include interviews and observations of how taxes influence the lives of the villagers and of how the system is organised and negotiated in practice. My account of the external taxes, paid until the middle and end of the twentieth century respectively, are also based on these registers supplemented with oral accounts.[17]

The main written source for this chapter, which for the sake of convenience I have called *Waltse tax register*, is a manuscript consisting of 136 un-numbered pages, folded and stitched to form a booklet (Fig. 6.1).[18] *Waltse tax register* contains two main texts. The first text covers 44 pages and contains the most recent version of the *bCa' yig* (lit. 'code of law', here 'the book of the *bca'* tax').[19] The term *bca' yig* is derived from *bca' khral*, i.e., the 'lease fee' charged for private lease of communal village land. The second text, called *Ban yig*, consists of 78 pages, plus 14 smaller pages inserted in the middle. The first section lists a type of taxes on private property called *ban dza*. I have not yet been able to

15 Elderly villagers reported that the taxes paid on natural resources included 'salt tax' (*tshwa khral*), 'gold tax' (*gser khral*) and taxes on the use of pasture (*rtswa rin*).

16 More detailed information about these three documents is provided in the relevant chapters.

17 There must have been documents issued by Nepali and Tibetan authorities as well, but the old administrative documents are scattered and some have reportedly been destroyed or lost. However, through interviews with elderly villagers and references in textual sources, I have been able to reconstruct a basic outline of the system.

18 The page numbers referred to in the book are my own.

19 Not to be confused with 'monastic guidelines', which is where the term *bca' yig* most commonly occurs. See Jansen 2013.

determine the correct spelling and meaning of the term, but *ban dza* could be a misspelling of *bad dza*.[20] The last section of the *Ban yig* includes a summary of some of the taxes previously paid to Tibet and Nepal as well as copies and summaries of a number of legal documents. If there ever was a title page of the *bCa' yig*, it has been lost, but page three—which was probably originally the first page—starts with the year 1915. The title page of the *Ban yig* gives the date Earth Mouse year of the fifteenth *rab byung* cycle (*rab byung bco lnga'i nang tshan sa byi lo*),[21] which corresponds to 1888. This year probably refers to either the introduction or a revision of the tax.[22] According to the senior villager who helped me read through the document, *Waltse tax register* was copied from an older original by Mee Guru, one of the former hereditary leaders (*'go ba*). This could in theory have happened any time between 1943, which is the year printed on the book's maroon textile cover, and 1980 when Mee Guru passed away, but judging from the names in the register and the inclusion of a number of abandoned and obsolete taxes to Tibet, I find it most likely that the book was composed around the middle of the twentieth century. The book is still in use and there are many additions by later scribes; the most recent was made in 2006. The additions reveal that the taxation system, which appears so rigid, has indeed been subject to revisions and adjustments. The book is quite disorganised with many loose sheets, some from older copies of the tax register, and it is sometimes difficult to read due to the different handwriting styles and the frequent misspellings.[23]

---

20 The spelling *ban dza* is the most frequently used in the tax register, but the form *ban rtsa* occurs in the opening verses. In his discussion of the term *pún* (spelling by Lyall, 1874) used to denote the grain tax in the *chos gzhis* in Spiti, Jahoda (2015: 73f) proposes that the correct spelling is *bon*, as the first syllable in *sa bon* (seed grain). It is possible that the *ban* tax in Limi has a similar etymology. Despite phonetic resemblance, it does not seem to be related to the term *bem chag* (lit. register') which occurs in tax registers from Mustang published by Ramble and Vinding (1987). However, I find it most likely that it is related to the words *be za*, *bun*, or *bed* which can all be translated as 'interest'. In their work on Nubri, Childs and Choedup (2019: 199) refer to local 'Interest documents' called *bad yig*.

21 Corrected from *rab 'byung cos lnga'i nang tshan sa byi lo*.

22 The original document may have been composed in 1888, but since the names listed in the register belong to a later generation, it is safe to conclude that the current register is a more recent version.

23 As mentioned in Chapter Five, the various styles of writing reflect the democratisation process in the community over the course of the last few decades, where the positions as village leader rotates and the erroneous spelling reflects the lack of education beyond one or two years of rudimentary primary school.

FIGURE 6.1 Reading the *Waltse tax register* during the village assembly meeting, 2011

FIGURE 6.2 Calculating butter taxes, 2011

6.2 Landownership and Other Bases for Taxation

Studies on Tibetan taxation practices show significant variation throughout history and between regions. The current taxes in Limi are calculated according to a number of different principles: landownership or user rights to land, herd size, number of 'taxable people' (*khral mi*) in a household, and household category.[24] The property taxes on fields and animals have been calculated according to estimated capacity rather than actual production.[25] The size of the grain taxes, for instance, are estimated according to the amount of seed grain (*sa bon*) needed, and the tax on animals is calculated according to the size of the herd and number of milking animals rather than the actual produce. As in other Tibetan areas, it is the household that is the main taxpaying unit.[26] It is often said that the *grong chen* families have to pay a full tax burden, the *grong chung* half a tax burden, and the *bom btang* a quarter, but as will become clear, this is a simplification that only holds true for taxes paid at fixed rates and for certain types of communal labour.

6.2.1 *Categories of Land and Landownership*

There are currently four main categories of land in Limi: privately owned land, land owned by the monastery, land owned by the village assembly, and communal land belonging to the three villages. Most of the households till a combination of privately owned fields, which constitute the majority of cultivated land, village fields, and monastery fields. Land at Limi territory outside the village boundaries is collectively owned by the three villages, and the management of its use as pasture or for harvest of winter fodder is strictly coordinated and regulated at three-village meetings.

If we are to take the oral historical accounts at face value, the first settlers in Limi migrated to what was presumably virgin territory.[27] How did some of the land become village property and some of the land the property of the monastery? Oral tradition in Til and Dzang claims that the king of Jumla donated land to Til Kundzom and Dzang Tilchen monasteries. This is confirmed both in the *Drigung history of Kailash*[28] and in the *Rinchen Ling monastery inventory*.[29] There is, however, no mention of such a donation of land to the monastery

24 A common principle for taxation in many countries is income, but in Limi—as in most other Tibetan societies—income has not been liable for taxation.

25 The *ban dza* tax described below seems to be an exception.

26 Carrasco 1959: 212.

27 See Chapter Three.

28 *Drigung history of Kailash*, f. 29b–30a.

29 *Rinchen Ling monastery inventory*, f. 3b–4a.

in Waltse, and there is no mention of similar donations of land to any of the secular village administrations.[30] When I asked people in Waltse how the village assembly and the monastery acquired their fields, they replied that all the property had been given by the villagers. When I asked them to explain how such donations had taken place, they said that in the case of the village land, fields were given back to the community when a household decided to leave the village or as payment of debt. The monastery would similarly receive its land either as payment of debt or as donations from villagers in order for them to acquire merit, something I will discuss in more detail in Chapter Nine.

6.3 Taxes Paid to Tibet and Nepal

Whereas the basic features of the central Tibetan tax system have been described and analysed, little is known about the tax system in Western Tibet with which Limi had fiscal relations before 1960. Even after the incorporation of Ngari with Central Tibet at the end of the seventeenth century, the province was only loosely connected with the central authorities. What we know about the tax system in Central Tibet is therefore not directly applicable to the Western Tibetan setting. The basis for the Central Tibetan taxation law was the *Iron monkey settlement* (*lCags spre zhib gzhung*) of 1740,[31] revised in the *Iron tiger settlement* (*lCags stag zhib gzhung*) of 1830.[32] However, as Surkhang noted in 'Government, monastic and private taxation in Tibet', Purang and a number of other 'districts' (*rdzong*) in Ngari were not included in the *Iron tiger settlement*. About the tax system in Ngari, he further commented that:

> In this province, there are very few monastic estates and no private estates at all.[33] The tax is not very high. Each *rZong* (sic) pays a sum of money called *sGrigs-'bul*.[34] After having provided the monasteries with their share, the *rZongs* (sic) *sdod* keeps the remaining amount of revenue.[35]

---

30 Folio 4a of the *Rinchen Ling monastery inventory* mentions that the Waltse temple and its 'estate' or 'property' (*mchod gzhis*) was given over to the Drigungpa. However, it does not say anything about the amount of land and how it had been acquired. The term *mchod gzhis* used in the inventory appears to be synonymous with *chos gzhis*. See *Bod rgya tshig mdzod chen mo*, pp. 858 and 842 respectively.

31 Surkhang 1984: 15.

32 Surkhang 1984: 20.

33 The absence of aristocratic landowners was noted also by Carrasco 1959: 106.

34 According to the glossary of taxation by Thupten Sangyay (1986: 44) *sgrigs 'bul* refers to the custom of giving rewards to a number of government offices '... in proportion to the amount of their offerings made voluntarily to *bLa Phyag Las Khung*.'

35 Surkhang 1986: 28.

Sherring, in the report after his 1905 expedition to Ngari, similarly noted that since the 'governors' (*sgar dpon*) and 'district commissioners' (*rdzong sdod* or *rdzong dpon*),[36] had to buy their posts, they were, '… entitled to put all revenue, fines and other State income into their own private purses'.[37] This appears to have been common practice.[38] Surkhang's comment further suggests that the district commissioners were the main tax collectors in Ngari and that the taxes were distributed to the monasteries through them. However, actual practice appears to have been much more complicated. Levine was able to conduct preliminary research on pre-1960 taxation in four communities in Ngari in 1990, which resulted in what remains the only western language publication on taxes in the province.[39] Her study of the taxes in Ruthog (Ru thog), Tholing, Purang, and Khochar shows 'tremendous regional diversity'.[40] It is also debatable whether it is correct to state that the taxes in Ngari were 'not very high'. The fact that there were few estates in Ngari does not mean that the inhabitants were exempted from fiscal burdens. We do not have enough knowledge about the taxation mechanisms, about how the tax system related to the overall economic situation of the population, and about how the taxes were experienced by those who had to pay. Carrasco noted that:

> The western province of mNga'-ris does not include any estate of the nobility. It is directly under the officials sent by the Lhasa government or under local monasteries. All local monasteries, however, are branches of the great monasteries of Central Tibet or of Bhutan.[41]

The fact that the monasteries were branches not only of central Tibetan monasteries but also of Bhutanese monasteries further complicated the picture. John Bray writes that Bhutan had an enclave in Ngari at Darchen (Dar chen) and controlled some monasteries in the Kailash area.[42] As mentioned in Chapter Three, some of these monasteries were originally Drigung Kagyu monasteries that had been 'lent' out to the Drukpa Kagyupas in the fifteenth century and

36 According to Sangyay (1986: 41) the official designation of the district commissioner (*rdzong dpon*) was *rdzong sdod*.

37 Sherring 1993: 146.

38 According to Travers (2023) and Goldstein (1968) it appears that the *rdzong sdod* commonly retained some of the taxes in other parts of Tibet as well.

39 Levine 1992 (republished in 2023). In addition, some information on taxation can be found in the *History of the three districts of Ngari* (1996) and there is also some scattered information in Tsering Gyalpo (2006) and Tsering Gyalpo et al. (2012).

40 Levine 1992: 322.

41 Carrasco 1959: 106.

42 Bray 2012.

had remained with the order since then,[43] whereas others (including Darchen) were donated by King Senge Namgyal (Seng ge rNam rgyal, r. ca. 1616–1642) when Ngari was conquered by Ladakh in the seventeenth century.[44] The monasteries had the right to collect taxes from affiliated villages for economic support. The Drukpa Kagyupas' influence in the area reportedly extended also to Humla as they were collecting taxes and other contributions from affiliated villages all the way down to the Nyinba villages near Simikot. Todpa, one of the Nyinba villages, used to belong to the Drugpa Kagyu order before it was converted to Nyingma. Similarly, also other Humli villages like Zangrak (s.u.) and Yarik (s.u.) were affiliated with the Drukpa Kagyu.[45] The complex religio-political relations in Humla and Ngari have been reflected in the taxation systems. Levine's brief but valuable overview of the tax systems in Purang and Khochar, with which Limi had fiscal relations, provides an instructive case for comparison.[46] Regarding the taxation systems in Purang, Levine writes that Purang was the wealthiest in the district, with a considerable amount of arable land.[47] The system of taxation in Purang was, according to her, closer to that of Central Tibet with the Tibetan government, Shephel Ling (bShad 'phel Gling) monastery, Tashigang (bKra shis sgang) monastery, and the Drukpa Kagyu *bla brang* in Darchen as the main landlords.[48] Levine further explained that,

> Some of the villages belonged in their entirety to one of these landlords, but there were other villages whose memberships were divided among government and monastic estates. Also the memberships of a few villages owed tax to several monastic institutions, although one of the monasteries clearly was dominant—in its control over local lands and its rights over local people—and readily identified as such. It is as if a large number of tax beneficiaries were vying for the support of a limited population in Purang.[49]

---

43 See for instance the *Drigung history of Kailash* f. 32b and Petech 1997: 319.

44 According to Ardussi (1977: 311) the Bhutanese enclave at Kailash must have been obtained some time between the Ladakhi king Senge Namgyal's conquest of Guge in 1630 and his death in 1642. See also Chapter Three.

45 Interview with Tshewang Lama, May 2013.

46 Levine 1992. The monasteries and *bla brang* belonging to the Bhutanese Drukpa Kagyu order are throughout Levine's article referred to as Drigung. In order to avoid unnecessary confusion, I have therefore changed the names when referring to the article.

47 Up to twelve times the size of that in Ruthog and Guge. Levine 1992: 332.

48 Levine 1992. Also the *History of the three districts of Ngari* (1996: 191) mentions that Khochar and Zher paid taxes to the Drukpa *bla brang* in Darchen.

49 Levine 1992: 333.

This statement suggests that the tax burden on the Purangbas may have been higher than Surkhang's description. Furthermore, it becomes clear from her article that the villagers in Purang paid both 'internal' and 'external' taxes. The former consisted mainly of work on monastery land, whereas the latter consisted mainly of different types of *'u lag* ('compulsory transportation service') and tea taxes referring to the compulsory purchase of tea from the holders of the government tea monopoly.[50] The tea was sold at high prices and had to be paid for in Indian rupees. Surkhang considered this tax as the most difficult for the subjects (*mi ser*) of western Tibet.[51]

The situation in Khochar was quite different in that all but one household were (*mi ser*) belonging to the Drukpa Kagyu monastic estate (*bla brang*) at Darchen.[52] When the Ladakhi king Senge Namgyal gave Darchen to the Drukpa Kagyupas in the seventeenth century, he also bestowed the order with Khochar and a few other villages for economic support.[53] Levine reports that the Bhutanese representative in Darchen was present only in the summer season, while the rest of the year Khochar was under the jurisdiction of the *rdzong dpon* (presumably the district commissioner of Purang) and the *sgar dpon* ('governor'). Taxes were paid both to the Tibetan and Bhutanese representatives, and Khochar is therefore another example of double taxation in the region.[54] Khochar monastery belonged to the Sakya school of Tibetan Buddhism,[55] and in the introduction to a joint trilingual publication on the Khochar monastery, Tsering Gyalpo writes that, '… the villagers of Khorchag did not have to pay taxes to or perform obligatory services for the monastery.'[56] On a similar note, Levine reports that the duty to plant and harvest the land belonging to Khochar Monastery '… rotated, following general taxpayer statuses in the village (…) although this seems not to have formed a part of the official Khochar tax responsibilities. That is, work for Khochar Gompa was described as "voluntary" and as not supported by external coercion.'[57] As we will see below, the boundary between 'voluntary' and 'compulsory' has been equally blurred in Limi. More research is needed to get a better understanding of the actual

50 Levine 1992: 335.

51 Surkhang 1986: 28. See also Bray 2012, Rauber 1982, Sherring 1993, and the *History of the three districts of Ngari* 1996: 191.

52 Levine 1992: 336. Corrected from Drigung Kagyu in the article.

53 Levine 1992: 335. See also Bray (2012) and the *History of the three districts of Ngari* (1996: 191).

54 Levine 1992: 335.

55 The conversion is described in Chapter Three.

56 Tsering Gyalpo et al. 2012: 25. English version translated by Christian Jahoda.

57 Levine 1992: 338f.

conditions, but it should be noted that although the Khochar monastery was not supported by local taxes it received taxes from other sources. The Humli Khyampas studied by Rauber became 'subjects' (*mi ser*) of the monasteries in Khochar and Purang[58] and, as I will discuss further below, the three villages in Limi also paid significant amounts of butter to these monasteries.

6.3.1 *Tibetan tax* (bod khral)

The taxes paid by the people in Limi to their Tibetan neighbours were often referred to as 'person taxes' (*mi khral*)[59] since they trace their early origins to the plateau. In the *Waltse tax register* the people's tax is simply referred to as 'Tibetan tax' (*bod khral*). The tax was collected in the individual villages and consisted of a variety of products transported in bulk to Purang *rdzong*. It must have been a sizeable contribution because the tax from Limi to Tibet is referred to as 'the great tax of Limi' (*sle mi khral mo che*) in the *History of the three districts of Ngari*:

> Annually, the three Limi villages offered fifty loads of butter to the lamps in Khochar monastery. On the twenty-fourth day of the tenth Mongolian month, the headmen of Limi met with the representative of Purang district and had to offer the butter without any omission. This was called 'the great tax of Limi'.[60]

Unfortunately, the book does not mention its sources, and this excerpt is probably based on memory, or it could be a summary of a more extensive text. The main entry about *bod khral* in the *Waltse tax register* provides a more detailed list of obligations.[61] According to the tax register, the 'Tibetan tax' was paid in butter, grain, money, dried turnips (*nyung skam*), meat, roasted barley flour (*rtsam pa*), wooden utensils (*chang* bottles, barrels, and buckets), and cheese. The majority of these items, although collected by the district commissioner (*rdzong sdod* or *rdzong dpon*) or his representative (*rdzong tshab*), appear to have been given to the three monasteries Khochar, Shephel Ling, and Gyangdrag. The entry in the tax register starts by specifying that the total amount of butter paid was 113 measures (*mar bre*).[62] The villagers explained

58 Rauber, personal communication January 2013. See also Rauber 1982: 165.

59 See also Goldstein 1974: 261.

60 My translation from the *History of the three districts of Ngari* (1996: 193).

61 *Waltse tax register*, pp. 80–82, 104, and 116.

62 I have not found this term in the dictionaries, but I presume this is the correct spelling. In local documents it is normally written *mer*, which is probably an abbreviation (*bsdus yig*) of *mar bre*.

that 1 measure of butter equals 8 *nya ga*, whereas 20 *nya ga* equals 1 *khal*. If we convert the 113 measures to *khal*, the butter paid by the Limigya amounted to 45.2 *khal*. According to Goldstein, butter tax (*mar khral*) in Central Tibet was measured in a special butter *khal* which weighed about 6.5 lbs.[63] If equivalent measures were used in Purang, the 45.2 *khal* of butter paid as the great tax of Limi would correspond to 293.8 lbs or 133.3 kg.[64] However, according to current practice in Limi and Nyin 5 *nya ga* equals 1 kg, and if using this as basis for calculation, the total amount of butter paid was 180.8 kg. Be that as it may, the amount was significant enough for the tax to deserve its name. The poorly spelled *bod khral* tax list is written in an abridged form, and it is not specified whether the amounts listed in the register are already included in the above, or whether they are to be paid by each of the households. Towards the end of the entry, it is specified that the responsibility to provide butter for the Khochar Jowo[65] should be divided between Waltse and Til; Waltse should pay 2/3, whereas Waltse and Til together should pay 1/3.

In addition, the *Rinchen Ling monastery inventory* mentions a tax to Gyangdrag *bla brang* from specified fields in the three villages. The contribution included five loads (*khal*) of dried turnips from Dzang, five measures (*bre*) of butter from Waltse, and various wooden items (two water barrels, two *chang* containers, and one bucket) made of good quality building material from Til. The tax should be paid annually and was established in an agreement (*gtan khra*) which was written by *sprul sku* Konchog Tenpa Rabgye (dKon mchog bsTan pa Rab rgyas) in two copies and bound by an 'oath' (*'ba' gan*) in 1789.[66]

6.3.2 *The Nepali Tax* (mon khral)

The *mon khral*, an outdated name for the tax paid to the Nepali government, was based on the fact that Limi is located in Nepali territory. These taxes have therefore also been referred to as 'land tax' (*sa khral*).[67] Historical documents say that the Yatse kings ruling Jumla from at least the twelfth until the fifteenth centuries donated land to the Drigung religious institutions in the

63 Goldstein 1971: 12.

64 Using this calculation method, the fifty *khal* mentioned in the *History of the three districts of Ngari* would correspond to 325 lbs, or 147.5 kg.

65 The Khochar Jowo is a triple statue of the Three Protectors (*rigs gsum mgon po*) representing the Bodhisattvas Mañjuśrī, Avalokiteśvara and Vajrapāṇi, often referred to as 'the three silver brothers' (*dngul sku mched gsum*). See for instance the *Catalogue of the three silver brothers* 1996 and Tsering Gyalpo et al. 2012: 48ff.

66 *Rinchen Ling monastery inventory*, f. 49a.

67 See for instance *Waltse tax register*, p. 73 and 106.

thirteenth century.[68] If they exercised such control over the territory, it is quite likely that they levied taxes as well. Their successors, the Kalyal kings, certainly did; they were notorious in Humla for their heavy taxation. The passage in the *Rinchen Ling monastery inventory* quoted in Chapter Three about the villagers in Dzang being so heavily taxed in the seventeenth century that they abandoned the village, is an extreme example.[69] Judging from oral accounts in Limi and Levine's reports from the Nyinba communities, heavy taxation by the Kalyal was a burden suffered by most Humli communities until the region was conquered by Nepal at the end of the eighteenth century.[70]

After the unification, the right to collect taxes was secured by the Kalyal descendants, the Thakuri *mukhiyā* who acted as representatives of the Nepali kings. According to Levine, the first known land registration took place shortly after conquering the area at the end of the eighteenth century.[71] The last reform, which took place in the Nepali year 2022 BS, corresponding to 1965 in the western calendar, is still remembered in Limi. Elderly villagers report that the Nepali officials came to register the number and size of the fields. They went from house to house to collect information which was subsequently recorded in the *lālpurja* records and stored in the land registration office (N. *malpot*) in Simikot.[72] The documents in the land registration office were recent, and the information I have on the *mon khral* is therefore limited to brief entries in the *Waltse tax register*, more recent practice, and oral accounts, which can be considered reliable because of the temporal proximity and because they conform to practices recorded by other scholars.[73]

The taxes to the Nepali government consisted of 'land tax' (*sa khral*), 'hearth tax' (*thab khral*)[74] and 'water mill tax' (*chu 'thag khral*) paid first in *Tam ka* coins.[75] An entry in the tax register specifies that each household should pay one *'go Tam*. Later the rates were 0.5 rupee per field for the land tax, 2 rupees per household for the hearth tax, and 5 rupees per water mill. Whereas expensive in the past, the fees have not been adjusted according to inflation, and

68 See for instance *Rinchen Ling monastery inventory*, f. 3b–4a and *Drigung history of Kailash*, f. 29a–30a.

69 See Chapter Three. The story is also briefly discussed in Hovden (2013: 215f).

70 Levine 1988a: 91–94.

71 Levine 1988a: 92. See also Regmi 1978.

72 Conversation with elderly villager, 16.01.12.

73 For an account of Nepali taxation in the Nyinba villages, see Levine 1988a: 91–93.

74 According to Ramble (personal communication) the corresponding term used in Mustang is *me khral*.

75 *Tam ka* is an old currency used in Tibet. For a brief overview of the history of Tibetan currencies, see Shakabpa 2010: 62–65.

during the last decades the taxes have therefore been very low. Regarding the procedures for the collection and payment of taxes to the Nepali authorities, Konchog Gyatso, one of the senior villagers, said that they used to collect *sa khral* along with the other taxes in the eighth Tibetan month. Representatives from Limi had to travel to Simikot, he said, and this was the task of the 'senior official' (*las 'dzin rgan po*), who would combine it with the 'autumn trade' (*ston tshong*) in Simikot. These taxes were paid until the Maoist insurgency in the 1990s.[76] In the last few years, there have been a few Limi villagers earning a Nepali salary, and they have to pay 1% income taxes to the central authorities. As part of the administrative reforms after the new 2015 constitution there will also be other taxes, including from the municipality. But at the time of writing, it was still uncertain when the municipality would complete the tax legislation.

6.3.3 *Fiscal Continuity*

The payment of taxes to the Tibetan side were abolished immediately after the demarcation of the border in 1960. One of the senior villagers put it this way, 'In the past, we were in the middle. The men in Limi were Tibetan whereas the land was Nepali. Then, the people also became included in the Nepali side.'[77] However, people in Limi decided to continue collecting some of the former *bod khral* and decided to use it for local purposes instead. The part of the tax that they decided to keep was the butter tax to the Khochar Jowo. The rationale, I was told, was that they felt that it was not good to stop offering butter to the Jowo, and they therefore decided to offer this butter for the lamps in their own monastery instead. However, it is likely that there were also pragmatic reasons; there was a need for butter for the lamps in Rinchen Ling and it was easier to continue an old tax than to impose a new one.

As mentioned above, the *mon khral* was paid to the district authorities in Simikot until the insurgency in the 1990s. During the turbulent time of the civil war, financial support to one party would be punished by the other. The three Limi villages fared much better than other communities in Humla, but some families were forced to give substantial contributions to the Maoists. This had to be kept secret from the government officials. The district government, severely crippled by the upheaval, stopped collecting taxes. Again, people in Limi chose to continue the taxes and added the money to the village funds for internal usage. The sum is only symbolic and does not pose any economic difficulty even for the poorest people.[78]

76 Conversation with senior villager, 16.01.12.

77 Conversation with senior villager, 16.01.12.

78 Compare with the continuation of obsolete taxes mentioned in Ramble (2008: 158).

6.4 Internal Taxes and Tax Collection Procedures

Apart from the few individuals who have to pay income tax, the villagers in Limi are paying only internal taxes, yet the system is relatively complicated. As mentioned in the previous chapter, the local taxes are mainly paid in agricultural produce and most of them are therefore collected in the late autumn. The collection of grain taxes takes place immediately after the harvest, normally in the eighth Tibetan month corresponding roughly to October in the western calendar. The monastery and the village assembly alternate in collecting the taxes first. The collection of grain taxes by the village assembly takes place under the supervision of the village leaders, whereas the collection of the remaining taxes takes place during the autumn village assembly meeting (Figs. 6.1–4). In 2011, the meeting lasted eight days, starting from the fifth of December. The taxes were calculated and collected during the first three days, whereas the last five days were spent on village administration as detailed in Chapter Five and the annual payment of debt. The first part of the meeting is referred to as the 'tax calculation' (*khral rtsis*) meeting and will be described in some detail here.

Early in the morning of the first day of the meeting, the village leaders sat down together with some of the most capable men in the centre and the other men spread out in a circle along the walls of the courtyard. Many of them also drank 'calculation beer' (*rtsis chang*) or 'taxation beer' (*khral chang*) which was provided by the *grong chung* families throughout the meeting. If a man was caught drinking his own *chang*, I was told that he would be fined. The man who revealed this information was trying to disguise the high quality *chang* he had brought from his home as water and apparently knew what he was talking about. The two senior officials (*las 'dzin rgan po*) brought the keys and the box containing the village archives and placed it in front of the village leaders. The seal was broken, the box opened and the leader took out the *Waltse tax register* and scrolls with the last year's population records and the number of cattle owned by each household.[79] A Tibetan calendar (*lo tho*) was brought to help check the age of the taxpayers and a leather hide was spread out on the ground in front. Most of the calculations were made by placing tokens on the leather hide according to an old system (see Figs. 6.3 and 6.4).[80] Although electronic calculators were also used, some of the taxes are easier to calculate according to the old system. In this way, the calculations were also visible to everyone present. During the first day, they updated the lists over 'taxable people' (*khral*

79 As mentioned in Chapter Five, there are very strict rules safeguarding the box with the village documents.

80 The use of the tokens is explained below.

mi) and people under the age of fifteen (*tongkhor*, s.u.), animals above three years except horses, the number of milking animals, and the number of fields per household. During the second day, the butter, cheese, and tea taxes were collected and on the third day of the *khral rtsis* part of the village meeting, the *'u lag* responsibility was calculated. The following paragraphs will discuss each of these taxes.

6.4.1 *Lease of Village Land and Compulsory Support for Meditating Monks*

The *bCa' yig*, the first book in the *Waltse tax register*, contains lists of two taxes: the *bca' khral* and the *sgrub grwa*. The *bca' khral* is a fee paid for the lease of communal village land, whereas the *sgrub grwa*, which in this context can be translated as 'retreat [tax]'[81] is collected annually for the sponsorship of four meditating monks. In the introduction to the list of lease fees it is written that the tax covers the expenses for the Tshechu (Tshes bcu) and Nyene (bsNyen gnas) festivals.[82] All households in the village have leased *bca'* fields belonging to the village assembly either for planting crops or building a house.[83] The villagers told me that the fees for leasing the old fields were fixed before living memory and are listed in the tax register under the names of late parents or grandparents of the current heads of households. When new fields are leased out, the tax is calculated according to the amount of seed grain needed.[84] The estimate is carried out by the two senior officials (*las 'dzin rgan po*) and is repeated three times. The median of the three estimates will determine the new tax. Even if the size of the tax is estimated based on the amount of seed grain, the land does not need to be productive and used for cultivation. This means that a lease has to be paid even for land that has been rendered temporary or permanently useless by natural hazards such as the recent years' floods.[85] The total amount of taxes from the *bca'* fields is just above 48.5 *khal* of grain.[86]

81 A more accurate translation would be '[allowance to support] monks in retreat'.

82 Tshes bcu, refers to the auspicious tenth day of the month, celebrated in commemoration of Padmasambhava. See Schwieger 1997: 851–57. The villagers convene twice a year for alternating *bsnyen gnas* (one day precepts) and *smyung gnas* (fasting) practice. For more details see Chapter Seven. *Waltse tax register*, p. 3: *wal rtse yul pa'i bsnyen [gnyen] gnas dang tshes bcu'i rgyu 'gro so sos [sros] bca' [ca] 'babs rnam kyi tho bkod [dkod] pa la.*

83 According to senior villager, 08.02.12.

84 This is the case for new fields, including fields used for house construction, but most of the *grong chung* and *mo rang* pay seven *bre* each.

85 A similar inflexibility in Ruthog in western Tibet was noted by Levine (1992: 324).

86 The lease fee has been calculated from the *Waltse tax register*. Some entries are difficult to read, but the total amount should be reasonably accurate. See list of measurements in Appendix III.

The retreat tax (*sgrub grwa*), the second tax in the *bCa'yig*, refers to a contribution intended to support monks undergoing the 'three years, three months' (*lo gsum zla gsum*) retreat. The sum is simply determined according to family category and is listed together with the lease fee in the register. Most of the *grong chen* households pay 13 *bre* of grain each, but a few have voluntarily donated fields for the retreat tax and pay more. Two former *grong chung* who were elevated to *grong chen* status pay 6.5 *bre* of grain for the retreat tax each, whereas two current *grong chung* pay 1 *bre* each. None of the other smaller households, including the *bom btang*, pay grain for this tax. In addition, the families have to provide a certain amount of butter (only the families who committed themselves in the past),[87] tea (only the *grong chung*), and firewood (all households) for the meditating monks. Each of the four monks receives annually: 5 *khal* and 5 *bre* of grain, 5 *mar bre* and 2 *nya ga* of butter, 10 loads (*khur bu*) of firewood, and 5 bricks (*sbag drug*) of tea.[88] The age of this tax is uncertain, but the fact that it is listed together with the lease fee shows that it is at least as old as the current tax register. There is a copy of an obligation contract (*gan rgya*) in the village tax register making village support to four meditating *dge slong* (fully ordained monks) compulsory. This agreement seems to have been the origin of the retreat tax which is listed together with the lease fee at the beginning of the book, dated in a Wood Dragon year. At first, I thought that the agreement was written in the fifteenth *rab byung* cycle, corresponding to 1904, but on page 92–93 in the register there is a list of retreat tax contributions from the Earth Rat year in the same *rab byung* (1888), which suggests that the tax is even older. The names in the list, however, were updated when the document was composed in the middle of the twentieth century.

Whatever the date, the agreement seems to be an internal Waltse decision as the other two villages are not mentioned and no external authorities are registered as witnesses or signatories in the copy. Unfortunately, I have not been able to see the original, but I suspect that the text in the tax register is an abridged version. A tentative translation follows:

> In the year of the Wood Dragon, on the first day of the fourth month, in front of [lit. to the feet of] the preserver of the two systems, the precious

87 *Waltse tax register*, list on p. 43. A copy of the same list can be found on p. 100. The text says that in the year of the Fire Mouse in the twelfth month, some households offered their goats to the monastery for the retreat tax (*sgrub grwa*), which will be used for butter. The *rab byung* cycle is not mentioned, but the year probably refers to 1936, because the names in the list are so old that they had to scribble new names under in order to recall which households the taxes apply to. See also conversation with senior villager, 08.01.12.

88 Conversation with former leader, 27.11.11.

> lord of the law, we, whose names, marks, and places of origin are clearly given below, present an agreement, [drawn up] freely and willingly, the subject of which [is as follows]: this year, according to an agreement that was concluded by the community of Waltse, concerning the accomplishment of a support fund for food provisions for four meditating *dge slong* [monks]. Capital should be provided from each household, irrespective of its size. Regarding the size of the endowment and regarding the establishment of the capital fund, until the world-ages end and as long as the Buddha's doctrine endures, [the contribution] shall be paid without interruption, irrespective of the size of the household. Each household should discharge all their duties in terms of obligatory payments and, at the very least, [contribute with] provisions of water and firewood, and they should follow the procedure that was established in the past. According to its wealth, each household should provide cash payment, grain from the fields, or butter, each year.[89] Henceforth, we shall not be deficient in these payments by so much as a sesame seed. The terms of the contract will not be transgressed and there should be no blame on others. [The contracting parties] shall not bring up again [the old stories of] the dispute,[90] raise dirt from the [water's] depth,[91] speak with two tongues from the same mouth, make cooked meat raw again, move mountains and dry up oceans, and carry the leader on the nape of one's neck etc.[92] In short, if the contract is violated, even to the size of a sesame seed, the penalty enforced by law [lit. the feet of the law] will be five *srang* of gold. In order to confer constant validity to this contract by the signatories, the seal has passed from hand to hand.[93]

I asked the villagers how this sponsorship of the four meditating monks became a tax responsibility, and they replied that it started as a donation that gradually became habitual until it became a compulsory tax. One of the former village leaders said that, during his ancestors' time, the supplies were given according to capacity as a virtuous action (*dge ba*).[94] The shrine keeper explained that

89 The meaning of *phyi 'jal* in the text is unclear. The translation of this line is therefore only tentative.

90 Mullard 2013: 190 n. 49. Schneider (2002: 425) proposes: 'to produce new ideas in the form of: "I have been thinking about it."'

91 Schneider 2002: 426.

92 The translation of the last saying was suggested by Nyima Drandul, personal communication December 2013.

93 *Waltse tax register*, pp. 108–110. My tentative translation.

94 Conversation with former village leader, 27.11.11.

in the past they had many monks in retreat, and they established the rule of providing the retreat tax to support them. Right now, none of the monks is doing the three-year retreat, so the tax is instead given to four monks on a rotational basis according to seniority.[95] In return, these four monks have to serve whenever the village requests ceremonies such as the rain-making ritual (*char 'bebs*), fire offering rituals (*sbyin sreg*), offerings to the wrathful aspects of Guru Rinpoche (*gu ru drag po gtor rgyag*), or whenever they need a lama for community rituals.[96] The three-day rain-making ritual performed in the early summer in 2011 can serve as an example of how the system works. At the autumn assembly in 2010, the retreat tax had been given to the four most senior monks in the village. In the last week of June, in order to get much-needed rain after the barley had been sown, the village leaders approached the four monks who had received the allowance and requested them to perform the rain-making ritual. The four monks had to accept and the *las 'dzin rgan po* and the *las 'dzin* officials facilitated[97] the ritual. The ritual went on for three days, but the monks told me that the length of the ritual depended on the villagers' wish and they would have prolonged it if the leaders had asked them to do so.

The retreat tax is of importance for several reasons. Firstly, the voluntary commitments from some of the individual households to support the meditating monks show that such patronage has been among the virtuous activities performed by the laity in order to obtain religious merit. But the conversion of these voluntary donations to a compulsory tax involving all households can be read as a sign that the community wanted to promote higher qualifications among the monks. As will be discussed in Chapter Seven, the three-year retreat is an important qualification for performing the monastic dances (*'cham*) and other major rituals in the village. However, even if there have not always been monks who would meditate the villagers decided to continue giving an annual allowance to four of the monks. The fact that the villagers demand something in return suggests that it has not always been easy to get the monks to perform these rituals. Moreover, this case illustrates that the boundary between voluntary donation and compulsory tax can sometimes be fluid.

---

95 The shrine keeper was one of four monks completing the *lo gsum zla gsum* retreat in 2005. Since then, none of the monks has undergone such long retreats.

96 Conversation with a monk official, 05.04.12. One of the senior monks (28.04.12) commented that this requirement is a new rule, suggesting that in the past, even if nobody meditated there would be no specific obligation to give anything back.

97 During the rain-making ritual, which takes place at the shrine of the serpent deities (*klu*) to the west of the village, the officials have to provide most of the offering items, cook, and serve tea for the monks.

6.4.2 *The* ban dza *Tax on Private Fields and the Collection of Alms and Allowances*

The second text in the *Waltse tax register* is the *Ban yig*. This book lists the *ban dza* tax, as well as the *bsod nyoms* (alms), *sos long* (spring provisions) and *ston long* (autumn provisions) contributions for the *bla brang* lama and the blacksmith. According to the register, it seems that the *ban dza* tax was newly established in the Earth Mouse year of the fifteenth *rab byung* cycle (1888).[98] However, the document is rather vague and the year could also refer to a tax reform. In fact, Regmi mentions a Nepali tax reform in 1888/1889. It is uncertain whether this was implemented in remote corners of the kingdom like Limi, but it is possible that this tax was originally an external Nepali tax.[99] The man who gave me the first introduction to the tax register, said that he found the *ban dza* puzzling, not only in terms of etymology and origin, but also in terms of how it is calculated.[100] The tax has to be paid by the *grong chen* households as well as 19 of the *grong chung* households. Many of the villagers pointed out that the larger and more wealthy households pay much less than smaller households. However, it is not only a divide between the *grong chen* and the other family categories, as might be thought. The greatest landowner, for instance, pays only a symbolic sum of 4 *bre* of barley, whereas another *grong chen* family with fewer fields has to pay 1 *khal*, which is five times as much. The total amount of grain paid as *ban dza* is 24 *khal* and 6.5 *bre*.[101] The only pattern the village people have identified in this tax is that the oldest *grong chen* families, directly descending from the village's founding families, pay less. This might also give us a clue as to how to understand this tax. Originally there were only seven *grong chen* households, whereas during fieldwork in 2012 there were thirty-one. The *ban dza* might originally have been a small tax on privately owned fields. The original seven households are likely to be larger landowners and more powerful than the others and a large fee may have been imposed on other households

98 *Waltse tax register*, p. 48, l. 2–3: *rab 'byung bco lnga'i nang gi sa byi lo nas bzung/ wal tse'i yul gyi ban rtsa'i khral 'babs kyi sgrig* [*bgrig*] *dan yang rig bgyis pa'i tho bkod* [*skod*] *par* / This is the only place in the register where the spelling *ban rtsa* is found. In addition, the spelling *ban khra* occurs once or twice in the Rinchen Ling monastery inventory.

99 Regmi 1978.

100 Senior villager, 20.03.12.

101 The calculation is based on the *ban dza* section in *Waltse tax register* (pp. 45–73). The entries are written according to household order (*grong mtshams*), with partitions and amendments added by different scribes. The text is not well organised and there might be some minor mistakes in my interpretation, but the total sum provided should be sufficiently accurate for the purpose of this book.

advancing to the *grong chen* category. Another possibility is that the *ban dza* refers to interest, at rates that have been higher for later households. In their account of taxes in Nubri, Childs and Choedup mention a *bad yig*, which they define as an 'interest document' that '... specifies the interest households must repay and the amount of grain sharecroppers must remit to support communal rituals.'[102] The phonologically related words *be za*, *bun* and *bed* can all be translated as interest.[103] Since the spelling of words in the Limi documents are often based on the vernacular this appears as the most likely translation.

Together with the *ban dza* tax, three other types of compulsory contributions are listed: donation of alms (*bsod nyoms*),[104] the collection of autumn provisions (*ston long*)[105] and spring provisions (*sos long*).[106] Alms were given to the annual begging missions from monasteries in Tibet, and later to pilgrims and other 'wanderers' (*khyams pa*). These donations must have been voluntary at first, but eventually became institutionalised and included in the tax register. The first recipients were groups of monks from monasteries in Ngari, but later the contributions were also given to various wanderers. The spring provisions and autumn provisions were allowances to the *bla brang* lama and to the blacksmith (L. *ada*, T. *mgar ba*), but the allowances have not been collected since the last resident reincarnation (*sprul sku*) in Limi passed away around 1980 and the last blacksmith left the village. Until the 1970s one Tibetan blacksmith family served all three villages in Limi. The Limi blacksmiths have been regarded as quite skilled and have cast a number of statues in Limi and the surrounding area. As has been reported from many other Tibetan communities, the blacksmiths and a few other families, who were regarded as belonging to lower lineages, were subject to various types of social exclusion and were not allowed to share cups with the rest of the villagers. This type of discrimination was mentioned as the reason why the last family left Limi. But materially they were reportedly well off; the blacksmith's family earned good money from their work, had houses in all three villages and according to the tax registers

---

102 Childs and Choedup 2019: 199.

103 The translations occur respectively in the RY, JV and IW dictionaries available at nithartha.org.

104 The total amount of alms (*bsod nyoms*) listed in the *Waltse tax register* is ca. 10 *khal* and 18 *bre*.

105 Autumn provision (*ston slong*) used to be paid by all *grong chen* households and only four *grong chung*. The total amount listed in *Waltse Tax register* is ca. 7 *khal* and 13 *bre* of grain.

106 Spring provision (*sos slong*) used to be paid by all *grong chen* households and and three *grong chung*. The total amount of grain listed in *Waltse tax register* is ca. 2 *khal* and 19.5 *bre*.

they were, at least in the second half of the twentieth century, entitled to these yearly allowances from the village taxes.[107]

6.4.3 *The Butter and Cheese Taxes*

A sizeable portion of the taxes collected in Limi are paid in dairy products. These taxes are simply referred to as butter tax (*mar khral*) and cheese tax (*phyur khral*) in the tax register. The butter and cheese are collected during the second day of the tax calculation assembly meeting. The cheese tax is paid only by the *grong chen* families, whereas the butter tax is paid by all households. One part of this tax is calculated according to the number of taxable people (*khral mi*) in a household,[108] another part according to the number of milking animals and a final part is based on landholdings, which are then converted to an equivalent in butter.

Some of the butter, which is used for the large butter lamps in the monastery's shrine rooms, is a continuation of the former butter tax paid to Khochar monastery, mentioned in the paragraph about *bod khral* above.[109] The butter tax actually comprises three different taxes that are collected separately during the meeting (see Fig. 6.2):

1) The old butter tax for Khochar monastery (part of the obsolete *bod khral*). Currently, this butter is used for butter lamps in the Mani temple as well as in the four shrine rooms in the Rinchen Ling monastery and is calculated according to the number of milking animals.
2) Butter used as an allowance to the four meditating monks (*sgrub grwa*), the shrine keeper of the Mani Lhakhang and the Rimchö lama. The remaining part of this butter is used for tea during the six annual Tshechu festivals for Guru Rinpoche organised in private homes. The tax is calculated according to the number of 'taxable people' (*khral mi*), people under the age of majority (*tongkhor*, s.u.), the number of fields and the

107 The Limi blacksmiths reportedly cast statues also in Khochar monastery and as far south as the Raling (Ra gling?) monastery in Nyin. In Tibetan and Himalayan societies blacksmiths have been regarded as belonging to 'unclean lineages' (*rigs btsog pa*) and subject to stigmatisation and discrimination (see e.g., Fjeld 2008 and Holmberg 2007). I do not have information to assess how the status of the blacksmiths in Limi compared with those in other societies.

108 A taxpaying person in Limi is between fifteen and sixty-five years old, and the number of taxpaying people in each household is converted into butter.

109 *Waltse tax register*, pp. 80–82, 104, and 116.

number of animals (converted to the equivalent of a yak according to a special system).[110]

3) Butter for the Lhabab festival (lHa babs dus chen) celebrating Buddha's descent.[111] The amount of butter is determined according to family category: *grong chen*—3 *nya ga*, *grong chung*—2 *nya ga*, *bom btang*—1 *khog ba* (s.u., a little less than a *nya ga*).

The villagers in Limi make butter either from the milk of yak cows (*'bri*), hybrids, cows, or goats, and all types are valid as tax payment. But since the three former are regarded as better for tea, the goat butter is used mainly for butter lamps. The butter for lamps is melted in large pots at the assembly meeting in order to prevent it from being appropriated and used for other purposes. The villagers are encouraged to keep as many milking goats as possible, and a fine has to be paid by those households who do not own goats.[112]

6.4.4 *Ritual Sponsorship*

In addition to the lease fee on village land, meditation support, *ban dza* tax on private property, alms, and allowances listed in the *Waltse tax register*, the document also contains occasional entries about ritual sponsorship. These are of different kinds, and because of limited information in the tax register, it is not always clear whether the contributions are already included in other taxes or represent extra commitments. A senior villager helped me go through some of the entries, which would otherwise have been incomprehensible. For instance, the sponsorship of the Tshechu and Nyene festivals mentioned on page 3 in the register are earmarked as the purpose of the village lease fees, but in addition there are various voluntary pledges to sponsor these two festivals, additional sponsorship of the meditating monks, the Saga Dawa (Sa ga zla ba)[113] festival, butter lamps for people who have passed away, and commitments to sponsor the large butter lamp in the Mani temple. These commitments are legally

110 The size of animal herds is traditionally counted in 'yak heads' (*g.yag mgo*). 'Yak head' is a unit for large bovines; and ovines are converted to bovines. The tax register also provided a key for calculating and converting the number of animals to the equivalent of a yak. In the case of the *bod khral* the conversion was calculated according to a 6:1 formula, whereas for the local tax they would count seven sheep or goats as equal to one yak. In 2004 there were reportedly 400 'yak heads' in Waltse, whereas the number calculated during the tax collection meeting in 2011 had been reduced to 267.

111 The Lhabab festival celebrates Buddha's descent from the heaven of the thirty-three (gods). See the list of rituals in the Appendix.

112 This was the case in 2012. When I returned to Limi in 2018–19 the villagers had sold their goats, and I presume the practice of fining the hoseholds has been discontinued.

113 The Saga Dawa (Sa ga zla ba) festival celebrates the Buddha's birth, enlightenment and *parinirvāṇa*.

binding, and some of the entries in the *Waltse tax register* appear to be copies or abridged versions of longer legal documents.

6.4.5 *Transportation*

In addition to the contributions in kind and money, there are two types of corvée in Limi: 'transportation tax' (*'u lag*) and 'communal labour' (L. *biri*, uncertain spelling and etymology, perhaps *spyi res*?). The *'u lag* service has traditionally been used for the transportation of taxes, goods, and messages to and from the administrations in Purang and Simikot. It is not known whether Limi also had to provide *'u lag* as part of their external taxes in the past, but there has always been a need for a transportation and communication facilities in the villages.[114] As the infrastructure in Limi is poor, the *'u lag* service is still used. But nowadays, it is restricted to the transportation of goods purchased for communal use, or to accompany monks or village leaders on official duty. A rudimentary internal postal service has also been used as a way of distributing the burden of sending messages to the other villages in the community whilst the only village with a phone was Waltse.[115]

There are three *'u lag* distances[116] and two additional transportation services in Limi today. The *'u lag* is the name for the longest distance from Limi all the way to Simikot. The medium distance, to Tshongsa at the other side of the Nyalu pass or to Zher at the Tibetan border, is called *bar 'gel*, and the shortest distance is called *thung lag* and refers to transportation to Janglungma or Talung. The *'u lag* requires both men and pack animals, whereas the other transportation services require either the provision of horses for 'riding' (*zhon*) or 'pack animals' (*khal ma*). Only the *grong chen* families are required to provide horses for *'u lag*, whereas the duty to send a man to lead the horses falls on the *grong chung* families.[117] Riding horses and pack animal services have to be provided by all households owning horses, irrespective of family category. People explained that because the horses grazed on communal land, this was

---

114 In the middle of page 73 in *Waltse tax register* there is an entry mentioning that four men from the small households did *'u lag* service for the Tibetan tax (*mi re ba rnam nas bod khral la mi re wa bzhi 'u lag songs*). Since this was mentioned randomly next to an entry specifying an amount paid as Nepali tax, I presume the *'u lag* involved transportation of the taxes and not a separate tax in itself.

115 The phone was established in the summer of 2010.

116 See also Ramble 2008c: 33. Three of the distances in the *'u lag* system in Te are referred to as *ring lag*, *bar lag*, and *thung lag*.

117 This tax would seem to be much more difficult for the *grong chung* families since they have to send men with the horses, whereas the *grong chen* only have to send their animals. Even so, the *grong chen* complained that this tax was much heavier for them.

FIGURE 6.3 Negotiating the transportation duty (*'u lag*)

what they had to provide in return. The duties are administered by the two senior officials (*las 'dzin rgan po*), who keep records of the service.

According to the established practice in Limi, the village leaders and monks are entitled to corvée for official purposes. In addition, the leaders' assistants, the female leaders, and road committee members are entitled to *'u lag* when needed.[118] The corvée transportation taxes are notoriously unpopular, but households that serve in any of the village management positions or perform other types of community service, are entitled to buy themselves out of the duty. This is regarded as a kind of allowance as these village positions and services are all unpaid. But since there are many duties that qualify for such exemption, the negotiations are often lengthy affairs. The calculation of services due takes place in the village assembly meeting in the following way: small wooden sticks are placed in a circle on the calculation mat with the names of the members of thirty of the *grong chen* families in front and the *grong chung* on the flip side. Then leaders distribute tokens (nuts, broken pieces of porcelain, and stones) symbolising the value of the work done for the village converted into *'u lag*: 4 nuts equals the short distance, 8 nuts equals the medium distance and 16 nuts the full *u'lag* distance (see Figs. 6.3 and 6.4).[119]

118 Village assembly meeting, 07.12.11.

119 Village assembly meeting, 07.12.11.

FIGURE 6.4 Tokens used to calculate taxes

However, even if the various tasks are supposed to be registered, this is not always done, and there is always protracted discussion of how much each household is required to contribute.

6.4.5 *Communal Labour and Other Obligations for the Village and Monastery*

The other type of corvée, locally referred to as *biri*, is communal labour for the village, monastery, or the community.[120] *Biri* is regarded as a type of tax obligation and is organised through the *tsho*, an administrative unit which for the present purpose can be translated as 'work group'.[121] Each of the taxpaying households in Limi is member of a *tsho* and as suggested in Chapter Three, it is possible that these *tsho* were based on clan membership in the past, but if so, that association has been lost. In Waltse there are currently three *grong chen tsho*: Drablasung, Serwa, and Khyungdruwa. In addition, there are three *grong chung tsho* and three *bom btang* (*mo rang*) *tsho*, but none of these are named.

120 The youth clubs also demand that their members participate in *biri* for the club. This work can be done on the youth club fields, for village purposes, or to raise an income for the club, for example when the members from the Youth Club in Waltse went to Til to help a sponsor with the harvest.

121 The only households not part of a *tsho* are the *khral med* who are not obliged to pay taxes.

The communal work carried out by the *tsho* normally consists of different kinds of construction work on communal property such as maintenance work on roads and bridges (Figs. 6.5 and 6.6), the monasteries and other important buildings, and in the case of Waltse, the building of embankments (Figs. 6.7 and 6.8). During the last couple of years, most of the *biri* work in Limi has been carried out on the road connecting the Limi valley with the new road from the Lapcha pass on the Tibetan border to the Salli River valley, a day's walk from Simikot. *Biri* is sometimes also done for the monasteries, but the duty is administered through the village assembly, and the monastery often contributes some provisions for the workers.[122] Communal labour is calculated as a flat tax and therefore differs from other types of taxes. Each household is required to contribute one representative irrespective of its size. Hence, a single woman from a *bom btang* household has to work just as many days as a member of a large *grong chen* household. The general rule in all three villages is that the labour is the responsibility of the *kha rgan* of the family, but the requirements vary with the season. During the winter season, while many of the men are away, the village assembly does not impose any fines if the men send female or monk family members as replacements, but during the summer season there is a fine. Depending on the situation, the duty to participate in communal work can be demanding, but when asked how they felt about the *biri*, many villagers told me that they often experienced participation as positive. They emphasised the fact that even if the work could be physically challenging, they cherished the sociability when people from all households were working together.

The obligation to participate in communal labour is connected with rights to land as illustrated by the following example: a couple of generations ago, a man decided to split from a *grong chen* house in Til and married as a *mag pa* into the household of his wife in Waltse. This gave him the position of *kha rgan* and entitlement to the fields as well as the responsibilities for taxes and other obligations. However, since the man also received a share of fields and a house from his paternal household in Til he also had to pay taxes to Til. His descendants, who still live in Waltse, have had to continue to pay taxes and perform *biri* work in both villages.[123] The descendants are not wealthy and have made requests to Til village for tax exemption many times. Each time they have been refused on the grounds that the village does not need more land, it

122 For the use of *biri* for monastic purposes, see Chapter Nine.

123 Normally this is avoided by making the person who is splitting off from a household sign a document specifying that the property should be returned to the main household upon his or her death.

FIGURE 6.5 Tents set up by the work groups for communal labour (*biri*)

FIGURE 6.6 Women carrying stones for bridge construction, December 2011

FIGURE 6.7 Winding gabion wire, autumn 2011

FIGURE 6.8 Building gabion walls, autumn 2011

needs people. But finally, a few years ago, the family was granted a temporary exemption from the tax payment to Til.

6.5 Credit and the Problem of Debt

Some of the revenue collected by the assembly is reinvested annually in the form of credit to the villagers. This rudimentary credit system is quite strict, as the loans have to be repaid exactly one year later with twenty per cent interest. The interest is added to the village fund together with the fines for various transgressions. Thus, the village fund is increasing year by year. The possibility of borrowing grain or money on credit has been an important lifeline in difficult times, but some households have ended up in a debt spiral. The debt must be repaid on a specific day, but if a household has not been able to save the money required, they have to ask their relatives for private loans. The villagers will then pay the debt with interest to the village assembly and take up a new and larger loan the next day to pay back their relatives. If the relatives deny a loan, a family may end up having to sell some of its valuables, or even give over fields to the village as a last resort. In these cases, the fields will be leased out to other villagers, and this is reportedly one of the main ways that the village in particular, but also the monastery, has acquired property. In cases when the family sees no other solution than to abandon the household, rather than leasing out the property piece by piece, the village assembly will sell the property to another household who will then take over the rights and duties of the old household. There are recent examples of this in all three villages in Limi.

6.6 Rigidity and Flexibility in the Local Taxation System

Today, the taxes are experienced as manageable by most of the villagers in Limi. This is partly related to the improved economic situation in recent years. However, up to the end of the twentieth century, a significant proportion of the villagers were relatively poor and there are many stories in all three villages about households getting into serious difficulties with problems in meeting the tax requirements. When a household is unable to pay, the procedures are as follows: First, the head of the household asks for a loan either from the village assembly, the monastery, or relatives in the village. If the situation is particularly difficult, for instance because of debt or the death of family members, a request for tax reduction may be submitted to the village assembly meeting.

If denied, the household has no other choice than to take up a loan, sell property, or abandon one or more fields. If accepted, a reduction or complete exemption will be given for a limited number of years.

Normally, only very severe economic problems will be accepted as valid reasons for tax reductions. Even if a household decides to leave some of the fields fallow, or if the fields have been destroyed by natural disasters, they must still pay their taxes. There were for instance a number of villagers asking for tax reductions after they lost some or most of their fields in the 2011 flash flood. However, the majority at the village assembly meeting decided that they would have to continue paying the same taxes as before.

If we look at the list of households in Waltse provided in Chapter Four, fourteen individuals were classified as *khral med* ('without tax') in 2019. The majority were elderly people living alone, but tax exemption is also given to other individuals in difficult life circumstances. There are several examples of people obtaining temporary tax reductions can be found in the *Waltse tax register*.[124] There are also examples of cases when the general level of taxation has been experienced as being too high, and the village assembly has decided to reduce the fees for all villagers. The Nyene and Tshechu list in the register, for instance, is an example of such a reduction of the fees collected for compulsory funding of the two festivals.[125] Hence, even if most of the taxes appear quite rigid, these entries show that flexibility is practised in difficult situations. During the last decades, it is the members of the village assembly who have had the authority to decide in such cases.

6.7 The Religious Purpose of Village Taxes

The taxes collected by the village assembly in Limi do not cover all village expenses. Some of the expenses, such as the costs for the school and the health post, are covered by NGO support and/or by the Nepali government.[126] Below, I have grouped the tax spending into five categories according to purpose.

124 There is for instance an entry detailing the five years' leave (*dgongs pa*) from the single woman tax (*mo rang khral*) category given to a woman, counted from the Earth Dragon year (1988). From the spring village assembly meeting in the Water Monkey year (1992) she should again pay the single woman tax. *Waltse tax register*, p. 129.

125 *Waltse tax register*, p. 122ff.

126 I do not have a complete list of the village expenditures, but through observations and a number of conversations I have managed to get an overview.

If there is anything left after these expenses have been met, the food provisions will be spent on other community rituals or on visiting Nepali officials:

1) Allowances
   - The monk serving as lama during the Rimchö festival
   - The shrine keeper of the Mani temple
   - Four monks in retreat (*sgrub grwa*)
   - Spring and autumn allowances for the lama (presently dormant) and blacksmith (until 1970)
2) Lay ritual expenses
   - The six annual Tshechu festivals (*chang*, tea, and food provisions)
   - The two annual Nyene festivals (*chang*, tea, and food provisions)
   - The Saga dawa festival (*chang*, tea, and food provisions, until ca 1985)
3) Butter lamps
   - Butter for the lamps in the monastery's shrine rooms (the old *bod khral*)
   - Butter for the lamp in the Mani temple
4) Alms (until ca. 1960)
   - For monks on funding missions, pilgrims, and other wanderers
5) Transportation and construction work
   - For the village community and the monastery according to need
   - Exemption from the *'u lag* duty is given as a kind of compensation for village service

This simple overview should suffice to show that most of the taxes collected by the village assembly are used for religious purposes.[127] The only exceptions include some of the transportation and construction work, the largely symbolic *mon khral*, and the former allowance to the blacksmith. Similarly, although we do not know how large a portion of the taxes was kept by the *rdzong sdod* in Purang, most of the pre-1960 *bod khral* seems to have been given to the three monasteries in Purang and the *bla brang* at Gyangdrag. If we look more closely at the actual spending today, it appears that much of the village assembly's religious spending is on lay rituals. However, the village assembly provides allowances for monks and lamas, and it provides butter for the lamps in the monastery.[128] The monastery collects its own taxes, so why does the village assembly also collect taxes that will be spent on monks and monastic rituals? The monastic tax system will be discussed in Chapter Nine, but a brief examination of the village taxes to the monastery should suffice to give a preliminary answer. The retreat tax is offered as support to individual monks,

127 This concurs with Schwieger's (2023) findings from Central and Eastern Tibet during the dGa' ldan pho brang government.

128 Taking care of the Mani temple is regarded as the responsibility of the laymen.

whereas the allowance to the lama will be given after the village assembly has requested that the lama take the position. As will be explained in greater detail in Chapter Seven, the Rimchö festival, even if it is the most important festival in the monastic calendar, is arranged as a joint venture between the village and the monastery. Moreover, it is the duty of the village leaders to request the most senior monk to perform the role of head lama during this festival. The allowance to the lama of the *bla brang,* which is currently dormant, is also regarded as separate from the *grwa tshang*. And finally, the sponsoring of butter for the butter lamps in the monastery is a continuation of the former *bod khral* which was part of Limi's external taxes in the past and therefore the responsibility of the village assembly. As all these examples show, the support to the monastery is not given to the monastic institution, or the *grwa tshang*, as such. Another important difference between the village community and the monastery as tax collectors is that the latter's basis for tax collection is land and recruitment. The village as tax collector has a wider basis and can collect resources from all social strata.

In this chapter I have given an overview of the main taxes collected by the village assembly in Limi since the end of the nineteenth century until today, and shown how they have been formed, maintained, and changed. The *ban dza* tax still remains obscure, but overall the tax register and people's comments provide sufficient evidence to trace the development of the main taxes. Some of the taxes currently paid are local adaptations of former external taxes to Tibet and Nepal, whereas others are religious donations that have gradually ossified into a compulsory tax. While the tax system in Limi bears some resemblance to the former tax system in Ngari, there are also significant differences, most importantly due to different patterns of landownership, and due to the fact that Limi also paid taxes to Nepal. Finally, the chapter has shown that the village, district, and state as tax collectors have not only been concerned with secular affairs, but that the majority of the village taxes are spent on religious purposes. The religious concerns of the village administration and its degree of involvement in monastic affairs will be further explored in the final part of the book.

CHAPTER 7

Monastic Rituals, Organisation and Management

In the summer of 2011, the monks from Waltse received an invitation from Kyabgön Rinpoche's office to participate in the winter teachings in Dehra Dun. This would also give them the opportunity to attend the Kālacakra initiation (Dus 'khor dbang chen), the world's largest Tibetan Buddhist ritual, which was to be arranged in Bodhgaya just a few weeks later.[1] Most of the monks said that they wished to attend, but the village assembly requested that they stay in the village for the Rimchö festival, which is held to protect the villagers from harm throughout the year. The 'eight pronouncements' (*bka' brgyad*) ritual complex, which forms the most potent part of the festival, requires a large number of qualified monks in order to be regarded as efficacious. It was therefore decided that only a small delegation of monks would be given leave of absence.

The Rimchö festival is regarded as so crucial to the community that absence is hardly tolerated and throughout history, several laws have been designed to ensure its proper performance. It is initiated and partly funded by the village assembly and the rest is funded directly by the laity as well as the *grwa tshang*. Rimchö may therefore serve to illustrate how the village and monastic institutions cooperate in the management of village affairs. Before investigating the festival, however, it is necessary to give an overview of the monastic complex and the ritual services performed. The Rinchen Ling monastery is located at the heart of the village and throughout the centuries, the villagers have gradually expanded and sustained it through numerous taxes and voluntary donations, enabling the monks to perform rituals for the wellbeing of all living beings inhabiting the local environment. I will give a brief introduction here in order to examine the scale and scope of the monks' activities and acquire a basic understanding of the ritual

1 The Kālacakra initiation conferred by the Dalai Lama in 2012 gathered as many as 200,000 participants from all over the world. Tantric initiations are highly esoteric, but in exile, the Dalai Lama has held more than thirty large-scale Kālacakra initiations.

 | DOI:10.1163/9789004714571_008

importance of the village monasteries. Thereafter, I will investigate the organisation of the monastic institution, its offices as well as the procedures for decision-making and conflict resolution. Finally, I will explore the monastery's relationship with secular authorities in the local community and on the national level.[2] Although the broader socio-economic, political, and cultural transformations of the region may have had less visible impact on the management of the monastic institution than on the village management discussed in the three preceding chapters, this is about to change, and it will not be possible to understand the dynamics in the monastic institution without taking these processes into account.[3]

7.1 The Monastery and Its Shrines

As detailed in Chapter Three, Rinchen Ling originally consisted of little more than the Vairocana temple, which currently forms the north-western corner of the monastic complex (Fig. 7.1). It was probably not until after the merger with the monasteries at Dzang and Til at the end of the seventeenth century that Rinchen Ling expanded into something near its present size. The villagers have expanded the buildings step by step in a combination of various types of voluntary donations, taxes and other contributions. According to oral tradition, the enlargement of the monastery complex was a joint venture between the three villages. The construction material and labour were provided by the local villagers, although it is likely that the monks were sent on fund raising missions to neighbouring communities as well. There have been several extensions and refurbishments also in more recent times. One such extension was made prior to Drigung Kyabgön Rinpoche's visit in 2008, with the rebuilding of the lama's quarters next to the scripture hall. Since then, monks and laity have repaired the roof, restored the monk cells, built a new kitchen and covered the inner monastery courtyard with stone slabs. The funding of these more recent repairs comes from different sources, including local taxes, private sponsorship, INGOs, and the Nepali state. The current monastery building is three storeys high and covers an area of 36 × 32 metres.[4] The compound includes

2 This theme will be continued in the subsequent chapters.

3 The outline of the monastery and its ritual calendar in the first part of the chapter is based on a combination of interviews, a study of the monastic complex, observations of ritual preparations and performances as well as records from the *Rinchen Ling monastery inventory* (*Rin chen gling gi gtan deb*) and the ritual calendar in the *Rinchen Ling list of ritual expenses* (*Rin chen gling gi mchod rgyun lag khyer*) from 1935(?) and 1995. The final part of the chapter detailing the monastic management system is based mainly on observations and interviews.

4 Measurements provided by Bidari 2004.

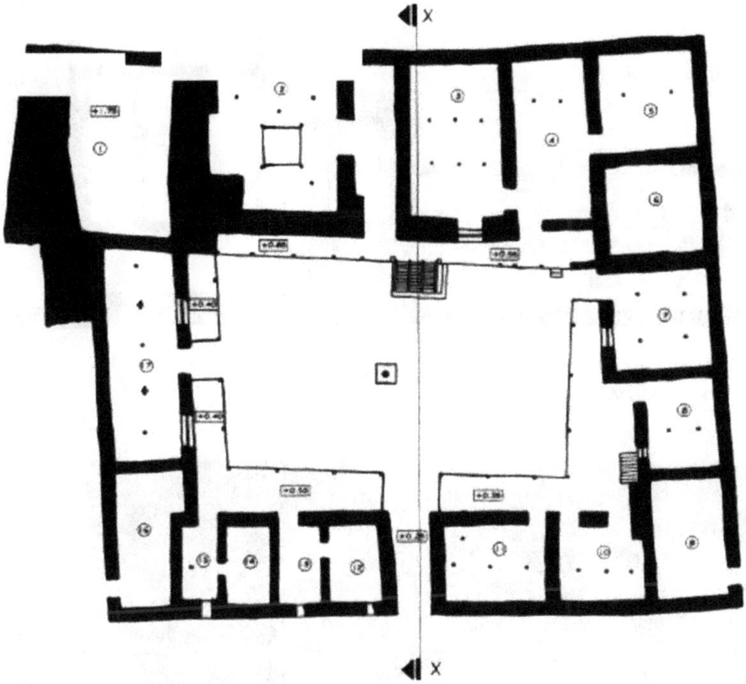

FIGURE 7.1 Plan of the ground floor of Rinchen Ling
© JOHN SANDAY ASSOCIATES 2003

two shrine rooms, an assembly hall, a scripture hall, two lama's quarters, monk cells, two kitchens and a number of storage rooms constructed around an inner courtyard, which will be described in the following paragaraphs.

When visiting the monastery, one first passes through a gate leading to the outer courtyard. An integrated bench in front serves as one of the most popular gathering points in the village, where opinions on politics, information and gossip are exchanged by monks and laity (Fig. 7.16). In the middle of the courtyard is the Mani temple (Mani lha khang, Fig. 7.3), surrounded in the summer season by patches of white and pink cosmos flowers. There is a flagpole in front, with the flags being changed by the laymen after the annual supplication ritual (*lha gsol*) to the territorial deity (*yul lha*) in the tenth Tibetan month. The Mani temple belongs to the lay village community and is maintained by shrine keepers from the *grong chen* and *grong chung* families according to a rotating schedule. The current temple was erected about one hundred years ago, replacing a smaller structure of unknown origin. The

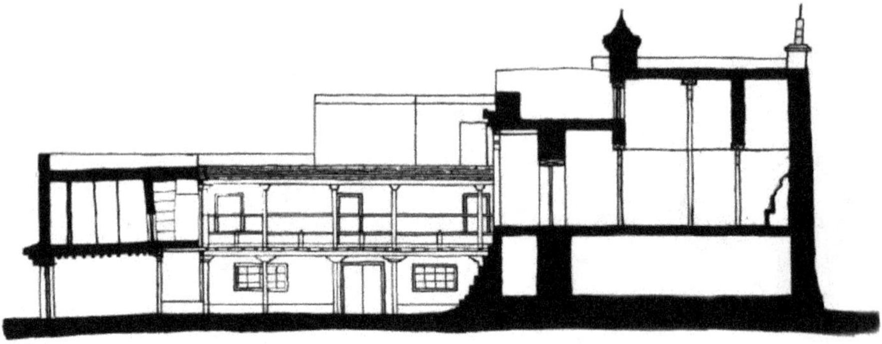

FIGURE 7.2 Cross section of Rinchen Ling
© JOHN SANDAY ASSOCIATES 2003

FIGURE 7.3 The Mani temple and the outer monastery courtyard

temple was sponsored by two of the most powerful men in the village, *'go ba* Dung (s.u.) from the Dzardziwa family and *'go ba* Lowe (s.u.) from the Kurgyab family (Figs. 7.4 a,b). The murals, including images depicting the two headmen on the western and eastern walls respectively, were painted by a local artist.[5] The scriptures that were placed inside the two large prayer wheels were

5 The name of the artist was Kushog Lhabri (sKu shogs lHa bris) from Til. The granddaughter of Mee Lowe is painted on his shoulder, reportedly because she was born in the same year the temple was built.

FIGURE 7.4 (a) Mee Dung from the Dzardziwa and (b) Mee Lowe from the Kurgyab family

reportedly carried all the way from Mustang.[6] Especially elderly villagers visit the temple frequently to spin the large prayer wheels on their daily circumambulation. The last few years, the public village phone has been moved to a room at the back of the temple serving as yet another of the village's main gathering points. Immediately to the north of the Mani temple is the gate to the inner courtyard and the monastery proper.

7.1.1 *The Protector Deity Chapel*

The 'protector deity chapel' (*mgon khang*) on the second floor in the north-western corner of the compound (Fig. 7.5) is where the villagers go to seek help from the Drigung protective goddess Apchi Chökyi Dröma. She is approached for everything ranging from small individual prayers, daily 'supplication rituals' (*gsol kha*) performed for the benefit of the households, to the village assembly asking for predictions (*rtags pa*) to help make major decisions. The importance of Apchi for the villagers can hardly be overestimated, and this is by far the most frequently used shrine room in Rinchen Ling. A 'medicinal clay' (*sman 'dam*) statue of the wrathful aspect of the Drigung goddess riding on a

6 Interview with young craftsman, 11.01.12.

FIGURE 7.5 The protector deity chapel

blue horse, is the main image and the focus of a majority of the monastery's rituals (see Fig. 7.6).[7] The statue is richly adorned with large silver amulet boxes (*ga'u*), pearl necklaces, turquoise, coral, and other precious stones.[8] In addition, the altar shelves (*kun dga' ra ba*) on the northern wall carry a large number of other statues. The murals, the most important of which portray Apchi and the four-armed Mahākāla (mGon po phyag bzhi), the six-armed Mahākāla (mGon po phyag drug), Tseringma (Tshe ring ma), as well as the Drigung founder Kyobpa Jigten Sumgön, are difficult to date. The varnish is very dark in places but given the former practice of repainting murals and statues, they are probably not much older than a couple of hundred years.[9]

Underneath the protector deity chapel there used to be a red temple for the *btsan* spirits (*btsan khang*), but this has been sealed off. The village is built in a precarious location just below a field of scree, and large boulders are strewn

7 *Rinchen Ling monastery inventory*, f. 9b, l. 4f.

8 Many of these objects were donated by either local villagers or visiting lamas or other pilgrims and are recorded in the *Rinchen Ling monastery inventory*.

9 It is unclear whether the inscription outside the assembly hall applies also to the murals in the protector deity chapel. But if so, the murals may have been repainted as late as 1918.

FIGURE 7.6 The central image of Apchi Chökyi Dröma in the protector deity chapel

amongst the houses. Some of the boulders are painted red, as they are regarded as abodes of *btsan*. If the spirits are angered, they may respond by sending environmental disasters, disease or other harm. Just like the *lha* and *klu*, these spirits must be appeased and ritually controlled in order to keep the local environment in balance.[10]

7.1.2 *The Assembly Hall*

The assembly hall (*'du khang*) is mainly used in the winter season (Fig. 7.7). Apart from the daily rituals to propitiate the protector deities and the monastic dances, virtually all rituals that require the participation of the whole congregation of monks take place in the assembly hall. It is located in the middle of the northern flank of the monastery, directly above the triple wooden staircase

10 See Hovden and Havnevik (2021) for a discussion of how these forces are kept at bay as part of the environmental management in Limi. See also Diemberger (2021) for an analysis of how these spirits and deities are both conceived of as beings in the landscape and features of the landscape itself, and how they '… emphasize the relational dimension of humans with the environment they inhabit and are therefore inherently connected to a morality of care as well as to local power relations' (*ibid*: 20).

FIGURE 7.7 Ritual in the assembly hall

leading up to the second floor. The western wall is covered by shelves carrying the *Tengyur* (*bsTan 'gyur*),[11] whereas the main altar is located along the northern wall. A large, gilded copper (*gser zangs*) statue of Jowo Śākyamuni is placed in the centre (Fig. 7.8), flanked by a brass (*rag li*) statue of Dorje Chang (rDo rje 'Chang, Skt. Vajradhāra) to the east and an image of Jigten Sumgön to the west. The Jowo statue is believed to be able to absorb the villagers' diseases, but it is the statue of Dorje Chang that is regarded as the most precious. The statue was made by the local blacksmith thanks to the sponsorship of the Drigung Chungtsang Tenzin Chökyi Lodrö.[12] The inventory unfortunately does not mention the date, but it is likely to have been crafted during or after the Rinpoche's visit in the winter of 1896. Two decorated thrones are placed in front of the altar. The highest throne belongs to the Chetsang and Chungtsang Rinpoches, and the lower belongs to the Limi reincarnation Senge Tenzin Rinpoche (Seng ge bsTan 'dzin Rin po che, b. 1981), all three lamas represented by large, framed photographs.

11 The *Tengyur* (*bsTan 'gyur*, lit. 'translated treatises') is the collection of the Tibetan Buddhist commentarial tradition.

12 *Rinchen Ling monastery inventory*, f. 4b, l. 5f.

FIGURE 7.8 The central Jowo image in the assembly hall

The eastern wall of the assembly hall is decorated by murals. Bidari, in his brief report on the monastery, writes that the murals both in the protector deity chapel and assembly hall date from the thirteenth century,[13] but that, I think, is

13 Bidari 2004.

very far from the case. No historical research had been conducted prior to the writing of the report and it therefore contains some errors and factual confusion. His report, however, is still valuable for its architectural information and simply because it was the first one ever written about Rinchen Ling monastery. Like Bidari, I initially hoped that the murals could provide information about the earlier history of the monastery, but, unfortunately, they have been repainted several times. One of the villagers showed me remnants of older layers at a spot where the murals have flaked. If my theory that the assembly hall was built only after the monastery's conversion to the Drigung school is correct, one can hardly expect to find an older layer of Sakya murals underneath the present paintings.[14] The current murals on the eastern wall of the assembly hall depict the successive Drigung lineage holders. The Sixth Chungtsang Rinpoche, Tenzin Chökyi Lodrö (1868–1906), is the last lineage holder painted on the wall, indicating that this section of the murals is not much older than one hundred years.[15] Like the other temples in the monastery, the assembly hall has been restored several times. The last major restoration took place before the present generation of senior monks. On a beam just outside the assembly hall gate, it is written that the murals in the temples were (re-)painted in an unspecified Earth Horse year.[16] My guess is that the restoration took place in the fifteenth *rab byung*, which would correspond to 1918, the year before the visit of Tenzin Zhiwe Lodrö (1886–1943), the Sixth Chetsang Rinpoche.

7.1.3 *The Vairocana Temple*

The Vairocana temple is the oldest part of the monastic complex which possibly stems from Rinchen Zangpo's time. This is normally the third temple the villagers visit for worship. The wooden threshold, which has a deep depression formed by innumerable footsteps throughout the centuries, was probably the original entrance to the temple. Today, the entrance is partly hidden behind the main staircase on the ground floor. The temple is two storeys high and, in addition to the four-fold Vairocana ensemble (Fig. 3.1) surrounded by twenty-five of the original thirty-two statues of the Vairocana mandala introduced in Chapter Three, it houses one of the statues of Rinchen Zangpo (Fig. 3.4) and a set of twelve old volumes of the *Prajñāpāramitā* (*'Bum, the*

14 There is a bronze of an unknown Sakya lama in the assembly hall likewise listed in the inventory (fol. 6a), but its origin and date are uncertain.

15 I am grateful to Kurt Tropper for pointing this out to me.

16 The inscription (*sa ta lo lha khang rnam rtsi sros*) is poorly spelled, but probably means that all the temples were (re-)painted in this year.

Perfection of Wisdom sūtras), protected by beautifully carved wooden book covers (*glegs shing*) (Fig. 3.2). These volumes are no longer read,[17] but are used for one of the annual circumambulations (*chos skor*) of the fields for protection of the crops (Fig. 7.12).[18] A study of the model of the ground floor of the monastery reveals that the walls surrounding the Vairocana temple and the sealed off *btsan khang* are considerably thicker than the other monastery walls (see Fig. 7.1). One of the elderly villagers, who had participated in the restoration of this temple in 1995,[19] noted that the old temple walls were constructed with a mixture of stone and mud packed in-between a wooden framework in the same way as the walls of Guge Dawa Dzong (Gu ge mDa' ba rDzong).[20] If confirmed, this could be another indication of the temple's old age.[21] The Vairocana temple is frequently visited for worship (*mchod mjal*) by local villagers, travellers, or pilgrims. Water offerings are placed on the small altar in front of the four-fold statue, and butter lamps are lit every day. However, the temple is seldom used for other ritual purposes. The monks perform an annual confession and purification ritual (*skong bshags*) for Vairocana, but since the ritual involves the whole monk assembly it takes place in the assembly hall.

7.1.4 *The Scripture Hall and the lamas' Quarters*

As the name suggests, the scripture hall (bKa' 'gyur lha khang), which is located just above the protector deity chapel on the third floor, houses the monastery's collection of the *Kangyur* (*bKa' 'bgyur*), the Tibetan version of the Buddhist canon. The volumes are stacked in shelves covering the northern wall, surrounding an old wooden Śakyamuni statue (Fig. 7.9). The other walls are covered by scroll paintings, and masks for the *'cham* dances are strapped to the beautifully carved central pillars of the hall. There is little ritual activity, but the annual reading of the *Kangyur*, which is organised in the first half of the second month, takes place in this chapel.[22] Like the *Prajñāpāramitā* in the

17 From the eleventh to the twelfth Tibetan month the monks go from house to house to read the villagers' private collections of the *Prajñāpāramitā*. This is regarded as part of the monks' duties performed upon request by the villagers.

18 This ritual, which takes place twice a year in Limi, is common in Tibetan Buddhist communities. For other accounts, see for instance Havnevik 2011: 241f, Childs 2005.

19 The year is painted on a beam in the ceiling outside the temple.

20 Interview with elderly villager, 05.08.10.

21 See Chapter Three.

22 During the first day of the New Year celebration, the elderly men perform court dances (*gar*) and barley beer is served to the male guests in this hall. Lo Bue (2003: 193) writes that *gar* dances were also performed during the New Year celebration in Lhasa.

FIGURE 7.9 Statue of Śakyamuni Buddha surrounded by the *Kangyur* in the scripture hall

Vairocana temple mentioned above, the volumes of the Buddhist canon are carried around the fields for protection once a year. A new set of the *Kangyur* was bought in 2010 and was carried from the road head in Dungling to Rinchen Ling on the backs of twenty young men and women from the village. The scriptures were welcomed at the entrance stupa of the village and carried in a procession led by all the monks, circumambulating the monastery three times before they were carried up to the scripture hall. The villagers lined up in the monastery courtyard and each presented a silk scarf and touched the scriptures with their foreheads to receive blessing (*byin rlabs*) (Fig. 7.10).

On the western and eastern flanks of the third floor there are two quarters (*gzims khang*) for high lamas. The former was refurbished in 2008 and is mainly reserved for Drigung Kyabgön Rinpoche but is also used as storage space for some of the masks and other equipment used during the annual *'cham* dances. The smaller quarters (*gzim chung*) on the eastern flank used to be the residence (*bla brang*) of the head lama, but in his absence the furniture, statues,

FIGURE 7.10 Villagers welcoming the new scriptures, October 2010

and ritual equipment have been moved to other locations, and the rooms are now used for meetings and hospitality purposes.[23]

7.1.5 *The Monk Cells, Kitchens, and Storage Rooms*

The monk cells (*shag*) are located on the second floor of the eastern, southern, and western flanks of the compound. These cells which were recently refurbished, are relatively spacious, and the monks live there during the busiest part of winter. In the past, the cells would be divided according to village affiliation, so that monks from each village would live together.[24]

There are currently two kitchens in the monastery. The main kitchen is located on the ground floor, to the east of the monastery courtyard. The kitchen is simply furnished, with a newly bought iron stove (the stove was purchased in Purang, and transported by truck to Dungling, dismantled and carried on the backs by young men and women to Waltse). The kitchen is looked after by

23 The objects are listed in the *Record of the resident lama's belongings*.

24 Organising the monks' living quarters according to place of origin has been common practice in Tibetan monasteries.

the steward (*gnyer pa*), assisted by local women according to a rotating schedule (Fig. 9.9).[25] The main storage rooms are located on the southern, western, and northern flanks of the monastery courtyard. The storage rooms house the monastery's provisions, grain reserves, firewood, and various types of equipment. Most of the masks for the monastic dances are stored in a room in the western flank. Once a year, the night before Rimchö, a 'supplication ritual for the masks' (*'bag gsol*) is performed in this room.

7.1.6 *The Inner Courtyard*

The inner monastery courtyard, an open space in the middle of the monastic complex measuring approximately 18 × 11 metres, is in constant use both for religious and secular purposes. Larger monastic rituals, such as the monastic dances during Rimchö, take place here; as does much of the practical work related to the day-to-day management of the monastery. Moreover, it is frequently used for conflict resolution in the monastic off-season. In the past, it was also a favoured location for weddings and other large festivities. Due to Kyabgön Rinpoche's ban on meat consumption within the monastery compound, such activities have been reduced in the last few years and the main part of the weddings have been moved to the recently renovated community hall.[26] In the middle of the courtyard is a large flagpole (*dar po che*). The monks change the flags once a year during the Festival of the fifteenth [day] (bCo lnga'i dus chen). A gallery lining all sides of the second floor supported by wooden columns (*ka ba*) provides sheltered seating and a walkway on the ground floor underneath. This is where the spectators are seated during large festivities and ritual events.

For large celebrations and festivals, the cooking takes place on iron tripods placed over open fires in the monastery courtyard. The sponsors have to provide a type of deep-fried oil bread (L. *bola*, s.u.) and other food items for the monks and guests. The distribution of oil bread during celebrations is so important that it has given its name to a genre of festivities and so much of this bread is needed that prior to large events the monastery courtyard is transformed into a virtual 'bread factory' (Figs. 9.10 and 9.11). While ritual services constitute the core responsibility of the monastery, a large proportion of the activities taking place in the monastic compound consists of various types of work. This includes both maintenance of these temples and chapels by monks themselves or villagers through compulsory labour (L. *biri*) as well as patronage and practical facilitation of the rituals.

25 The duty to serve in the monastery is detailed in Chapter Nine.

26 See Chapter Four.

7.2 Ritual Life in the Monastery

The ritual life in the monasteries in Limi is sharply divided between the winter and the summer seasons. All the monks convene in the monasteries[27] from the time of the Lhabab Festival (lHa babs dus chen), celebrating Buddha's descent from heaven, on the twenty-second day of the ninth Tibetan month until the Göku Festival (Gos sku dus chen)[28] commemorating Kyobpa Jigten Sumgön, on the twenty-fifth day of the fourth month. This is the time for most of the extensive rituals in Limi, culminating with the *'cham* dances during the Rimchö festival celebrated in Waltse at the end of the twelfth month. During the five summer months, the monks are largely free to stay where they want, and most spend the season engaging in income-generating activities for their families.[29] As will be detailed in the following two chapters, the reasons for this particular arrangement seems to have been practical: in order to fulfil their sponsorship duties, the households depend on the contribution of the monks.[30] During the summer, there are therefore few monks available, but a ritual of supplication (*gsol kha*) to Apchi Chökyi Drölma is performed every day by the shrine keeper, who is on duty all year round. Some of the monks also perform rituals for agricultural purposes[31] and other rituals upon request in the summer season. In cases of extensive rituals to ward off illness or if someone passes away, the number of monks required will be called back to the village to participate.

The ritual calendar in Limi includes a great variety ranging from the daily rituals mentioned above, to seasonal rituals to ensure a good harvest,

---

27 The monks have to pay a fine if they fail to show up. The fine is relatively high for monks holding special positions in the monastery.

28 The Göku festival has received its name from the display of a great brocade image (*gos sku*) of the founder of the Drigung Kagyu order.

29 Such seasonal monk service has been practiced also elsewhere. See for instance Jahoda 2015: 123, n. 225 and 125, n. 231, and Shakya, Rabgyas and Crook 1994: 624.

30 Monks have traditionally engaged in agricultural work, animal husbandry, trade and crafts. In the past, it was normally the monk brother who polished and varnished the wooden bowls that Limi is famous for. Nowadays, many monks spend the monastic off season performing religious services in neighbouring communities. Some monks also spend the summer season studying either in Dehra Dun in India or in Kathmandu. The households' duties towards the monastery are discussed in Chapters Eight and Nine.

31 Including amongst others the three fire offering rituals (*sbyin sreg*), the offering of a *gtor ma* to a wrathful form of Padmasambhava (*gu ru drag po gtor rgyag*), as well as various rituals to maṇipulate the weather, such as the *char 'bebs* ritual to persuade the serpent deities (*klu*) to make rain.

to elaborate commemorative festivals, life cycle rituals, and other rituals to serve the needs of the villagers.[32] These monastic rituals can be categorised in a number of ways. Here, I have chosen to distinguish between rituals that form part of the monastic calendar and are largely sponsored by the monastic community (*grwa tshang*) and those that are performed at the request of the village assembly or individual households. This distinction helps to understand how the religious and secular institutions cooperate administratively and economically in the management of basic services to the villagers. The rituals that are arranged and performed by the laity form another major category, showing that the local monastery does not have a 'ritual monopoly' in the villages.

7.2.1 *Rituals Sponsored by the Monastic Community*

During the seven winter months, the monastic community arranges twenty-two annual rituals, some of which last for several days. With the exception of the Rimchö festival, which is co-organised with the village assembly, these rituals are financed either through particular monastic sponsorship responsibilities discussed in Chapter Nine, or from the monastery's general fund. In addition, individual households frequently sponsor meals or other parts of the expenses as a virtuous activity (*dge ba*).[33] It is the duty of all monks to be present during these rituals.

TABLE 7.1 The main rituals in the monastic ritual calendar

1st month	**3rd month**
sKong bshags—3 days	Mi 'khrugs cho ga
Ma ṇi dus chen—9 days	Tshe chog
Kun rig	
bLa ma mchod pa	**4th month**
	Gos sku dus chen
2nd month	
bKa' 'gyur recitation—15 days	
Tshogs	

32 Only a selected number of rituals will be described and analysed in the book. A complete overview of the rituals is provided in Appendix IV.

33 See Chapter Nine.

TABLE 7.1 The main rituals in the monastic ritual calendar (*cont.*)

9th month	**11th month**
lHa babs dus chen (sKong bshags)	Grwa ba'i lo gsar
	sKong bshags
10th month	
sKu gnyer rtsis sprod	**12th month**
dGa' ldan lnga mchod (sKong bshags)	bCo lnga dus chen
Dgu gtor	'Cham rtsis
gNam gang	Sa 'dul
	gSar ma'i 'cham
	rNying ma'i 'cham
	gNam gang

These rituals are part of the general repertoire of Drigung Kagyu monasteries and, as we will see below, constitute only a portion of the monks' ritual activity.

7.2.2 *Rituals Performed on Behalf of the Village for Wellbeing and Environmental Management*

The rituals requested by the village assembly are often categorised as either rituals for wellbeing (*bde rim*) or annual rituals (*lo rim*). But there are also rituals to manipulate the weather and for managing the environment, e.g. the *char 'bebs* (lit. 'to cause rain to fall') ritual (see Fig. 7.13). The village assembly also requests rituals for special events, such as the protection of the village and monastery against flood.[34] Fire offering rituals (*sbyin sreg*) are performed annually to ensure a good harvest (*zhing gi sku rim*). It should be mentioned that except for the rain making ritual, most of these rituals are part of a general repertoire that can be performed for a broad variety of purposes. The fire offering rituals, for instance, are part of a standard set of four types corresponding to the four kinds of virtuous action (*zhi, rgyas, dbang* and *drag*), but currently only three of them are performed in Waltse. The first is a pacifying fire offering (*zhi ba'i sbyin sreg*) performed after the first irrigation and after the first sprouts emerge from the fields. This is done in order to avoid crop damage by insects. The second is an extensive fire offering (*rgyas pa'i sbyin sreg*) performed after the 'eyes' appear on the grain (*mig don*) in order to avoid a particular plant disease (see Fig. 7.11). The third is a powerful fire offering (*dbang gi sbyin sreg*) performed in the community hall after the cutting of the barley, but before

34 See also Hovden and Havnevik 2021.

FIGURE 7.11 The second of the annual fire offering rituals (*sbyin sreg*) to protect the crops

threshing, in order to increase the yield. In the past, the monks would also perform a wrathful fire offering (*drag po'i sbyin sreg*) in the monastery courtyard, but nowadays they perform a ritual to the wrathful aspect of Guru Rinpoche (*gu ru drag po'i gtor rgyag*) in the community hall instead. This ritual is generally performed to remove obstacles and diseases for the monks and the laity.[35]

Since 2006, a significant number of rituals have been performed to protect the village and monastery from floods.[36] These rituals have been performed both by the monks and the laity and form part of a larger ritual repertoire employed more generally to avert misfortunes and obstacles, and more specifically in order to modify the weather and the outcome of agricultural work. While these rituals have been performed locally, the type of ritual response has often been decided by external high lamas at the request of the village assembly or directly by the monastic community. For flood protection, Drigung Kyabgön Rinpoche has advised the monks in Rinchen Ling to recite the *Kangyur* carefully (see Fig. 7.14) and continue performing supplication rituals to Apchi Chökyi Drölma. Another high lama belonging to the Nyingma

35 Interview with one of the monks, 04.06.11.

36 See also Hovden and Havnevik 2021.

FIGURE 7.12 Carrying the *Prajñāpāramitā* around the fields for protection

FIGURE 7.13 Performing the rain making ritual (*char 'bebs*) by the shrine for the *klu*

FIGURE 7.14 Monks reading the *Kangyur* for flood protection

FIGURE 7.15 Ritual dedication of a yak to the deities (*lha g.yag*) for flood protection

order has recommended the monks to perform a yak offering ritual (*lha g.yag*), which entails the dedication of a live animal to the gods (see Fig. 7.15). David Holler argues that despite the highly different concepts of liberation at play, *lha g.yag* can be characterised as a sub-category of *tshe thar* (life liberation) rituals.[37] This rinpoche has suggested that the cause of the flood is the disturbance of the territorial deities, and the offering of a yak to the deities will appease them and he also advised the villagers to construct a stupa (*mchod rten*) in order to stop the flood. Most of this ritual activity has been sponsored by the village assembly.

7.2.3 *The Rimchö Festival*

Rimchö is the name of the most important festival in Limi and is celebrated at separate times in all three villages. The order of the celebrations was reportedly once established by lottery: the first celebration takes place in Dzang at the end of the tenth month with liturgy from the wrathful guru (*gu ru drag po*) cycle; the next takes place in Til in the eleventh month with liturgy from the Mahākāla (*mgon po*) cycle; and finally, the most extensive celebration with liturgy from the eight pronouncements (*bka' brgyad*) cycle takes place in Waltse Rinchen Ling at the end of the twelfth month (Figs. 7.16 and 7.17). The monks in Dzang and Til perform only the new monastic dances (*gsar ma'i 'cham*), whereas the monks in Waltse also perform the old monastic dances (*rnying ma'i 'cham*).[38] Despite the different ritual texts, a shorter list of *'cham* dances in Dzang and Til, as well as some differences in funding and organisation, the celebrations in the three villages appear quite similar. The senior monks acquired their ritual experience before the split of Rinchen Ling monastery, and some of the younger monks are observing the celebrations in the other monasteries as guests.[39] I attended the festivals both in Til and in Waltse, but the following account will be mainly based on the latter.

The festival features many similarities with celebrations elsewhere, for instance the Mani Rimdu festival, originating in the Nyingmapa Mindroling (sMin grol gling) monastery, which was established by Dzatrul Ngawang Tenzin Norbu (rDza sprul Ngag dbang bsTan 'dzin Nor bu, 1867–1940) at Dza Rongphu (rDza Rong phu) monastery on the northern side of Mount Everest and later on in several monasteries in Solu Khumbu, carefully analysed by Richard Kohn.[40] The festival also shares some features with the Namthong (Nam mthong) festival

---

37 Holler 2008: 208, 218.

38 The dances are described in the *Drigung dance manual*, p. 29ff and p. 14ff respectively.

39 During Rimchö in Waltse in 2012, for instance, eight young monks from Dzang visited in order to study the dance steps and the ritual procedures.

40 See e.g., Kohn 2001.

FIGURE 7.16 Anticipating the Rimchö festival

FIGURE 7.17 Watching the play in the monastery courtyard during Rimchö

in Khochar and is probably directly influenced by it, as a number of Limigya visit Khochar for the event.[41] But the liturgy and the monastic dances performed in Limi are specific to the Drigung Kagyu order of Buddhism, and certain other parts of the festival have a distinctly local flavour.

According to the *Drigung dance manual*, the Drigung Kagyu tradition of performing *'cham* started with the tenth throneholder Dorje Gyalpo (rDo rje rGyal po, 1284–1350).[42] Togden Rinpoche (rTogs lDan rin po che) explains that the sixteenth century throneholder Rinchen Phuntsok (Rin chen Phun tshogs, 1509–1557) combined teachings from the Nyingma and Kagyu traditions and introduced the *bka' brgyad dbang sgrub*.[43] Throughout the centuries there have been several other additions, but among the most important were the dances of the protector deities, including the dances of the four armed Māhakāla and Apchi, introduced by the Second Chetsang Rinpoche Trinle Sangpo ('Phrin las bZang po, 1656–1718). Today these dances form part of the so-called new dances (*gsar ma'i 'cham*).

The *Rinchen Ling dance manual* states that it was Konchog Trinle (dKon mchog Phrin las), the vajraholder at Kailash and a close disciple (*dngos slob*) of the Fifth Chungtsang Rinpoche Chönyi Norbu (Chos nyid Nor bu, 1827–1865), who started the tradition of performing the exorcism rites and dances of the eight Herukas (*sgrub pa bka' brgyad kyi gtor zlog gar 'cham*) in Rinchen Ling (Fig. 7.20).[44] The year is not specified, but since he was a disciple of the Fifth Chungtsang it must have taken place in the second half of the nineteenth century. The manual then states that during his visit to Limi in 1895, the Sixth Chungtsang Rinpoche Tenzin Chökyi Lodrö corrected the melody, dance steps, and use of musical instruments, so the ritual could be performed according to tradition.[45]

The Rimchö festival requires substantial preparation, both by the monks and the laity. The main preparations start between three and four weeks prior

41 Monks and laity from Limi receive invitations to attend similar festivals in Purang district, but because of the Chinese restrictions on travel, the villagers have only attended the festival in Khochar in the last few years. These visits have contributed to the spread of styles of performance throughout the ages. The Namthong festival is described by Tsering Gyalpo et al. (2012: 221–53).

42 The *Drigung dance manual*, p. 3.

43 Teaching by Togden Rinpoche <http://www.coreofculture.org/a-sacred-drikung-teaching-on-cham-by-his-eminence-togden-rinpoche-of-phyiang-monastery.html>, accessed 18.07.15

44 The *Rinchen Ling dance manual*, lines 40–41.

45 The *Rinchen Ling dance manual*, lines 41–43.

to the festival. First, the village headman requests the most experienced monk to serve as Rimchö lama. Then, the monks start practising monastic dances (*'cham*) in the monastery courtyard (Fig. 7.18). On the fifteenth or sixteenth day, the monks are assigned the characters they are to represent, and on the seventeenth day of the month, the villagers are invited to attend the final *'cham* rehearsal (*'cham rtsis*) as spectators. The rehearsal starts with a recitation of the dance manual (*'cham yig*) (see Fig. 7.19). The text was composed by the Sixth Chungtsang Rinpoche Tenzin Chökyi Lodrö during his visit in 1895 and is written on a scroll measuring approximately 2.5 metres long, richly decorated with a dragon motif on both sides (see Fig. 7.20).[46] On this day the monks are clad in red robes and rehearse the most difficult dances.

The laity also has a special role in the festival. The female heads of the *grong chen* households have the duty to perform an ancient type of dance (*shon*) from Western Tibet (Fig. 7.23).[47] The most experienced *shon* dancer in Waltse told me that there are twenty-five different songs.[48] Whereas only a selection of these were performed during Rimchö in Waltse, the full set was performed in Til. The *shon 'go* ('head of the *shon* [dancers]') of the *shon* performers (*shon ma*) has the responsibility to lead the dances and invite the other performers to her house for rehearsals.[49] This is a compulsory rotating duty assigned during the autumn village assembly meeting. During the same meeting a dance master (*gar dpon*) and a dance attendant (*gar g.yog*) are appointed according to a list of male heads of the *grong chen* households. These two men have the responsibility to lead the *gar* dances[50] and ensure that the dancers know their steps. In Limi there are six main types of *gar* dances performed according to the men's position in the local hierarchy (Fig. 7.24).

46 The *Rinchen Ling dance manual* 1895.

47 According to Tsering Gyalpo et al. (2012: 274) the *shon* dances go back at least to the late tenth century.

48 In an article about a song tradition in Porong (sPong rong) belonging to the *shon* genre Ramble (2002: 66) quotes a source explaining that there are traditions of twenty-five, eighteen, and thirteen *shon* songs.

49 The *shon* are also performed during *lha gsol* for the local deities, and occasionally also during other festive events. Elderly people in Limi lament that the song traditions are disappearing, but so far, the enforcement of the duty to perform *shon* during major festivals contributes to keeping the traditions alive.

50 The performance of *gar* dances is another ancient tradition from Western Tibet. The king of Ladakh sent a group of dancers to the Fifth Dalai Lama in the seventeenth century, after which the tradition was adopted by the government of the Dalai Lamas, who kept professional *gar* dance troupes. See for instance Lo Bue (2003: 193).

FIGURE 7.18 Novice learning from the senior monks during *'cham rtsis*

FIGURE 7.19 Reading the *'Cham yig* during the final rehearsal before Rimchö

FIGURE 7.20 The *'Cham yig*

FIGURE 7.21 The two Atsaras scattering *rtsam pa* for wealth and fertility

The day after the *'cham* rehearsal, the monks start building the extensive sacrificial cakes (*gtor ma*) and preparing the 'magic weapons' (*zor*), which are placed in the assembly hall. Then, between three and five in the early hours of the morning from the twentieth to the twenty-ninth day of the month, the monks recite the *bKa' brgyad* text. The eight pronouncements, or the eight great *sādhanā* teachings (*sgrub pa bka' brgyad*), refers to a set of Mahāyoga teachings believed to have been transmitted in Tibet by Padmasambhava. The teachings and associated ritual complex focus on the eight Herukas, with the supreme Heruka (Che mchog He ru ka) as the central deity. During the last three days of the liturgy, monastic dances are performed during the daytime. The Rimchö festival normally requires the participation of at least fifty monks. As will be discussed in the next chapter, this was one of the main explanations given for the need of the compulsory recruitment of monks in Limi through levy.[51] Senior monks reported that in the past, the liturgy used to be performed

51 See Chapter Eight.

FIGURE 7.22 Sogra (Sog ra), one of the retinue of Namse during the second day of Rimchö

FIGURE 7.23 Women performing *shon* dances

FIGURE 7.24 Man performing the ancient *khrom srung ba'i gar* dance

by two teams of monks, one reciting texts during the night shift, and the other group performing the monastic dances during the daytime. But now, with only thirty-five monks (including novices), they have to work double shifts. The programme on the first day starts in the afternoon and, except for the taming of the ground by the two *garuḍas*, consists mainly of amusing and entertaining plays. The programme on the second day starts early in the morning and consists of dances of the protector deities, the so-called 'new monastic dances', interspersed with performances of *shon* and *gar*. The programme on the final day culminates with the exorcism ritual and the throwing of magical weapons.

TABLE 7.2 The main rituals during the Rimchö festival

The first day (27/12): Taming the ground (*sa 'dul*)	
1)	Performance by two *atsara* (*a tsa ra*) (Fig. 7.21)
2)	The dance of the *garuḍas* (*bya khyung*)
3)	Play of the men from the southern valleys (*rong pa*)
4)	Play of the Thakuri king
5)	Play of Nyene (s.u.), the young rinpoche
6)	Circle dance around a bonfire in the monastery courtyard

TABLE 7.2 The main rituals during the Rimchö festival (*cont.*)

The second day (28/12): The new monastic dances (*gsar ma'i 'cham*)	
1)	Supplication to the deities to ask for permission to wear the masks (*bag gsol*)
2)	Performance by two *atsara*
3)	Dance of the blood drinking Mahākāla (*mgon po khrag 'thung rol pa*)
4)	The women perform *shon* dances
5)	Individual dance of Apchi (*a phyi'i sger 'cham*)
6)	Dance of the four guardians of the teachings (*bka' srung bzhi*)
7)	The women perform *shon* dances
8)	Dance of Vaiśravaṇa (*rnam sras kyi 'cham*) (see Fig. 7.22)
9)	Performance of *gar* dance by the guardians of the festival place (*khrom srung ba'i gar*) (Fig. 7.24)
10)	The play about the protectors of sacred places, represented by male and female monkeys (*zhing skyong yab yum*)
11)	Dance of the Dharma protector and the King of the *rgyal po* spirits (*chos skyong dang rgyal po*).
12)	Performance of *gar* dance by the dance leader and his servant (*gar dpon dang gar g.yog*)
13)	The first display of Mahākāla (*mgon po 'don dang po*)
14)	Performance of *gar* dance by the village leaders (*dbon po'i gar, drug bcu pa*)
15)	The second display of Mahākāla (*mgon po 'don gnyis pa*)
16)	The women perform *shon* dances (Fig. 7.23)
18)	The third display of Mahākāla (*mgon po 'don gsum pa*)
18)	The women perform *shon* dances, then they are joined by the men and perform combined *gar shon*
19)	Circle dance around a bonfire in the monastery courtyard
The third day (29/12): The old monastic dances (*rnying ma'i 'cham*)	
1)	Performance by two *atsara* (*a tsa ra*)
2)	Drum dance (*rnga 'cham*) (Fig.7.25)
3)	The four keepers of the gate (*sgo ma bzhi*) bring the effigy (*nya bo*) concealed under a piece of black cloth (Fig. 7.26)
4)	Dance of the *'dzam chen po gnyis*
5)	The dance of the two deer (*shwa ba pho mo gnyis*), who uncover the effigy with their antlers
6)	The dance of the two buffaloes (*ma he pho mo gnyis*)

TABLE 7.2 The main rituals during the Rimchö festival (*cont.*)

7)	Dance of the supreme Heruka (*che mchog he ru ka*). The other monks receive him while playing horns and cymbals.
8)	The dance of accomplishment (*sgrub 'cham*), featuring the eight principal Mahāyoga tutelary deities.
9)	The dance of magic weapons (*zor 'cham*), also called black hat dance (*zhwa nag 'cham*). The effigy is killed by the *kīlaya*. (Fig. 7.27)
10)	The play of the grandmother and grandfather (*a phyi dang mes mes* or *rgan rgon gnyis kyi zlos gar*).
11)	Play of two monks checking if the effigy is really dead, followed by the performance of *gar* dance by the same two monks.
12)	'Liberation' dance (*bsgral 'cham*). All monks available participate in this dance, the *nya bo* effigy is cut up and its consciousness liberated.
13)	Dance of the swirling dust storm (*rlung nag 'tshub*).
14)	Libation offering (*gser skyems*) and throwing of magic weapons (*zor*). Each of the different types of *zor* have the power to prevent different types of harm and are shot or thrown in the four cardinal directions.
15)	Circle dance (Fig. 7.28)

After the throwing of the magical weapons, the Rimchö lama gives blessings to all spectators seeking an audience, and then everybody climbs down the stairs to the courtyard. The grand finale of the festival appears almost chaotic: The monks start carrying the remaining offering cakes and effigies down to the monastery courtyard and play cymbals and horns preparing to cast out the offering cakes (*gtor rgyag*), while groups of laity join in a number of simultaneous song and dance performances. Women from the *grong chung* families perform a different type of song (simply referred to as *gzhas*), a long line of brocade clad boys and men wield swords and shields and shout *tsheyah, tsheyah* (s.u.). The festival is complex with many layers of meanings and functions for the monks and the lay audience and participants as well as the local environment. It is regarded as crucial for village life, and the villagers therefore spend a considerable amount of time and administrative, economic and labour resources, involving all sections of society, to ensure a successful performance. The system for sponsoring and facilitating it constitute a central part of the village and monastery's local governance.

FIGURE 7.25 Monks performing the drum dance (*rnga 'cham*)

FIGURE 7.26 The four gate keepers carrying the effigy

FIGURE 7.27 The lead dancer during the magic weapons dance (*zor 'cham*)

FIGURE 7.28 Circle dance in the monastery courtyard after the Rimchö festival

7.2.4 *Rituals Performed at the Request of Individual Households*

I have chosen to distinguish between rituals that the households sponsor on a regular basis, and those that are requested when needed. Both categories include general rituals to overcome obstacles and prevent or cure diseases, and increase prosperity and wellbeing, but the latter also include life cycle and other rituals. The capacity of both monks and laity is reduced during the summer season and because of the high demand for rituals in the village and the Rinchen Ling monks' obligation to serve the villagers' ritual needs, the majority of the more extensive rituals are timed to fit the monastic schedule. In Waltse, individual households have committed themselves to sponsor a wide range of rituals annually or biannually:[52]

- Offering to the wrathful aspect of Guru Rinpoche (*gu ru drag po gtor rgyag*). The ritual is sponsored by one *grong chen* family every two years and requires the participation of all monks.
- High praise of the warrior deity (*dgra lha dpangs bstod*).[53] The ritual is performed by the shrine keeper (*sku gnyer*) and one monk in combination

52 The list was provided by one of the most experienced monks (04.06.11), and the items have later been confirmed by other monks and laity.

53 Nebesky-Wojkowitz (1996: 318–40) devotes a whole chapter to the warrior deities (*dgra lha*). The *dgra lha dpangs bstod* ritual performed in Limi is similar to his description on pp. 335–38.

with a *lha bsang* ritual. The ritual is arranged every year in the tenth Tibetan month by twenty *grong chen* and seven *grong chung* families. Prayer flags are raised at the respective shrines of the 'ancestral deities' (*pho lha*)[54] shrines. High praise of the warrior deity always takes place on auspicious days and is performed also at other occasions.[55] (Fig. 7.29)

- Rituals to secure prosperity (*g.yang 'gugs*) (one lama + the shrine keeper)—sponsored by five *grong chen* families every two years, and one *grong chen* family every three years.
- Extensive offering feasts (*tshogs rgya*) (the shrine keeper + four monks)—sponsored by three *grong chen* families every year, one every two years, and one every three years.
- Four hundred offerings for removing obstacles (*brgya bzhi*) (two monks)—sponsored by fifteen *grong chen* and six *grong chung* families every year.
- Liturgy from the Heart Sūtra for expelling demons (*Sher snying bdud zlog*) (four monks)—sponsored every year by five *grong chen* and two *grong chung* families.
- Propitiation rituals (*bskang gso*) (four monks)—sponsored by twenty-eight *grong chen* and seven *grong chung* families every year.
- Four-mandala ritual (*maN Dal bzhi chog*) to Tārā (four monks)—sponsored every year by one *grong chen* family.
- Extended supplication rituals (*gsol kha*) to Apchi Chökyi Drölma (two monks)—sponsored by twenty-nine *grong chen* and eight *grong chung* and five *bom btang* performed prior to the annual reading of the *Prajñāpāramitā*. In addition, most households sponsor the ritual performed by the shrine keeper monk once a month. (Fig. 7.30)
- The reading of *Prajñāpāramitā* in all households owning the scriptures. In other households the monks read the collection of religious works (*gzungs bsdus*) instead. In 2012 it took the monks a whole month to go from house to house and read the texts.
- Fumigation offering to purify the deities (*bsang*)[56] (one monk)—one time every month by thirty-one *grong chen* and twenty-nine *grong chung*. The *bom btang* sponsor the ritual according to their wish; perhaps every two to three months.

54 As explained in Chapter Three, 'household god' is probably a more appropriate translation of *pho lha*.

55 The *dgra lha dpangs bstod* ritual is also performed as part of the celebrations to the *pho lha*, and as a ritual for the wellbeing (*bde rim*) of the village.

56 The texts used for the fumigation rituals (*bsang*) in the three villages are of varying lengths and have been slightly adapted to include local deities.

FIGURE 7.29 Ritual for the praise of the warrior deity (*dgra lha dpangs bstod*)

FIGURE 7.30 Preparing *gtor ma* for the supplication ritual to Apchi Chökyi Dröma

In addition to the large number of regular rituals the monks also perform rituals when needed for reasons such as illness, obstacles in school and business, life cycle rituals and so forth.

7.2.5 *Rituals and Festivals Arranged and Performed by the Laity*

There is a striking difference, between Limi and the Tibetan communities further south in Humla, which are largely Nyingma, in the virtual absence of tantric practitioners (*sngags pa*), spirit mediums and their priests (N. *dhami* and *dangri*)[57] and other non-monastic specialists. While part of the reason may be ascribed to differences between the Nyingma and Drigung schools of Buddhism, it is tempting to ascribe it to ritual 'streamlining' due to the strong monastic presence in Limi over a long period of time.[58] Yet, the monasteries do not have a ritual monopoly in the villages, and as mentioned in the previous chapter about village taxes, the laity also performs a number of extensive rituals. As with so many of the communal activities in the village, participation and patronage are compulsory and is organised at household level.

In Waltse, the most important rituals performed by the laity include the six annual rituals on the tenth of the month (Tshes bcu),[59] and two fasting rituals (bsNyen gnas smyung gnas), which are largely funded through the village taxes. Mani recitations where representatives from each household convene in the community hall to recite religious texts and mantras for one or more days are arranged according to need and for a variety of purposes. In 2012, for instance, *maṇi* recitations were arranged for fifteen days in a row to pray for protection from flooding. In addition the villagers arrange annual supplication rituals (*lha gsol*) for the territorial deities (*yul lha* and *pho lha*), and rituals which the monks are hesitant to perform because they are regarded as morally dubious, such as rituals to avert the negative influence of 'gossip' (*mi kha*).[60] Finally, the laity arrange a number of festivals such as the extensive New Year celebrations, Dunchang (Dus chang?), and 'opera' (A ce lha mo) performances.

57 See for instance Levine 1989. The only other village in Humla with a monastery is Yalbang (Yul dbang). The Namkha Khyung Dzong (Nam mkha' Khyung rDzong) monastery was founded in 1985 and currently houses approximately 150 monks.

58 From this point of view, Limi religious life appears more like practices in communities with similar local monasteries in Central and Western Tibet.

59 The Tshechu festival is arranged on the following dates: 10/10, 11/10, 12/10, 1/10, 1/15, 2/10. See also the ritual calendar in Appendix IV.

60 Rituals to avert gossip are frequently performed in the villages. A ritual text to avert gossip (*mi kha*), which is used further south in Humla, has been translated by Kapstein (1997: 527–37).

These are more secular events but are initiated by libation offerings (*gser skyems*) to the tutelary, protective, and local deities, and have important religious components.

A detailed discussion of these rituals and festivities is beyond the scope of this book, but I will provide a brief overview of the most important. Tshechu (lit. the Tenth day [ritual]) commemorates Guru Rinpoche, and in Waltse it is compulsory to perform the ritual at least six times each year. However, this ritual is also frequently performed on other occasions, especially in cases of disease. The ritual takes place in the private shrine rooms of the large households in Waltse (see Fig. 7.31). For Tshechu, there are four lay chant masters (*dbu mdzad*) and a list of rotating patrons and hosts. The role of chant master is inherited from father to son in four families. These men have learned how to prepare the Tshechu offering cakes (*gtor ma*) and perform the ritual for the morning session and during the afternoon session, representatives from the other households also participate. Participation in Tshechu is compulsory among both the *grong chen* and *grong chung* families, and each household must send one representative aged between eighteen and sixty. Those who are literate bring their own prayer books, whereas those who are not recite mantras. There is a strong gender division here: the only woman I have seen among the men reciting texts during these rituals is the nun in Til. The main text recited in the second part of the Tshechu is a short version of the *Life story of Guru Rinpoche* (*Pad ma bka' thang*), which many of the male villagers know by heart.

The two fasting rituals (*smyung gnas*) are arranged in the first and fourth Tibetan months respectively. One monk serves as tantric master (*rdo rje slob dpon*) supervising the ritual and instructing the lay participants. The villagers have made participation in this ritual compulsory for the *grong chen* families; each household has to send one representative aged between eighteen and sixty. The ritual is arranged twice a year: the first is an eight-day ritual taking place in the community hall in the first month, and the second is a two-day ritual performed during the month of Saga Dawa in a private house. The responsibility to host the event rotates, and so does the duty to participate. The villagers reportedly became reluctant to participate, and it was therefore decided at a village assembly meeting that the upper and lower divisions (*grong stod* and *grong smad*) would alternate.

The Tshechu, fasting rituals, and *maṇi* recitations are important opportunities for the laity to earn religious merit and though they are regarded as less effective than monastic rituals, they can to a certain extent be seen to be 'functionally equivalent' and constitute an alternative when monks are not

FIGURE 7.31 Private altar during Tshechu

available.[61] For instance in case of serious disease, the villagers may convene to perform Tshechu, either on their own initiative, or as recommended by local monks or lamas from outside—something that occurred a number of times during my stay in Limi. In general, all these rituals are ways for the laity to contribute ritually. Occasionally skilled laity even step in to perform less complex rituals together with the available monks in the monastic off-season.

7.3 Monk Offices and Decision-making

To ensure the smooth performance of the rituals described above, the Limigya have developed a strict and detailed system of monastic management, recruitment, and funding. The formal positions in the monasteries and the hierarchy of which they form a part have not changed much during the last century,[62] but the socio-economic and political changes have had important consequences for the management of the monasteries. Although the monastic

61 See for instance Metcalf 1981.

62 The administrative documents that I am basing my observations on date back to the end of the nineteenth century.

administration is separate from the village government, this and the following two chapters will explore the degree of mutual influence between the two.

The administrative structure of Tibetan Buddhist monasteries varies with the type, size, and location of the institution. Moreover, the size of the affiliated village(s) and the ownership of land and other resources influence the administrative needs of the monastery. The Kyilung (pseudonym) monastery in Ladakh studied by Paljor Tsarong, for instance, was, with its thirty-four monks, almost exactly the same size as Rinchen Ling, which in 2012 hosted a monk population of thirty-five.[63] However, although both belong to the same sub-school of Buddhism, the former serves a larger number of villages which is also reflected in a slightly different administrative structure.

In Limi, most of the decisions concerning the day-to-day management and regulation of the monastery are taken either within the monastery itself or by a joint assembly of monks and lay villagers (*skya ser*). This gives the decision-making procedures a democratic character and seems to be a common feature of local monasteries.[64] In cases of major importance, advice is sought from Drigung authorities and occasionally also from high lamas of other Buddhist schools. The Limi villagers have particularly close connections with the Nyingma lamas belonging to Dudjom Lingpa's tradition, based at the Namkha Khyung Dzong monastery in Yalbang and in Kathmandu.[65]

7.3.1 *Religious Authority*

The highest religious authority[66] in all Drigung monasteries belongs to the Drigung throne holders: the Drigung Chetsang and Drigung Chungtsang Rinpoches.[67] Throughout history, several of the Drigung hierarchs have visited Limi as part of their pilgrimages to Mount Kailash. Although, as the next chapter will show, reforms instigated during their visits could have serious consequences for a local community, they were generally not able to engage

63 Tsarong 1987.

64 See for instance Crook and Shakya (1994: 581), who characterise the management system as 'remarkably democratic'.

65 The biographies of two religious masters belonging to the lineage report that they spent time in Limi. See Chapter Three.

66 For a discussion of religious authority in Tibetan Buddhism, see Mills 2003.

67 The system with one Chetsang and one Chungtsang Rinpoche was established in the seventeenth century after Konchog Rinchen (dKon mchog Rin chen, 1590–1664) and Rigdzin Chödrak (Rig 'dzin Chos grags, 1595–1659), the last heirs of the Kyura lineage, passed away. The two brothers have retrospectively been referred to as the first Chetsang and Chungtsang Rinpoche. The history is presented in the article "A Brief History of the Drikung Kagyu Lineage of Tibetan Buddhism"at the official Drikung website n.d. a).

directly in the management of the remote monasteries in the past. The present Chungtsang Rinpoche resides in Lhasa and exercises little influence over monastic affairs outside China's borders.[68] The Chetsang Rinpoche[69] established a new centre for the order in Dehra Dun in the 1980s[70] and has since worked continuously to strengthen the order's already existing monasteries in areas outside China. He has also established a number of monasteries and Buddhist centres across the world.[71] So far, Chetsang Rinpoche has made two visits to Limi. The first took place in 1993 and the second in 2008. These visits, which have already been referred to in previous chapters, are of great importance to the community and are frequently mentioned by the villagers.[72] With the recent improvement of communications and infrastructure, contact has become frequent and Chetsang Rinpoche has been asked by the monastics as well as the laity for advice on a number of matters in Limi.

The three monasteries in Limi also have an incarnated lama, often referred to as 'the Limi *sprul sku*'. The current *sprul sku*, Senge Tenzin Rinpoche, is regarded as an incarnation of the thirteenth-century Drigung master Senge Yeshe[73] and was recognised by Kyabgön Rinpoche in 1994.[74] In addition to the monasteries in Limi, Senge Tenzin Rinpoche has the responsibility for his home monastery Gungphur (dGung 'phur) in Purang and Gomoche (sGo mo che?)[75] in Dolpo. He also runs two Dharma centres in Taiwan, where he is currently residing. The Limi *sprul sku* visited Limi for the first time in 2003, and

68 The Chungtsang Rinpoche is currently deputy secretary general of the Office of Religious Affairs in Lhasa. See the article "His holiness the H.h. Drikung Kyabgon Chungtsang", Drikung website n.d. b).

69 Elsewhere, I have referred to the current Drigung Chetsang as Kyabgön Rinpoche, as this is the way he is normally referred to in Limi. It should be noted, however, that *kyabgön* (*skyabs mgon*) is part of the title of both Drigung hierarchs.

70 The consecration of Jangchub Ling (Byang chub Gling) monastery took place in 1985 and the inauguration in 1992. See the article "Drikung Kagyu Institute—history", Drikung website n.d. c).

71 An overview of worldwide centres is provided on the Drikung website n.d e). See also Gruber's (2010) biography of Kyabgön Rinpoche.

72 The visits are described on the Drigung website, in Konchok Pasang (2008), in the Limi Youth Society magazine and are also mentioned in Gruber (2010: 271f, and 302 n.11).

73 See Chapter Three for a brief account of Senge Yeshe's three years' stay in Limi in the first part of the thirteenth century.

74 See the Kailashzone website 2010.

75 I have not been able to find the correct spelling of the name of this hermitage, but since it is located at the foot of the Crystal Mountain (Shel dkar ri?) the spelling sGo mo che (lit. 'The great gate') is at least not unlikely.

a second time together with Kyabgön Rinpoche in 2008.[76] However, his visits to Kathmandu are more frequent and many Limigya meet with him there. He is involved in various forms of engaged Buddhism, and after the earthquake in 2015, he sponsored relief to some of the hardest hit communities, and a team of young people from Limi distributed the aid. While the Rinpoche does not seem to intend to take up residence in Limi, he has officially stated that he '… wishes to take full responsibility for finding sustainable solutions for both the spiritual and financial requirements of his monasteries and people.'[77] I will return to some of his initiatives in Chapter Nine.

7.3.2 *Local Monastery Management System*

The day-to-day management of the monasteries is carried out by a number of monk officials (*las thog*),[78] who have the authority to make routine decisions regarding their assigned tasks. However, in cases of major decisions, higher levels of authority are consulted. As will be explained below, the procedures and level of official involved depend on the type and gravity of the matter. In order to be allowed to take up the monk office positions, the monk's household must have completed a minimum of six years of compulsory ritual sponsorship.[79] Currently, most of the monk offices rotate according to seniority, but in the past, when all the monks from the three villages in Limi convened in Rinchen Ling, the order of office holders depended on availability.[80] The highest ritual positions, such as lama for the Mani and Rimchö festivals, also require certain religious qualifications and are taken up at the request of the monks and the village assembly respectively. Recently, the monks taking up the position of administrative leader (*sbug pa*) have been appointed by Kyabgön Rinpoche.[81] The following list of positions in the monastery is arranged according to rank:

1. Resident lama (*bla brang bla ma*) is the title conferred on the religious head of the monastery. The position used to be held by the Limi *sprul*

76 At the time of manuscript submisssion, he embarked on a two-year restreat in Chökhor Tse together with a group of monks mainly from Limi as well as one nun.

77 See the Kailashzone website 2010.

78 For an overview of monk offices mentioned in monastic guidelines (*bca' yig*), see Jansen (2015: 86–105).

79 See Chapter Nine for details about the sponsorship requirements.

80 The principle of seniority also applied in the past, but the possibility to pay for a replacement (see Chapter Eight) made the order more random in practice. The split of the monasteries is briefly described in Chapter Three and below.

81 The position of administrative leader of the monastery changed during my fieldwork in 2011–12, and the monks showed me the decision letter from Kyabgön Rinpoche's office in Dehra Dun.

sku. However, the position has been vacant for several decades since the untimely passing away of Kushog Ramjor (sKu zhabs Rab 'byor), who was the last resident *sprul sku*.[82] According to the *Rinchen Ling monastery inventory*, a *bla brang* ('lama's residence') had already been established by the king of Jumla in the thirteenth century, but no details are provided.[83] The lama's residence, fields, and a number of religious objects follow the position and are recorded in a separate document.[84] As mentioned above, the current Limi *sprul sku* Senge Tenzin Rinpoche has established himself in Taiwan.

2. Officiating lama during tantric rituals.[85] Since the *bla brang bla ma* post is vacant, the monastery's most senior monks have served as lama. As long as the monks from all three villages still convened in Rinchen Ling, it was reportedly no problem to fill this position, but after the split, a new system was established. The most extensive rituals, such as the Rimchö, the Gutor (dGu gtor), and the Mani festivals, require an officiating lama. The village community has the responsibility to request the most senior monk to take on this role. For the other rituals, it is the monk assembly that makes the request. Finding a monk to take on the role as officiating lama has become difficult in Dzang and Til, where, because of the flexibility in the enforcement of the levy,[86] most of the senior monks do not stay in the village. In Til, they therefore made a new rule demanding that one senior monk would have to be present each year and that this responsibility should rotate. The position of lama is regarded as an honour, but the performances of the most powerful rituals are also a great responsibility requiring the right empowerments and monastic training.
3. The senior monk (*bgres song*) category refers to monks who have assumed all monastic posts (*las thog*) and completed the payment of the compulsory ritual expenses (*gtong sgo*). The senior monks are given the highest seats during rituals and have special authority in general decision-making, and particularly in conflict resolution.

82 Kushog Ramjor passed away at an early age due to an epidemic at the end of the 1970s or beginning of the 1980s. His remains were embalmed in salt and enshrined in a stupa located next to the school.

83 *Rinchen Ling monastery inventory*, f. 3b.

84 The lama's residence was kept separate from the rest of the monastery economically, this becomes clear from the *Record of the resident lama's belongings*.

85 Lama is normally translated as 'teacher', but the term has been used in a range of different contexts. See Samuel (1993: 280f) for an overview of the different meanings of the term 'lama'.

86 The monk levy is discussed in Chapter Eight.

4. The post of administrative leader (*sbug pa*) of the monastery is held jointly by two monks, one senior and one junior. Their main duty is the overall administration of the monastery. The two *sbug pa* have to buy supplies and equipment for the monastery, settle minor disputes between monks, and have the responsibility to decide which ritual texts should be used. Before the split between the three monasteries, there were three *sbug pa*, one from each village so as to ensure that monks and laity from the three villages would get equal treatment. Previously the position of *sbug pa* would rotate according to seniority, but in recent years, the monks have asked Kyabgön Rinpoche for advice in choosing the leader. The term of office has recently been extended to six years.
5. The disciplinarian monk (*dge bskos*) has the responsibility to maintain discipline in the monastery, to organise recruitment of new monks, to process villagers' requests for more complex rituals,[87] and to implement the orders of the administrative leader. The disciplinarian also has the authority to order and to carry out corporal punishment. The disciplinarian is appointed for one year, and the post rotates according to seniority.
6. The cantor (*dbu mdzad* or *dbu chos*) leads the recitation in the major rituals. This post, too, lasts for one year and rotates according to seniority. In addition to the ritual responsibilities, the cantor cooperates with the disciplinarian and the steward during tax collection and decision-making related to patronage of certain rituals.
7. The steward (*gnyer pa*) is the keeper of the monastery's storerooms and is responsible for food management. The position is for one year and, like most of the other monk offices, rotates according to seniority. The steward supervises the measuring of all donations of food to the monastery, including the tax collection after the harvest, the monks' compulsory ritual patronage (*gtong sgo*), as well as donations for individual ritual requests. The steward also supervises the activities in the kitchen and the serving of tea and food and is therefore often unable to participate in the rituals. He is assisted by the rotating fire-tenders, tea servers and water carriers as described in Chapter Nine below, and on the occasions of large festivities, the *las 'dzin* officials and several other helpers.
8. The shrine keeper (*sku gnyer*) is responsible for the daily water offerings (*yon chab*), butter-lamps (*chos me*), the daily supplication ritual (*gsol kha*) to Apchi Chökyi Drolma, offering of incense, and sweeping floors.

87 Simple rituals like supplications (*gsol kha*) to A phyi will be agreed on directly with the shrine keeper, and similarly, for the equally frequent purification rituals (*bsang*), the monks will be requested directly.

The post lasts for four years. During the first two years, the monk must pay twenty *khal* of grain as a fee to the monastery (*grwa tshang*). During the next two years, the position is nicknamed *za ba po* ('eater'), because then he does not pay a fee but is allowed to keep all the grain offerings from lay people as well as the grain grown in the monastery fields. The shrine keeper also has the right to keep any money offerings made in front of the statues in the protector deity chapel (*mgon khang*). So, whilst the position requires a lot of work, it is regarded as lucrative.

9. The conch blowers are called *dung mkhan*. This task rotates annually and is normally held by two young regular monks.
10. Most monks are referred to as regular monks with intermediate vows (*bar shar ba*). They are called on to help the administrative leader bringing supplies to the monastery from Purang and Simikot. They also assist the steward, and they step in when there are no lay people available for serving tea, bringing water and lighting fire. The novices have to be able to recite the *Kangyur* before they can become a regular monk. The transition from novice (*grwa chung*) to regular monk (*bar shar ba*) normally takes place when the boy is around fifteen years old, but sometimes earlier, if he is talented. The ordination always takes place on the first day of the second month.
11. The novice monks are called *grwa chung* from the time they enrol at the age of eight until they are approximately fifteen years old. The novices are in a learning position, and often have to practise recitation in the monastery courtyard while the senior monks are performing rituals. At other times, they are seated in the lower row and participate in ritual performance. The most senior novices participate in the recitation as much as they can and sometimes they are also assigned additional tasks such as looking after animals that have been donated to the monastery.

The three first positions on the list are the highest in the monastery, but the monks holding these posts are not part of the daily monastic administration and only participate in deciding matters that have not been settled by the monk officials. If someone has made a request to the monastery that cannot be decided by the individual officials or if there is a conflict involving one or more monks, the decision-making process in the monastery follows the following pattern of ascending authority:

First, the officials (*las thog*) in the monastery administration, number four to eight on the list above, will try to make a decision. If they are not able to reach an agreement, the issue will be forwarded to the senior monks (*bgres song*), who have completed all monastic offices, and therefore have more authority. If the senior monks also fail to solve the case, it will be presented to the lama. If even the lama is unable to find a solution, all the monks will be called together for a meeting.[88]

7.3.3 *Conflict Resolution*

The procedure for conflict resolution in the monastery is organised according to a model that parallels the 'village court' and at higher levels the two are merged.[89] Attempts are made to solve cases internally, but if that fails, the lay community is called upon to help. If that, too, fails, representatives from the three villages are summoned, and finally as a last resort, external authorities, religious or secular, will be asked to intervene. One senior monk explained that in the past, if the monks were unable to resolve a conflict themselves, they would turn to the hereditary headmen (*go 'pa*) or the chief (*spyi khyab*) of the three villages. Elderly monks reported that the hereditary village leaders had no formal authority over other aspects related to monastery administration; it was only in cases of serious conflict that they would be requested for conflict resolution. Stories about major decisions in the past suggest that the more powerful among the headmen nevertheless exercised significant authority also over monastic affairs.

Currently, if the monastery asks the village leaders to help with conflict resolution, they will arrange a joint meeting in which both laymen and monks (*skya ser*) participate in the resolution. The result will be written down in a legal document and stored in the monastery archive. One of the senior monks gave an example, 'These days there is a small conflict in the monastery. The monk administration will reconcile it. If it had been a big conflict, we would have requested the laymen for help.'[90] Eventually it turned out that the monks were unable to solve the conflict, and the youth club intervened and tried to resolve the case through mediation (*slong 'bebs*),[91] but it was not resolved until it reached the '[council of] the fifteen'. The '[council of] the fifteen' is the next step after the *skya ser* meeting, and as mentioned in Chapter Five, it was established in 2009 in order to reduce favouritism and to solve more serious disputes at the village level so that three-village meetings could be avoided. The establishment of the new council must be considered a consequence of the overall changes of the village government system. The council was set up just a few years after the hereditary leaders were more or less forced to resign. The young and inexperienced leaders, who are chosen by lottery, do not have

88 Interview with senior monk official, 07.04.12.

89 An overview of the 'village court' was provided in Chapter Five.

90 Interview 13.04.12.

91 The role of the youth club has been discussed in Chapter Five.

as much authority as their predecessors and the establishment of the council may have been an attempt to compensate for this. Moreover, although the villagers did not say so explicitly, the split of the monastery increased the conflict level between the three villages, and this is likely to have strengthened the desire to keep the resolution processes within the individual villages. Another important change was explained to me by one of the senior monks: 'In the past, the monks and laity would only gather in order to resolve very big conflicts. Small and medium sized conflicts would be handled by the village and monastery separately. Nowadays, however, laymen even participate in small conflicts in the monastery, (...) and monks and laity convene and make new regulations (*'grig khrims*) together.'[92] The regulations he referred to were made during a joint meeting of laity and monks (*skya ser*) in 2009 and deal with a variety of topics ranging from proper conduct for monks and laity during rituals and festivals to regulations on use of communal property, recorded in a legal contract (*Contract by the assembly of laity and monks*), which will be discussed in Chapter Nine.

7.4 The Splitting and Rebuilding of the Monasteries

Chapter Three told the story of how the monasteries in Limi were merged in the seventeenth century as a way of escaping the heavy taxes imposed by the Kalyal kings, and how they split again in the 1980s. The disagreement that led to the partition mainly concerned the use and distribution of resources and access to monastic services, but it also had significant consequences for other aspects of the monastery management. Decision-making in monastic affairs had previously been carried out within the monastery itself or in meetings with monks and lay representatives from the three villages. After the split, decision-making was in most cases scaled down from the three-village level to the single-village level.[93] While Rinchen Ling continued to serve the community in Waltse, the small village temples in Dzang and Til were rebuilt and transformed to fully fledged monasteries. This facilitated greater interaction between the village government and the monastic administration and consequently created a greater demand for monks.

After the split, the monastery in Waltse had to manage with a greatly reduced number of monks, whilst the temples in Dzang and Til, which had

92 Interview 13.04.12.

93 The different implementation of the recruitment rule discussed in Chapter Eight is an example of the consequences.

formerly been looked after only by shrine keepers, had to be extended into full-fledged monastic institutions to cater for the religious needs of their communities. In Dzang and Til, monks and villagers had to upgrade and extend the buildings of the old temples, establish monastic offices and administrative routines, purchase scriptures and ritual equipment, determine the ritual calendar, and decide how to implement the recruitment rules.[94] The expansion of the old temple buildings in Til and Dzang into monastic institutions required significant mobilisation. The monks in Til explained:

> In the beginning there was no time to think about the rituals; we were only concerned about how to get funding and manage the extension of the monastery. We had to build the kitchen, the assembly hall, and the monks' and lama's quarters. We begged the village people for money to buy beams and the villagers contributed with food, money and other donations. In the past, there had been only one shrine keeper and just an absolute minimum of equipment in Til Kundzom. There were only three pots—not even a 'portable fire bowl' (*me slang*) for keeping the tea warm. Everything had to be acquired [when we expanded the monastery]. We received many donations from households for the merit of people who had passed away. We held a meeting and decided to go also to Waltse, Dzang, and to Purang to beg our relatives and acquaintances (*ngo shes*) for donations. We also begged acquaintances among the Byansi[95] and nomads from Ngari, who donated sheep and goats. For the money we received from selling these animals we bought golden statues. It was important that the statues would be made of durable material; clay, for instance, will dissolve after some time. [The extension of the monastery took several years.] In 1993 we put the stone slabs on the floor, and during Kyabgön Rinpoche's visit, the monastery was consecrated. [Although some of the sponsors were external], most of the contributions were made from the village, and the villagers did all the construction work, including carrying all the beams and stones.[96]

94 For economic implications of the split see Chapters Three and Nine; for consequences for recruitment, see Chapter Eight.

95 The Byansi or Bura, referred to as *byang pa* (lit. 'people from the north') by the Limigya, is an ethnic group living in the Humla and Darchula districts, and the Indian state of Uttarakhand. See for instance Levine 1987: 77f.

96 Interview with the monks in Til, 05.03.12.

This massive effort over the course of several years can be read as a clear sign of the importance placed on the monastic institution in the three villages. Not only its religious significance, but its function in providing services to ensure the health and wellbeing of the villagers, and its function to appease and keep in check threatening forces from outside and within. Since basic biomedical health services, education, and other social services have been largely absent throughout most of Limi's history, this role of the monastery is experienced as particularly important.

When rebuilding the two new monasteries in Dzang and Til, Rinchen Ling in Waltse served as model in terms of management structure and ritual service. The lists of ritual expenses and other administrative documents, for instance, were simply copied and adapted from the Waltse register. Similarly, the ritual calendars in the two villages were based on the calendar from Waltse. As will be explained in the following chapter, the recruitment rules were continued and even strengthened in all three villages.[97] Several meetings were held, both among the monks and combined meetings between monks and lay representatives, in order to make decisions and muster support for the monasteries. Such a restructuring of the monastic landscape could have led to other reforms in monastic management, but fear of further fragmentation and spill over effects on temporal village management made the villagers choose a model based on continuity. However, it is worth noting that contrary to the situation when the first temples were established hundreds of years back, the initiatives were now purely local.

7.5 The Monasteries' Relationship with Temporal and Religious Authorities

As mentioned in Chapter Three, the monasteries in Limi have been connected with a network of monasteries in Tibet and Nepal throughout history. Since the thirteenth century, the monasteries in Dzang and Til were branch monasteries of Gyangdrag, the Drigung stronghold at Kailash, but the monasteries in Limi have also had strong connections with a number of other monasteries in Central Tibet, especially with Yangri Gar and Drigung Thil, and in Ngari with Shephel Ling, Khochar, Gungphur, and Sera Lung (Se ra Lung). Moreover, monks and laity in Limi have interacted with monks from various smaller

97 See Chapter Eight.

institutions in other communities further south in Humla. Elderly villagers also tell stories of local monks and lay pilgrims who ventured further east to Mustang and all the way to Kathmandu.[98] Such long-distance travel in the past was, however, extremely time-consuming and communication with religious and secular authorities outside Limi was therefore restricted. It was common to send orally transmitted or written requests to the Drigung rinpoches with the men who were going to India in the winter season to fetch maple burls for the wooden drinking bowls. Most of the maple hunters spent some time in Dehra Dun and acted as intermediaries between monks and laity at home and the lamas. Improved infrastructure and communications have facilitated better and more frequent relations with a number of religious authorities in exile; this was particularly noticeable after Nepal Telecom set up a satellite phone in Waltse during summer of 2010. Recently, Waltse and Rinchen Ling has both wifi connectivity and mobile phone coverage, and many of the monks are now linking up with religious authorities and others on social media and this is likely to have significant impact in the coming years.

The most important monastery outside Limi is Jangchub Ling, the main Drigung monastery in India and the seat of Kyabgön Rinpoche. However, since the Limi *sprul sku* established himself in a Buddhist centre in Taiwan, stronger connections have been made with the Taiwanese sangha and with some of the order's American supporters. When some of the villagers started to migrate to Kathmandu in the 1990s, they also established closer contact with the Drigung lamas in the city. After the Drigung lamas inaugurated Rinchen Palri (Rin chen dPal ri) monastery in 2007 and the Drigung Kagyu Rinchen Ling monastery in November 2009, monks from Limi enrolled in both institutions, and members of the Limi community in Kathmandu regularly participate in the monastic events. Until recently, the Nepali government has shown little interest in, and has consequently had little influence over, the monasteries in Limi. But since 2000, the three monasteries in Limi have been registered with the Buddhist Philosophy Promotion and Monastery Development Committee, which is an office under the Ministry for Federal Affairs and Local Development. This has provided the monasteries with some funding. Just as the village assemblies' relationship with the central authorities has changed, so has the monasteries': the last few years, the contact with the Nepali central government has become much more frequent, and the monasteries now have special committees dealing with government budgets.

98 Though sharing the same *sprul sku* with Gomoche monastery in Dolpo, interactions between the communities have probably been minor.

Overall, the local management system has been negotiated in the light of larger socio-economic and political transformations in the region over the last six decades. These larger transitions have also had effects on monastery management, but to a more subtle degree. The outline of the monastic management system in this chapter described the formal positions in the monasteries as being largely the same as in the past. The decision-making and conflict resolution procedures, however, have become more democratic, and partly due to the downscaling of monastic decision-making to the village level after the split of the monasteries there has been a greater degree of interaction between village and monastery. The following chapters, however, will show that the monastery has, in certain ways, become more conservative as a response to increased pressures and challenges, especially in the area of monastic recruitment.

CHAPTER 8

Monastic Recruitment

> On an early December morning in 2011, three eight-year-old boys from Waltse were led by their parents to the Rinchen Ling monastery and clad in robes.[1] The parents first offered tea (*mang ja*) to the assembly of monks, then the lama cut a lock of hair (*skra gcod*) from each of the young novices and instructed them to abandon all sinful activities and to practice virtuous deeds.[2] The parents then offered prayers that the young monk recruits (*grwa chung*) would have long lives and perform many good deeds as monks. After presenting a mandala offering to the lama, the parents distributed ceremonial scarves (*kha btags*) together with a small donation of money to all the monks in the assembly. When the ceremony was over, the young boys took their seats at the lower end of the novice row and tried their best to imitate the senior monks in the complicated liturgy[3] for the day's ritual (Fig. 8.1).

∴

The monastic disciplinarian (*dge bskos*) had visited the three families a year in advance[4] and announced that it was time for the parents to send their sons to the monastery.[5] The visit was, however, only a formality. In Limi, providing a son as monk to the monastery is part of the households' obligations to

1 In Limi, the recruitment of novices always take place during the Ganden Ngamchö (dGa' ldan lnga mchod) festival, which commemorates the passing away of Tsong kha pa on the twenty-fifth of the tenth Tibetan month. The boys were actually only seven years old, but the Limigya follow the Tibetan custom of adding the birth year when calculating people's age.

2 In the past, the *Limi monastery regulations* (*Sle mi dgon gyi bca' yig*) from 1806 would be read out loud at this point, but this is no longer practised.

3 The liturgy for Ganden Ngamchö is the *Na rag skong bshags* ritual for purification of the lowest hells. Contrary to practice in Lhasa and other Gelug dominated places (see e.g., Richardson (1993 and Mills (2003: 352), the festival is not celebrated by the laity in Limi. See also Appendix IV.

4 The reminder is given during the Saga Dawa festival.

5 Interview with senior monk official, 07.03.12.

 | DOI:10.1163/9789004714571_009

the institution, and the parents had therefore known about it since the birth of their sons. While dedicating the second son to a monastery has been a widespread ideal in many Tibetan Buddhist communities, the recruitment of monks through levy has been far less common. In Limi, the system of monk levy has been practised at least since the end of the nineteenth century with important implications not only for monastic life and social organisation but also for the governance of the three villages. To provide historical context, I will first explore some of the known examples of monk levy from edicts and historical works from Western Tibet. Then, I will provide a translation of the nineteenth-century recruitment contract and a brief discussion of how the system was established and developed in Limi. Based on interviews, observation, and household surveys, the following part will study how the system has been implemented over the last few decades and discuss examples of how the rules have been variously endorsed and challenged by the villagers. Particular attention will be given to some of the consequences of increased availability of secular and religious education as well as other socio-economic and political changes for monastic recruitment. As suggested in the opening vignette of the book, the monk levy represents a big dilemma for many households. The final part of the chapter will address these dilemmas and discuss how the monastic obligations are negotiated today and offer some tentative thoughts about why they have been maintained.

FIGURE 8.1 The young novices during Ganden Ngamchö, 2011

8.1 Recruitment by Law

The dictionary term for compulsory recruitment or monk levy is 'monk tax' (*grwa khral, btsun khral, ban khral*), but this term is not used in Limi and, as we will see below, is not mentioned in the recruitment contract—instead recruitment is part of the duties referred to by the phrase *grong pa la dgon pa'i khral*, literally 'the households' obligations to the monastery' or *dgon pa'i khral*, 'monastic obligations', for short. In Limi, these monastic obligations include not only recruitment, but also the closely associated sponsorship duties, which will be detailed in the following chapter.

'Monk tax' has generally been understood as a monastery's right to conscript recruits in order to ensure a stable monk population. While not very common, the phenomenon has a history of several hundred years and has been found across the Tibetan plateau and adjoining areas, but its implementation has varied considerably. In Tibet, the practice was forcefully ended with the Chinese annexation, whilst in some of the frontier enclaves in the Himalaya it survived for longer. Currently, I am only aware of the levy being practised in Limi. Probably the most commonly quoted account of monk tax is Goldstein's article about taxation in Samada (Sa mda') village in Tsang (gTsang), which gives a brief description of the duty to provide monks for the local Drigung monastery.[6] A more detailed treatment of the topic has been provided by Cassinelli and Ekvall in *A Tibetan Principality: the Political System of Sa-skya* (1969).[7] Basing their analysis on interviews with four exiled members of the Sakya ruling family, Cassinelli and Ekvall's account provides insight into the elite's understanding of how the 'monk tax' system functioned, but their analysis lacks the perspective of those who were subjected to the rule. These and most other works, moreover, have tended to focus on only single cases of the practice. Consequently, Jansen's comparative study of the prevalence and many meanings of the term 'monk tax' in available textual sources from pre-1950 Tibetan Buddhist areas is particularly welcome, providing much needed nuance to aid our understanding.[8]

8.1.1 *Historical Precedents*

King Yeshe Ö's 988 decree (*chos rtsigs*) on secular and religious law cited in Chapter Three contained what is probably the first known example of compulsory monastic recruitment. The decree stated that except for the heir to

6 Goldstein 1971b: 20.

7 Cassinelli and Ekvall 1969: 294–311.

8 Jansen 2023.

the throne, all his brothers should be ordained as monks.[9] The rule, which seems to have applied only to the royal family, had the function of keeping potential contenders for the throne at a safe distance and at the same time retain the ruler's control of the newly established monastic institutions.[10] Whereas it is important not to overstate the historical link, the legal regulation of the relationship between monastery and community in Western Tibet, and the priority of the former over the latter, has its historical origin in this period. Another example that is often mentioned in Limi is that of Krācalla, the thirteenth-century king of Jumla, who became a staunch supporter of the Drigung Kagyupas after his conversion by Chenga Lingpa. According to the *Rinchen Ling monastery inventory*, the king ordered two of his sons be ordained, while the youngest was placed on the throne.[11] Like the more famous king Yeshe Ö, the example of Krācalla may have functioned as a historical 'model' in the region.

The earliest extant written formulation of a compulsory recruitment system for commoners in Western Tibet that I have come across dates from the middle of the sixteenth century. The *Ladakh chronicles* (*La dwags rgyal rabs*) state that at the invitation of King Tashi Namgyal (bKra shis rNam rgyal, r. ca. 1550–75) the Drigung vajraholder at Kailash (Chos rje lDan ma Kun dga' Grags pa, d.u.)[12] founded Phyang (Phyi dbang)[13] monastery and instituted the rule of monk levy in the adjoining villages.[14] After the former Western Tibetan kingdoms came under the sway of Central Tibet in the seventeenth century, the Ganden Phodrang (dGa' ldan Pho brang) government decided to strengthen Tholing as the religious centre of Ngari and an edict was issued stating that each family of Guge was obliged to send the middle son to become a monk.[15] Although

9 Vitali 1996: 193. The original text of the decree has not been preserved.

10 Monastic recruitment has contributed to reduce the pressure on inheritance also in regular households (see e.g., Goldstein 1981c), but at the same time secular manpower has tended to be in high demand.

11 *Rinchen Ling monastery inventory*, f. 3b, ll. 5–8. See also Chapter Three above.

12 After more than a century of decline, Chos rje lDan ma Kun dga' Grags pa was appointed head (*rdor 'dzin*) of the Drigungpas in Ngari at Gyangdrag monastery and managed to strengthen the order's position. In addition to the foundation of Phyang monastery, according to local tradition quoted in Petech (1978: 324), he also received Lamayuru (bLa *ma g.yu ru/g.yung drung*) monastery and has since been credited with the spread of the Drigung school to Ladakh.

13 The full name of the Phyang monastery is sGang sngon bKra shis Chos rdzong.

14 Francke 1999 [1914] vol. 2: 37f: "*yul yul nas btsun khral btab*". See also his translation and comment on p. 103f.

15 Vitali 1999: 50, n71. 'In the later part of the life of the rGyal.dbang sku-phreng lnga.pa, sGar dpon Bu.chung (…) and, during the war, rgyal.po Dga' ldan Tshe.dbang dpal.bzang paid

similar recruitment rules may have existed before, the Ganden Phodrang government may have used the monk tax at least partly as a strategy to spread its influence and control over the religious institutions throughout its newly acquired territory. The Fifth Dalai Lama also issued similar edicts in other locations on the geographical margins of the Tibetan state. A well-known example is the edict from 1680, which introduced compulsory recruitment in Tawang (rTa dbang), a small principality located south-east of Lhasa on the border with Bhutan, translated by Michael Aris.[16]

The Ngari edict from 1687 enforced monk levy not only in the monastery at Tholing, but also in its twenty-five branch monasteries (*dgon lag*), including monasteries belonging to the Sakyapa and Drugpa schools of Buddhism. Vitali writes that the government's decisions were carried out by the 'war-time king' (*dmag dus kyi rgyal po*) Ganden Tshewang together with the 'governor' (*sgar dpon*). The establishment of the recruitment rule is also mentioned in the regent Sangye Gyatso's (*sde srid* Sangs rgyas rGya mtsho, 1653–1705) religious history of the Gelug order, the *Yellow beryl* (*Baidurya ser po*, 1698). The regent writes that the number of monks in Tholing had dwindled to thirty and that the following measures were taken:

> From fire hare (1687), at the beginning of the twelveth (sic) *rab.byung*, in addition to the original thirty monks, 160 new [Tho.gling] monks were gathered by means of *ban.khral*.[17]

Sangye Gyatso and the Ganden Phodrang government invested great efforts into establishing control over the newly conquered region. In order to strengthen its ties with Central Tibet, the regent introduced a new system for appointing abbots to Tholing, who would subsequently become 'throne holders' at Ganden monastery (*dga' ldan khri pa*). The abbatial succession seems to have functioned for some time,[18] but the monk levy apparently failed because

particular attention to mTho.lding dgon.pa. By gathering the middle sons in the families to become monks from the ten directions of Gu.ge *phyi.nang* ("external and internal"), they appointed it the mother dgon[.pa] of the twenty-five branch monasteries, including Sa[.skya.pa and] 'Brug[.pa] monasteries, they not only expanded it but gave to it a stable organization. This is a sign of its greatness during the intermediate period.' Quote from Tashi Tsering (ed) 1996, Tibetan text in appendix 8, p. 204.

16 Aris (1980: 13ff) provides a version of the edict together with his translation. See also Jansen (2023), who interprets the instalment of the monk levy in Tawang as a way of securing monks to newly founded monasteries.

17 Translated by Vitali (1999: 53), Tibetan text p. 205.

18 Vitali 1999: 52.

a new edict had to be issued in 1738, during the reign of the Seventh Dalai Lama. As was the case with the previous edict, it ordered all families in the region to send sons to Tholing and its branch monasteries.[19] Dieter Schuh has translated a fragmentary legal document from Tholing dated 1741, which seems to have been issued to enforce the implementation of the Seventh Dalai Lama's 1738 edict.[20] Another recruitment document translated by Schuh was issued twenty years later in 1761, during the reign of the Eighth Dalai Lama.[21] Both documents detail the reinforcement of the obligation of farming and nomadic households belonging to Tholing and its branch monasteries to send the middle of three sons to the monastic community with which they were affiliated. The number of legal documents written to reinforce the rule within a relatively short time span suggests that the duty must have been resented by the local population. The resentment can also be read from the documents themselves; in particular the document from 1761 explicitly refers to local resistance to the levy. Compulsory recruitment may have been implemented for some time, but yet again, in 1847, another edict was issued to enforce the recruitment rule in order to improve 'the pitiful conditions' of Tholing:

> During the period 1847–1849 he [i.e. gNod sbyin Phun tshogs, the newly appointed "plenipotentiary" of the area] visited mNga' ris sGar twice. On these occasions he saw the pitiful condition in which Tho.ling was lying. Similar to the ordinance issued in the period of Sgar.dpon Bu.chung and dGa'.ldan Tshe.dbang dpal.bzang, he issued an authoritative edict in fire sheep (1847) ordering all families of the region to give their middle sons to become monks at the *dgon.pa*-s, and not to create obstacles to those who had faith in the religion, so that they could renounce secular life.[22]

The Gelugpa presence and the influence of the Ganden Phodrang government seem to have been weaker in Purang.[23] There is no mention of Purang in these edicts, and none of the monasteries there are included in the lists of Tholing's branch monasteries.[24] However, the Indian Civil Service officer

19 Vitali 1999: 186.

20 Schuh 1981: 75ff.

21 Schuh 1981: 113ff.

22 Vitali 1999: 56.

23 Apart from Shephel Ling and a couple of branch monasteries, the only other known Gelug monastery in the Purang district was a small monastery called Serchung (Ser chung), founded by lHa dbang bLo gros in the fifteenth century (Vitali, personal communication 2014 and 1990: 38).

24 Vitali 1999: 109–114.

Charles Sherring noted in his travel account from the beginning of the twentieth century that monk conscription was indeed practised in Shephel Ling, the main Gelugpa monastery in Purang.[25] Unfortunately, no legal documents are available, but since Shephel Ling was founded by the above-mentioned Ganden Tshewang just after the incorporation of the Western Tibetan kingdoms in Central Tibet, it is not unlikely that the same recruitment rule as that which applied to Tholing was introduced there as well. Levine writes that monk conscription was practised in neighbouring Khochar, which belonged to the Sakyapas.[26] Moreover, as mentioned above, variants of the monk levy system have been reported from Sakya,[27] Dingri (Ding ri),[28] Samada,[29] and Kyirong (sKyid grong).[30] On the Nepali side of the border, compulsory recruitment could for instance be found in Baragaon, in the Mustang district[31] and in Dolpo. Hence, although we do not know how strongly it was enforced, this system of recruitment appears to have existed in a number of locations in Western Tibet and affiliated regions.[32] However, the three monasteries in Limi seem to have been the only institutions in Humla with such a recruitment system.

In some cases, as in the examples from Ladakh and Tawang, the rule appears to have been introduced with the foundation of the temples and monasteries to ensure a stable community of monks.[33] However, in other places it was probably more commonly implemented later, after the first small structures had been expanded and developed into institutions and often because of monastic population decline. Although far from exhaustive,[34] these historical examples from Western Tibetan areas should suffice to show that the immediate reasons for the introduction of the rule of monk conscription varied and that it was met with various degrees of resistance. Although no reasons for this resistance are provided in the available legal documents, it is easy to imagine that a newly conquered region, weary after a series of wars and general decline,

25 Sherring 1993: 188.

26 Levine 1992: 344.

27 Cassinelli and Ekvall 1969: 294–311.

28 Aziz (1974: 180 and 274) provides brief accounts of compulsory recruitment to *ser khyim dgon* as well as to monasteries in Dingri. Her overview of the tax responsibilities in the region (pp. 395–97) lists the number of monks conscripted from different villages.

29 Goldstein 1971b.

30 Schuh 1988: 52f

31 Ramble (2008a: 180–83) writes that monk levy has been prevalent in Baragaon and provides an account of how the system dissolved in Te. See also Aziz 1974: 180, 274, Cassinelli and Ekvall 1969: 294–311, Goldstein 1971b: 20 and 2010: 9 and Schuh 2000: 295.

32 Compulsory recruitment was also practised in Derge (see Thargyal 2007: 159).

33 This is also pointed out by Jansen (2023).

34 See Jansen (2023) for more examples.

would be reluctant to accept a rule that would demand so many of their sons. The rule was never needed in the largest monastic institutions in Central and Eastern Tibet; instead, these monasteries had to impose certain restrictions on enrolment.[35] However, the levy was implemented in relatively large regional monasteries, like Sakya, Shephel Ling, and Tawang, which had several hundred monks. In all the examples, mentioned above the introduction of the rule seems to be closely associated with the attempt of the government or the head of a religious order to maintain and spread its influence and control. But what was the reason for establishing the practice in a small community like Limi? As we will see below, the monastery's proximity to Mount Kailash seems to have been at least part of the explanation.

8.1.2 *Signing the Contract*

In 1894, the thirty-third Drigung lineage holder, Drigung Chungtsang Tenzin Chökyi Lodrö, went on a three-year pilgrimage to Kailash and Manasarovar.[36] He spent the last winter of his pilgrimage, from 1895–96, in Limi.[37] During his stay he witnessed the Rimchö festival and, apparently not completely satisfied with the local conditions, he corrected the monks' performance of *'cham*,[38] commissioned the composition of a new 'dance manual' (*'cham yig*, Fig. 7.20), and demanded a strengthening of monastic recruitment practices. In order to accomplish the latter, monk and lay representatives (*skya ser*) from the three villages were called to a meeting. An agreement was eventually reached and detailed in a written contract (*gan rgya*) entitled: *Yul tsho gsum na bu gnyis byung phyin bu re chos sgor zhugs rgyu gan rgya* (…)[39] ('Contract [regarding] the obligation for each [household] with two sons in the three villages to [make] one son enter the monastery'). The contract consists of sixteen lines, and as the norm is with this type of legal documents,[40] it is written in cursive script (*'khyug yig*) on a scroll of Tibetan paper. A few of the syllables are illegible, but in most cases it has been possible to infer the content from the context.[41] The contract is authenticated by nine stamps including those of the Drigung Chungtsang Rinpoche, the Ngari district governor (*spyi khyab*),

35 Jansen 2015: 57ff.

36 See also Chapter Three.

37 He wrote the *Drigung history of Kailash* towards the end of this pilgrimage.

38 The corrections are detailed in the *Rin chen gling 'cham yig* composed in 1895. This *'cham yig* is read on the final public rehearsal (*'cham rtsis*) before the annual festival. See Chapter Seven.

39 The last two syllables are illegible.

40 Schneider 2002: 417.

41 I am grateful to Charles Ramble, Nyima Drandul, and Per Kværne for valuable suggestions.

a representative from Purang *rdzong* and the Shephel Ling monastery, as well as the stamps from the three villages in Limi and Rinchen Ling (see Appendix 1).[42] Since the document is crucial for the regulation of the lay—monastic relationship and by extension for the governance of the villages even today, I have attempted a translation of the full text below. The transcript of the text can be found in Appendix 1:

> **Contract [regarding] the obligation for each [household] with two sons in the three villages to [make] one son enter the monastery (...)**
> The following is the true content of the unchanging agreement[43] [submitted] in the year of the Fire Monkey [1896], on the fifteenth day of the third month, in the presence of the outstanding source of benefit [and happiness], the highest precious preserver of the law. The two parties below confer constant validity to the original tenor of the contract[44] [which was issued] from the office of the counsellor of the three districts [of Ngari], in the Earth Monkey year [1848? 1908?].[45] Concerning the monks in the Limi monastery, according to the order of His Holiness, the Drigung *sprul sku* Rinpoche, you, [the representatives from] the villages and the monastery, monks and laymen, have come to an actual agreement to continue (*rgyun 'khyongs*) the unchanging definite meaning of the 'legal arrangement' (*sgrig bca'*).[46] [As] necessary observations from Purang district [and Shephel Ling] monastery, the seals were brought down [to Limi][47] on the sixth (?) day of the fourth (?) month[48] in the year of the Fire Monkey [1896].
>
> Authenticated by the signature of the [contracting parties] listed below, in a state of unchanging voluntary acceptance, the original meaning of the contents of the obligation submitted in its full length, will be taken to heart.[49] In the Limi monastery, the [tradition of performing] the

42 I have not been able to identify the last stamp.

43 *gan rgya'i nang don* (*Bod rgya tshig mdzod chen mo*)

44 Based on Schneider's (2002: 420) translation of the *sanctio*: *slar yang gan don 'di rang la sor gnas rgyun 'khyongs yong ba gyis.*

45 The Earth Monkey year may refer to 1848, the date of an earlier contract, which may or may not have been issued by the office of the district governor of Ngari. Another possibility is that the date refers an authorisation rather than first instalment of the contract in 1908.

46 This could refer to the renewal of the contract.

47 The phrase *tham pa phab pa yin* could mean that the two seals were brought from Purang to Limi.

48 The dates in the document are unclear.

49 Schneider 2002: 419f.

'cham dances of all the protectors of the teaching has been flourishing. Moreover, the monastery performs many religious activities and duties (*byed sgo*). Meanwhile, the number of monks has decreased. At the occasion when Drigung Kyabje Rinpoche Konchog Tendzin Chokyi Lodro steered his horse to Mount Kailash for pilgrimage, he stayed one winter in Limi. Having observed that the number of monk recruits (*grwa rgyun*) was dwindling, for the performance of the dances of the guardians of the teaching and the many religious offerings and rituals, [he said that] there need to be approximately fifty monks. There is no other solution. Even since early times, in order to avert misfortune from the three villages in Limi, and to bring guidance and protection for this and future lives, this monastery was established. Having seen the great abundance and prosperity, [the Rinpoche ordered that] when the large households from the three villages have two sons, one son should be placed in the monastic community (*chos sgor grwa tshang*). There is no other solution. 'Please send [your sons to the monastery]'. As a result of [the Rinpoche's] insistent request, [and] not being able to withstand his urge, [the representatives] from the three villages, [after adding the rule that] the small households with three sons should send one son to the monastery, [they] voluntarily accepted and replied 'we shall comply'.[50] Henceforth [they] acted according to the definite meaning [of the contract].[51]

In a case where the son [taking care of] the household passes away, the son who has entered the door of the Dharma should return [to take up the responsibility of householder]. If a monk in the monastery breaks the rules, he has to [pay] a fine of half a *srang* of gold as punishment for the violation. [Having] once more [returned to] the religious life, until the time of death, [he] is not allowed to leave.[52] Moreover, there can be no dispute[53] no matter the reason, all [you] can do is to negotiate the size of the fine; you cannot argue about the decision. [You] cannot return to the question [about] who started the fight. Within the monastery, apart from [issues like] who is powerful or weak, who is senior or junior,[54] discussion is not allowed. Even when [monks] from the monastery visit

50 The sentence is difficult to translate, but it seems that the *grong chen* did not accept until the *grong chung* were included.

51 Tentative translation.

52 This means that breaking the monastery's rules on purpose in order to get dismissed is not an option.

53 Lit. 'making what falls down return upwards'.

54 Rank according to either status or age.

other villages, the local customs should be respected,[55] whether great or small. [The monks] should not act individually. To [put it] concisely, the content of this agreement should not be transgressed by [conduct such as saying] 'it is not me, it is him', bring up again [the old stories of] the dispute,[56] raise dirt from the [water's] depth,[57] [talk with] two tongues in one mouth, hide the faults of the right [hand] from the left, make cooked meat raw again, (…),[58] carry the master on one's shoulders, move mountains and dry up lakes and so on. In conclusion, the terms of this contract, from the point of view of monks and laymen, shall not be transgressed, not even to the size of a sesame seed. If the rules are broken, the penalty enforced by law [lit. 'to the feet of the law'] will be ten *srang* of gold … again, conferring constant legal validity to the tenor of this agreement,[59] the seals are offered: [Among the representatives from] Til village the seal has passed from hand to hand, [among the representatives from] Waltse village the seal has passed from hand to hand, [among the representatives from] Dzang village the seal has passed from hand to hand, [and among the representatives from] the monastery, the seals have passed from hand to hand.[60]

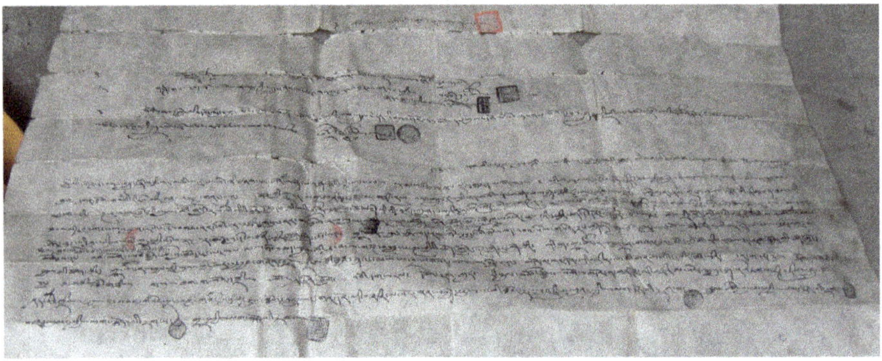

FIGURE 8.2 The *Monastic recruitment contract*

55 Tentative translation.

56 Translation based on Mullard (2013: 190 n. 49). Schneider (2002: 425) proposes: 'to produce new ideas in the form of: "I have been thinking about it."'

57 Schneider 2002: 426.

58 The document writes *'bam dags ral.* I have not been able to translate this phrase.

59 Schneider 2002: 420.

60 According to Schneider (2002: 416) *lag bskor zhus pa'i rtags* refers to a practice in which the seal is passed from hand to hand of all members of a signing party.

The document starts with a list of the authorities involved. Whereas the initiative was taken by the Drigung hierarch, the legal process demanded authorisation from the Ngari governor's office (*spyi khyab lhan khang*), as well as the district administration in Purang *rdzong*, and the main monastery in the district, Shephel Ling. Even though Shephel Ling was a Gelug monastery it also exercised authority over other monasteries in the region, regardless of religious affiliation.

The monks in Limi think that the compulsory recruitment system may be older than this contract, and there are reasons to believe that the contract could be a renewal of an earlier original that is no longer extant. The year Earth Monkey provided in line three does indeed seem to refer to an earlier date.[61] At first, I thought that Earth Monkey (1848 or 1908) would have to be a misspelling of Fire Monkey, but it is not likely that a mistake should have been made with regard to such an essential point. Some of the phrases in the introduction seem to refer to an earlier practice; for instance, the phrases *rgyun 'khyongs* ('continue') in line three and *sngar nas bzung* ('since the past' or 'always') in line six suggest that the recruitment rule may be a continuation of an earlier practice. A similar example, in which two different dates provided in the same document refer to a renewal of an earlier recruitment contract, has been found by Vitali in the 1847 edict issued by the minister (*bka' blon*) Nöjin Phuntsok (gNod sbyin Phun tshogs) after his second visit to Ngari.[62] Judging from the available documents, monk levy in Ngari seems to have been introduced both in the form of general edicts (*bka' shog*) and more specific legal contracts (*gan rgya*) as in the case of Limi. Because no former contract has been found in the Limi archive, there is no mention of monk levy in the *Limi monastery regulations* (*bca' yig*) from 1806, and since there is no *explicit* reference to an earlier agreement in the recruitment document, I suspect that if there ever was a former regulation, it must have been of a more general kind.

The *narratio* starts by establishing the religious importance of the local monastery and praises the monastery for keeping the tradition of performing the *'cham* dances, but states that the number of monks is not sufficient to perform the rituals properly. The rinpoche reminds the villagers of the importance of the rituals and argues that the villages are wealthy enough to establish a compulsory recruitment system. The negotiations must have been tough, however, as the text is explicit about the rinpoche having to 'urge insistently' (*bka' nan*

61 The date of the visit of Drigung Chuntsang Rinpoche in the Fire Monkey year (1896) is confirmed by the *Drigung history of Kailash* which he composed at the end of his stay, and by a number of other sources.

62 Vitali 1999: 56, 186–89.

che ba). Line ten in the document shows that the *grong chen* households did not consent until the *grong chung* households were also included. The *grong chung* recruitment rule is added as subscript and written with a thinner pen, authenticated by a stamp.[63] Interestingly, this contract specifies that the large households (*grong chen*) have to send the youngest of two sons while the small households (*grong chung*) will have to send the middle of three sons, which seems a particularly strict rule for the large households, as the standard formula elsewhere seems to be the middle of three sons. We do not know the population size in 1896, but one possible reason could be that this was the only way to recruit as many as fifty monks, which was said to be a minimum requirement for performing the rituals during Rimchö.

The next section provides details about how the rule should be enforced and how to deal with monks wanting to escape. The text makes it clear that this type of recruitment is a lifelong obligation but recognising the importance of the householder for the survival of a family, it is specified that the only acceptable reason for withdrawing from the monastery is the death of the monk's elder brother. Then the text states that the monks cannot evade their responsibility by deliberately breaking the monastery's rules so as to get expelled. Whatever the crime, after paying a fine, the offending monk would still have to remain in the monastery. If my reading of the contract is correct, this appears as a particularly strict enforcement of the levy, and represents a notable deviation from general monastic discipline, according to which grave misconduct would be punished by expulsion.[64]

Finally, the *sanctio* consists mainly of standard obligation contract (*gan rgya*) formulae; a long list of sayings common to the genre are quoted, and the size of the fine for breaking the contract is set to ten *srang* of gold, a considerable amount at the time. The contract was concluded after passing the villages' and monastery's seals from hand to hand through the congregation, whereupon the document was stamped, finalising the agreement.

8.1.3 *Later Implementation of the Contract*

The resistance and need for the Rinpoche to put pressure on the villagers, as expressed in the contract, indicates a lot of resentment. Unfortunately, the sources do not tell us how the villagers reacted after the Rinpoche left and how the new rule was implemented in this early period. But Limi monks and

63 It is possible that the subscript was added later, but I find it most likely that it was included as part of the original negotiations.

64 See for instance Jansen (2015: 209ff) for a study of what kind of transgressions would lead to expulsion in a number of monastic guidelines (*bca' yig*).

laity have shared their experiences since the middle of the twentieth century onwards, a period that is still part of living memory. Throughout these decades, the villagers in Limi have been sending their second or third sons to the monastery at the age of eight, but the implementation of the levy has varied.

The rule applied to all households with the required number of sons, but not to the blacksmith family, who had an inferior status and was exempt from regular taxation.[65] However, whilst the rinpoche's stipulated minimum of fifty monks was in force, the monks did not all necessarily remain in the monastery. Elderly monks recall that in the past there used to be sufficient leeway if some of them wanted to devote longer periods for retreats or to seek religious instructions in one of the order's main monasteries, or if they had to, or preferred to, work to sustain their families. A monk would be allowed to seek leave on condition he found a replacement for the years when he was supposed to serve as monk official[66] and his household was able to pay an annual fine to the monastery.[67] This flexibility in the implementation of the recruitment rule meant that some of them were monks in name only and others, while others were only periodically so. But as long as Rinchen Ling recruited from all three villages, keeping enough resident monks was reportedly no problem.

This situation changed when monks from Dzang and Til decided to split from Rinchen Ling in Waltse and re-establish the monasteries in their own villages in the 1980s. The full list of ritual services that previously used to be performed only in the monastery in Waltse were now performed also in the two other village monasteries, something that created a greater demand for resident monks. The population in Limi increased in this period,[68] and the numbers of *grong chen* and *grong chung* households were extended, but this did not suffice to make up for the sudden reduction of monks in Waltse and to supply enough monks for Dzang and Til. As mentioned in Chapter Seven, much of the decision-making regarding monastery affairs, which had previously been made at joint meetings between laity and monks from the three villages, was now scaled down to the level of individual monasteries and

65 The Tibetan blacksmith family moved from Limi in the 1980s. See Chapter Six for more details about the special status assigned to this family.

66 See Chapter Seven.

67 Villagers and people from other communities in Humla occasionally commented that this led to a certain skewing of the socio-economic background of the monk population; the wealthy families were able to pay themselves out of the obligation, whereas the poor monks had to remain in the monastery. However, for generations, the monastery has had several monks from the best-known families who decided to stay for reasons of religious aspirations or the status and power which could be obtained within the monastery, or both.

68 See Chapter Four.

villages.[69] Consequently, slightly different strategies were chosen in Waltse, Til, and Dzang. The Rinchen Ling monastery, which was still the largest, continued the tradition of performing 'the dances of the eight Herukas' for the Rimchö festival, requiring the number of monks to be kept as high as possible. The villagers in Waltse therefore opted for a strict interpretation of the recruitment rule and removed the former possibility to escape the duty by paying for a substitute. One of the senior monks explained:

> After the monasteries split, the villagers in Waltse made it compulsory to stay in Rinchen Ling monastery. Before, [if the monks wanted leave] they would just pay the fine and it was acceptable. The villagers made the rule preventing monks from going outside because if all monks left, the monastery would collapse (*thor zhig*).[70]

In Dzang and Til the villagers chose a less strict implementation of the obligation to stay in the monastery. In these villages, the monks were still able to pay an annual fine if they wanted to be exempted from their duty. Monks seeking leave from a formal position would have to find a replacement (*tshab*) and offer part of the fine as payment to him. This worked well for a while, as there was a strong motivation to support the newly established monasteries. However, as we will see below, the many push and pull factors for outmigration mentioned in Chapter Four gradually made it more difficult to retain the monks.

8.2 'Life Entrustment', Other Reasons for Enrolment and Opportunities for Nuns

In addition to conscription, there are also other reasons for monastic recruitment in Limi. In general, sending a son or daughter to the monastery has been viewed as a good opportunity for the child. Firstly, because it is regarded as generating religious merit both for the child and the family and for protection from harmful spirits. Disease, disabilities, and other forms of misfortune are generally perceived as being caused by harmful spirits and premature death or sickness was the reason that was most often cited for voluntarily sending a child to the monastery. For example, if a son has been sick the family may entrust him to the monastery in the hope that this will save his life. In Limi, this category of monks is referred to as *tshe bcol*, lit. 'life-entrusted' monks.

69 See Chapter Seven.

70 Interview with senior monk, 21.08.10.

If enrolling in one of the local monasteries, the *tshe bcol* monk and his family will have to follow the same rules as the levied monks, with the important exception that the *tshe bcol* monk will have the option to return to lay-life if he later wants or needs to.

Studies of monastic recruitment often list economic and social concerns among the more worldly reasons for monastic recruitment, for instance in cases when families have had too many mouths to feed.[71] In some Tibetan Buddhist societies, there were economic incentives for monastic recruitment, whereas in others, sending a son or daughter to the monastery simply meant that the family did not need to worry about his or her livelihood.[72] The organisation of the monk levy in Sakya, for instance, entailed not only tax reduction for the monk's household, but also the statistically rare, but nevertheless lucrative, possibility to earn a position as revenue collector or administrator in monasteries outside the principality.[73] However, in many cases, especially in small village monasteries, the families would have to continue to support their monks and nuns. Hence, economic concerns have hardly been a motivating factor for recruitment in the local monasteries in Limi and sending a son to the monastery as a monk places a significant burden on the household economy; the family not only loses much of his 'productive capacity' but will also have to continue to provide his food and clothing and sponsor a number of extensive monastic rituals.

Monks and nuns sent from Limi to monasteries in Kathmandu or India are not part of this funding system and currently all receive sponsorship in their respective monasteries. Most of them stay either in Jangchub Ling, Kyabgön Rinpoche's seat in Dehra Dun in India, in the recently founded Rinchen Ling monastery in Kathmandu or in Rinchen Palri in Balambu, but there are also a few monks from Limi in Drigung Kagyu monasteries and centres in other countries. The nuns tend to stay either in Samten Ling (bSam gtan gling) nunnery in Dehra Dun or in Rinchen Palri (Rin chen dpal ri) monastery in Kathmandu. In this category we find monks and nuns who are enrolled because of a handicap as well as those who have been ordained because of their own religious aspirations (*chos sems*). However, because of the system of child enrolment, the latter type is relatively rare. Religious sentiment may of course develop

---

71 See for instance Tsarong (1984: 58f), Goldstein and Tsarong (1985: 20), Goldstein (1998: 17) and Mills (2003: 40).

72 Goldstein 1998: 17. See also van Lochem 2004: 12f. Van Ede (1999: 120f) notes that orphaned nuns among the Sherpas in Nepal hardly received any economic support from their relatives apart from the first tea ceremony and the robe.

73 Cassinelli and Ekvall 1969: 296–300, 305–11. See also Ramble's (2008: 184) account of the economic advantages of the nominal monks in Te.

later, and my interlocutors emphasised the strong religious motivation of some of the monks and nuns. This applied both to monks who had been levied and those who had been ordained in monasteries in Kathmandu or India.

8.2.1 *The Empty Seats in the Nuns' Row*

Currently, there is only one nun doing monastic service in Limi—the young nun in Til. When I asked if there were nuns in the Rinchen Ling monastery in the past, people replied that there had not been any within living memory. But in the past, there must have been some, they added, because one of the rows in the assembly hall is called 'the nuns' row'. I enquired also whether girls from Limi enrolled as nuns in nunneries in Ngari in the past, but nobody had heard any mention of this. They said that there were very few nunneries in Ngari; instead nuns would live in separate nuns' quarters in the same monasteries as monks.[74]

I discussed with people in Limi why there were no longer nuns in the nuns' row in Rinchen Ling and why there were so few nuns from the villages in monasteries elsewhere. The reasons given were related to education and economy. The monks in Til, for instance, commented that, 'nowadays girls go to school and in the school there is no difference between the genders. Here [in Limi] the tradition is for boys to enrol as monks, there is no tradition for nuns.'[75] Following up on the topic, the monks explained that the main reason why there were so few nuns was that girls from wealthy families, who have time and can afford it, will go to Kathmandu or India for studies, whereas those who have to stay in the village would have too much work to do to consider taking up a monastic life. The nun who is currently in the monastery has physical disabilities, preventing her from engaging in the hard manual work of her fellow sisters in the valley.[76]

In addition to this nun in Til, there were six nuns from Limi living in monasteries in Kathmandu or India in 2012.[77] Physical disability was the most common reason why parents would send their daughters to monasteries outside the valley.[78] In spring 2011, the father in the house where I was staying told me that he was planning to send his daughter to a nunnery in India.

---

74 This can be seen also in Sherring's (1993: 188f and 207) account of the nuns associated with Shephel Ling monastery in Purang, and the nuns in Khochar monastery in 1905.

75 Interview with the monks in Til, 06.03.12.

76 Interview with the monks in Til, 08.03.12. According to Gutschow (2004: 6 and 34), a nun in Zangskar is not necessarily free from work duties in her natal home. See also Childs and Choedup (2015).

77 The number of nuns from Limi was still the same in 2019.

78 Informal conversations with the parents.

TABLE 8.1 Total number of nuns from Limi, 2011

Name of village	Number of women	Nuns	Percentage of women
Til	132	1	0.8
Waltse	235	4	1.7
Dzang	191	2	1
Total	558	7	1.3

She had sustained serious injuries from falling off the roof while playing as a child. The family had spent all their savings on trying to get her to a hospital, but the hospital in Purang refused her admission. Eventually, they found a doctor who could help her, and after a long and arduous process she recovered. Although she was functioning normally again, her parents feared that she would struggle with the demanding physical labour that women must do in Limi and decided a nunnery would be a more suitable environment for her.

8.3 Monastic Demography

It is commonly estimated that the number of monks in Tibetan monasteries in the middle of the twentieth century constituted between 20–30% of the male population[79] distributed among approximately 2,700 monasteries.[80] Samuel, however, argues convincingly that these numbers are probably too high. Since there are no reliable data for the whole region, he bases his estimates on available numbers from societies that have been studied in more detail. He suggests a more moderate percentage of 10–12% *celibate* monks in centralised agricultural communities and a lower percentage in more peripheral agricultural and pastoralist communities.[81] In other Tibetan Buddhist societies, Samuel notes, there may have been between 15–20% married clergy, which he refers to as 'lay *chos pa*'.[82] The number of nuns is even more uncertain, but Hanna Havnevik

79 For comparison, Goldstein refers to Tambiah's study from Thailand which relates that '… only about 1–2 percent of the total number of males were monks and most of these were not life-long permanent monks.' Tambiah 1976: 266–67 in Goldstein 2010: 3.

80 Goldstein 2010: 3.

81 Samuel (1993: 582) reserves the terms 'monk' and 'nun' for celibate monastics.

82 Samuel 1993: 582. For a discussion of the different categories of clergy, see Samuel (1993: 274ff).

quotes an estimate of 27,180 nuns living in the 818 nunneries in Tibet in the same period.[83] Although Samuel's distinction between religious communities in three different types of societies (centralised agricultural, remote agricultural and pastoral areas) helps to nuance the picture,[84] it provides only a rough estimate. To discern the causes for variation in monastic demography, it is necessary to take factors such as monastery type, recruitment method, taxation[85] and other socio-economic and religious conditions into account. Moreover, over the last few decades, political conditions and issues of ethnic identity have become increasingly important factors in influencing people's choice for entering a monastic institution.[86]

Although Goldstein did not pay much attention to the monasteries in Limi, he noted that in 1974 there were fifty monks in the three villages.[87] Harka Gurung, who visited Limi just three years later, reported that there were about forty monks.[88] However, it is unclear to what extent these figures reflect the actual number of monks at the time since no records are kept in Rinchen Ling's archive. Goldstein's figure corresponds to the stipulated minimum in the recruitment contract, and this was also the number the monks provided when I enquired about the size of the monastic population in the past. However, counting the exact number of monks in Limi is not straightforward and depends on how one understands the category 'monk'. Samuel, who, based on Goldstein's article, calculated that 12.5% of the male population in Limi were monks, categorised them as lay *chos pa* or *ser khyim*.[89] My own demographic survey of the three villages in Limi, conducted almost forty years later, provides figures for the total monk population and levied monks:

As shown in table 8.2, the total number of 119 monks represented more than a doubling of the figure given by Goldstein and with 23.2% of the male population it conforms to the highest estimates of the size of the monk population in Tibetan societies. However, this figure gives an exaggerated impression as it includes both levied and voluntary monks, nominal and actual, who are residing in Limi or monasteries elsewhere. Monks enrolled in monasteries outside the valley are unlikely to have been included in Goldstein's or Gurung's

83 Havnevik 1989: 37.
84 Samuel 1993: 310. The different types of societies are defined on p 115f.
85 See Chapter Nine.
86 See for instance Havnevik (1996: 260ff) for a discussion of the reason of nuns' ordination in contemporary Tibet.
87 Goldstein 1974: 266. The comment was made in the caption of a photo in his first article about the community.
88 Harka Gurung 1980: 115.
89 Samuel 1993: 581. For an explanation of how I use the word 'monk', see Chapter One.

TABLE 8.2 Total number of monks from Limi, 2011

Name of village	Total population	Number of men	Total monk population	Percentage of males	Levied monks	Percentage of males	Resident in Limi 2011–12
Til	227	95	18	18.9	18	18.9	8
Waltse	424	192	43	22.4	35	18	27
Dzang	419	227	58	25.6	46	20.3	17
Total	1070	514	119	23.2	99	19.2	52

estimates, but even if we count only levied monks, the number has increased by as much as 98% from Goldstein's fieldwork in 1974 to 2011. As detailed in Chapter Four, the total population growth in the three villages in the same period is 35.8% and explains at least some of this rise. The high demand for monks after the split of the three monasteries (which took place after Goldstein and Gurung collected their data) caused the villagers to implement the recruitment rule more strictly, and this is probably another major reason for the increase. A final reason may be related to the way of counting. It is likely that Goldstein counted only those monks who actually did monastic service in Rinchen Ling, and it is possible that so long as the required number of fifty monks was serving in the monastery the number of levied monks exceeding that number could be allowed to be absent.[90]

At the time of this survey, the total proportion of monks was highest in Dzang and lowest in Til. The discrepancy between the two villages may partly be due to differences in family composition, residence pattern and work opportunities and partly due to the absence of monks who have enrolled for other reasons than conscription in Til. Table 8.2 shows that twelve monks from Dzang and nine from Waltse have enrolled for other reasons than conscription. In a society with compulsory recruitment this number is quite high. However, with the exception of some of the so-called 'life entrustment' (*tshe bcol*) monks discussed above, none of these reside in any of the monasteries in Limi. If we compare the number of monks serving in the village monasteries during the winter 2011–12, the attendance of the levied monks was in fact higher in Til (44.4%) than in Dzang (37%). Monastic attendance is determined by laws

90 This was a time when the monk levy was implemented more loosely, and eventual surplus monks were not forced to return if they could pay the fines.

TABLE 8.3 Number of monks according to household category and reason for recruitment, 2011

Family category	Number of inhabitants	Number of men	Total no. of monks	Levied monks	Other monks	Percentage of males
Large househ.	194	96	28	24	4	29.1
Small househ.	157	75	9	6	3	12
Single woman	70	21	6	5	1	28.6
Tax-exemption	3					
Total population	424	192	43	35	8	22.4

passed by the respective village assemblies, and because of the strict enforcement of the levy in Waltse, attendance is normally close to 100%.[91]

The total number of monks in Waltse is forty-five, and thirty-five out of these are levied. In a normal year, all, except two monks who have received special permission to work for the Limi *sprul sku* in Taiwan and two runaway monks who have abandoned the village are resident in Rinchen Ling. Table 8.3 breaks down the numbers according to reason for enrolment and social stratification and shows that the majority of the conscripted monks (68.6%) in Waltse come from the large households, whereas only 17.1% come from the small ones. This difference can be explained by the stricter recruitment requirement and the larger family size of the *grong chen* households.[92] More surprising, perhaps, is the fact that as many as 14.3% of the levied monks were from the single woman household category.[93] The majority of these monks originally belonged to larger households but split off to establish new subsidiary households together with their partners. These monks will have to continue their duties in the monastery, but since monks are not entitled to any share of the family property they are not counted as heads of the *bom btang* household, and the sponsorship of the monastic ritual expenses (*gtong sgo*) and other parts of the 'monastic obligations' (*dgon pa'i khral*) remain with their old households.[94] The only

91 The reduction to 77% this particular year was due to six monks being on a special mission in India and two being allowed absence on a more permanent basis to serve Senge Tenzin Rinpoche.

92 See also Chapter Four.

93 In Dzang, there are five monks in the single woman household category, whereas in Til there is only one.

94 The high number of monks establishing subsidiary households has been possible after the work opportunities for single women in Purang improved. See Chapter Four.

exception among the five levied monks in the single woman category is one of the young novices mentioned in the introduction to this chapter. He is the youngest of three brothers, and according to the rules described in Chapter Four, the family will be upgraded to the *grong chung* category when the eldest son turns fifteen, hence the monastic recruitment and patronage obligations apply also to this household.[95] This is the only single woman household with three sons in Waltse, but even if it is a rare case, it illustrates the logic of the system.

8.4 Training of Monks

All the monks in Limi receive basic training qualifying them for monastic service in the local community.[96] Young novices are taught the alphabet and how to read by monk relatives and often practise recitation together under the supervision of one of the older monks (Fig. 8.3). There are often at least two generations of monks within the same family, and in these cases the teacher tends to be the novice's uncle. The ritual procedures will be taught by the monk disciplinarian (*dge bskos*). Other basic skills are learned largely by copying older monks. The most complex and important ritual is the above-mentioned dances of the eight Herukas[97] performed during the Rimchö festival. During the one-month preparation for the *'cham* dances, the young monks learn the elaborate steps by dancing next to the more experienced monks. Since the split of the three monasteries in the 1980s, Waltse Rinchen Ling has been short of monks, so the novices have had to participate in the performance during the festival.

The monasteries in Limi are primarily ritual institutions and the monks are trained to become ritual specialists. There has never been any college for scholastic training in Limi; neither have the monasteries in the community had any preceptor (*mkhan po*),[98] at least not within living memory. Monks have, however, had opportunity—although to a limited extent—to travel to other monasteries for training. The lack of qualified teachers in Limi, combined with the strict implementation of the recruitment rule and the associated restrictions of movement, however, have made it difficult for monks to aspire to higher

95 See Chapter Four about village organisation.
96 The rituals are detailed in Chapter Seven and the ritual calendar in Appendix 1.
97 See Chapter Seven.
98 The term *mkhan po* can also mean 'abbot,' but the monks in Limi use the term in the meaning of a 'teacher' or 'scholar monk.'

FIGURE 8.3 The steward supervising the novice's recitation

monastic education. The general level of education in the three monasteries is low, and the majority of the young monks have received only lay vows (*dge bsnyen*). Some of the regular monks have received novice vows (*dge tshul*), while only a few of the senior monks have taken full *dge slong* vows. There are also a number of monks from the three villages with full ordination residing in monasteries in India and Kathmandu.

To receive advanced instruction, empowerments, and vows, the monks must travel to one of the larger Drigung monasteries. In the past, the monks from Limi travelled all the way to Drigung Thil for higher training.[99] Senior monks say that they all undertook the three-month journey when they were young. In addition, instruction and empowerments used to be sought from incarnate lamas and other religious masters visiting the area when they came on pilgrimages to Mount Kailash. For the three decades between the crackdown on monasteries in Tibet and the reestablishment of Drigung monasteries in exile, access to higher instruction was limited, but especially after the inauguration

99 Goldstein and Tsarong (1985: 18) report that the monks from Kyilung (pseudonym) in Ladakh would also travel to one of the main Drigung monasteries in Central Tibet for training in the past.

of Jangchub Ling (Byang chub Gling) in Dehradun in 1992,[100] and more recently Rinchen Palri (Rin chen dPal ri)[101] and Drigung Kagyu Rinchen Ling ('Bri gung bKa' brgyud Rin chen Gling)[102] in Kathmandu in 2007 and 2009 respectively, it has become easier for the monks to seek advice and receive instruction. Many of the monks from Limi travel to these monasteries during the summer months, and some stay on for meditation and more advanced studies. It is also primarily in these monasteries that monks who are not conscripted, as well as outmigrated monks from the two villages with lighter implementation of the monk levy, reside. In their study of migration from Nubri, Childs and Choedup point out that such exile monasteries recruit actively from remote high mountain communities and constitute important pull factors for outmigration.[103]

Whereas the possibility of receiving scholastic training has been limited for monks from Limi, the numerous hermitages in the valley bear witness to a long tradition of retreats. Some, like the Chaye hermitage built by *sgrub thob* Senge Yeshe at the site of the old meditation hut of Rinchen Zangpo, have been used by many visiting religious adepts.[104] Other hermitages, however, are used primarily by local monks and lay people. The latter tend to perform shorter retreats in small meditation huts owned by their families, especially during the economically unproductive winter season, whereas the former perform their retreats in larger hermitages in the summer. The main hermitage in Waltse is Chökhor Tse (Chos 'khor rTse) located high up on a ridge about an hour's walk to the west of the village (Fig. 8.4). According to local tradition, the hermitage dates from the thirteenth century, and one of the huts is supposed to have belonged to Drigung Chenga Lingpa. The hermitage has recently been extended and now consists of approximately ten secluded cells. In addition, there are three hermitages on the mountainside immediately to the east of the village, two of which are still in use.

The lack of competent teachers is a big problem in Limi, and some years ago, the monks requested Drigung Kyabgön Rinpoche to send a qualified teacher (*mkhan po*). In 2002, Lama Öser (bLa ma 'Od zer) came to stay for three years and under his guidance four of the monks from Waltse underwent the

---

100 Jangchub Ling in Dehradun is the main Drigung monastery in exile and the seat of Kyabgön Rinpoche.

101 Rinchen Palri monastery in Kathmandu was established by Sonam Jorphel Rinpoche (bSod nams 'Byor 'phel Rin po che) from Lama Yuru (Bla ma g.Yu ru) monastery in Ladakh.

102 Drigung Kagyu Rinchen Ling in Kathmandu was established by *sgrub dbang* Konchog Norbu Rinpoche (dKon mchog Nor bu Rin po che 1921–2007) and consecrated in 2009.

103 Childs and Choedup 2019.

104 See sub-chapter 3.3.

FIGURE 8.4 Chökhor Tse hermitage

three-year retreat (*lo gsum phyogs gsum*)[105] in Chökhor Tse hermitage. A number of other monks have also undertaken retreats for longer or shorter periods. Although retreats are strongly encouraged, they are always voluntarily undertaken according to the monks' own aspirations. As noted in Chapter Six, the community finds it so important that monks complete the three-year retreat that it has established a special 'retreat tax' to secure patronage for the practice.[106]

The monastery has provided literacy not only for its monks, but also to some degree for the laity. In the past, there was no secular institution in the village where children could learn how to read and write, and several laymen told me that they had received instruction from monk relatives when they were young. The man who used to serve as village astrologer in Waltse, studied astrology and learnt how to make dough offerings (*gtor ma*) and perform rituals under the monk from the leading Dzardziwa family. After the first young villagers were sent to Kathmandu and India for secular education, and after the introduction of village schools in Limi, the prospects and expectations of young men, both

105 In Limi the three-year retreat is normally referred to as *lo gsum zla gsum* (*zhag gsum*).

106 See Chapter Six for details about the 'retreat taxes' (*grub grwa*) collected by the village assembly to support meditating monks.

monks and lay, have changed. As secular education became an alternative for the young, some families in Waltse have sought permission to send their sons to school before enrolling them in the monastery and have been granted up to two years' leave for education. In addition, some of the young monks attend classes at the local school in the summer season, during the break in the monastery's ritual calendar. In Til and Dzang the situation is different because of the more flexible enforcement of the monk levy. If the parents can afford to pay the fines, they are free to send their monk sons for longer education outside the valley. After the establishment of large Drigung monasteries in exile, some monks from Dzang and Til (as well as voluntary monks from Waltse) have received higher monastic education in Kathmandu or Dehradun. But this opportunity is not available for the levied monks in Waltse and places the young monks in a difficult situation. The story of one of the monks illustrates the dilemma:

> When I was a young novice, if I compared myself with the other children [in the village] I felt lucky. There was no proper school at the time, and the other kids were sent out to collect cow dung and do other types of work, whereas I was allowed to perform rituals. Although I didn't reflect much about it, I was content to be a monk. But after I turned fifteen or sixteen years old, that changed. I wanted to get an education, I wanted to learn different subjects and how to speak English, but there was no option. I had to stay [in the monastery] because of the monastic regulations (*dgon pa'i sgrig khrims*).[107]
>
> (…)
>
> A few years later, I left the monastery without asking for permission. I went to Dehradun and was planning either to study or to meditate. Then I realised that I was already too old for school, but I felt too young and inexperienced to go into retreat. I therefore asked an administrative officer for permission to stay in the [Jhangchub Ling] monastery. While in India I learned many skills, such as how to perform rituals, debate, and to speak a bit of English. I also taught some Ladakhi monks how to play the shawm (*rgya gling*). But after seven months, I received the message from Rinchen Ling saying that wherever I was, even if I was in the sky, I had to come back. This was a difficult situation, but I decided to return to the village.[108]

107 This was the time when the villagers in Waltse decided to adopt a stricter implementation of the recruitment rule.

108 Interview with a monk from Waltse, 30.04.12.

Although not denying that part of his monk career had been difficult, the monk told me that he was again content about his situation and that even after his return to Rinchen Ling he had had several opportunities to travel outside the village to gain religious empowerments. Not all monks share his urge to leave the valley to pursue further studies, but his story illustrates the sometimes conflicted position of monks in Limi.[109]

In addition to the restriction on educational possibilities, the compulsory monastic recruitment rule has consequences for the implementation of monastic discipline. The recruitment contract states that if a monk breaks the monastery regulations, he will have to pay a fine, but he will still have to remain in the monastery.[110] One of the monks explained:

> The monasteries in Limi are very different from other monasteries in Kathmandu and India. There, when you enrol as a monk, you'll have to study the monastery's rules and regulations. If a monk breaks these rules, he will get expelled. Many monks get expelled in this way. Here in Limi, however, even if a monk makes a very big mistake, he will only have to pay a fine; he will not be expelled but has to stay. This is the old system here.[111]

This is due to the special clause in the recruitment contract mentioned above, specifying that the levied monks would be monks for lifetime, even if they committed serious crimes. The monks who have outmigrated from Limi and taken secular jobs are therefore still regarded as being eligible for service in the local monasteries. In many monasteries they would be unwanted and classified as *grwa log* or *ban log*, but as Jansen points out, there have been many ways of handling such cases throughout history and some of the transgressors would even remain to fill important functions in their monastery.[112] In Limi, monks who have left the monastery have been called back for monastic service according to need.

---

109 The pressure is higher on monks, but as discussed in Chapter Four, young laymen—or women—are also called back to the villages by their parents to take up the role of householder, often having to interrupt their education. Because of the legal regulations, Limi appears to put very strict demands on its youth, but as discussed for instance by Childs et al. (2014), the conflict between parents who want their sons and daughters to come back to maintain the traditional village life is shared by numbers of families in other small communities across Nepal.

110 See the *Monastic recruitment contract*, line 11.

111 Interview with a monk from Waltse, 30.04.12.

112 Jansen 2015: 100 ff.

Visiting lamas have occasionally tried to tighten the monks' discipline. For example, as in many other village monasteries, monks in Limi used to drink barley beer and eat meat, but in recent years visiting lamas have disapproved. When Drigung Konchog Norbu (dKon mchog Nor bu) Rinpoche came to Limi for the first time, the villagers asked for empowerments, but he reportedly refused until all the monks in Rinchen Ling agreed to stop drinking *chang*. Meat was abandoned more recently during the visit of Drigung Kyabgön Rinpoche. He ordered a prohibition of meat within the monastery compound, a prohibition that also included the laity. This led the monks and lay patron families to start buying a variety of vegetables and spices from Purang, and the monks to build the first greenhouse in the valley.[113]

8.5 Conflicting Concerns—the Relationship between Monks and Households

The facts that the three monasteries recruit only from their respective villages, that the households must sponsor their monks, and that the monasteries are situated in the heart of the village in Waltse and Dzang and within 'calling distance' (*rgyang grags*) in Til, create close bonds between monastery and village, households and monks.

8.5.1 *Adaptation to Village Life*

Mills suggests a perspective on monastic ordination '… not as a single leap from householder to monk, but rather as a series of grades of possible renunciation'.[114] The monks within a monastery are therefore found on many different stages of the path to renunciation. In order to distinguish levels of renunciation from monastic ordination, he refers to withdrawal from the productive and reproductive capacities of the household as 'clerical renunciation'.[115] This is also a useful perspective to understand renunciation in Limi. Renunciation in the three village monasteries is generally weak, but some monks have taken full ordination and strive to keep their vows. All the monks, however, participate in

113 Vegetarianism is a relatively new phenomenon in Tibetan societies. The vegetarianism movement, which was initially started by *mkhan po* 'Jig phun in Eastern Tibet and rapidly spread also to the exile community, has been analysed for instance by Gayley 2011 and Gaerrang 2011.

114 Mills 2003: 74.

115 Mills 2003: 74f.

varying degrees in village life, and many families are dependent on the monks' labour for their sustenance.[116]

In the Nyingma and Kagyu schools of Buddhism, which have a '... legacy of permitting individuals to act in the dual capacity of householder and lama', the boundaries between monks and lay religious adepts are often fluid.[117] Such a fluidity is also common in Limi. As mentioned above, only a few monks in the three monasteries in Limi have taken *dge slong* vows. Some of the monks at lower ordination levels do not place too much importance on the vow of celibacy, and can in many respects be compared with 'householder monks' or 'householder lamas'.[118] However, since they are generally not allowed to act as head of a household, the monks in Limi are different from the lamas in Lubra (Klu brag) and the clergy in Te discussed by Ramble, the *ser khyim* monks discussed by Aziz, and the householder lamas discussed by Childs and Clarke.[119]

At the time of my original fieldwork, virtually all families in Limi with two or more sons married them polyandrously. As described in Chapter Four, the younger brothers would automatically join their elder brother's household; and this practice also included monks. While the polyandric practice has now been abandoned, monks are still regarded as part of their natal household and special rules apply. If a monk brother decides to split from his natal house, he will not have the right to inherit land, nor will he be entitled to the political rights of a lay householder. He may be allotted a share of land, depending on the generosity and means of his sibling(s), but normally only with temporary usufruct rights, and he will end up in the *bom btang* category. A monk in a *bom btang* household will still have the duty to serve in the monastery, but the associated obligation to provide monastic patronage will remain with his former household.[120]

Although there are a number of regulations to keep the roles of householder and monk separate in Limi, many of the monks occupy intermediate positions between the two ideal types. During the seven winter months when the monks in Limi are required to serve in the monastery, they wear robes and crop their hair short. But as mentioned in Chapter Seven, the monk cells are only used during the most intensive period of ritual practice; during the rest of the year

116 The monks participate in most types of work, except for ploughing and slaughtering animals.

117 Childs 1997b: 142.

118 For an overview of different categories of religious practitioners, see Samuel 1993: 270ff.

119 Ramble 1984 and 2008, Aziz 1974, Childs 1997b and Clarke 1980.

120 The patronage obligations are discussed in Chapter Nine.

the monks live in their respective homes.[121] Since it is the monks' families who provide their food, except during rituals, this arrangement is seen as a practical solution. In order to maintain distance from the lay members of their family, senior monks often occupy the shrine room of their house.[122]

8.5.2 *Calling the Monks Back*

Whereas all the monasteries in Limi are flexible regarding the monks' degrees of renunciation, Rinchen Ling is stricter when it comes to other aspects of the monks' duties. As discussed in the paragraph above on the implementation of the recruitment contract, the monks from Waltse are not allowed to leave the monastery during the seven winter months, and unless special permission has been received, they are not allowed to stay in other monasteries and few situations are considered valid reasons for absence. Occasionally, if some of the monk officials are sent on special missions, or if the monks have received an invitation to religious events, like Drigung Kyabgön Rinpoche's winter teachings in Dehradun in 2011–12 described in the opening vignette of the previous chapter, leave of absence may be granted so long as the villagers' need for ritual services are met. Otherwise, the only absence that is tolerated, and even encouraged, is solitary meditation. But unless the monks embark on retreats outside the valley, or perform the full three-year retreat, they may still be called back to the village to participate in important rituals.[123]

The flexible interpretation of the old recruitment rule in the monasteries in Dzang and Til, eventually resulted in so many absentees that the villagers decided to make the rules stricter. During the winter of 2011–12 only seventeen out of the forty-four levied monks from Dzang and eight out of seventeen from Til were staying in their respective monasteries, close to the minimum needed to keep the monasteries running. Both the resident monks and the villagers saw such low attendance as a serious problem. A senior villager told me that in Dzang, they '... feared that the monks might abandon the monastery. Therefore, they made the rule that a minimum of thirteen monks should stay in the monastery. These monks are chosen annually by lottery'.[124] He further elaborated that the laity took the initiative to establish this rule whereas the subsequent increase in the size of fines in Dzang several years later was

121 This is a recent adaptation; in the past, when Rinchen Ling recruited from all three villages, the monks had to stay in the cells for longer periods.

122 See also Mills 2003: 65f. He points out that the monastic cells are being owned by the households and this can be seen as an example of ordinary monks' ambiguous status.

123 One of the *dge slong* from Waltse, who spent the winter meditating in Chökhor Tse, for instance, was called back to perform Rimchö in 2012.

124 Interview 19.04.12.

decided on the initiative of the monks themselves. At the time of the original research, fines in Dzang were NPR 9000 per year for a regular monk, and NPR 100 000 per year for a monk in office (*las thog*); in Til the fines were NPR 13 000 and 100 000 respectively. As will be explained towards the end of the chapter, however, the increased fines did not suffice to ensure minimum recruitment in Dzang.

The experience of the three generations of levied monks from a family in Til may serve as an example of how demands from the villagers drive the parents to call back their sons. This family has three monks, one from each generation. The elder monk served all his years as monk official (*las thog*) in Waltse, but later moved to Til and is now a *dge slong* in Drigung Kagyu Rinchen Ling in Kathmandu. The monk from the second generation, the brother of the householder, currently lives abroad but served all the required years as a monk official in Til Kundzom before departing. The monk from the youngest generation, a man in his early twenties, was called back to the village to serve his first year as steward (*gnyer pa*) in 2011–12. One of his relatives related:

> It was a difficult decision to call him back to the village. His great-uncle monk is too old to step in as representative for our family; he has finished his duties, but we still have to pay 13 000 NPR annually in addition to a package of butter as a fine for his absence during the Saga Dawa ritual. We spoke with his monk uncle abroad, but he was unable to return to the village. He said that he regretted that he had never received proper education and told us to pay the fines for his nephew too, so that he could get good training in the Nayapati monastery [in Kathmandu].[125] However, we received a lot of pressure from the other villagers and eventually, we decided to call back our son.[126]

The number of monks residing in Til is generally low, and many of them have little experience. Worrying about the quality of the ritual performance and the training of the novices, the villagers therefore decided that as an absolute minimum, one senior monk would have to stay in the monastery. Since none of the monks volunteered, they decided to institute an annual rotation system among the senior monks.

125 Drigung Kagyu Rinchen Ling is often referred to according to its location as the Nayapati monastery.

126 Interview, 24.01.12.

8.5.3 *Tension between Religious Aspirations and the Households' Economic Concerns*

Several researchers writing on monastic organisation maintain that families, although seeing monkhood as an asset, are reluctant to send their children to the monastery for economic reasons.[127] In addition there are potential conflicts between individual aspirations and family obligations.[128] Such tensions between religious ideals and economic concerns can be seen in Limi. The following story of one of the monks in Waltse is special, but may serve to illustrate the dilemma:

> I was the youngest of three brothers, and according to the regulations for the small household category I enrolled when I was eight years old. However, after a few years my father and two elder brothers passed away and my mother therefore called me back from the monastery. But I really wanted to remain a monk; I remember I used to have dreams about climbing the stairs to the monastery. When I was eleven or twelve years old, Gelong Pandi (dGe slong Pandi) from Sera Lung Monastery (Se ra Lung dGon pa)[129] came to Waltse, and my mother asked him to perform a divination (*phyag mo*) to help her decide. The result of the divination was that I should return to the monastery. I followed Gelong Pandi's advice, but because of the difficult situation in the family I was called back one more time. I was persuaded to marry and had three daughters and two sons. My mother said that as a layman I would have much more freedom and begged me to stay in the house. Yet, I decided to return to the monastery. But since my family had so little money, we made a request to the monastery and were allowed to pay half taxes. Because I went back and forth between the household and the monastery I don't feel like a proper monk; I feel that I am only a monk who has taken refuge in the monastery, not a monk according to the rules. However, being a monk is very important for me.[130]

Like the monk quoted above, most of the monks I spoke with in Waltse and Til expressed positive feelings about their monastic life, although they performed

127 See for instance Aziz 1974: 180 and Jansen 2023.

128 See Childs and Choedup (2019) for comparable instances of the conflict between individual aspirations and family obligations.

129 Sera Lung is the name of a small Drigung Kagyu monastery located at the north-eastern shores of Manasarovar, with which the monasteries in Limi previously had a lot of contact.

130 Interview, 21.08.10.

their duties with varying degrees of diligence. However, some also stated that religious service was only a duty, and that they would do only the minimum required, but otherwise preferred to work as traders.

The economic role of monks in their respective households varies, but virtually all have to contribute to some degree. Because the monastic calendar obliges the monks to stay in the monastery during winter only, most of the monks are economically active in the summer months, and it is probably no coincidence that the main ritual season starts after the harvest. But some monks also contribute to their households between their ritual duties. Like their lay brothers, most monks are skilled craftsmen and used to have the task of carving, polishing and varnishing the wooden bowls that Limi is famous for.[131] Another task commonly undertaken by monks is leatherwork, such as production of saddlebags and other horse equipment. However, the productive capacity of the monks is necessarily limited, and the daughter of one of the senior monks in Waltse, while proud of his religious accomplishments, also complained that her father contributed so little to the economy of the household as he spent most of his free time meditating. This example shows the ambiguity that many families feel about monkhood and economic concerns, an ambiguity that will be further explored in the following chapter dealing with monastic economy and compulsory patronage.

8.5.4 *The Recruitment Dilemma*

In recent years, the majority of levied monks from Dzang and Til have chosen to outmigrate, and this has created an acute recruitment problem. The staffing of the local monastery has become particularly difficult in Dzang, and this situation was one of the immediate triggers preceding the young men's request to abolish the local laws mentioned in the opening vignette of the book. Although the attempt was not successful and the laws were reestablished after a few months, the problem persisted: most of the levied monks were absent and there were hardly any new monk recruits. One of the monks put it like this: 'nowadays fewer couples are giving birth, and less babies give less monks.'[132] The villagers felt that their need for basic ritual services were not met and

131 As soon as the elder brothers arrived from their hunt for maple burls in the Indian forests, it would be time for the monks to work. However, the men stopped going to India to fetch burls a couple of years after my PhD fieldwork and nowadays monks do other types of work. In the summer season they are commonly reciting rituals, doing wood carvings or other types of craft in Purang and elsewhere.

132 Interview with a senior monk from Dzang, 04.12.18.

demanded a higher number of monks serving in the monastery.[133] In 2017, they therefore called another meeting with all the levied monks and laypeople in Dzang. During this meeting, most households voted for the continuation of the monk levy, even if that meant that they would be forced to abandon the village themselves.[134] The debates were reportedly heated as the vast majority of the outmigrated monks were not willing to come back. Eventually, they ended up with a compromise: the monastery should be staffed for a period of three years at a time by a minimum of five monks who would be given salary for their service. The traditional administration and patronage system[135] was abolished and a committee of nine members consisting of one monk, three women and five laymen were given the responsibility for the funding. Absent monks would still have to continue to pay fines, which would contribute to the salary of the five monks in service. However, many problems persisted; the villagers experienced that the five monks did not suffice and demanded at least nine resident monks. During my last fieldwork in 2019, villagers expressed that the situation was so difficult that they feared for the future of the monastery. By the time of writing, it is not clear how the dilemma will be solved, but it seems to be linked closely to the destiny of the village.

8.6 Why Is the Monk Levy Still Kept?

When the monk levy was (re-)established at the end of the nineteenth century, the stated purpose was the ritual importance of retaining a sufficient number of monks, but there were probably other strategic reasons as well. After a series of political setbacks, and especially after the inclusion of Ngari into the central Tibetan state at the end of the seventeenth century, the Drigung position in the Kailash region weakened. Keeping a certain number of monks in the monastery in Limi may therefore have been seen as a strategy to maintain Drigung presence in the region. However, the monk levy would probably not have been enforced in a place like Limi had it not been for the arrival of the Drigung hierarch, who would probably never have visited Limi if it was not so conveniently located near Kailash.

133 The experience of one of my host families can serve as an example: When the grandfather passed away, they had to beg the monks to return to the village so that they could perform the death rituals. The monks accepted the request, but many villagers were deeply worried that they would end up in similar situations.

134 This was observed also by Yeh (2021).

135 The funding system is detailed in Chapter Nine.

These reasons for the compulsory recruitment rule being introduced do not explain why the villages in Limi still keep it when the practice seems to have been discontinued in all other Tibetan communities. While the reasons are complex, the main explanation given by monks and laity alike is the fear that the monks would abandon the monastery and that this would have a number of negative consequences for the villages. One of the monks expressed the view that 'If the rules and regulations were not so strict, all the monks would go for study or business.' 'How would the villagers react to that?', I asked.

> The villagers wouldn't allow the monks to leave in the first place because of the laws (*khrims*). The villagers would say that we survive because of you [the monks], everything we do here depends on the monastery and the rituals performed. Then the lay people would say—if you leave, why shouldn't we? And the village would eventually be abandoned.[136]

Such comments were frequently repeated during my fieldwork in 2010–12, showing the fear that if the system of monk levy is discontinued, it will have consequences for most aspects of social organisation and village management described in the previous chapters. This fear is probably one of the main reasons why the rule is maintained. By 2019, Dzang was already becoming depopulated, but apparently for the opposite reason: that the villages are still enforcing the monk levy. The households do not feel that they can call back their sons any longer and those who have the resources to establish themselves in Kathmandu therefore abandon the village.[137]

136 Interview with one of the monks from Waltse, 30.04.12.

137 As of the time of printing, Dzang has been abandoned, the monastery's belongings are being moved to Kathmandu and there are only a few people left in the village.

CHAPTER 9

Financing the Monasteries

The ones who perform the extensive rituals,
are the assembly of monks from our own village.

The ones who provide food supplies to the monastery,
are the groups of men from our own village.

The ones who provide firewood to the monastery,
are the groups of women from our own village.[1]

∴

This illustration of the reciprocal relation between the monks and the lay villagers are verses from a song called the 'Village prayer' (*yul gyi ma ni*), usually sung during harvest in Limi. The monks perform a staggering number of rituals, all of which require plenty of food supplies and firewood. I asked the steward about the number of rituals performed in a year in Rinchen Ling. He replied that he performed supplication rituals to Apchi Chökyi Drolma every day, often several rituals simultaneously. Virtually all of the eighty or so households arrange monthly supplication rituals, totalling a thousand supplication rituals per year for which the monks prepare about 34,000 dough offerings.[2] Furthermore, most families also sponsor purification offerings (*bsang gsol*), performed by a single monk in their home, at least once a month. That means another thousand rituals. In addition, there are a variety of other rituals initiated by the villagers or the village assembly, as well as the more extensive rituals prescribed in the monastic ritual calendar. All these rituals require a significant amount of butter, grain, *rtsam pa*, and other ingredients for the dough offerings, butter lamps, food and drinks as well as a small payment (*phogs*) for the officiating monks. Rooted in an agrarian economy, the expenses are

1 Excerpt from a song called '*The village prayer*' (*Yul gyi ma ni*) sung in Limi during harvest, which exists in many versions. As discussed in Chapter Four, it is in reality the women who produce most of the food items needed to sustain the monastery.

2 Thirty-four offering cakes are made for each supplication ritual.

 | DOI:10.1163/9789004714571_010

paid largely in kind and are covered by a number of different funds, including monastery taxes, village taxes, rotational sponsorship duties, and voluntary patronage. The ritual responsibilities are a key aspect of the monastery's contribution to local governance and the performance and management of these is supported through significant effort by the villagers.

9.1 Basic Outline of the Monastic Economy

The system for villagers' support of monasteries has its roots at the very beginning of Buddhist monasticism in Tibet. Already at the establishment of Samye (bSam yas), the first monastery in 775 AD, King Trisong Detsen (Khri srong lDe btsan, r. 755–797/804) allocated a certain number of households to the monastery for the sustenance of its monk population.[3] Karmay writes that at the request of the abbot, the king and the government granted:

> two hundred families for the fund of the religious offerings in the temples, and three families to provide the provisions of each monk. There were, therefore, 1100 families working for the monks in bSam-yas alone. This lay community was called *lha ris*, "domain of the gods". They were exempted from civil and military service as well as from all taxation. The monastery had absolute authority over them.
>
> (…)
>
> A few decades later, this same system was further strengthened. Instead of three families, the king Khri gTsug-lde-btsan (805–838) ordered seven families to be allocated to each monk living in the religious communities. (…) Buddhist monastic communities therefore began from the very beginning to have their own properties in much the same way as the nobles, however contradictory to the Vinaya principles it would seem. The only difference seems to be that the nobles worked for the state whereas the monastic communities did not.[4]

Whilst such a large number of sponsoring families per monk must have been exceptional, Karmay's account shows that the system of funding by allocating families to the monasteries goes back to the very beginning of Buddhist monasticism in Tibet. Yet, since few studies have been devoted to the field, our knowledge about how the monastic economy has been organised across the Tibetan Buddhist world, and about how it has changed throughout the

3 Karmay 1988: 7ff.

4 Karmay 1988: 7.

centuries is limited.[5] What we do know is that there have been great differences between the Tibetan Buddhist monastic institutions in terms of the size of their wealth, sources of income, and expenses. The way the monastic economy has been organised and its relation to the state and local communities has similarly varied. Many, especially among the larger institutions, have held significant land endowments, animal herds, or have been the seats of high lamas, who have attracted affluent sponsors from far and near. Goldstein notes that some of the individual monks from these institutions still had problems sustaining themselves.[6] Like them, many monks and nuns in small village monasteries have had to spend a great deal of time on income-generating activities. These small village monasteries, and particularly nunneries, have had a limited base for funding.[7] As has been pointed out by Jansen, there has generally been a strict division between the economy of the monastic community (*grwa tshang*) and the individual monks.[8] There has also been a division between the economy of the lama's residence (*bla brang*) and the monastery.[9] In Limi, the lama's residence has been vacant since 1980 and this chapter will therefore only deal with the economy of the monastic community.

Many monasteries have provided some income for the monks. Shakya, Rabgyas, and Crook, for instance, write that the monks in Zangskar are sustained partly by 'monk fields' (*grwa zhing*) that are cultivated by the monk's family and partly by a share from the revenue of land rented out to villagers (*khral zhing*).[10] Jahoda similarly notes that the monks in Tabo would traditionally be entitled to the produce of 'monk fields' (*grwa zhing*),[11] whereas Goldstein and Tsarong report that in Kyilung monastery (pseudonym) in Ladakh each monk has usufruct rights over an agricultural field, a so called 'salary field' (*phog zhing*).[12] A number of writers on Tibetan monasticism point out that the income was not sufficient for sustenance, and the distribution among the monks has varied.[13] In Limi, there has been no *grwa zhing*, but

5 Contributions to our knowledge of Tibetan Buddhist monastic economies in more recent history include Miller (1961), Tsarong (1987), Nornang (1990), Shakya, Rabgyas and Crook (1994), Ekvall and Cassinelli (1969), Jahoda (2015), Grimshaw (1983b), Gutschow (2004), Jansen (2015) and Goldstein and Tsarong (1985: 22–23). See also Ramble's (1984) detailed analysis of the ritual economy of the householder priests in Lubra.

6 Goldstein 1998: 21.

7 On the financial situation of nunneries, see for instance van Ede (1999), Grimshaw (1983b), Gutschow (2004) and Havnevik (1989).

8 Jansen 2015: 110.

9 The economy of the Drigung *bla brang* has been studied in detail by Tsarong 1987.

10 Shakya, Rabgyas and Crook 1994: 603f.

11 Jahoda 2007: 229.

12 Goldstein and Tsarong 1985: 22. See also Tsarong 1987: 59.

13 See e.g., Goldstein 1998: 21–22 and Jansen 2015: 117.

usufruct to fields has been temporarily given to the families of monks with special patronage responsibilities. The responsibility of feeding the monks rests mainly on their respective households. The only exception is when the monks participate in rituals, or if they undertake the three years, three months (*lo gsum zla gsum*) retreat.[14]

The monasteries in Limi depend on five main types of income, see Table 9.1.[15] While the funding is largely provided by the local villagers, the income also includes sponsorship from Drigung Kyabgön Rinpoche, the Limi *sprul sku*, as well as Nepali government allocations and some NGO funding.[16] The monasteries have received donations also from tourists, but the amount is reportedly small.

TABLE 9.1 Monastic income

Category	Income source
Monastery taxes (collected by the *grwa tshang*)	– Revenue from fields (*'bca*) – Ritual sponsorship (by *las sne* monks)
Village taxes (collected by the village assembly)	– Butter lamps – Meditation allowance (*grub grwa*) – Transportation (partly as village taxes, partly by individuals according to need, partly as donations giving merit) – Labour
Donations (regular and at special occasions)	– Ritual sponsorship – Other donations
Interest from loans (collected annually after the payment of taxes)	– Interest from grain loans – Interest from monetary loans
External contributions	– Sponsorship from Drigung lamas – Allocations from the Nepali government – NGOs – Donations from tourists and other visitors

14 In this case they will receive the retreat tax (*sgrub grwa*) from the village assembly taxes (described in Chapter Six).

15 This outline and discussion of the monastic economy in Limi is based on interviews and observations as well as a number of administrative documents from Waltse.

16 The Nepali government funding was provided in the early 2000s after the monasteries were registered at the Buddhist Philosophy Promotion and Monastery Development Committee, which is an office under the Ministry for Federal Affairs and Local Development. The monasteries have also received some support from the Nepal Trust and other NGOs.

TABLE 9.2 Monastic expenses

Category	Expenditure item
Rituals	– Offering items – Food and tea for the monks – Allowance (*phogs*) for the monks – Food and salary for extra staff and helpers (*lag sde*)
Religious items	– Ritual equipment – Religious texts
Administration	– Food and drinks during meetings – Correspondence – Office equipment
Hospitality	– Food and drinks for visitors
Maintenance	– Daily maintenance – Transportation – Upkeep of the buildings and statues (equipment, food and labour)
Travel	– For administrative and funding purposes – For the purchase of food, drinks, butter for the lamps and other goods – To Dehra Dun and other monasteries for rituals and meetings with rinpoches

The sources are so scattered that I will not provide a detailed analysis of the monastery's income and expenditure. Instead I will go through each of the main categories to explain the system. The monasteries own several fields, and this property functions as an important basis for the monastic economy. However, most of the ritual activity in the monastery is funded directly or indirectly through various categories of donations. The monastery's main expenses are listed in table 9.2.

Chapter Seven distinguished between rituals arranged by the monastic community (*grwa tshang*), those arranged by the village assembly (*yul ba*), and individual requests. The majority are arranged on a recurring basis according to a fixed schedule, and the sponsors can therefore calculate the expenses in advance. Much of the funding is collected just prior to the ritual in question, other funding is collected at specific times of the year according to rotating schedules and collected by various monk officials (*las thog*), or lay officials (*las 'dzin rgan po*) in the monastic off season. The system of patronage is quite complicated and in my overview below I will distinguish between rituals funded largely through monastery taxes, and the numerous rituals funded by the village and through voluntary donations.[17]

The ritual expenses consist mainly of food items for the monks and offerings. Some of the simpler rituals, like fumigations (*bsang*) and supplications (*gsol kha*), require only one monk and simple serving of food and tea. Others, such as confession and purification (*skong bshags*) rituals, require the whole assembly and repeated serving of food and drinks. In addition, offerings such as *rtsam pa*, grain, and butter are needed,[18] and each monk will be given an allowance (*phogs*). The size of the allowance varies with the ritual in question, but in Waltse the villagers and monks have agreed on a low allowance fee. Some of the larger rituals also require an additional donation to the monk assembly and the size of this can be determined by the patron. Some of the more extensive rituals require extra helping hands (*lag bde*), who have to be served food and drinks and given an allowance.[19] Occasionally the monastery needs new ritual equipment and texts. As I will show below, many of these items have been offered as donations to the monastery. But when Rinchen Ling needed a new set of the *Kangyur* in 2010, the costs were covered by the monastery itself. The administrative costs to cover equipment, food and drink needed during administrative meetings are relatively low. These meetings are held on a rotational basis and are, except for the increased allowance and privileges described in Chapter Seven, unpaid. In addition, funds are also required for routine maintenance work, hospitality purposes and travel. A growing trend since my first fieldwork in 2010 has been the monasteries' role in generating income for the community through larger networks of Buddhist patronage, tourism, and development projects. Initially, this was small scale, but it has increased with the recent improved connectivity and higher numbers of tourists. The great value of the monastery as heritage has been successfully used as argument for both flood mitigation support and the many initiatives taken to promote tourism, not only in the village but throughout the new municipality.[20]

---

17 See Chapter Seven for more details about the different types of rituals.

18 Some of the extensive tantric rituals, such as the *gu ru drag po gtor rgyag* and especially the exorcism ritual during Rimchö, require rare and costly offering items. Most of these ingredients have to be provided by the patron.

19 See also Grimshaw 1983b.

20 The Rinchen Ling monastery has been prominently featured in many of the initiatives to bolster tourism organised by ICIMOD and Namkha Rural Municiaplity. See for instance Namkha Rural Municipality and ICIMOD 2020.

FIGURE 9.1 The Rinchen Ling tax register

FIGURE 9.2 Rinchen Ling's list of regular ritual expenses

9.2 Taxes and Other Compulsory Contributions

Taxation has been a major source of income, especially for the larger monastic institutions in Tibetan areas. However, the importance of taxes for the monastic economy has varied greatly throughout the Tibetan Buddhist world, but because of the lack of sufficient sources, there has been no attempt at a systematic study of the monastic economy in the pre-1959 Tibetan world—a lacuna that has been noted by several scholars.[21] As mentioned in Chapter Six, some of the activities in the monastery are covered by taxes collected by the village assembly. However, there seems to be a clear distinction between monastery and village taxes. The former are used to finance the monastery's core activities, whereas the latter are largely used to support other monastic activities.[22] Here I will examine the taxes, services, and fees that are extracted by the Limi monasteries.[23] Although there have been important changes, especially with the split of the monasteries in the 1980s, the basic system is an ancient one. The monasteries in Limi collect revenue from their land, but the greater part of the regular expenses is covered by a combination of compulsory and voluntary contributions from the monks' households and the rest of the villagers. I will start with a brief description of the monastery's land endowments.

9.2.1 *Monastic Land ownership*

Most of the fields in Waltse are privately owned, and Rinchen Ling is the largest single landowner in the village. But how did the monastery acquire its property? In Dzang and Til it is commonly held that the majority of the fields were given to the respective monasteries by the Jumla king.[24] The story of the

---

21 See for instance Miller 1961, Dreyfus 2003, Strøm 2001 and Jansen 2015.

22 The butter for the large butter lamps was previously a tax obligation to the monastery in Khochar, the allowances for the meditating monks (*sgrub grwa*) is an investment in higher qualifications among the monks, the Rimchö festival is cosponsored by the village assembly and the monk assembly, and the allowance for the Rimchö lama is part of the former's share of the expenses. See also the discussion about the religious purpose of village taxes in Chapter 6.

23 The current taxes are recorded in the *Rinchen Ling tax register* (*Chu 'brug zla 8 nang gi* [*kyi*] *bca'* [*ca*] *yong 'bab* [*bab*] *zhal 'bru* [*brus*] *tho bkod* [*skod*] *pa la*), a stitched booklet of seven handwritten pages, first written in the year of the Water Dragon (Fig. 9.1). The sixty-year (*rab byung*) cycle is not specified, but judging from the names in the list, who were the heads of the households two generations back, it seems safe to assume that it was composed in 1952. Some updates have been added with a more recent pen. The book is kept in the monastery archive and is consulted only during the annual tax collection meeting.

24 The thirteenth century king of Jumla was reportedly a dedicated patron of the Drigungpas.

land endowments granted by the king of Jumla quoted from the *Rinchen Ling monastery inventory* in Chapter Three mentions the Drigung monasteries in Dzang and Til, but not the Sakya temple in Waltse.[25] It cannot be ruled out that Rinchen Ling received similar donations from one of the regional kings, but so far I have not found any mention of this in historical documents. The villagers I spoke with in Waltse thought that Rinchen Ling's fields had probably been donated by the villagers themselves.[26] In both the *Rinchen Ling monastery inventory* and the *Rinchen Ling list of ritual expenses* (Fig. 9.2) there are several entries about new fields being donated to the monastery for the merit of deceased relatives. Fields have also been given to the monastery as payment for debts. Just like the village assembly, the monastery has had an important function as credit institution, and in cases where the debtor was unable to pay off his debt by other means, fields would be given as a last resort.[27] A number of the monastery's and village assembly's fields have reportedly been acquired this way.[28]

As explained in Chapter Six most of the households in Waltse cultivate a combination of three types of fields: some are private property, some are leased from the village, and others are monastic property. The monastery fields can be roughly divided into a further three main categories. The first and most common is property leased out to the villagers for house building or to cultivate the fields. The usufruct rights to this land, but also the duty to pay taxes, is hereditary. Most of the households in the village cultivate at least one such field. The second category covers fields that have been donated for the merit of a deceased family member[29] and in respect of this the household will have to provide a set amount of grain or butter to the monastery annually. The amount of grain or butter paid from these fields is generally higher than the revenue taken from the leased fields. The third category of fields functions as 'capital' (*ma rtsa*) for monks having particular sponsorship duties (*las sne*)[30] and is cultivated by their families. It is only the first type of fields that are regarded as

25 *Rinchen Ling monastery inventory*, f. 3b–4a.

26 See for instance interview with former village leader, 27.11.11 and senior monk official, 07.04.12.

27 Debt was reportedly the main reason why households in rare cases would be abandoned. I was given two examples from recent times in Dzang and Til.

28 Interview with former leader, 27.11.11.

29 See for instance the interview with a senior monk official, 07.04.12.

30 The terminology and system are explained below.

taxable fields, *bca' khral*,[31] which can be translated as a 'lease fee' levied on the usage of monastery land.[32]

9.2.2 *Revenue from Leased Fields*

The collection of taxes from the leased fields (*bca' khral*) takes place immediately after the harvest, normally in the eighth or ninth Tibetan month, and lasts for two days. Grain is collected from all households tilling monastery land, in other words, most households in the village,[33] but the amount of grain varies with the size, type, and quality of the field. The lease fee is calculated according to the amount of seed grain needed, as well as the quality of the field and distance from the village. But on the average, households have to pay 4 measures of grain as tax per 1 measure of seed grain.[34]

The day before the tax collection, the novice monks are sent to inform the households that it is time to pay taxes. The next morning, the monks convene in the monastery for a serving of tea and then go down to the Lhazhing (lHa zhing) field below the monastery for the collection. The monks have different tasks: the administrative leader (*sbug pa*) reads the tax document[35] and informs the villagers how much they have to pay. It is the steward's task to measure the grain, and the disciplinarian checks the quality of the grain. [See fig. 9.3–5] If the steward needs a break, it is the cantor's responsibility to step in. Serving tea, carrying water, and tending the fire are the responsibilities of the lay people and rotate among the large households.[36] The water carrier also has to sift the grain. The grain has already been sifted by the households, but

31 Among the various spellings occurring in the tax register *bca' khral* seems to be the correct one. As explained in Chapter Six, *bca' khral* is also collected from leased fields belonging to the village community.

32 Interview with senior monk official, 07.04.12.

33 Only forty-nine households are mentioned in the old tax register, while some of the small households which partitioned after the register was written tend fields leased in the name of large households.

34 Interview with senior monk official, 07.04.12. Compared with Surkhang (1984: 24) this is a high tax. He writes that the households would have to pay 1 *khal* tax per 1 *khal* of seed grain for the *rgyal po'i lo khral* tax.

35 Tax documents are seldom updated in Limi, and the names listed belong to the ancestors of the contemporary villagers. All the tax documents are written according to a special order, however, so at least in theory it should be possible even for young villagers without knowledge of their ancestors' names to identify the households.

36 The *grong chen* households have the responsibility to serve during the tax collection meeting. As explained below, the duty to perform these tasks on a regular basis rotates among all the households.

FIGURE 9.3 Monk measuring one *bre* of barley

FIGURE 9.4 Payment of grain tax to the monastery

FIGURE 9.5 Monks supervising the collection of grain tax

not so carefully. The young monks hold the sacks and carry the grain up to the monastery, while the more senior monks measure dried cheese (*phyur ba*). In the past, when the monks used to drink alcohol, *chang* would be served during tax collection. It was an established tradition that both the novices and young monks would 'steal' a bit of grain for making *chang* when carrying the grain up to the monastery. After the ban on *chang*, this tradition had been abandoned.[37]

According to the *Rinchen Ling tax register*, there are 49 households paying taxes for cultivating monastery fields. The low number can partly be explained by the fact that the register was written in 1952, when there were fewer households in Waltse, and partly by the fact that most of the *bom btang* households have only limited user rights and pay a portion of the taxes due from the *grong chen* or *grong chung* household from which they partitioned. The total amount of revenue from these fields in 2011 was 63 *khal* and 5 *bre* of grain, which constitutes just a small portion of the monastic income.[38]

37 Interview with a monk official, 07.04.12.

38 In comparison the lease from the village fields totals a little bit more than 48.5 *khal* of grain.

FIGURE 9.6 Temporary storage of barley in the monastery courtyard

9.2.3 *The* las sne *Sponsorship Responsibilities*

The households who provide a monk for the monastery through the monk levy also have a duty to sponsor a number of monastic rituals.[39] This is the second of the monastic obligations (*dgon pa'i khral*) discussed in Chapter Eight. This sponsorship obligation is not specified in the *Monastic recruitment contract*, however, suggesting that the rule was instituted at a different time. The actual costs of the sponsoring duties are detailed in the *Rinchen Ling list of regular ritual expenses*, which is kept by the steward. The responsibility is organised as part of a number of rotating monastic positions called *las sne*.[40] The household of a *las sne* monk has to pay the expenses (*gtong sgo*)[41] for five different

39 The rituals funded through the *las sne* system are the regular monastic rituals described in Chapter Seven.

40 *Las sne* is often translated as 'monk official', but in Limi the term *las thog* is used for 'monk official' whereas the term *las sne* is reserved for sponsoring positions.

41 The spelling *gtong sgo* is used in Kyabgön Rinpoche's letter about monastic patronage. The most common spelling in the *Rinchen Ling list of ritual expenses*, is *stong dgos*. According to Tsarong (1987: 84), the term *gtong dgos* ('that which must be given') is used in the Kyilung monastery.

rituals, a duty which takes fifteen years to complete. The requirements of the *las sne* sponsorship involve sponsorship of the following rituals and meals:

TABLE 9.3 List of rituals sponsored by the households of the *las sne* monks

The Mani festival (Mani dus chen)	3 years patronage
Regular meals (*rgyun thug*, lit. 'regular soup')	3 years patronage
Confession and purification ritual (*skong bshags*)	6 years patronage
Commemoration of Jigten Sumgön (Gos sku dus chen)	2 years patronage
Confession and purification ritual for Vairocana (gTing skong bshags)	1 year patronage

A similar system for ritual funding through *dgon pa'i khral* is described by Tsarong in his study of Kyilung, pseudonym for a Drigung monastery in Ladakh, suggesting that the system may have been common within the Drigung order.[42] However, whereas the monks in Kyilung have to provide *gtong sgo* only for three years, as opposed to 15 years for the monks in Limi. The duty is enforced strictly; even if the monk runs away, the family will have to fulfil the *las sne* sponsorship.[43] The only exception is on the death of a monk when his family will not have to pay *las sne*, the tax is 'cut' and the family will be regarded as having completed its duty.[44]

The responsibility to sponsor rituals starts while the monk is still a young novice. The first responsibility is six years' patronage of the purification and confession rituals (*skong bshags*), which the monastic community arranges eight times per year. As mentioned in Chapter Seven above, completion of these first six years of patronage is a precondition for taking up positions as monastic officials (*las thog*). The following list provides an overview of the expenses for the *skong bshags* ritual performed during the Lhabab festival:[45]

- 70 *nya ga* of butter[46]
- 9 packages of Tibetan tea
- 49 *bre* of roasted barley flour (*rtsam pa*)
- 3 *bre* of barley flour for soup (*thug thal*)
- 8 *bre* of rice

42 Tsarong 1987: 83f.

43 There are examples of this in recent history. See for instance interview with elderly villager, spring 2012.

44 See Chapter Eight above.

45 Conversation with a monk official, 02.10.10.

46 See the list of measurements in Appendix III.

- 1 *bre* of barley grain
- 8 portions (*lhu*) of meat[47]
- 4 silk scarves
- 3 *bre* of buckwheat flour
- 2 *bre* of peas
- 16 *bre* of wheat flour
- 2 *bre* of salt
- 1 *bre* of dried cheese

Until the practice was abandoned in 2008, many of the rituals would require serving of meat which made the *las sne* sponsorship expensive,[48] and luxury items like tea would also have been costly in the past. In order to help the households of the *las sne* monks to acquire funding for the rituals, the monastery provides capital (*ma rtsa*) for the patronage. The capital is provided in the form of fields or 10 *khal* of grain. The fields are cultivated by the monks' households and the grain is either sold or lent to other villagers against interest. Possible profit or interest thus accumulated will help the monks' households to pay the ritual expenditures. At the annual meeting at the end of the monks' *las sne* duty (*las sne rtsis sprod*) on the tenth day of the third Tibetan month the old *las sne* monks have to hand the start capital over to the new *las sne*.[49]

There have been great differences in the economic situation of the households, but for most of them the ritual expenses of the *las sne* monks was a very heavy burden as the monastery requires fifteen years of ritual sponsorship per monk. Households in which the uncle, brother, and son of the *kha rgan* are monks end up with an almost continuous patronage duty (see Table 9.3 above). *Las sne* monks are therefore entitled to seek leave from the monastery to help their household accumulate the required funding. This obligation is also one of the main reasons why the monks convene only in the economically unproductive winter season. Especially in the past, when most of the villagers were poor, many households of *las sne* monks had to take out loans to fulfil the duty. The interest rate was generally high and, as mentioned earlier, in all three villages there are stories about families who were caught up in a debt spiral; in the most tragic cases the families eventually had to sell their property and abandon their households. Senior monks in Waltse and Dzang explained that

47 Meat is normally measured in *lhu* (portions of an animal's body). In Limi one yak, for instance, is divided into eighteen *lhu*. Since the ban on meat, the households have to pay money instead.

48 The eating of meat in the monastery was abandoned after Kyabgön Rinpoche's visit in 2008.

49 The procedures are described in the *Rinchen Ling list of ritual expenses*, f. 14b.

FIGURE 9.7 Monk officials going through the monastic expenses during the annual *rtsis sprod* meeting

because many households had problems covering the expenses, they called a meeting with representatives from the monks and laity (*skya ser*) in the three villages in order to try to lighten the economic burden on the monks' families.[50] This meeting is testified in the *Rinchen Ling list of ritual expenses*: On folio 22a it is written that in the year of the Earth Monkey (1968) they reduced the *gtong sgo*. Then follows a summary of the budget cuts made during the meeting.[51]

Despite this adjustment, the expenses were still high, and Drigung Kyabgön Rinpoche when visiting in 2008 decided to provide temporary patronage to relieve the *las sne* monks from their sponsorship duties, which was much appreciated in the three villages. Since the patronage was intended to cover the expenses of the *las sne* monks, they did not need the fields which had previously provided them with capital. The monk assembly in Waltse therefore requested the villagers to cultivate the fields instead. However, the revenue was high; for every *bre* of seed grain 5 *bre* had to be paid to the monastery. Eventually the villagers decided to distribute the fields by lottery. According

50 Interviews with senior monks in Waltse and Dzang, April 2012.

51 *Rinchen Ling list of ritual expenses*, f. 22a.

to the women who ended up cultivating the fields, the deal was not a good one. They said that after the revenue had been subtracted, they were left with hardly any surplus from the fields. Since the harvest is measured in baskets of 'heads of barley' (*nyog*)[52] and the revenue is measured in *bre* of grain it is not easy to calculate the exact surplus. But the women estimated that 1 basket of *nyog* would equal approximately 10 *bre* of grain, and then gave the following example:

> If we use 5 *bre* seed grain to plant a field, it will yield between 30–40 *bre* depending on the harvest. But after we have paid 25 *bre* of grain to the monastery we are left with only 5–15 *bre* of grain as surplus.[53]

Considering that 5 *bre* would have to be set aside as seed grain for the next year, the women risked ending up with very little surplus or none at all. They said that the main benefit from cultivating the *las sne* fields is the grass surrounding the fields and the hay, which they use as fodder for their animals. Cultivating fields is hard work, and in the summer of 2010, the women therefore visited the monastery to request a better deal, however the request was turned down.[54] The following year, the villagers received a letter from Kyabgön Rinpoche's office informing them that he had to withdraw the sponsorship. The letter starts with an account of how the patronage was established, and then it explains that because of lack of funds Changchub Ling will not be able to continue the patronage. The letter ended by recommending the villagers to resume their traditional system for monastic funding.[55] Consequently, the *las sne* fields were returned to the families of the *las sne* monks.

9.2.4 *Labour and Transportation*

Whereas the *las sne* sponsorship duty affects only households with a levied monk, all households have to contribute to the daily service in the monastery and must take turns serving tea, fetching water, collecting firewood, and tending the fire in the monastery kitchen (Figs. 9.7–9.9 and 9.11). The villagers must also take turns shovelling snow from the monastery roof in the winter, participate in various kinds of construction work in the monastery, and provide transportation service (*'u lag*) for monks. The workload is distributed according to household category.

---

52 *Nyog* is the term used in Limi for *snye* or *snye mgo* ('heads of barley').

53 Interview with the women cultivating the former *las sne* fields, 24.03.12.

54 Such inflexibility is characteristic of the taxation and ritual funding system in general.

55 Letter from the office (*phyag drung khang*) of Drigung Kyabgön Rinpoche, 03.03.12.

- Snow shovelling:
  - In the eleventh month, only the *grong chen* families clear the snow from the monastery, whereas in the twelfth month, both *grong chen* and *grong chung* families clear snow.
- Collecting firewood:
  - Green wood (*shing rlon po*) for the big stove (*thab chen*) used when all monks assemble—the *grong chen* households have to provide 2 loads, the *grong chung* households provide 1 load. In Limi, collection of firewood is always done by women. It is prohibited to collect firewood near the village, and the women have to walk a long way to be able to collect enough.
  - Dry wood (*shing skam po*) for the small stove (*thab chung*) used when only the monk officials assemble—the *grong chen* households provide 2 loads, the *grong chung* households provide 1 load, whereas the *bom btang* households provide 0.5 load.[56] The collection of dry firewood is regarded as the most difficult of the work duties.
- Carrying water:
  - Water is carried from Chunyal, the spring to the east of the village, to fill the container in the monastery kitchen. The *grong chen* households have to provide a full unit, the *grong chung* households half a unit, and the *bom btang* households a quarter of a unit according to the monastery's need. Again, it is the women who carry the water.
- Tea serving:
  - Tea for the monks has to be served only by the *grong chen* and the *grong chung* households. The former have to serve twice as many times as the latter, but special rules apply to certain larger festivals like Rimchö. The work can be done by both genders, but it is most frequently done by women.
- Transportation (*'u lag*):
  - Whenever a monk needs a horse for an official purpose the villagers will have to provide a riding animal. This duty befalls all households with horses, regardless of which social stratum they belong to. The officials (*las 'dzin*) have a list of all the horses in the village and make sure that the duty rotates.[57] This duty generally falls on the men.
  - If the monk officials need transportation of equipment, the *grong chen* provide two horses or pack animals (*khal ma*) whereas the *grong chung* provide people to walk with the animals. The actual number depends on

56 1 load (*khur bu*) of firewood equals 50 *rgya ma*.

57 See Chapter Six about the possibilities to buy oneself out of this duty.

the destination and on how many people are travelling. Monk attendants (*zhabs phyi*) are not entitled to use the pack animal service.[58]

Other tasks requiring participation from the villagers is maintenance and construction work. This requires one representative from each of the households to contribute with labour, often for several consecutive days. However, the monastery does not have the authority to demand free labour directly, but has to request the village assembly, and the work will be organised as *biri* through the work groups (*tsho*).[59] In contrast to communal labour performed as part of the village taxes, the monastery normally has to provide food for the workers, and in special cases also a salary. For instance, during the winter of 2012, when the monastery in Til needed repair work, the *grwa tshang* provided all meals for the workers. The work groups put up tents outside the monastery, which served as kitchens and resting places, and worked from morning till evening until the restoration was complete (see Fig. 9.8). If the monastery needs more help, for instance in the kitchen or with other more specialised tasks not covered by the regular rotating service, lay people may be hired, but this will be paid work.

Both men and women can perform these duties, but except for the transportation service and some of the construction work, they are most often performed by women. The long lists of grain, *rtsam pa*, butter, and dried cheese paid to the monastery are all products of the women's careful sowing, irrigation, weeding and harvesting of fields, milking animals, and churning milk to butter. It is also the women who spin the wool and weave the cloth used for the monks' robes, and who fetch all the firewood and water needed for the numerous tea servings. The latter used to be paid work but has now been made compulsory and rotates among the households. When reading the documents, the labour contributions are not very visible—but it is the continuous contribution of the women that keeps the monasteries alive. The administrative documents simply list the expenses to be covered, without specifying how much work is needed, how it is organised and who performs it. Other source material containing reports on religious donations also tends to focus simply on the amount donated and if the contribution is large, will also give the name of the sponsor. This shows that more work needs to be done on women's contribution to the monastic economy.[60]

58 See interview with the monk official and one of the senior monks, 07.06.11.

59 For a more detailed description of the organisation of communal labour, see Chapter Six.

60 The great work contribution of women is often underplayed. Except for the works by Grimshaw (1983a, 1983b, 1994) on nuns' and lay women's work in Ridzong (Ri rdzong) monastery in Ladakh and Gutschow (2004), there has been very little research on the subject.

FIGURE 9.8 Labour for the monastery in Til, 2012

FIGURE 9.9 On duty in the Til Kundzom monastery kitchen

FIGURE 9.10 Women preparing food for a ritual in the monastery courtyard

FIGURE 9.11 Deep fried bread (L. *bola*) served during a ritual

FIGURE 9.12 Measuring butter donated for the Göku festival

9.3 Voluntary Sponsorship and Donations

Various types of voluntary sponsorship account for a significant percentage of the monastery's income and possessions, including much of its land, as outlined above. Voluntary sponsorship is a broad category that I have roughly divided into two main types according to whether it is a recurring or a one-time donation. Moreover, a distinction can be made between sponsorship of rituals, on the one hand, and donations of provisions, money, texts, and ritual objects and so forth on the other.

9.3.1 *Ritual Sponsorship*

The different categories of rituals studied in Chapter Seven are sponsored either by the monk assembly, village assembly, or individual households according to the costs listed in the *Rinchen Ling list of ritual expenses* (Fig. 9.2). This is commonly referred to as the 'food book' (*za deb*), because essentially, what it contains is a long lists of food items needed for the rituals, either to feed the monks during rituals or as 'food offerings for the deities' (*zhal zas*).[61]

61 The book was written in the year of the Wood Pig, probably in the sixteenth *rab byung* cycle, which would correspond to 1935. It opens fittingly with a prayer to Namse (rNam

In addition, the villagers frequently offer sponsorship of parts of, or entire, rituals which would otherwise be covered by the monk assembly. The reading of the *Kangyur* can serve as an example. The reading is one of the regular rituals performed annually in the second Tibetan month by all the monks in Rinchen Ling. The first days of the reading are sponsored by the monastery and the final five days are sponsored by large households. In 2011, the monks performed a particularly thorough reading because they had bought a new set of the canon from Lhasa, and Kyabgön Rinpoche had advised the monks that a thorough reading could help protect them against flood. Even if the funding of the recitation was already established as part of the monastery's regular expenses, as many as forty households sponsored tea, a meal, and a little money for each of the monks, while four households covered all the costs for a full day ritual. Such patronage gives religious merit to the donors and considerable surplus to the monastery. When the monastery gets an unexpected sponsor for rituals already budgeted by the *grwa tshang*, the food items of the original funding can be sold and reinvested.

One of the monk officials provided a list of sponsors and the amount contributed to a reading of the *Kangyur* in 2011. A closer look at the list of sponsors tells us something about the economic condition of the society. One of the senior villagers pointed out that:

> if you look at the rituals performed by the monastery throughout the year, there are many privately sponsored confession and purification (*skong bshags*) rituals. Nowadays everybody is well off compared with in the past, when only few families were able to sponsor this kind of extensive ritual. Another example is the recitation of *Prajñāpāramitā* (*'Bum*). Nowadays, it takes almost one month to recite [because so many households own a set of the scriptures, and the monks have to go from house to house for the recitation]. There are also so many private propitiation (*bskang gso*) rituals that the monks are busy in the monastery every day. Because of this, the monks hardly have time to practice *'cham* anymore.

sras, Vaiśravaṇa), the god of wealth, and thereafter follows the lists of food and offering items required for all the regular rituals arranged by the monastery. It should be noted that many of the rituals arranged by the village or private sponsors mentioned in Chapter Seven are not included. This book therefore shows only a part of the monastic activity. While the book was composed in 1935, passages have been added as needed and the most recent additions were written only a few years ago. The book, consisting of twenty-nine folios stitched together to form a booklet, is kept by the steward (*gnyer pa*) together with a more recent summary (1995) and is frequently consulted. Similar books, based on the 'mother document' (*ma yig*) from Waltse, are kept in the monasteries in Dzang and Til.

The most striking feature is that a significant number of these sponsors come from the single-woman household category. The patronage by the single-woman households, a category that was economically disadvantaged in the past, has become possible due to the work opportunities in Purang in recent years.[62] The sponsorship of rituals can thus be seen as an indicator of the economy and wellbeing of the community. But the increase in ritual activity also points to the value that continues to be placed on the monastery in society.

9.3.2 *Donations from Far and Near*

Apart from a brief historical section at the beginning, the *Rinchen Ling monastery inventory* consists of long lists of objects belonging to the monastery.[63] Many of these objects have been donated by named persons. Most of the local names are unknown to the present generation, but some are identified by household. In many cases it is specified that the donation is given for the sake of obtaining liberation in a later lifetime (*phyi ma rnam grol thob phyir*). Many of the donations listed in folios 40b–49b are meant as capital for specific rituals. The entry on folio 49a about a particularly generous couple can serve as an example:

> In the year of the Earth Hare (1939?) when the monastery made the new brocade image (*gos sku*) of Kyobpa Rinpoche, grandfather Tashi Tsering and grandmother Jamyang Angmo from the upper division in Waltse [made a donation] in order to obtain liberation in a later life. [They] gave a golden lotus petal adorned with spotted turquoise stone ornaments and pearls as an offering for the commemoration at the value (*rin thang*) of 200 coins of foreign currency (*phyi sgor*) and 120 *go Tam*.[64] From the compound interest (*skyed thog*) of the 200 *phyi sgor*, the monastery will give[65] 4 *khal* of grain to each of those who are paying *gtong sgo* every year.[66] From the 120 *go Tam*, 60 should be given to the two shrine-keeper monks as capital for 4 *bre* of butter. The compound interest from the remaining 60 should be distributed by the monastery management to each of the

62 See Chapter Four.

63 The *Rinchen Ling monastery inventory* is the main source, but entries on donations are also included in the *Rinchen Ling list of ritual expenses*. In addition, there are a few donations to the *bla brang* listed in the *Record of the resident lama's belongings* (1949).

64 *go Tam* probably refers to Gorkha *ṭam* (*'go Tam*). One *Tam* equals half a rupee. See e.g., Ramble 2008b: 497.

65 *spya bre*—as lease?

66 It seems like this is meant as a relief for the large expenses (*gtong sgo*) which have to be paid by the *las sne* monks.

FIGURE 9.13 The brocade image of Kyobpa Jigten Sumgön during the Göku festival

> monks, 2 *nag Tam* coins should be offered to each monk when gathering for the [*gos sku*] ritual.[67]

This brocade image (Fig. 9.13) is still displayed every summer in the monastery courtyard during the Göku festival (Gos sku dus chen) commemorating Kyobpa Jigten Sumgön on the 25th of the 4th Tibetan month. In addition to the donations from the local villagers, the text says that statues, scroll paintings, scriptures, printing blocks, and other religious items were donated by lamas, adepts, and rinpoches—sometimes from monasteries far away. In addition to attesting to frequent contact with other Buddhist institutions, such gifts contributed to strengthening links between them. The *Rinchen Ling monastery inventory* provides names of some of the donors; four of the successive Drigung hierarchs are the most prominent among them, but there are also donors from as far west as Ladakh and as far east as Khams. The names of several hermits (*mtshams pa*) also occur in the lists, suggesting that many of the foreign donors were pilgrims to Kailash who were meditating in the caves and hermitages in Limi. The support went both ways. Some of these hermits also received food and other donations from villagers. The Dzogchen (rDzogs chen) masters Tshogkhang Rinpoche, who spent the last ten years of his life meditating in Chaye hermitage in Limi,[68] and Serta Rinpoche were both sponsored by families from Til Village.[69] Another, more famous Dzogchen master, Shabkar (Zhabs dkar, 1781–1851), recorded in his autobiography that he received plentiful donations when he visited Limi as part of his pilgrimage to Kailash (1814–18). Most of the gifts were given by anonymous donors, but the donation of 50 *zho* of gold from a certain Dorje Wangchug from Limi, was so generous that Shabkar chose to name him in the autobiography.[70] Shabkar wrote that he received in total 700 *zho* of gold from patrons in Limi and elsewhere in Ngari and decided to use the donations to construct golden victory banners, a spire, and a dharma wheel flanked by two deer on the roof of Shephel Ling monastery

---

67 *Rinchen Ling monastery inventory*, f. 49a f. My tentative translation.

68 According to the *Great biography of the Kagyu masters*, the Ye shes rdzong hermitage in Chaye was built by *grub thob* Senge Yeshe during his three-year stay here in the thirteenth century. See Chapter Three.

69 See *The Biography of Tshogkhang Rinpoche* and *The Biography of Serta Rinpoche*. Tshogkhang Rinpoche, alias E ta rā dza or Pad ma bde ba'i rgyal po (1873–1933) and Serta Rinpoche alias Padma Lung rtogs rGya mtsho (1891–1964) were both disciples of Dudjom Lingpa (bDud 'joms Gling pa, 1835–1904).

70 Ricard 1994: 321, 328.

in Purang. In addition, he donated many ritual objects which were placed inside the temple and bestowed the monastery with a permanent ritual fund.[71]

9.4 The Monastic Credit System

This combination of compulsory and voluntary donations described above creates a surplus, which is reinvested in loans to the villagers. It seems to have been quite common that monasteries, as landlords and recipients of donations, also acted as rudimentary credit institutions, through which parts of the taxes and donations circulated back into the local economy. One example is Drepung monastery, which according to Goldstein was '… heavily involved in money- and grain lending and had huge capital funds with thousands of loans outstanding at any given time.'[72] This may seem contradictory to the frequently cited Vinaya prohibition of the handling of money by monks, but as Gutschow points out, this restriction applied only '… to individual monks, the collective treasury (*spyi mdzod*) of the monastery was explicitly encouraged to loan out its endowments in this fashion'.[73] Gregory Schopen has in a number of articles showed that, whatever the Vinaya may say, monks have always handled money.[74] Buddhist monasteries functioning as credit institutions and granaries seem to have roots at least back to the time of the *Mūlasarvāstivāda Vinaya*. Schopen quotes a *Vinayavibhaṅga* in which the Buddha is said to have permitted the monks to accept permanent endowments from donors and to lend them out against interest.[75] Moreover, after problems with repayment, the text states that the Buddha gave '… detailed instructions on how to make a loan and how to write a written loan contract'.[76] The Indian Buddhist monasteries were owned by lay patrons, and the reason given for the Buddha's instruction was the need to secure continuity in the funding for the institutions, even after the original donors passed away.[77] The monasteries' function as credit institutions

71 Ricard 1994: 328f.

72 Goldstein 1998: 22.

73 Gutschow 2004: 90.

74 See for instance the articles in Schopen 1997 and 2004.

75 'The Blessed One said: "Perpetuities for the sake of the Buddha and the Dharma and the Community are to be lent on interest. What is generated from that, with that accrued revenue (*siddha*), worship is to be performed to the Buddha and the Dharma and the Community."' Quoted in Schopen (2004: 48)

76 Schopen 2004: 29ff. The full text is provided in Schopen (2004: 47–49).

77 Schopen 2004: 69f.

is therefore not a Tibetan invention, but a practice that is probably as old as Buddhism itself.

We have very little knowledge about how the credit system has been organised in Tibetan Buddhist monasteries, but it appears to have been common and there must have been significant variation. In Limi, the monastery has lent out both cash and grain to the local villagers. In the past, when the cash economy was less developed and with lower availability of grain, the latter was the most important. Today, there is more cash circulating, and more goods and provisions can be bought for money. The administrative leader of Rinchen Ling explained how the system of grain loans used to work in Limi which reflects the monastery's role in an agrarian economy:

> In the past, most households in the village would exhaust their grain reserves during the winter. Then, in the spring, they would request the monastery for seed grain. The monastery would give double amount to the *grong chen* families, for instance 2 *khal* of grain to the *grong chen*, and 1 *khal* of grain to the *grong chung*. The loan had to be paid back exactly one year after, and the interest was fixed at 10 per cent. This was cheaper than the private loans given by wealthy households in the village, and therefore much sought after.[78]

In the past, when paying back the loans, the villagers would sometimes ask the monastery if they could repay with rice instead. This would seem counterintuitive, as rice was a luxury that had to be transported from afar. However, since the monastery would give a more favourable exchange rate of 10 *bre* of rice to 20 *bre* of grain this would actually represent a cheaper solution for the debtor. Some people would request permission to repay some of their debt in *chang*. This would be a good deal for the villagers, because 2 *bre* of grain would be deducted from their debt as 'labour cost'. Although the amount of grain needed to brew a canister (*thrungma*, s.u) of *chang* was 4 *bre*, it would be counted as 6.[79] Levine notes a similar practice in her account of the lending system in Humla: the interest rate could be lowered if the debtor agreed to pay the debt with a more valuable grain.[80]

In Limi, the interest rate on cash loans is 20 per cent which may seem high but compared to the interest rate on cash loans in Dagpo Shedrup Ling (Dwags po bShad grub Gling) monastery in Central Tibet it appears relatively modest.

78 Interview with a monk official, 07.04.12.
79 Interview with a monk official, 07.04.12.
80 Levine 1988b: 222.

According to Ngawang Nornang's calculations, the debtors had to pay 16 per cent interest per year for a minimum period of 3 years, which would eventually amount to a staggering 48 per cent of the sum originally borrowed.[81] In Waltse, the village assembly has also been given the responsibility of managing the monastery's credit. During the village assembly meeting in the autumn 2011, for instance, the debt and interest were first collected for the village assembly fund, and then for the monastery's fund.

As in most questions related to the allocation of resources or distribution of rights and duties in Limi, the size of the loan has been decided according to social stratification, rather than actual economic situation. After a loan is made, the amount borrowed and the name of the debtor are written on a scroll of paper and stamped with his household's seal.[82] Just as in the case of loans from the village assembly described in Chapter Six, there is no leeway for debtors who are unable to pay back their loan.[83] Debtors who have been unsuccessful in accumulating sufficient funding will therefore end up in a debt spiral, a common solution for which is to sell some assets such as jewellery or, in more serious cases, private fields.[84]

Another way of transforming the monastery's surplus to cash is the annual auction of donated goods.[85] With the sponsorship of rituals, it is often expected that the patron (*sbyin bdag*) should make a donation (*zhal 'debs*) and for certain rituals, like the confession and purification (*skong bshags*), a donation of cash or objects is compulsory. The size of this donation varies according to the patron's means. The donations are made both in money and in kind, and in case of the latter, the objects are subsequently sold. In February 2012, just after the Rimchö festival, the monks in Rinchen Ling arranged their annual auction. Among the goods were rings, earrings, and other jewellery, there were children's and adults' clothes, and they sold rolls of home woven cloth (*snam bu*). The money earned from the sales would be loaned out to traders who had to repay it with interest the year after.

81 Nornang 1990: 255. See also Shakya, Rabgyas and Crook 1994: 601f.

82 I was shown a couple of such debt documents, but on the condition that I did not publish them. Even though the *Rinchen Ling monastery's old debt letters* were about twenty years old and all settled, they contained sensitive economic information about villagers still alive.

83 For more details, see the discussion on the problem of debt in Chapter 6.

84 Levine (1988b: 224f) describes similar repayment options in her analysis of the problem of debt in Humla.

85 Such auctions have ancient roots. According to Schopen (2004: 37) monastic auctions are described in the *Mūlasarvāstivāda Vinaya*.

9.5 Writing New Laws to Make the Patronage System More Just

In her discussion of the Buddhist economy of merit in Zangskar, Gutschow points out that the '... public nature of many rituals encourages an inflationary cycle of spending, of ever more spectacular gifts and rites'.[86] According to the villagers in Waltse, such an inflationary cycle also developed in Limi. The households competed to serve the most sumptuous meals and employ the largest number of helping hands; the system of ritual patronage grew out of control and eventually became too expensive for many of the families. There were also complaints that some of the monks would favour the houses with the wealthiest patrons, and a number of people requested guidelines to make the patronage system more just. The monastery's ability to handle the situation was reduced after the long-lasting conflict, which led to the partition of the monasteries. Similar problems with an escalating pressure on serving the guests and helpers were also felt when arranging lay-religious events, such as the Tenth day recitation (*Tshes bcu*) for Guru Rinpoche, and when asking relatives and other villagers for help with construction work on houses or with work in the fields. Moreover, after the transition from hereditary village leaders to a system of election through sortition, an increasing number of disciplinary problems occurred in the village and in order to deal with these problems, the villagers eventually decided to make a new set of laws (*'grig khrims*). Hence, in the summer of 2009, a large meeting was called with representatives of the 'monks and laity' (*skya ser*). The members of the '[council of] the fifteen' (mentioned in Chapters Five and Seven) functioned as leaders. A set of new laws were agreed upon, enforced with fines, and recorded in a legal contract (Fig. 9.14).[87]

The first rule in the contract regards the arrangement of the confession and purification ritual (*skong bshags*) and specifies that organising the ritual from outside the village is not permitted. Villagers sponsoring the ritual are permitted to serve deep fried bread and dishes of rice, *rtsam pa*, and barley for the monks, whereas fruit and barley should be provided for offerings. The number

86 Gutschow 2004: 86.

87 The *Contract by the assembly of laity and monks* (T. *lHa thog gnyis skya ser gnyis nas 'grig khrims kyi [khrim gi] gan rgya yin*) details a new set of laws and disciplinary rules from the '[council of] the fifteen', mainly regulating the relationship between monks and laity. The copy from 2011, which I was allowed to read, is kept by the '[council of] the fifteen' and consists of thirty-one poorly spelled lines written in cursive script (*'khyug yig*) on a scroll of Tibetan paper measuring approximately 60 × 100 cm. The original contract, which was written in 2009, is kept in the village archive.

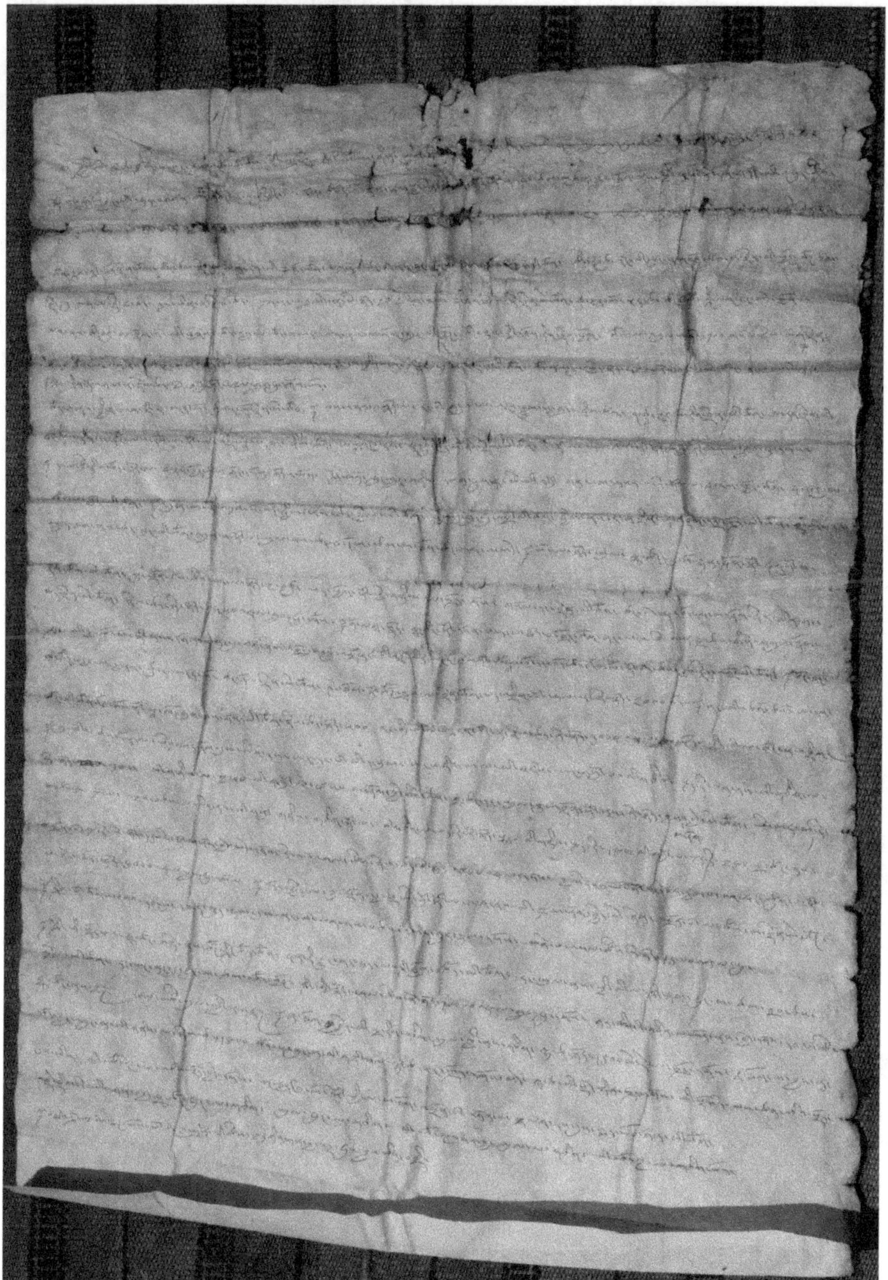

FIGURE 9.14 Copy of the contract detailing the new village and monastery laws in Rinchen Ling

of helping hands (*lag bde*) to prepare the food and assist with the serving and other practicalities is restricted to a maximum of seven.[88] It is permitted to serve barley beer and locally brewed alcohol to these helpers, but not other drinks that would have made the total costs very expensive.[89]

Among the laws are also several other rules relevant for the monastic patronage system: the maximum allowance (*phogs*) for each regular monk is set at NPR 100 per ritual,[90] which is regarded as an affordable price. Monks with specific responsibilities receive more: the lama receives a double share, whereas the cantor, steward, and disciplinarian are paid one and a half shares.[91] The contract also lists rules made to ensure that the laity dress properly when entering the monastery, and that monks dress properly when conducting rituals in the villagers' houses.[92] In most cases it is not permitted to serve barley beer and stronger liquor to the guests. A moderate maximum number of helpers (*lag sde*) is established, as this previously constituted a significant expense. Finally, it is specified that monks should not be served sweet tea and sweet drinks during rituals and even the number of dumplings (*mog mog*) served for the monks is set at seven. These rules may sound trivial, but the regulations have enabled more households to sponsor rituals. As has been argued about other aspects of village and monastery management in the chapters above, these new rules can be seen as part of a process of democratisation resulting in increased equality between villagers and transparency in the administration of monastic affairs.

9.6 The Cost of Rituals

This chapter has investigated the complex mechanisms for funding of the monastic institution in Limi through a combination of village and monastic taxes, voluntary sponsorship, capital investments, and external contributions. All households contribute with different types of taxes collected by the village and monk assemblies respectively, but the largest economic responsibility is borne by the households of the levied monks. Because of the monastic obligations (*dgon pa'i khral*) these households have to contribute with monk recruits as described in Chapter Eight, and they also have to cover the expenses (*gtong*

88 For some other rituals, the number was fixed at five or ten.

89 The *Contract by the assembly of laity and monks*, l. 2–4.

90 The fee for some of the simpler rituals, such as *gsol kha* and *bsang*, is lower. Interview with senior villager, 17.06.11.

91 Interview with senior villager, 17.06.11.

92 The *Contract by the assembly of laity and monks*, l. 15–16.

sgo) of a number of extensive rituals through a system of *las sne* positions lasting in total fifteen years. In addition to the obligatory patronage, all households also make voluntary donations in order to obtain religious merit.

The grain the monastery receives through taxation and the objects donated are generally sold and the capital is reinvested in the form of loans. These loans have been much sought after since the interest rates and conditions are more favourable than is the case with loans obtained from private households. The role of the monastic institution in the village economy is therefore not simply that of recipient of taxes and donations; through its function as granary and creditor, a part of the monastic income feeds back into the local village economy. While this has been the case far back in history, it should be noted that the economic role of the monastery in the village is changing. The importance of the monastery's function as granary, for example, has greatly dwindled with the downscaling of agricultural work. The monastery's role as creditor also has its disadvantages such as people ending up in debt spirals. While this is a general feature of the credit system in the village, Levine's study of the problem of debt in other communities in the district[93] and reports from Ngari[94] suggest that it has been a problem throughout the region. Moreover, many villagers, both lay and monastic, have experienced the sponsorship duty as difficult to fulfil and it has been most pronounced in some of the less economically advantaged households with levied monks having to provide fifteen years of compulsory ritual patronage as part of the *las sne* system. This has resulted in two major adjustments to the regulations the last fifty years. The first one, in 1968, reduced the general cost of the rituals (*gtong sgo*), and the second, which took place in 2009, aimed at reducing the inflation in food, allowances, and services provided to the monks and thus made the sponsorship system more just. While important, these reforms have been implemented in only one of the villages, and they are limited in their scope.

9.7 Searching for Sponsors Online

On the website of the charitable foundation Kailashzone, five young monks from Limi appeal for sponsorship. Three of them are levied monks from the local monasteries in Dzang and Til seeking higher education in India, and two, originally from Dzang and Waltse, are monks who have taken ordination for other reasons. Kailashzone is headed by the Limi *sprul sku*, Senge Tenzin

93 Levine 1988b.

94 See for instance the *History of the three districts of Ngari* 1996.

Rinpoche, and chaired by *mkhan po* Tashi Kailash (bKra shis Kailash). In the announcement the *mkhan po* first explains that since the monks' respective households have to cover all the monastic expenses, the monks are forced to work to help their families to accumulate the necessary funding. Then he continues:

> Senge Tenzin Rinpoche, Kailashzone, and the abbots of the Limi monasteries[95] wishes (*sic*) to break the tie between the monks and their households. Then the monks wouldn't need to take part in their household affairs and would be able to pursue their spiritual goal. To accomplish this, they need to find alternative financial sources to maintain the traditional monastic rituals and to finance the needs of the monks.[96]

While the statement '… to break the tie between the monks and their households' could mean the abolition of both the recruitment and patronage system, it is clear from the context that it was the patronage that the Rinpoche wanted to focus on. The website from 2005 has not been updated since, so I do not have information on how it was received by potential sponsors. Be that as it may, the high patronage costs (*gtong sgo*) for the monks' households have been a concern as far back as the villagers remember. Patronage has caused so many problems throughout history that there is a strong wish among the villagers to become relieved of this duty. Kyabgön Rinpoche's funding to cover these expenses for a couple of years was therefore very popular in the community. External sponsors could possibly also provide financial relief in the future, but the monks' dilemma is far more complex than it appears. The monk levy and the monastic patronage system are such an integrated part of the way the community is organised that it would not be easy for the villagers to devise a new way to sustain the monastery without repercussions for the community's overall governance.

---

95 As explained in Chapter Seven, the monasteries in Limi do not have any abbots, but the term *mkhan po* presumably refers to the *sbug pa*, the administrative leaders of the monasteries.

96 The Kailashzone website 2005.

CHAPTER 10

Charting a Course In-Between

> I remember my first conversations with Tshewang, a politician and intellectual from Humla, also known as Chhakka Bahadur, in 2009 and 2010. We spoke about the challenges that Limi and other communities in Humla were facing. 'Humla is in a state of betwixt and between', he said. 'The old barter economy has crumbled, but the communities have not yet completed the transition to market economy.' Tshewang further explained how Humla was also in a state of transition politically. He pointed out that Limi was unusual as they had managed to preserve their own system of governance, and he highlighted the important role of the local monasteries in the management of the community. While parts of the traditional management system needed reform, it was very efficient as there was no room for corruption, and he opined that it was important to preserve its good qualities. He explained that other communities in Humla had experienced a variety of problems when discarding their traditional forms of local governance. The current system in Nepal is ridden with fractionalism and corruption, it '… does not fit with our environment and socio-economic context. To improve it, one needs to fuse it with [the] indigenous system.'[1]

∵

Much has changed since 2009, but Limi is still in a situation of 'in-betweenness'. Revisiting these conversations thirteen years later, Tshewang's words continue to speak directly to the dilemmas that many Limigya find themselves in, which are discussed throughout this book. In my study of how this small Himalayan mountain community has governed itself throughout times of great socio-political, economic and cultural transformation, I have taken a longitudinal village centred approach. While the worldly and religious administrations were explored in different parts of the book, in this final chapter

1 Fieldnotes and personal communication with Tshewang Lama.

 | DOI:10.1163/9789004714571_011

I wish to reflect on the roles the two institutions play in local governance. I return to the dilemma with which the book started and consider how some of the mechanisms designed to support the worldly and religious institutions are experienced as increasingly out of sync with modern life. This situation of 'in-betweenness' has been exacerbated by the improved connectivities, outmigration, environmental challenges, the transition to a monetary economy and the requirements, challenges and opportunities presented by the Nepali state.

What does 'the art of governing' Limi entail? In this book I have used 'art' in a suggestive manner to emphasise the fact that governing a place such as Limi requires mastery, creativity and insight in navigating complex loyalties and senses of belonging. These loyalties are reflected in their 'in-betweenness' in terms of geographical location at the frontier, as well as a number of other socio-cultural, religious, political, environmental and economic relations and processes. The literal translation of Limigya (Sle mi rgya), as the 'people from the Land in-between' thus becomes an effective metaphor of their positioning. The Limigya are place focused and yet networked as highlighted by Saxer and they navigate the borderland through their multiple affiliations as illustrated by Yeh and Saxer.[2]

The 'governing' in the title has been used in a flexible manner to capture collective decision-making mechanisms in this local context. Since the role of the state in Limi is limited, I have chosen a working definition that is deliberately broad to encompass local structures and practices without being constrained by theoretical debates. I have tried to use the English word in a way that matches as closely as possible with the vernacular. There is a metaphor in old Tibetan legal culture where national (lit. royal) law is likened to a golden yoke and religious law to a silken knot.[3] This analogy, which denotes the different qualities of the worldly and religious laws and a model of governance that encompasses both, has roots at least as far back as the eleventh century and can be found in texts as early as the *dBa' bzhed*.[4] Villagers in Limi recall that in the past, their grandparents used to cite this saying. Childs and Choedup, in their description of the political system in Nubri further east on the Nepali-Tibetan border, add a third dimension to the metaphor likening village law to an iron

2 Saxer 2013 and 2017, Yeh 2021.

3 See for instance French 2002. Pirie (2017: 42) points out that it is not clear what these 'laws' actually referred to, and that instead of describing two concrete sets of laws, Tibetan authors employed the phrase '... to evoke an ideal realm in which political and worldly practices were conducted in harmony with Buddhist principles and practices'.

4 Wangdu and Diemberger 2000. See also Diemberger 2021.

ring.[5] While this version of the metaphor is not common in Limi, it can serve as a figure for reflection on the triple sources of national, religious and village law that the Limigya have to navigate.

For the Limi villagers, 'the golden yoke of national or royal law' has been represented by shifting state configurations in the region throughout the centuries. For a long historical period, the Limigya's relation to national state administrations seems to have been predominantly through taxation as well as conflict resolution in the few cases that the community have not been able to solve internally. During recent years, however, this has changed due to a confluence of multiple factors, including improved connectivities and the Nepali administrative reforms following in the wake of the 2015 constitution.[6] After being merged with other VDCs to form Namkha Rural Municipality in 2017, the Limigya have engaged more actively with the state. In this process, the villagers have discovered that they have potentially much to gain, but also a lot to lose. Since my first visit in 2010, the Limi leaders have acquired increasing experience and network in the Nepali bureaucracy, making it easier to get access to state resources. However, together with the stronger interaction with different parts of the state apparatus also comes more exposure to corruption, political fractionalism and other issues that plague the young democracy in Nepal. Moreover, the Nepali legal culture is still largely unknown to most villagers in Limi, and the local leaders' lack of formal education added to the lack of proficiency in Nepali language make it challenging to take fully advantage of the system. Another concern is related to the loss of authority within the newly merged municipality. As mentioned in Chapter Five, villagers experience that the continued attempts at encroachment from communities that were previously separate administrative units threaten their traditional management of natural resources.[7] Recent well-intended government plans for biodiversity conservation by designating Limi territory with protected status may entail further centralisation of control over local natural resources. By sidelining the effective traditional resource management system, it risks alienating the local population.[8] If the villagers could manage to get their indigenous system

5 *Rgyal khrims gser gyi gnya' shing/_yul khrims lcags kyi a long/_chos khrims dar gyi mdud ba.* Childs and Choedup 2019: 36 and 184, note 26.

6 See for instance Chapter Three for an overview of state relations throughout history and Chapter Five for a more comprehensive discussion of recent political changes.

7 See also Bhattarai et al. (forthcoming), Havnevik, Hovden and Rinchen Loden (forthcoming), and Gurung et al. (forthcoming).

8 As argued by Bhattarai (2021: 3), 'None of the existing federal policies adequately address the issue of recognition of traditional institutions or practices or knowledge systems in natural

formally recognised, however, Gurung points out that Limi could serve as a model for other communities in Nepal.[9]

What is meant by 'the silken knot of religious law' varies according to context.[10] Here I have used 'religious law' to designate the laws and regulations administered by the monastery that apply to the laity. I have also used it as a means to discuss the many direct and indirect ways the monastic institution contributes to local governance. As has been studied in detail in Chapters Eight and Nine, it is the monastic recruitment law with the associated funding mechanism, locally referred to as the households' obligations to the monastery (*grong pa la dgon pa'i khral*) as well as the monastery's role as landowner that places the strongest legal restrictions on the villagers. While the recruitment law was made by the Drigung hierarch at the end of the nineteenth century, it seems nevertheless up to the local community to keep it, adjust it or dissolve it.

The silken knot of religious law is a figure of speech that has been engaged with in many different ways. French quotes the Dalai Lamas' dGa' ldan Pho brang code describing the silken knot as smooth,[11] whereas the leader quoted in Childs and Choedup's book rather emphasises the fact that the knot can be adjusted and made tighter.[12] History shows that also the Limigya have tightened or loosened the knot depending on what the circumstances require. Before the split of the monasteries in the 1980s for instance, the laws and regulations were implemented in a relatively flexible way. In order to meet the increasing demand for monks with the (re-)establishment of monasteries in all three villages from the 1990s onwards, however, the enforcement of the recruitment rules had to be intensified. We also see that even if the three villages in the community largely share the same laws and regulations, they do not necessarily enforce them in the same way. Nowadays, Waltse has chosen to tighten the knot, whereas Til and Dzang have opted to loosen it.

One of the particularities of Limi compared to other Tibetan speaking communities in Humla is the involvement of the monastic institution in local

---

resource governance.' At the time of writing, the government had still not decided which conservation model to apply. See Bhattarai et al. (forthcoming).

9 Janita Gurung personal communication. See also Gurung et al. (forthcoming) and Bhattarai et al. (forthcoming).

10 As pointed out by Pirie (2017), there does not seem to be any clear consensus of what 'the silken knot of religious law' refers to. It has often been discussed in terms of religious influence on general laws as such, including references to the ten virtues (*dge ba bcu*) or Guru Padmasambhava quotes from the *Pad ma bka' thang*. However, the details of that debate are beyond the scope of this book; here I apply the metaphor as an analogy.

11 French 2002: 1.

12 Childs and Choedup 2019: 36.

governance.[13] However, it is important to understand the way this involvement functions: monks are not allowed to participate as representatives in village assembly meetings,[14] but they are involved in civil decision making in special cases such as *skya gser* meetings, conflict resolution and through participation in the [Council of] the fifteen. Local monks or higher lamas also perform divination on behalf of the village assembly for certain larger decisions, such as when they consulted A phyi as to whether they should join the PRC at the beginning of the 1960s, or more recently when they asked A phyi for advice on whether they needed to relocate the monastery to protect it from flooding.

The monastery caters for all sorts of small and large concerns in the lives of the villagers. People consult the local monks for the appropriate predictions and rites when they are sick, as well as for success at school or in business. The Limigya see their local landscape as inhabited by numerous spirits and deities that influence their lives and livelihoods and the monastery has a key role in appeasing these numina. This social service function is also relevant from a governance perspective. Many rituals, such as those performed in order to manipulate the weather and secure a bountiful harvest, are performed for the benefits of the whole community at the request of the village assembly, showing how the two institutions cooperate.[15]

The village assembly is responsible for the village laws. The Nubri leader quoted in Childs and Choedup emphasise the malleability also of this 'iron ring of village laws'. While iron does not strike as particularly malleable, it can be hammered out and shaped.[16] Chapters Three, Five and Six have shown that while the 'iron ring' of village law in Limi is very strict, it has been repeatedly reforged in response to internal and external triggers throughout history. The local administrative documents contain several examples of this, for instance of tax relief given to struggling households. The documents record also revisions of the laws to make them more just, or to preserve larger parts of the local forest as happened in Waltse in 2009,[17] but also to adapt to the shifting requirements from the Nepali state, to mention but a few. Yet, community members also voice their complaints, and arguably the most critical dilemmas include the differences between the rights and duties of the various social

13 The other Tibetan speaking communities in Humla are predominantly Nyingma with religious specialists functioning as householder lamas. The only other sizeable monastery in Humla, Namkha Khyung Dzong in Yalbang, is a very recent institution that engages with worldly authorities in different ways.

14 There are occasional exceptions to this rule.

15 See also Hovden and Havnevik 2021.

16 Childs and Choedup 2019: 36.

17 *Contract by the assembly of laity and monks* 2011 [2009].

strata, the position of women in the local hierarchy,[18] and those cited in the opening vignette of the book, where religious law forces young men to serve as monks in the local monastery, and village law forces young laymen back to the village to take over the responsibility as heads of the households. In recent years, these rules have been met with increasing resistance and have caused a lot of tension. Opposition to the rules has, together with pull factors such as specialised job opportunities and other attractions in the city, led many households to abandon the valley threatening the future existence of two of the villages. One senior man from Limi, who said he was familiar with the version of the metaphor about the three types of law used in Nubri, likening the village law to an iron ring, explained it a bit differently. He said that iron is a strong material, and this applies to the village laws as well. But then he added that just like iron, the village laws need to be maintained properly, so that they do not rust (*g.ya' pa med pa*).

Why are the majority of the villagers continuing to vote in support of these laws despite the critiques? Even the village that temporarily decided to renounce their old village and monastery laws in favour of the Nepali national laws cited in the opening vignette of the book, reverted to their traditional laws after only a few months.[19] It is the monastery that seems to be at the crux of the local dilemma. The villagers are afraid that the monastery will fall apart without the strict rules. They say they are completely dependent on the monastery for its ritual services, but without the strict recruitment rules the monks will leave, and if the monks leave, the others will also leave.[20] The population in Dzang, and to a lesser extent Til, is currently falling at a dramatic rate. Interestingly, many of the households that abandon the village due to the recruitment rules are voting in support of their strict implementation.[21] There are obviously complex dynamics at play, and there are several voices and opinions, but my many conversations with Limigya about their own traditional way of governing themselves versus the Nepali system yield some possible answers why they keep these laws. Contrary to what one might expect, the strictness of village and religious law is often cited as an asset. There are several reasons for this, including the predictability and significant degree of

18 See Havnevik, Hovden and Rinchen Loden (forthcoming) for a discussion of the women's situation.

19 As discussed in Chapter Eight, in a meeting two years later it was decided to staff the monastery with a minimum of five monks. These monks were given salary, and a monastery committee was established with the responsibility to secure funding and administration. The villagers did, however, not find this system sufficient to meet their ritual needs.

20 See Chapter Eight.

21 This seeming contradiction was also pointed out by villagers quoted in Yeh (2021).

transparency in the system, which effectively hinder corruption. The system is also considered to be efficient, with all the management posts tailored to take care of natural resources and to align with local livelihoods. Another important reason is the fact that these laws have developed organically within the community. Although some drivers of change throughout history have been external, the agency remains local. The laws seem to have a value in themselves for the shared sense of belonging to the place. Conscious of the strength of their traditional system of self-governance, the Limigya frequently speak about the laws with pride, and they seem to serve as a point of reference with intrinsic value beyond the actual content. When I discussed the failed attempt at abolishing the local customary laws in the 2015 meeting with villagers from Dzang four years later, they explained that the Nepali rules were not felt to be relevant to their community, whereas their own village laws were moulded to their needs, to ensure the sustainable management of the environment, to support the local livelihoods, and not the least to secure their monastery. To understand the value placed on the local system it is important to include the roles played by the monastery in local governance and to the way it caters to the spiritual needs of the villagers and contributes to local resilience.[22]

An unforeseen event that took place after my final fieldwork in 2019, the onset of the Covid-19 pandemic, highlights some more of the strengths and ductility of the local system as well as some of the challenges that remain. As in the rest of the world, the pandemic struck as an unexpected stressor that put local governance to the test. Lockdowns were imposed everywhere out-migrated Limigya were living; schools, workplaces and markets were closed. Travel across international borders was either forbidden, as in the case of China, or severely restricted, as in the case of India. In this initial phase of the pandemic, the villages that so many Limigya had left behind in search of a better life were revalued as the safest place to be. Hence, a large number of out-migrated villagers were tested for Covid, successfully negotiated travel permits, secured seats on one of the few flights to Humla and returned to the Limi valley: children came back from boarding schools in India and Kathmandu, and seasonal workers returned from Purang, Kathmandu and India.[23] Suddenly there were many more mouths to feed, while monetary income and access to

22 See also Hovden and Havnevik 2021 and Gurung et al. (forthcoming).

23 These returnees had to spend long time in quarantine before being allowed back into the villages. Limi closed its borders, partly at the instruction of national law, and partly on the model of the community's historical responses to epidemics. This strategy seems to have been successful as there was no spike in death rates as one would have expected if Covid had reached a community without any hospital.

markets on the Chinese side of the border as well as in the district headquarters in Simikot were lost.

This situation forced the villagers to revert to agriculture for sustenance.[24] As mentioned in Chapter Four, over the last few years, many fields had been left fallow, and the villagers had become increasingly dependent on earning an income in Purang and on access to cheap (but low quality) food items there. Now, the villagers started recultivating their fields. In Waltse, the assembly voted for an adjustment to village law, making it obligatory to cultivate previously fallow fields. Yet, although output increased, it has never been possible to survive on agriculture alone. Those among the households with several fields and full storerooms managed well, while those without (mainly single women and the elderly), were dependent on help from relatives. But this relief would only be possible as long as there was grain left in the storerooms. Not knowing how long the border would be closed, the villages therefore called an assembly meeting, during which they decided to request food aid from the Nepali government. A group of villagers marched over the almost 5000 metre Nyalu pass, wading through snow up to their hips, in order to get to Simikot and then to Kathmandu to put their case to the relevant authorities (Fig. 10.1). However, while requests for food aid are not new, now the whole process was thoroughly documented, and got coverage on social media, in newspapers, radio and even on TV.[25] The villagers were successful and in November 2021, food and other basic necessities were airlifted to Limi (Fig. 10.2). The monastery performed rituals in order to secure a successful outcome. Such a combination of efforts—leveraging local institutions and village laws to maximise resource use, appeasing the local deities to ensure spiritual grounding, and requesting national government support—serves as an example of how the strengths of all three systems can be utilised.

Tshewang's advice from the opening vignette—to continue to build on the strengths of the indigenous governance system—might offer a sustainable way forward for the Limigya. Such an approach might help them to stay clear of the worst pitfalls of the Nepali governance system, which so far has been riddled with problems. However, it would require at least a minimal acknowledgement of the indigenous system by the Nepali state, and some necessary updates by

24 See also Chapter Four.

25 See for instance the article "Help extended to Humla residents facing shortage of rice" by Chhapal Lama 2021. Considering how little experience the villagers had with Nepali authorities in 2010 when I first visited the valley, the contrast is striking.

COLUMNS

The Nepali state in the Himalaya

The food shortage in Limi Valley has highlighted Nepal's weak state presence in the Himalayan borderlands.

Photo Courtesy: Paljor Tamang

FIGURE 10.1 Wading in snow over high passes to seek help for food shortage
© THE KATHMANDU POST

KARNALI PROVINCE

Help extended to Humla residents facing shortage of rice

Kantipur Media Group, KL Dugar Group and Summit Air deliver rice to shortage-hit Humla villages.

The three organisations flew 136 rice bags each weighing 25 kg to Humla on Wednesday. Chhapal Lama/TKP

FIGURE 10.2 Food aid finally secured
© THE KATHMANDU POST

the Limigya to adapt to modern society.[26] This would entail finding ways to address several dilemmas caused by their multiple states of 'in-betweenness', discussed throughout the book. These dilemmas include devising sustainable mechanisms for monastic recruitment and funding, providing access to adequate education, healthcare and sustainable livelihoods and motivating young people to continue living in the villages. The pandemic revealed what many Limigya had feared for a long time: that an excessive reliance on Purang is risky. Developing more localised solutions and creating ways to offer relevant job opportunities to some of the educated youth might at least help reduce the massive out-migration.[27]

If the village laws are completely discarded or made too weak, there may be a real risk that the society will collapse, as so many Limigya say they fear. However, the senior villager quoted above also cautioned against the opposite scenario: if the iron ring of village law is made too tight and not treated properly, it may go rusty. Six hundred years ago, Thangtong Gyalpo (Thang stong rgyal po) blended some arsenic into the iron rings used for his suspension bridges to effectively prevent them from rusting.[28] When properly handled iron is a strong material that is also ductile and able to flex without breaking. Perhaps the Limigya could incorporate an anti-corrosive into the iron ring of their village law to maintain its flexibility. Considering such an update to the village law might prove helpful as the Limigya chart a course for their society in-between.

---

26 This point is discussed in Bhattarai (2021), Gurung et al. (forthcoming) and Bhattarai et al. (forthcoming).

27 See Chapter Four and Bhattarai et al. (forthcoming).

28 Kalmus 2015 and Wolf 1993. I am grateful to Diemberger for pointing this out to me.

APPENDIX 1

Excerpts

Excerpt from the *Rinchen Ling monastery inventory*, f. 9a, l. 2–3
yang lo tsa+tsha ba rin chen bzang po'i 'dra sku rje de nyid kyi sku gdung gi cha las bzhengs [gzhengs] pa pad sgrags kyi dpangs [dpang] su khru gang sor gsum yod pa byin ldan gcig/_yang sman 'jim las grub pa'i lo tsa+tsha ba'i 'dra sku khru gang sor bzhi pa gcig/

Excerpt from the *Rinchen Ling monastery inventory*, f. 2b–3a
gu ge zhang zhung gi yul stod du sku 'khrungs pa'i/ lo tswa ba [bas] rin chen bzang po zhes mtshan yongs su grags pa de nyid kyis [kyi] gu ger tho ling gser khang gi gtsos pa'i bstan gzhi gtsug lag khang brgya rtsa brgyad bzhengs [bzheng] pa'i phyi mtha' sku tshe'i smad la grub par bskrun pa'i gnas gzhi 'di nyid dang nye ba'i sgrub gnas lha sdengs su sku'i bkod pa dag zhing du bsdus pa/

Excerpt from the *Rinchen Ling monastery inventory*, f. 3b–4a
sras nu bo rgyal srid du skur bas chab srid rgyas pa lung bstan pa dang bcas [cas] kyi gus 'dud du _sle mi yul 'dzang du gnas gzhi til chen [chung]/ _til [stil] du kun 'dzom dgon dang_bla brang [grang] sa yul bdag thob dang mchod gzhis yon bdag so so'i rnyed bkur [skur] gang bgyis sdud [sdu] len sogs ji srid bar 'gog med du/ _rgyal po yab sras gsum gyi bka'i gnang ba rgyas bcad du thob pas _ti se rgyang grags dgon gyi ya gyal dang khongs su 'thus pa.

Excerpt from the *Rinchen Ling monastery inventory*, f. 4a
dbal rtse lha khang du sa skya pa'i sku gnyer ba de khas _'bri gung pa'i grwa [gra] rigs zhig grub mtha'i phyogs 'dzin gyi rkyen lam du btang nas lha khang rgyang skyur gyis bros bud du song bar rtsa 'dzin thabs bral du song gshis bcas kyis _rgyal po gtso phal rnams kyi bka' khrims las _dbal rtse lha khang mchod gzhis bcas pa 'bri gung pa'i grwa pa'i stong bcal du rtsa len ji srid bar 'jags gnas su bcad brtsal du byung ba _de kha'i lha khang lte ba mdo sbug rten mchod.

Excerpt from the *Rinchen Ling monastery inventory*, f. 4a
de rjes rang re 'bri gung pa'i 'dzin bdag 'dzang gi til chen dgon pa'i mi sde zhabs 'degs pa rnams mon rong spun lnga pa'i khral khrims [mkhrim] gyi mnar spyod che bas [ba'i] bud stongs thor zhig du song shis _ dgon gnas bla grwa [gra] rnams la gzan rgyag [zan gyag] ches pas [pa'i] 'khra tshugs ['khra' tshugs] ma thub nas/_rten [brten] gsum mchod cha rnams dbal rtse'i lha khang du gdan drangs pa bcas.

 | DOI:10.1163/9789004714571_012

Excerpt from the *Rinchen Ling monastery inventory*, f. 50a, l. 3ff.
gdung brgyud rgyal po mgon gsum nas rim par mon rgyal po/_la dwags rgyal po/_bod rgyal po dga' ldan tshe dbang gis [gi] mnga' dbang bsgyur nas da lta yan chod la sngar bdag snyon med dang _snga khyun 'jags gnas yin pa kun shes ltar la _bye brag sle mi nang mtshan yul mtsho so so'i sa mtshams rnams/_so so'i ma yig ban khrar gsal ltar la.

Excerpt from *Waltse tax register*, pp. 108–110
shing 'brug zla pa'i 4 pa'i tshes 1 la _ lugs [lug] gnyis gong ma khrims bdag rin po che [krim bdag rin por che] zhabs drung du /_zhu ba _bdag ming rtags khungs [gungs] gsham [sham] gsal rnams [rnam] nas blos blangs [blos bslang] mi 'gyur med gyi gan tshig rtsang ma phul snying la don rtsa /_'di lo dbal rtse yul tsa'i kha 'cham [cham] mthun ['thun] grub thog sgrub grwa [gra] dge slong [slongs] bzhi pa'i gsol rgyags grong pa [grongs] so so nas sbyor 'jags ['byor 'byags] che chung thog ma rtsa [mar rtsa] gtsugs thog skal pa nam stongs rgyal bstan [tshan] ji srid [sid] bar phyag [chag] med byed rgyu grong che chung med gyi 'jal ['byal] dgos byed sgo thams cad [thamd] dang tha na chu shing sogs [sog] la sngar bkod [ngar kos] gdong len [dang len] byed dgos grong so so nas rang rang gi rgyu lag thog phyi 'jal ['byal] sog sa zhing 'bru mar lo lo bzhin phul ba dang smar lag thog du phul ba sogs la phyin chad mi 'grub pa'i zha chag [phyag] til [stil] 'bru tsam me byed zhu zhing 'di las mi 'gal ba'i _nga min kho yin _dran gtam gsar skyes [dran stam gsar skyed]_ rnyog ma gting slong [rnyog pa rting log] kha gcig [cig] lce [ce] gnyis_ btsos sha rjen log [rtsos sha sbyin log]_ ri sgul mtsho skyom [ri gu tshe skyong] _ dpon ltag khur [pon rta gur] sogs byas mi chog pa dang mdor ['ngor] na gan don 'di bzhin la mi [sme] gnas pa til [stil] 'bru tsam shar tshe gong ma khrims zhabs su 'ba' [khrim zhab su 'ba] gser srang [ser sang] lnga gtsang [rtsang] 'bul dang slar [blar] yang gan don 'di bzhin [zhin] la sor gnas byed zhu ba ming thog rtags [rta] 'zhu ba'i [be] yul tsa'i lag [legs] skor ba'i rtags /

The *Monastic Recruitment Contract*
Title on the scroll:
yul tsho gsum na bu gnyis byung phyin bu re chos sgor zhugs rgyu gan rgya (...)[1]

Title on the front page:
1) gsham gsal gan don bzhin sor gnas yod pa byed / [large red square stamp]

1 The last two syllables are illegible.

Introductory lines (2–5):

2) me spre [1896] zla 3 tshes 15 la ___ phul byung phan ba'i 'byung gnas[2] gong ma khrims bdag rin po che'i zhabs drung du[3]

3) gsham gsal gnyis mos gan rgya'i 'bru don la sor gnas rgyun 'khyongs yong ba gyis ___ [subscript: skor gsum spyi khyab lhan khang nas] [black square stamp] ___ sa spre zla tshes la / [black square stamp][4]

4) gsham gsal sle mi dgon du grwa chos bzhugs skor[5] skyabs rje[6] 'bri gung sprul rin po che'i bka' don ltar khyed rang yul dgon ser skya nang mos mthun grub pa'i sgrig bca'[7] dngos 'brel yin tshe nges don sor gnas rgyun[8]

5) 'khyongs dgos rgyu'i spu hreng rdzong chos nas tham pa phab pa yin ___me spre zla tshes // [square black stamp, Purang *rdzong*] [circular black stamp, Shephel Ling monastery]

Main text:

6) ___zhu ba ___ bdag ming rtags [brtags] khungs gsham gsal rnams nas blos blangs mi 'gyur ba'i gan tshig (?) gtsang mar phul snying la _don rtsa sngar nas bzung

7) sle mi dgon du bka' bsrung rnams kyi gar 'chams [mchams] dar rgyas che zhing lhag par dgon gyi mchod las byed sgo'i rigs mang ba bcas _bar skabs dge 'dun zhal grangs nyung zad la song skabs _ 'bri gung skyabs rje _ rin po che dkon mchog bstan 'dzin chos kyi blo gros nyid gangs rir gnas gzigs la chibs bsgyur gnang bar

8) thug _dgun thog gcig gi ring sle mir bzhugs 'jags gnang ba dang _dgon gyi grwa rgyun kha grangs shin tu nyung bar gzigs nas _bka' bsrung rnams kyi gar 'chams [mchams] dang mchod las byed sgo'i rigs mang zhig la brten _dge 'dun zhal grangs lnga bcu'i skor tsam zhig med thabs mi

9) 'dug zhing _snga nas kyang sle mi yul tsho gsum nas tshe 'di'i rkyen zlog dang phyi ma'i 'dren skyabs su chos sde 'di nyid btsugs 'dug dpal shin tu legs tshogs che bar gzigs nas _yul tsho gsum gyi grong chen re la bu gnyis re byung tshe bu re chos sgor grwa tshang du ma btsug

10) thabs med 'dug pas _'jug rogs [rog] zhes bka' nan che bar _brten gsung nan ma theg nas yul gsum nas [stamp and subscript with thinner pen: grong chung ba

---

2 Probably short for the standard phrase: *phul byung phan dang bde ba'i 'byung gnas* meaning 'the outstanding source of benefit and happiness'. See the THL dictionary and Schneider 2002: 419.

3 This is a standard phrase in the *inscriptio* of a *gan rgya* document, see Schneider 2002: 419.

4 It is not clear which line this date belongs to.

5 The syllables are illegible, but Ramble suggests *bzhugs skor*.

6 The syllables are unclear.

7 Especially the syllable *bca'* is uncertain.

8 The three last syllables are unclear.

bu gsum re la bu re grwa rtsar[9] 'jugs rgyu] lhag bsam dang len thog legs so khas len zhus shing phyin chad nge don ltar byed zhus pa dang _gal srid grong gi bu de bzhin tshe 'di ma 'tshog tshe chos

11) sgor zhugs pa'i bu yi [subscript with thinner pen: nyes chad sgrub lam zhus thog bu de bzhin phyir slog byed dgos] las sde [half red stamp] grwa spyi[10] 'dres ltar khur thog bu de bzhin phyir slog byed dgos [half red stamp] grwa (tshang nas)[11] kyang phyin chad nag nyes byung tshe nyes chad 'ba' sel gser srang phyed re sgrub thog slar yang chos sgor nam 'chi bar sdod pa las _phyir 'gro mi

12) chog pa dang bab log yang rkyen rtsa su thog tu la (?) _yas mas nyes chad sgrub lam zhu ba ma gtogs _bslab pa snga phyi'i rtsod gleng sogs byed rgyu med cing _'di thad grwa tshang nas kyang drag gzhan rgan gzhon [zhon] gyi go rim dang _ma zad nag skyon gyi rtsod gleng

13) byas mi chog cing _grwa tshang nas kyang phyi yul kyi lar rgya rgyab gnon rjes 'brang ci khyon _byed pa las ya bral so sor ma song bar byed rgyu dang _mdor na gan don 'di bzhin la mi gnas pa'i nga min kho yin_dran (gtam) gsar skyes _rnyog ma gting

14) slong _kha gcig lce gnyis _g.yas khag g.yon dkris _rtsos sha rjen rlog _'bam dags ral _dpon rtag khur _ri sgul mtsho skyom sogs mdor [mdon] na gan don 'di bzhin la ser skya su thad nas 'gal rigs _til 'bru tsam

15) shar tshe khrims zhabs su 'ba' gser srang bcu gtsang 'bul zhus thog slar yang gan don 'di bzhin la sor gnas byed zhus pa ming thog rtags phul _til yul spyis lag skor ba'i rtags [black circular stamp] wal rtse yul spyis lag skor ba'i rtags [black thumb shaped stamp][12]

16) 'dzang yul spyis lag skor ba'i rtags [black circular stamp] grwa spyi lag skor ba'i rtags [black square stamp]

Excerpt from the *Rinchen Ling monastery inventory*, f. 49a

sa yos zla nang wal tse grong stod mes mes [me me] bkra shis tshe ring dang i pa'i 'bya' g.yangs dbang mo nang tshang gnyis nas phyi ma rnam grol thob phyir 'di lo grwa [gra] tshang gzhung nas skyob pa rin po che'i gos sku gsar bzhengs [gzhengs] snang skabs rten[13] 'di la mchod 'bul dus mchod [chod] ma rtsa [mar tsa] gong ming dags rgan [rgon] gnyis nas rgyu dngos gser kyi pad 'dab g.yu khras rgyan pa phom dang mu tig bcas [cas] rin thang phyi sgor nyis brgya [rgya] dang go Tam dngul brgya dang nyi shu byas par phul ba'i phyi sgor nyis brgya grwa tshang gzhung la phul ba'i skyed thog

9 *grwa tshang*?

10 Short for *grwa tshang dang spyi pa*.

11 The syllable is almost completely covered by a black stamp.

12 This is different from the stamp they are using today.

13 *sten*?

gzhung [bzhung] nas lo ltar spya (?)[14] bre 'bru khal bzhi re gtong sgo [stong ko'i] rgyu 'gro byed du snang dgos dang _go Tam dngul drug bcu sku gnyer [snyer] gnyis la mar bre [mer] bzhi'i mar tsar sprad pa dang _go Tam dngul bcu grwa tshang gzhung la phul ba'i skyed thog grwa [gra] gzhung tshogs thog sku 'gyed nag Tam gnyis re 'bul dgos.

14 *dpya*?

APPENDIX 2

Glossary

The translations of Tibetan terms in the glossary are brief versions of terminology as they are used in the book. Fuller explanations are provided in the relevant chapters. Approximate spelling is suggested for most of the terminology and proper names not found in dictionaries.

Technical Terms

Wylie Translation
a ce lha mo Tibetan opera
a ni nun
a phyi grandmother
'ba' gan oath
'bag gsol supplication ritual for the masks
ban khral monk tax, monk levy (syn. *grwa khral, btsun khral*)
ban dza (s.u.) type of tax paid on private property in Limi
ban yig (s.u.) book of the *ban dza* tax
bar 'gel the medium *'u lag* distance in Limi
bar shar ba regular monk, who has taken the middle precepts
bca' khral lease fee, taxes paid on village and monastery land
bca' yig monastic regulations, book of the *bca'* tax
bco lnga village council in Waltse ('[council of] the fifteen')
bde rim welfare rituals
bgres song senior monk, who has completed all monk offices
bka' blon minister
bka' brgyad, sgrub pa bka' brgyad eight pronouncements, the eight great *sādhanā* teachings
bka' 'gyur lha khang scripture hall
bka' shog ordinance, edict
bka' shog chen mo the great edict
bka' stsal pronouncement
bla brang a lama's residence
bla brang bla ma resident lama
bod sil bu'i dus the 'age of fragmentation' in Tibet, between the early and later diffusions of Buddhism

 | DOI:10.1163/9789004714571_013

bod khral Tibetan tax, tax paid to Tibet before 1960
bom btang Limi term for *mo rang* household, short for *bu mo btang*?
bre volume measurement, approximately 1 litre
'bri yak cow
brgya bzhi four hundred offerings for removing obstacles
'brog pa nomad
'bru tsha type of Tibetan headless script
bsang, bsang gsol fumigation offerings
bskang gso propitiation ritual
bsnyen gnas the one-day precepts
bsod nyoms alms
bstan pa phyi dar the second dissemination of Buddhism in Tibet
btsan a type of spirit
btsan khang shrine for the *btsan* spirit
btsun khral monk tax, monk levy (syn. *grwa khral, ban khral*)
bu tshab adoption
byang pa Byansi or Bura (lit. 'people from the north')
byin rlabs blessing
chang Tibetan barley beer
chad pa fine (usually in grain or cash)
'cham monastic dance
'cham rtsis final public *'cham* rehersal
'cham yig monastic dance manual
char 'bebs rain making ritual
chos khrims religious law
chos me butter-lamp
chos pa religious practitioner
chos sgar religious encampment
chos grwa religious school
chos gzhis religious estate or property (also spelled *mchod gzhis*)
chos sems religious aspirations, religious mind
chos skor here: the practice of carrying Buddhists scriptures around the fields for protection
chos rtsigs decree
chu 'thag khral water mill tax
dar po che large flagpole
dbang gi sbyin sreg powerful fire offering
dbu chos cantor, chant master
dbu mdzad cantor, chant master
dga' ldan khri pa throne-holder at Ganden monastery

dge ba virtuous action
dge bskos monastic disciplinarian
dge bsnyen person who has taken layman's (upāsaka/upāsikā) vows
dge slong fully ordained monk (bhikṣu) or nun (bhikṣuṇī)
dge tshul person who has taken novice (śrāmaṇera) vows
dgon lag branch monastery
dgon pa monastery, lit. 'secluded place'
dgon pa'i khral monastic taxes or obligations
dgongs pa here: temporary leave from tax obligations
dgra lha warrior deity
dgra lha dpangs bstod high praise of the warrior deity
dgun nyal low income manual labour in Humla, lit. 'hibernation'
dkar chag a literary genre (lit. 'list of contents')
dkon mchog gsum lit. 'the three jewels', The Buddha, Dharma, and Sangha
dmag dus kyi rgyal po war-time king
dngos slob close disciple
drag po'i sbyin sreg wrathful fire offering
'dre type of angry spirit
'du khang assembly hall
'du ma assembly, here: usually village assembly meetings
dung mkhan conch blower
ga'u charm box
gan rgya legal contract, obligation contract
gangs skor circumambulation of a mountain (here: Mt. Kailash)
gar dance, here: ancient West Tibetan court dance
gar dpon dance leader
gar g.yog dance attendant
gdung rten reliquary
glegs shing wooden book covers
gnas bdag guardian deity, 'lord of the place'
gnya' bo the groom's party
gnyer pa steward, general term for village and monastic positions
'go ba headman, village leader
'go Tam probably Gorkha ṭam (half rupee)
gos sku brocade image
'grig khrims regulations, law
'gro stangs procedure
grong chen large household
grong chung small household
grong mtshams household order

grong pa estate, household
grub chu sacred spring (lit. 'accomplishment spring')
grub thob siddha
grwa khral monk tax, monk levy (syn. *ban khral, btsun khral*)
grwa pa monk
grwa tshang monastic community, monk assembly
grwa zhing lit. 'monk fields', fields for the sustenance of monks
gsar ma'i 'cham new monastic dances
gser gi mdo li golden palanquin
gser khang golden temple
gser khral gold tax
gser skyems libation offering
gser thog golden roof ornament
gser zangs gilded copper
gsol kha supplication ritual
gtan deb lit. 'permanent inventory', type of adm. document
gtan khra agreement, decree
gtong sgo ritual expenses
gtor ma offering cake or effigy
gtor rgyag casting of dough effigies
gtsug lag khang temple
gu ru drag po gtor rgyag offering to the wrathful aspect of Guru Rinpoche
'gur lha class of deities
g.yag 'go animal calculation unit, (lit. 'yak head')
g.yang 'gugs ritual to secure prosperity
g.yar to lend
g.yung drung swastika, L. *yugrum*
gzhas song
gzim chung here: the lesser of the two quarters for high lamas
gzims khang here: quarters for high lamas
gzhu 'doms armspan
gzungs bsdus collection of religious works
hrul skyon tattered
ka ba wooden column
kha btags ceremonial silk scarf
kha rgan male head of the household
khal a load, quantity of twenty
khal ma pack animal
khral tax, obligation
khral chang beer drunk at tax collection meetings (syn. *rtsis chang*)

khral dgongs pa application for tax reduction or temporary exemption
khral gcog lit. 'to break the taxes', taking leave from the village
khral mi taxable person, used for calculating poll tax
khral med without tax obligations
khral pa taxpayer
khral rtsis autumn tax collection meeting
khral zhing taxable fields, fields for lease
khrims law, rule, code of conduct
khrims khang court
khrom srung ba disciplinarian, lit. 'guardian of the festival place'
khur bu load of firewood
khyams pa migrant, wanderer, pilgrim
khyim mtshes lit. 'neighbour', here: member of partitioned household
'khyug yig Tibetan cursive script
klu serpent deity, nāga
kun dga' ra ba altar shelves
lag sde helping hands (i.e., helpers during rituals and festivities)
las 'dzin official, annually rotating post in the Limi village adm.
las 'dzin rgan po senior official
las 'dzin rtsis sprod the spring assembly meeting in Waltse, Limi
las pa oficial (syn. *las 'dzin*)
las sne monastic sponsorship position
las thog monk official
lcags spre zhib gzhung the Iron Monkey settlement
lcags stag zhib gzhung the Iron Tiger settlement
lha bsang fumigation offering for the pho lha and yul lha
lha gsol supplication ritual to local deities
lha g.yag ritual dedicating a yak to the gods
lha khang temple, shrine
lha mo here: short for a ce lha mo, Tibetan opera
lhu portions of meat
lo gsar New Year
lo gsum phyog gsum the three years three months retreat
lo gsum zla gsum the three years three months retreat
lo rags type of watchman
lo rim annual ritual
lo tho Tibetan calendar (lit. 'year list')
lo tswa ba translator
lta rtog pa type of watchman
lug rdzi shepherd

ma rgan female head of the household
ma rtsa capital
ma yig main document (lit. 'mother document')
mag pa here: uxorilocal/matrilocal groom
maN Dal bzhi chog four-mandala ritual to Tārā
mang ja offering of tea to the monk assembly
mar butter
mar bre measurement of butter
mar khral butter tax
mchod mjal religious visit to a place of worship
mchod rten stupa
mdzo yak-cow hybrids
me slang portable fire bowl for keeping the tea warm
mes mes grandfather
mgar ba blacksmith, L. *ada*
mgon khang protector deity chapel
mgur lha class of deities
mi kha gossip
mi khral person tax, poll tax
mi re partitioned household (lit. 'man by himself'), (syn. *grong chung*)
mi rtsis attendance
mi ser subjects
mkhan po preceptor or abbot
mo rang single woman household
mog mog Tibetan dumplings
mon pa non-Tibetans living south of the border
mon khral Nepali tax
mthu destructive spell
mtshams khang retreat hut or hermitage
nag snyil black fringes
nag Tam old coin used in Tibet
nang khral internal tax
ngo shes fictive kin, ritual friendship (N. *mit*), (lit. 'acquaintance')
nya ga weight measurement
nyin thig 'sun line', observance of the sun light to determine the timing of agricultural work
snye (L. nyog) 'heads of barley'
nyung skam dried turnips
'om bu a type of tamarisk (Lat. *Myricaria dahurica*)
pha'i spun the bride's party lit. 'kinsmen of the [bride's] father'

pha rnying old paternal home
pho lha territorial or ancestral deity (lit. 'paternal deity')
phog zhing lit. salary field', field for the sustenance of monks
phogs allowance for officiating monks
phor pa, phor bu (L: furru) wooden bowl
phyi ba temporary mingrants, lit. 'outside [travellers]'
phyi khral external tax
phyi ma rnam grol liberation in a later lifetime
phyi sgor foreign currency
phyur ba dried cheese, L. *churbi*
phyur khral cheese tax
ra rdzi goatherd
rab byung calendrical cycle of sixty years
rab byung ordination vows (short for *rab tu byung ba*)
rab gnas consecration
rab tu byung ba ordination vows
rag li brass
rdo rje slob dpon tantric master
rdor 'dzin title given to the Drigung representatives at Kailash
rdo rje 'dzin pa title given to the Drigung representatives at Kailash
rdza clay
rdzong district, Tibetan administrative unit (lit. 'fortress')
rdzong dpon district commissioner
rdzong sdod same as *rdzong dpon*
rdzong tshab representative of the district administrative officer
rgya gling shawm
rgyal khrims civil law
rgyan rgyag to draw lots
rgyang grags calling distance, 500 arm-spans (*gzhu 'doms*), ideal minimum distance between village and monastery
rgyas pa'i sbyin sreg extensive fire offering
rgyun thug meals served in the monastery, (lit. 'regular soup')
ri khrod hermitage
rin thang value
rigs gsum mgon po the 'protectors from the three [Bodhisattva] families': Mañjuśrī, Avalokiteśvara, Vajrapāṇi
rigs lnga the five Buddha families
rkang gnyis/ka ni entrance stupa
rnam rtog scepticism, hard-headednes, superstition
sbyin bdag patron, sponsor

rnying ma'i 'cham old monastic dances
rong pa people from the southern valleys
rtags pa here: prediction ritual
rtsam pa roasted barley flour
rtsis chang beer drunk during tax collection (lit. 'calculation beer')
rtswa rin grazing fee
sa bon seed grain
sa 'dul taming the ground
sa khral land tax
sa ma 'brog agro-pastoralist (lit. 'neither [fully] peasant nor nomad')
sbag drug bricks of tea
sbug pa title of the adm. leaders of the monasteries in Limi
sbyin sreg fire offering rituals
sde pa governor
sde pa gzhung old term for the Tibetan government
sde srid regent
sdig pa sin, moral wrongdoing
ser khyim householder monk/priest (lit. 'yellow householder')
sgar dpon governor
sgra bla warrior deity
sgrib defilement, ritual pollution
sgrig bca' legal arrangement
sgrig khrims law and order, agreement
sgrub grwa here: retreat tax or allowance to support monks in retreat
sgrub thob siddha
shag monk cells
shing rlon po green wood
shing rta 'khor lo wooden carts
shing skam po dry wood
shon ancient West Tibetan song type
shon ma shon performer
shon 'go head of the shon dancers
skong bshags confession and purification ritual
skra gcod cutting a lock of hair during monastic ordination
sku gnyer shrine keeper
skya ser assembly of monks and laity (lit. [wearers of] grey and yellow [robes])
skyed thog compound interest
slong 'bebs mediation
sman 'dam medicinal clay
sman mo female wrathful spirits

smyung gnas fasting ritual
snags pa tantric practitioners
snam bu woollen cloth
sos long spring provisions
sprul sku here: reincarnated lama (lit. 'emanation body')
spyi khang community hall
spyi khyab chief
spyi khyab lhan khang governor's office
spyi mdzod the collective treasury of a monastery
srang unit of money, weight
ston long autumn provisions
ston tshong autumn trade
stong sgam lit. box with 1000 coins
Tam ka old currency used in Tibet
thab chen large stove
thab chung small stove
thab khral hearth tax
'thor ba fragmented
thug thal barley flour used for soup
thung lag the shortest *'u lag* distance in Limi
tsha khral salt tax
tshab replacement, representative, substitute, proxy
tshe bcol ordained to protect from misfortune (lit. 'life entrusted')
tshe phyid Nyinba word for low-income work (lit. 'life sustenance')
tshe thar ritual freeing of animals (lit. 'life-liberation')
tshes bcu the tenth day ritual
tsho type of social organisation (lit. 'group')
tshogs rgya extensive offering feast
tshong ra market
tshwa rin grazing fee
'u lag transportation duty, transportation distance
yon chab water offerings
yul ba villagers, village assembly
yul 'dzin gsum gyi 'du ma three-village meeting
yul lha territorial deity
yul gsum the three villages [in Limi]
yul gyi khral village taxes or obligations
yul gyi khrims village laws
zangs yig copper plate inscription
zhabs phyi monk attendant

zhal 'debs donation
zhal zas food offering *gtor ma*
zhi ba'i sbyin sreg pacifying fire offering
zhing gi sku rim rituals for the fields (to ensure a good harvest)
zhing skyong territorial protector deity
zhon riding
zhor las manual labour in Purang (lit. 'side job')
zor magic weapons
zwa stinging nettle, Lat. *Urtica dioica*

Proper Names

Abi Genmo Dzong A phyi rGan mo rDzong
Alchi A lci
Amgon Zangpo A mgon bZang po
Apchi A phyi
Apchi Chökyi Dröma A phyi Chos kyi sGrol ma
Changchub Ö Byang chub 'Od
Changra Cham lCang ra 'cham
Chaye sPya ye
Chaye Namkha Dzong sPya ye Nam mkha' rDzong
Chaye Yeshe Dzong sPya ye Ye shes rDzong
Chemchog Heruka Che mchog He ru ka
Chenga Lingpa sPyan snga Gling pa
Chetsang Rinpoche Che tshang Rin po che
Chogro Cog ro, lCog ro
Chogrowa Cog ro ba
Choprang Ganga Choprang (s.u.) sGang ga
Chödzong Nyinda Khabjor Chos rdzong Nyi zla Kha sbyor
Chökhor Tse Chos 'khor rTse
Chönyi Norbu Rinpoche Chos nyid Nor bu Rin po che
Chugpo Zangzhung Phyug po Zhang zhung
Chugpo Zhanang Phyug po Zhwa nang
Chungtsang Rinpoche Chung tshang Rin po che
Dagpo Shedrup Ling Dwags po bShad grub Gling
Darchen Dar chen
Demchog bDe mchog, Skt. Cakrasaṃvara
Dingri Ding ri
Dondrup Chögyal Don grub Chos rgyal

Dorje Chang rDo rje 'Chang, Skt. Vajradhāra
Dorje Gyalpo rDo rje rGyal po
Drablasungwa sGra bla srung ba?
Drabli Gyalmo sGra bla'i rGyal mo
Drepung 'Bras spungs
Drigung Chetsang 'Bri gung Che tshang
Drigung Chungtsang 'Bri gung Chung tshang
Drigung Kagyu 'Bri gung bKa' brgyud
Drugchu Lung Drug bcu lung
Drukpa Kagyu 'Brug pa bKa' brgyud
Drusha Bru sha
Druwa Bru ba
Dungling s.u.
Dzang mDzang/mDzangs/'Dzang
Dzardziwa rDza rtsibs ba
Dza Rongphu rDza Rong phu
Dzatrul Ngawang Tenzin Norbu rDza sprul Ngag dbang bsTan 'dzin Nor bu
Dzogchen rDzogs chen
Ganden dGa' ldan
Ganden Ngamchö dGa' ldan lnga mchod
Ganden Phodrang dGa' ldan Pho brang
Ganden Tshewang dGa' ldan Tshe dbang
Gangkar Lhamo Gangs dkar lHa mo
Gangri Lhabtsen Gangs ri lHa btsan
Ghuya Gangpa G+hu ya sGang pa
Gomoche sGo mo che (?)
Göku Düchen Gos sku dus chen
Gönpo Chakzhi mGon po phyag bzhi
Guge Gu ge
Guge Dawa Dzong Gu ge mDa' ba rDzong
Gungphur dGung 'phur
Guru Rinpoche Gu ru Rin po che
Gyalpo rGyal po
Gyalwang Kunga Rinchen rGyal dbang Kun dga' Rin chen
Gyalwang Rinchen Phuntsok rGyal dbang Rin chen Phun tshogs
Gyangdrag rGyang grags
Gyanyima rGya nyi ma
Heruka He ru ka
Hrakya Sra skya?
Humla 'Om lo, Wom lo

Jangchub Ling Byang chub Gling
Jao Lhadeng Bya'u lHa gting/lding
Jomo Ling Jo mo Gling
Jowo Jo bo
Kailash Gangs dkar Ti se, Gangs Rin po che
Kangyur bKa' 'gyur
Katse Kā rtse, Kha rtse
Katse Gokhar Kha tse Go khar, Kā rtse O dkar
Khochar, Khorchag Kho char, 'Khor chags
Khochar Jowo Kho char Jo bo
Khyithang Khyi thang
Khyungdruwa Khyung bru ba?
Khyungpa Khyung pa
Konchog Samten dKon mchog bSam gtan
Kumbum sKu 'bum
Kurgyab sKu rgyab?
Kushog Ramjor sKu zhabs Rab 'byor
Kyide Nyimagön sKyid lde Nyi ma mgon
Kyil dKyil
Kyirong sKyid rong
Kyobpa Jigten Sumgön sKyob pa 'Jig rten gSum mgon
Lama Kundzom Bla ma Kun 'dzom
Lama Yuru Bla ma g.Yu ru
Ladakh La dwags
Larung Gar Bla rung sGar
Lhabab festival lHa babs dus chen
Lhadeng lHa sdengs
Lhadrön lHa sgron
Lhadzin Gompa lHa 'dzin/rdzing dgon pa?
Lapcha Shar La rtse Shar
Lhazhing lHa zhing
Limi Sle mi
Limi Chumig Lhadzing Sle mi chu mig lha rdzing
Limi River Sle mi Chu
Lo Monthang Glo sMon thang
Lubra Klu brag
Mani festival Mani dus chen
Mani temple Mani lha khang
Mapham Yumtsho Ma pham g.Yu mtsho
Mangyul Mang yul

Maryul Mar yul
Memo Nagnyil sMan mo Nag snyil
Mepo Changthang Med po Byang thang
Mepo Thaljor Med po Thal 'byor?
Mepo Zhaphug Med po Zha phug?
Miluwa Mi lus ba?
Mindroling sMin grol gling
Mön Mon
Nagtsho Tshultrim Gyelwa Nag mtsho Tshul khrims rGyal ba
Namkha Rural Municipality Nam mkha', Nep. Namkha Gaunpalika
Namkha Khyung Dzong Nam mkha' Khyung rDzong
Namse rNam sras, Skt. Vaiśravaṇa
Namthong Nam mthong
Nganglag Tshakha Ngang lag Tshwa kha
Ngari mNga' ris
Ngari Gar mNga' ris sGar
Ngorchen Kunga Zangpo Ngor chen Kun dga' bZang po
Nöjin Phuntsok gNod sbyin Phun tshogs
Nyene bsNyen gnas
Nyinba Nyin pa
Nying sNying
Nyingma rNying ma
Nyingmapa rNying ma pa
Ombu Lungpa 'Om bu Lung pa
Omlo 'Om lo
Purang sPu hreng (sPu hrengs, Pu hrang, Pu rang)
Pel Yeshe dPal Ye shes
Phelgye Ling 'Phel rgyas Gling
Phulgong Lhä 'Phul sgang lHas?
Phyang Phyi dbang
Rakarwu Ra dkar dbu, Ra dkar rus?
Räni Rad nis
Rewingo Re wing go
Rimchö rim mchod
Rimdzöwa Ri mdzod pa?
Rinchen Ling Rin chen Gling
Rinchen Palri Rin chen dPal ri
Rinchen Phuntsok Rin chen Phun tshogs
Rinchen Zangpo Rin chen bZang po
Rongchung Rong chung

Ruthog Ru thog
Saga Dawa Sa ga zla ba
Sakya Sa skya
Sakyapa Sa skya pa
Samada Sa mda'
Samten Ling bSam gtan Gling
Samye bSam yas
Sangye Gyatso Sangs rgyas rGya mtsho
Senge Namgyal Seng ge rNam rgyal
Senge Tenzin Rinpoche Seng ge bsTan 'dzin Rin po che
Senge Yeshe Seng ge Ye shes
Sera Se ra
Sera Lung Se ra Lung
Serchung Ser chung
Serta gSer thar
Serta Rinpoche gSer thar Rin po che
Serwa gSer ba?
Shabkar Zhabs dkar
Shephel Ling bShad 'phel Gling
Shiwar Shi war
Songe Srong nge
Songtsen Gampo Srong btsan sGam po
Sönam Tse bSod nams rTse
Tagri Trawo sTag ri Khra bo
Takhyung Karpo rTa khyung dKar po
Tashigang bKra shis sgang
Tashi Lhunpo bKra shis Lhun po
Tashi Namgyal bKra shis rNam rgyal
Tashigön bKra shis mgon
Tawang rTa dbang
Tengyur bsTan 'gyur
Tenzin Chökyi Lodrö bsTan 'dzin Chos kyi bLo gros
Tenzin Pema Gyaltsen bsTan 'dzin Pad ma rGyal mtshan
Tenzin Zhiwe Lodrö bsTan 'dzin Zhi ba'i Blo gros
Tholing Tho ling, (mTho lding, mTho ling/gling, and Tho gling)
Til Til
Tilchen monastery Til chen dgon
Til Kundzom Til Kun 'dzom
Todpa sTod pa
Togden Rinpoche rTogs lDan rin po che

Trinle Zangpo 'Phrin las bZang po
Trisong Detsen Khri srong lDe btsan
Trongtö Grong stod
Tsang gTsang
Tsede rTse lde
Tseringma Tshe ring ma
Tshamdo mTshams mdo?
Tshechu Tshes bcu
Tshogkhang Rinpoche Tshogs khang Rin po che
Tshongsa Tshong sa
Waltse dBal rtse
Wangde dBang lde
Welchen Gekhö dBal chen Ge khod
Welse dBal gsas
Yakba (s.u.)
Yalbang Yul dbang
Yangrigar Yang ri sgar
Yangkur gYang skur
Yatse Ya rtse
Yeshe Ö Ye shes 'Od
Yugrum Ri Yung drung Ri
Yulsa Yul sa
Zhangzhung Zhang zhung
Zher Zher
Zhiwa Ö Zhi ba 'Od
Zurkhang Zur khang

APPENDIX 3

Measurements

Butter (weight):
5 *nya ga* = 1 kg
1 *mar bre* = 8 *nya ga*
20 *mar nyag* = 1 *mar khal*

Grain (volume):
3 thowa (s.u.) = 1 bre
4 jul/zhul (s.u.) = 1 bre
6 *phul* = 1 bre
1 *khal* = 20 *bre*

Meat:
1 yak = 18 *lhu* (portions of meet)
1 front leg of a yak = 2 *lhu*
1 back leg of a yak = 3 *lhu*

Animals:
1 *g.yag 'go* = 6 sheep or goats (Tibetan tax)
1 *g.yag 'go* = 7 sheep or goats (village tax)

Chang:
1 *thrungma* (s.u.) equals 6 *changgar* (s.u.)

Length:
khru—cubit
sor—finger width

'U lag distances:
'u lag—long (from Limi to Simikot)
bar 'gel—medium (from Limi to Tshongsa or to Zher)
thung lag—short

 | DOI:10.1163/9789004714571_014

APPENDIX 4

List of Rituals and Festivals

The list is an excerpt from my fieldnotes between 2010 and 2012, giving an overview of the major rituals and festivals performed by monks and laity during the year in Waltse. The Tibetan date is given in the left column, the middle column provides basic information about the name, performers, and organisation of the event, whereas the right column gives a brief summary of sponsor arrangements. In addition to the rituals listed below, individual households sponsor a significant number of supplication, purification and other rituals. More information about these events are provided in Chapter Seven.

Date	Name and description	Patronage
1/3–5	**sKong bshags (monastery)** Three days of *skong bshags*, from the 3rd to the 5th of the 1st month. On the 5th day the ritual is performed for rNam par snang mdzad.	The ritual is sponsored by the *grwa tshang* through the *las sne* system. 1 monk per day.
1/6–16	**Mani dus chen (monastery)** The monks recite mantras in the monastery assembly hall. During the first day the monks take their seats (*mani gral 'dzin*), the shrine keeper and the disciplinarian give details regarding organisation and ritual procedures. The recitation takes place the following 9 days and nights.	The ritual is sponsored by the *grwa tshang* through the *las sne* system. 2 monks.
1/1–8	**bsNyen gnas smyung gnas (the laity)** Alternating *bsnyen gnas* (precepts with food) and *smyung gnas* (fasting) in the community hall. One monk (*rdo rje slob dpon*) gives teachings to the laity for eight days. It is compulsory for each *grong chen* household to send a representative between 18 and 60 years old. In addition some elderly people participate voluntarily. A few years ago the villagers decided to alternate participation between the *grong stod* and *grong smad* households.	The sponsorship duty rotates among the *grong chen* households. Two households share the costs every year.

 | DOI:10.1163/9789004714571_015

(*cont.*)

Date	Name and description	Patronage
Variable date	**Sa gsol (monastery)** Two days' supplication ritual for those who have left the village for the winter (*phyi ba*).	Sponsored by the village community.
1/8–9	**rNam sras kyi dus lha (the Miluwa households)** *lHa gsol* celebrated by the Miluwa households. In Til and Dzang the celebration is grand, whereas in Waltse, the celebration is smaller because the small number of households belonging to this *pho lha*.	Jointly sponsored by the Miluwa households.
1/10	**Tshes bcu (the laity)** One *grong chen* family hosts the festival. Compulsory participation, one member from each household.	Village taxes.
1/15	**Tshes bcu (the laity)** One *grong chen* family hosts the festival. Compulsory participation, one member from each household.	Village taxes.
	Mani (the laity) Two-day recitation of mantras in the community hall. Normally the villagers raise a tent in the Lhazhing field below the monastery. The festival is also referred to as E ma ho (exclamation from the Pad ma bka' thang).	Sponsored by the village community.
1/17–19	**Kun rig (monastery)** Three-day purification ritual for rNam par snang mdzas performed by the assembly of monks.	Sponsored by the *grwa tshang*, but there are often voluntary donations.
1/20	**bLa ma mchod pa (monastery)** Half-day *bla ma mchod pa* ritual. *Tshogs* are distributed to all the monks.	Sponsored by the *grwa tshang*, but there are often voluntary donations.
1/16–25 (the 19th was cut)	**Mani (the laity)** The laity performed nine-day recitation of Vajraguru mantras in the community hall for the protection from flooding. The ritual was performed after Kyabgön Rinpoche had performed *phyag mo*.	Sponsored by the village community.
1/21	**Tshogs rgya (monastery)** Extensive *tshogs* offering ritual performed by all the monks.	Privately sponsored by a *bom btang* household.

(*cont.*)

Date	Name and description	Patronage
1/21–23	**Bom btang tshogs rgya (monastery)** Extensive *tshogs* offering (*tshogs rgya*) arranged by the *bom btang* households. This is an old tradition. Almost all the monks participate, and in the evening the villagers gather in the community hall and drink *chang* and eat meat.	Sponsored annually by the *bom btang* households. The old *'go ba* families provide carpets and tables and serve as *lag bde*.
1/23–29	**bsKang gso (monastery)** Seven-day *bskang gso* ritual arranged by the villagers in 2012 to prevent flooding. The ritual was performed after Kyabgön Rinpoche had performed *phyag mo*.	An equal amount of *rtsam pa* was collected from each household. The other provisions were sponsored by the village assembly.
1/30	**sKong bshags (monastery)** Annual *skong bshags* ritual performed by all the monks.	Sponsored by the *grwa tshang*. The expenses are covered by 1 *las sne* monk.
2/2–2/8	**bsKang gso (monastery)** Seven-day *bskang gso* ritual arranged by the villagers in 2012 to prevent flooding. The ritual was performed after Kyabgön Rinpoche had performed *phyag mo*.	Sponsored by the *grwa tshang*. Extraordinary ritual 2012.
2/1–15	**bKa' 'gyur (monastery)** The monks read through all volumes of the Kangyur. In 2012 they read the volumes thoroughly because of Kyabgön Rinpoche's advice that this may help protect the village from flooding. The time needed varies between 12 and 15 days, depending on the monks' reading speed. If they have leftover supplies from *bsnyen gnas smyung gnas* this will be used, otherwise the three *grong chen tsho* will provide and cover the expenses.	The *Grwa tshang* covers the first 4 days (2 *las sne* monks have to sponsor 4 days each.) Then the *grong chen* families sponsor 5 days.
2/10	**lHa gsol for the *yul lha* (the laity)** Celebrated in the morning. The shrine keeper monk performs *bsang* and *gser skyems* at the shrine of the *yul lha*. Only men participate, except two young girls who serve *chang*. The men burn juniper incense, hoist new prayer flags, and give the shrine a fresh stroke of paint. Then the men celebrate with *chang* and *gar* dance performance.	Sponsored by the village community.

(*cont.*)

Date	Name and description	Patronage
2/10	**Tshes bcu (the laity)** Two *grong chen* families alternate hosting the festival. Compulsory participation.	Village taxes and one *grong chen* household.
2/22	**Tshogs (monastery)** Kangyur *tshogs*. Performed by the monk assembly.	Sponsored by the *grwa tshang*.
2/23	**sKong bshags (monastery)** Private *skong bshags* for a woman from Waltse.	Privately sponsored.
2/24–26	**Popzang (s.u.) (monastery/villagers)** Just before sowing the crops masked dances and plays are performed hoping for a good growing season. The festival is alternately arranged by the monks and the villagers and is called the Spring festival (*sos ka'i dus chang*) if arranged by the latter. Popzang takes place in the monastery courtyard. The monks/laity perform Tibetan opera and arrange horseriding competitions for 3 days.	The festival is arranged alternately by the monastery, the village, and recently also the youth club. Donations are made by all villagers at the end of the festival.
2/28	**sKong bshags (monastery)** *skong bshags* ritual performed in the assembly hall of the monastery by all monks available. This particular ritual was performed for the benefit of a sick uncle of the sponsor.	Privately sponsored.
2/28–29	**Cog ra gi dus lha (Chogrowa)** Two-day celebration of Gangri Lhabtsan. The *gtor ma* are prepared on the 27th day. The *grong chung* celebrate on the 28th day and the *grong chen* on the 29th. The men ride up to the shrine in the morning followed by horse race, and in the afternoon of the 29th *gtor rgyag*, and finally merrymaking inside a private house.	The hosting of the celebration rotates among the Chogrowa families. 4 monks are needed for the *lha gsol*.
Not fixed (3/2, 2011)	**bDe rim (monastery)** Threefold ritual performed in the monastery in order to increase *rlung rta*. The *dgra lha dpangs bstod* ritual takes place in the courtyard at the left wing of the 3rd floor and is performed by three monks (2 senior monks and 1 young helper). The rest of the monks perform *gsol kha* and *bskang gso* (performed simultaneously) in the protector deity chapel.	1 gnyer chen and 6 gnyer chung are chosen from the 6 upper tsho.

(*cont.*)

Date	Name and description	Patronage
3/5 (2011)	**Tshes bcu (the laity)** A villager had not recovered after an operation and the ritual was performed for her quick recovery.	Privately sponsored by the patient's family.
3/11–13	**Mi 'khrugs cho ga (monastery)** Akṣobhya ritual. Part of Nya skam mchod pa festival. If some of the *las sne* are changing, they will hand over the responsibility to the next monk at this time.	Sponsored by the *grwa tshang*.
3/14–16	**Tshe chog (monastery)** Rituals for procuring long life. Part of the Nya skam mchod pa festival.	Sponsored by the *grwa tshang*.
2nd or 3rd month	**Chönchang (s.u.) (the laity)** The festival takes place the day after the *phyi ba* arrive. Celebrated for 3 days with chang, tea, songs, dances, *lha mo* performance. [In 2010 the celebration took place very early, at the end of the 1st month because of the snow conditions. In 2009 in the 2nd month.]	
3rd or 4th month, after sowing the fields	**Spring village assembly meeting (change of *las 'dzin*)** The meeting normally lasts for three days. The first two days for the *grong chen* households and the last day including the *grong chung*. The old *las 'dzin* hand over the equipment (*chang* bottle, stamp, measurement equipment) and pass over the responsibilities to the new ones. After the meeting is over, villagers may present requests in front of the assembly.	Sponsored by the village community.
4/15	**Sa ga zla ba (the laity)** The villagers in Waltse perform *bsnyen gnas smyung gnas* for two days. The shrine keeper has to perform the role as *rdo rje slob dpon*. An extensive celebration takes place in the monastery in Til, attended mainly by the Tilwa.	Village taxes.
4/25	**Gos sku dus chen (monastery)** Display of the brocade image of Kyobpa Rinpoche in the monastery courtyard.	Sponsored by the *grwa tshang*. Two *las sne* monks sponsor two years each.

(*cont.*)

Date	Name and description	Patronage
4/26	**rTsis sprod (monastery)** 5–6 young monks perform *gsol kha*, while the senior monks calculate the whole year's expenses. This marks the end of the ritual season in the monastery.	Sponsored by the *grwa tshang*.
5th or 6th month	**Kong bskyur bola (s.u.) (the women)** (*Kong bskyur* is the name of a weeding instrument, *bola* (s.u.) means deep fried bread.) The women's summer festival. After the first weeding the women invite the men to a party in the community hall. Each male guest should ideally donate NPR 100 per day for the tea and chang, but this is not compulsory.	Sponsored by the women.
5th or 6th month	**dByar ka'i bola (s.u.) (the men)** The men's summer celebration.	Sponsored by the men.
5th or 6th month	**Kong bskyur bola (s.u.) (the elderly)** The old people's summer celebration.	Sponsored by the elderly.
6/ 29	**Sa srung 'khor lo (the *las 'dzin*)** Celebrated on an auspicious day after the barley takes its shape. The *las 'dzin* put a land protecting wheel at the *rkang gnyis mchod rten*.	Sponsored by the village community.
7/4 the date is not fixed.	**Chos skor (the laity) and sbyin sreg (four senior monks)** A group of villagers carry 12 volumes of *'Bum* around the fields. The procession is led by the shrine keeper. The lama performs *sbyin sreg* assisted by three monks. The *las 'dzin* fascilitate the ritual.	Sponsored by the village community.
7/8 the date is not fixed.	**Chos skor (the laity) and sbyin sreg (four senior monks)** A group of villagers carry the volumes of the *Kangyur* around the fields. The procession is led by the shrine keeper. The lama performs *sbyin sreg* assisted by three monks. The *las 'dzin* fascilitate the ritual.	Sponsored by the village community.

(*cont.*)

Date	Name and description	Patronage
7/10–13 the date is not fixed.	**Chumbe (s.u.) dus chang (the laity)** Festival traditionally performed before the late weeding (*phyi yur*), now they celebrate after. The festival lasts for 3 days. In the past the festival was celebrated in a very elaborate way, now it is mostly attended by old people because the young people are all busy working in Purang.	Sponsored by the village community.
9th month	**Weddings** In 2011 three weddings were celebrated.	
	sByin sreg (two senior monks) Two senior monks perform *sbyin sreg* in the community hall.	Sponsored by the village community.
9/22	**lHa babs dus chen (monastery)** This is the day when the monks convene in the monastery after the summer holiday. The monks perform sKong bshags.	Sponsored by the *grwa tshang*.
9th month	**Collection of monastery taxes** This takes place just after the harvest, normally at the end of the 9th month. All monks available should be present, but if some of the younger monks are away, they won't be called back. It is compulsory for the monk officials to attend.	The *grwa tshang*.
10/3–4	**sTon ka'i dus chang (the laity)** Autumn festival celebrated after the harvest, when the villagers come back from Purang.	Sponsored by the villagers.
10/10	**Tshes bcu (the laity)** Six *grong chen* families rotate the responsibility for arranging the festival. Compulsory participation.	Village taxes.
10/3–5	**sKu gnyer rtsis sprod (monastery)** Changing of the *sku gnyer* every second year. The event lasts for three to five days. All the objects of the *sku gnyer* are handed over to the new one. The monks also perform a two-day *bskang* ritual for the *sku gnyer*, but the time is not fixed. Only the monk officials participate.	The old *sku gnyer* provides 4 tea servings and 2 meals and the new *sku gnyer* provides 1 tea serving. The rest is sponsored by the *grwa tshang*.

(*cont.*)

Date	Name and description	Patronage
9th or 10th month, not fixed.	**Thachang (mtha' chang?) (the laity)** Final celebration before the departure of those who spend the winter months working outside the village (*phyi ba*).	Sponsored by the villagers.
10/23	**Las thog rtsis sprod (monastery)** *Las thog rtsis sprod* takes place every second year when the disciplinarian, cantor and the steward rotate their posts.	Sponsored by the *grwa tshang.*
10/25	**dGa' ldan lnga mchod (monastery)** New monks are recruited, and their parents have to offer *mang ja*. The monks perform *na rag skong bshags.*	Sponsored by the *grwa tshang* through the *las sne.*
10/26–29	**Dgu gtor (monastery)** On the 26th they build the *gtor ma*. From the 27th to the 29th they perform the *dgu gtor gtor rgyag* ritual in order to dispel evil spirits. The *gtor ma* are cast on the 29th.	The *grwa tshang*. In the past the monks should bring *rtsam pa.*
10/30	**gNam gang (monastery)** For the sake of Lama Konchog Trinle Wangchug who passed away they perform *bDe mchog gi cho ga.*	Sponsored by the *grwa tshang* through the *las sne.*
11/1–2	**Grwa ba'i lo gsar (monastery)** New Year celebrations. The monks celebrate in the monastery courtyard.	Sponsored by the *grwa tshang.*
11/1–3	**Mes mes kyi lo gsar (the grandfathers)** The grandfathers and the men celebrate New Year in the community hall.	The grandfathers.
11 /4–6	**Slob phrug gi lo gsar (the school children)** New Year festival arranged by the school. Family members are invited to watch song and dance performances in the community hall.	The families of the school children.
11/7–9	**A phyi rgan mo'i dus chang (the grandmothers)** The grandmothers celebrate New Year in the community hall.	The grandmothers.
11/10	**Tshes bcu (the laity)** One *grong chen* family hosts the festival. Compulsory participation, one member from each household.	Village taxes

(*cont.*)

Date	Name and description	Patronage
11/10–12	**sNa byung gi dus chang (s.u.) (young women)** Young women's festival in the community hall.	Young women.
11/5	**Na rag sKong bshags (monastery)** On the 5th day the ritual is sponsored by the *grwa tshang*, and from the 6th day onwards it can be sponsored by lay people. In the recent years the number of lay patrons has increaed.	Sponsored by the *grwa tshang* through the *las sne* system.
	In 2012 the monks performed *na rag skong bshags* for private families for nine days in a row.	Private families upon request.
11/6–7	**Gsol kha (monastery)** Prayer for the health and wellbeing of those away from the village	Sponsored by the village community.
11/8–12/11	**'Bum (monastery)** The monks recite *'Bum* (*Prajñāpāramitā*) in all the private houses who own a set of the scriptures. In the houses of the other families, the monks read *gZungs bsdus*, the collection of religious works. There will be a lottery deciding which monks go to which family.	Private families upon request.
11/23	**Tshes bcu (the laity)** Private Tshechu for the recovery of a seriously ill villager.	Private sponsorship.
11/30	**gNam gang (monastery)**	
12/8–9	**rGyal po'i lha gsol (Rimdzöwa)** The adherents of the *pho lha* rGyal po celebrate for two days. Monks perform the *dgra lha dpangs bstod* ritual. The lay villagers gather in a private house for recitation and merrymaking.	Sponsored by the Rimdzöwa.
12/10	**Tshes bcu (the laity)** One *grong chen* family hosts the festival. Compulsory participation, one member from each household.	Village taxes

(*cont.*)

Date	Name and description	Patronage
12/10–17	**'Cham practice (monastery)** One week is set aside for the monks to practice *'cham* in the monastery courtyard. The young monks learn from the more experienced ones. In 2012 the practice was delayed because of an extraordinary number of requests for *skong bshags* rituals from the laity.	Sponsored by the *grwa tshang.*
12/15	**bCo lnga dus chen (monastery)** The *gnas bcu gtor ma* are prepared the night before. *gNas bcu* ('the ten topics') is recited in the morning of the 15th, then they put new flags on the flagpole in the monastery courtyard. In the early afternoon they practice *'cham* and in the late afternoon they perform the One hundred offerings (*brgya mchod*).	Sponsored by the *grwa tshang.*
12/18	**'Cham rtsis (monastery)** The monks invite the laity to watch the final rehersal of the *'cham* dances without masks. Starts by reading the *'cham yig*. Also the young monks are allowed to perform in order to practice.	Sponsored by the *grwa tshang.*
12/19	**Sa gsol (monastery)** A combined *sa gsol* for the men who have travelled to India in order to fetch maple burls for *phor bu* and the children in boarding schools. Normally they would get one day each, but this year the monks were very busy.	Sponsored by the villagers.
12/19–20	**Rim mchod preparation (monastery)** Practice of *'cham*. The monks prepare the *gtor ma* for the *bka' brgyad* recitation.	Sponsored by the *grwa tshang.*
12/21–26	**Rim mchod preparation (monastery)** The monks recite *sngon 'gro* and *sngon gzhi* every night until the 29th. During daytime they practice *'cham* and prepare the offerings. From the night of the 24th, the monks also receite *zlog pa*.	The first 7 days lunch is provided by 4 *grong chen* households. The monastery collects tea and butter from all *grong chen*. The remaining meals and drinks are provided by the *grwa tshang.*

(*cont.*)

Date	Name and description	Patronage
12/26	**Practice of *shon* (women from *grong chen* households)** The *shon 'go* invites all the *shon ma* to the community hall where they practice all the twenty five *shon* dances.	The *shon 'go* sponsor the practice of *shon*.
12/27	**1st day of Rim mchod—Sa 'dul (monastery)** – Performance by two *atsara* (*a tsa ra*) – The dance of the *garuḍas* (*bya khyung*) – Play of the men from the southern valleys (*rong pa*) – Play of the Thakuri king – Play of Nyene (s.u.), the young rinpoche – Circle dance around a bonfire in the monastery courtyard	Lunch provided by the *grong chen*, the tea is provided by the monastery, the other meals by the monks' families.
12/28	**2nd day of Rim mchod—gSar ma'i 'cham (monastery)** – Supplication to the deities to ask for permission to wear the masks (*bag gsol*) – Performance by two *atsara* (*a tsa ra*) – Dance of the blood drinking Mahākāla (*mgon po khrag 'thung rol pa*) – The women perform *shon* dances – Individual dance of Apchi (*a phyi'i sger 'cham*) – Dance of the four guardians of the teachings (*bka' srung bzhi*) – The women perform *shon* dances – Dance of Vaiśravaṇa (*rnam sras kyi 'cham*) – Performance of *gar* dance by the guardians of the festival place (*khrom srung ba'i gar*) – The play about the protectors of sacred places (*zhing skyong yab yum*) – Dance of the Dharma protector and the King of the *rgyal po* spirits (*chos skyong dang rgyal po*). – Performance of *gar* dance by the dance leader and his servant (*gar dpon dang gar g.yog*)	The *grwa tshang* provides tea (in the past also meat). The rest of the food is provided by the monks' families. The *grwa tshang* used to serve meat for the *'khrom srung ba*, the drummer and the *gar dpon* and *gar g.yog*, but now they give money instead. In the past they would also serve meat for the *spyi khyab* and *'go ba*.

(*cont.*)

Date	Name and description	Patronage
	– The first display of Mahākāla (*mgon po 'don dang po*) – Performance of *gar* dance by the village leaders (*dpon po'i gar, drug bcu pa*) – The second display of Mahākāla (*mgon po 'don gnyis pa*) – The women perform *shon* dances – The third display of Mahākāla (*mgon po 'don gsum pa*) – The women perform *shon* dances, then they are joined by the men and perform combined *gar shon* – Circle dance around a bonfire in the monastery courtyard	
12/29	**3rd day of Rim mchod—rNying ma'i 'cham** – Performance by two *atsara* (*a tsa ra*) – Drum dance (*rnga 'cham*) – The four keepers of the gate (*sgo ma bzhi*) bring the effigy (*nya bo*) concealed under a piece of black cloth – Dance of the *'dzam chen po gnyis* – The dance of the two deer (*shwa ba pho mo gnyis*), who uncover the effigy with their antlers – The dance of the two buffaloes (*ma he pho mo gnyis*) – Dance of the supreme Heruka (*che mchog he ru ka*) – The dance of accomplishment (*sgrub 'cham*) – The dance of magic weapons (*zor 'cham*), also called black hat dance (*zhwa nag 'cham*). The effigy is killed by the *kīlaya*. – The play of the grandmother and grandfather (*a phyi dang mes mes or rgan rgon gnyis kyi zlos gar*). – Play of two monks checking if the effigy is really dead, followed by the performance of *gar* dance.	

(*cont.*)

Date	Name and description	Patronage
	– 'Liberation' dance (*bsgral 'cham*). The *nya bo* effigy is cut up and its consciousness liberated. – Dance of the swirling dust storm (rLung nag 'tshub). – Libation offering (*gser skyems*) and throwing of magical weapons (*zor*).	
12/30	**gNam gang (monastery and village)** The *gar dpon* invites all the men in the village for leftover *chang* and calculations. This is also the time to pay fines issued during Rim mchod, for instance those *grong chen* families not providing *shon ma* will have to pay fines. In the monastery all the masks and other equipment for the Rim mchod festival is packed. Then the monks arrange an auction.	The *grong chen* provide lunch, the rest is sponsored by the *grwa tshang*.

References

Aase, Tor H., Prem Chapagain and Hemanta Dangal 2018. "Multi-sited Himalayan households and the misleading rural—urban dichotomy." *Area* 51(1): 1–8.

Adhikary, Surya M. 1997. *The Khaśa kingdom. A trans-Himalayan empire of the middle age*. New Dehli: Nirala Publications.

Acharya, Anurag 2011. "A decade of democratic deficit. Local elections needed to spur local development, most survey respondents say." *Nepali Times* no. 553 (13 May 2011–19 May 2011). https://archive.nepalitimes.com/news.php?id=18193

Ardussi, John 1977. "Bhutan before the British: a historical study." PhD dissertation, The Australian National University, Canberra.

Aris, Michael 1980. "Notes on the history of the Mon-yul corridor." In Michael Aris and Aung San Suu Kyi (eds), *Tibetan studies in honour of Hugh Richardson. Proceedings of the International Seminar on Tibetan Studies Oxford 1979*. Warminster: Aris & Philips Ltd.

Armington, Stan 2001. *Trekking in the Nepal Himalaya*. Hawthorn VIC and Oakland CA.: Lonely Planet Publications.

Aziz, Barbara N. 1974. "The people of Dingri: a socio-historical portrait of a district in S.W. Tibet." Unpublished PhD dissertation, University of London.

Basnet, Govinda and Ram Prasad Chaudhary 2017. "Indigenous system of pasture-land management: A case of Limi in the Kailash sacred landscape, Nepal." In Madhav Karki, Rosemary Hill, Dayuan Xue, Wilfredo Alangui, Kaoru Ichikawa and Peter Bridgewater (eds), *Knowing our Lands and Resources. Indigenous and Local Knowledge and Practices related to Biodiversity and Ecosystem Services in Asia*, pp. 86–93. Paris: UNESCO.

Bauer, Kenneth M. 2004. *High Frontiers: Dolpo and the changing world of Himalayan pastoralists*. New York: Columbia University Press.

Beall, Cynthia M. and Melvyn C. Goldstein 1881. "Tibetan fraternal polyandry: a test of sociobiological theory." *American Anthropologist*, 83(1): 5–12.

Bellezza, John V. 2005. *Spirit-mediums, sacred mountains and related Bon textual traditions in Upper Tibet: calling down the Gods*. Leiden: Brill.

Bellezza, John V. 2010. *Antiquities of Zhang Zhung: A Comprehensive Inventory of Pre-Buddhist Archaeological Monuments on the Tibetan Upland. Volume 1: Archaic Residential Monuments*. Edited by Geoffrey Barstow, Mickey Stockwell and Michael White, published online by THL: https://dev.thlib.org/bellezza/essays/bellezza_antiquities_part1.pdf

Bellezza, John V. 2011. "Territorial characteristics of the pre-Buddhist Zhang zhung paleo-cultural entity—a comparative analysis of archaeological evidence and popular Bon literary sources." In Henk Blezer (ed), *Emerging Bon: The Formation of Bon Traditions in Tibet at the Turn of the First Millennium* AD. PIATS 2006: Tibetan Studies: Proceedings of the Eleventh Seminar of the International Association for Tibetan Studies, Königswinter 2006, pp. 51–116. Andiast: International Institute for Tibetan and Buddhist Studies.

Bhattarai, Ishwari 2021. "Roles of the Three Tiers of Governments in Institutionalizing Traditional Natural Resources Management Systems: A Case of Limi Valley in Nepal." Unpublished research report, written for KSLCDI and HimalConnect.

Bhattarai, Ishwari, Binaya Pasakhala, Janita Gurung, Srijana Joshi, and Sunayana Basnet (forthcoming). "Dilemmas of Traditional Natural Resource Management Systems in the Nepal Himalaya: A Case Study from Limi, Humla." In Riamsara Kuyakanon and Hanna Havnevik (eds), *Changing climate and communities in high places and icy spaces*. Cambridge, UK: Open Books Publishers.

Bidari, Keshav 2004. "Halji monastery—a hidden heritage in North-West Nepal". *Ancient Nepal* 155 (June 2004): 1–5.

Bishop, Barry C. 1990. *Karnali under stress. Livelihood strategies and seasonal rhythms in a changing Nepal Himalaya*. Chicago: The University of Chicago Press.

Brauen, Martin 1980. *Feste in Ladakh*. Graz: Akademische Druck und Verlagsanstalt.

Bradley, Becky, Dave Bradley, Sitar Lama, Khendrap Lama, and Rinjin Lama 2004. "Demographic Survey Report: Limi Valley, Humla, Nepal." Unpublished report compiled for the Nepal Trust.

Bray, John 2012. "Ladakhi and Bhutanese enclaves in Tibet." *Journal of Bhutan Studies*. 28(1): 1–20.

Brown, Garret W, Iain McLean, and Alistair McMillan 2018. *A Concise Oxford Dictionary of Politics and International Relations* (4 ed.). Oxford: Oxford University Press.

Bubriski, Kevin and Abhimanyu Pandey 2018. *Kailash Yatra. A Long Walk to Mt Kailash through Humla*. Kathmandu: ICIMOD.

Buchroithner, Manfred F., Jan Kropáček, Jacob Trültzsch, Thomas Himpel, Astrid Hovden, Nicolai Holzer, Tino Piezconka, Ralf Rosenau, Steffen Schöley, and Benjamin Schröter 2014. *Kailash / Gurla Mandhata Trekking Map 11 (Tibet / Nepal 1:100.000)*. Institute for Cartography of the Dresden University of Technology, 1st edition.

Buckley, Michael 2008. *Shangri-la: a travel guide to the Himalayan dream*. Chalfont St. Peter: Bradt Travel Guides.

Buffetrille, Katia 2003 [1998]. "Reflections on pilgrimages to sacred mountains, lakes and caves." Reprinted in Alex Mckay (ed), *The history of Tibet, volume II, The medieval period: c. 850–1895, the development of Buddhist paramountcy*, pp. 233–246. London: RoutledgeCurzon.

Carney, Diana (ed) 1998. "Sustainable rural livelihoods. What contribution can we make?" Department for International Development (DFID), London.

Carrasco, Pedro 1959. *Land and polity in Tibet.* Seattle: University of Washington Press.

Cassinelli, C.W. and R. Ekvall 1969. *A Tibetan principality: the political system of sa skya.* Ithaca, N.Y.: Cornell University Press.

Central Bureau of Statistics, National government of Nepal 2014. "National Population and Housing Census 2011 (Village Development Committee/Municipality): Humla."

Chambers, Robert and Gordon R. Conway 1992. "Sustainable rural livelihoods: practical concepts for the 21st century." Brighton: IDS.

Childs, Geoff 1997a. "A note on the Tibetan origins of the Sherpa Serwa (Gser-ba) clan." *Himalayan Research Bulletin* 17(2): 23–25.

Childs, Geoff 1997b. "Householder lamas and the persistence of tradition: animal sacrifice in Himalayan Buddhist communities". In Helmut Krasser, Michael Torsten Much, Ernst Steinkellner, and Helmut Tauscher (eds), *Tibetan studies. Proceedings of the 7th seminar of the International Association for Tibetan Studies, Graz 1995*, pp. 141–155. Vienna: Verlag der Österreichischen Akademie der Wissenschaften.

Childs, Geoff 2000. "Claiming the frontier: a note on the incorporation of Nubri within the borders of Nepal." *Studies in Nepali History and Society* 5(2): 217–26.

Childs, Geoff 2005. "How to fund a ritual: notes on the social usage of the Kanjur (bKa' 'gyur) in a Tibetan village." *Tibet Journal* 30(2): 41–48.

Childs, Geoff and Namgyal Choedup 2015. "From servant (g.yog mo) to disciple (slob ma): modernity, migration, and evolving life course options for Buddhist nuns." In Hanna Havnevik and Charles Ramble (eds), *From Bhakti to Bon: festschrift for Per Kvaerne.* Oslo: Novus.

Childs, Geoff and Namgyal Choedup 2019. *From a trickle to a torrent: education, migration, and social change in a Himalayan valley of Nepal.* Oakland, CA: University of California Press.

Childs, Geoff, Sienna Craig, Cynthia M. Beall, and Buddha Basnyat 2014. "Depopulating the Himalayan highlands: education and outmigration from ethnically Tibetan communities of Nepal." *Mountain Research and Development,* 34(2):85–94.

Church, Mimi and Mariette Wiebenga 2008. "A four-fold Vairocana in the Rinchen Zangpo tradition at Waltse in Nepal." *Asianart,* October 21, 2008. Available at: http://www.asianart.com/articles/halji/index.html

Citrin, David M. 2010. "The anatomy of ephemeral health care: "health camps" and short-term medical voluntourism in remote Nepal." *Studies in Nepali History and Society,* 15(1): 27–72.

Citrin, David M. 2012. "The anatomy of ephemeral health care: health, hunger, and short-term humanitarian intervention in Northwest Nepal." Unpublished PhD dissertation, University of Washington.

Clarke, Graham E. 1980. "The temple and kinship among a Buddhist people of the Himalaya." Unpublished PhD dissertation, University of Oxford.

Craig, Sienna R. 2020. *The Ends of Kinship: Connecting Himalayan Lives Between Nepal and New York*. Seattle, WA: University of Washington Press.

Crook, John 1994. "Social organisation and personal identity in Zangskar." In John Crook and Henry Osmaston (eds), 1994, *Himalayan Buddhist villages: environment, resources, society and religious life in Zangskar, Ladakh*, pp. 475–518. Delhi: Motilal Banarsidass Publishers.

Crook, John, and Henry Osmaston (eds) 1994. *Himalayan Buddhist villages: environment, resources, society and religious life in Zangskar, Ladakh*. Delhi: Motilal Banarsidass Publishers.

Crook, John, and Tsering Shakya 1994. "Monastic communities in Zangskar: Location, function and organisation." In John Crook and Henry Osmaston (eds), *Himalayan Buddhist villages: environment, resources, society and religious life in Zangskar, Ladakh*, pp. 559–600. Delhi: Motilal Banarsidass Publishers.

Cüppers, Christoph (ed) 2000. *Religion and state (chos srid zung 'brel) in traditional Tibet. Proceedings of a seminar held in Lumbini, Nepal, March 2000*. Bhairahawa: Lumbini International Research Institute.

Davidson, Ronald M. 2005. *Tibetan renaissance: tantric Buddhism in the rebirth of Tibetan culture*. New York: Columbia University Press.

Dalton, Jacob P. 2011. *The taming of the demons: violence and liberation in Tibetan Buddhism*. New Haven and London: Yale University Press.

De Vries, Klaas 2014. "A Sociolinguistic Survey of Humla Tibetan in Northwest Nepal." SIL International.

Diemberger, Hildegard 2021. "When lha lu spirits suffer and sometimes fight back: Tibetan cosmopolitics at a time of environmental threats and climate change." In Kuyakanon, Diemberger and Sneath (eds), *Cosmopolitical Ecologies Across Asia: Places of Power in Changing Environments*, pp. 19–42. London: Routledge.

Diemberger, Hildegard, Astrid Hovden, and Emily T. Yeh 2015. "The honour of the mountains is the snow: Tibetan livelihoods in a changing climate." In C. Huggel, J.J. Clague, A. Kääb, and M. Carey (eds), *The high-mountain cryosphere: environmental changes and human risks*, pp. 249–71 Cambridge: Cambridge University Press.

Diemberger, Hildegard and Samantha Skrivere 2021. "Piles of Plastic on Darkening Himalayan Peaks: Changing Cosmopolitics of 'Pollution' in Limi, Western Nepal." *Worldwide Waste: Journal of Interdisciplinary Studies*, 4(1), p. 6.

Dotson, Brandon 2012. "At the behest of the mountain: Gods, clans and political topography in post-imperial Tibet." In Cristina Scherrer-Schaub (ed), *Old Tibetan Studies: Proceedings of the Tenth Seminar of the International Association for Tibetan Studies, Oxford 2003*, pp. 159–204. Leiden: Brill.

Dreyfus, Georges 1995. "Law, state and polity in Tibet." *Journal of the International Association for Buddhist Studies*, 18(1): 117–38.

Dreyfus, Georges 2003. *The sound of two hands clapping: the education of a Tibetan Buddhist monk.* Berkeley: California University Press.

Ede, Yolanda van 1999. "House of birds: a historical ethnography of a Tibetan Buddhist nunnery in Nepal". Unpublished PhD dissertation, University of Amsterdam.

Ellis, Frank 2000a. "The determinants of rural livelihood diversification in developing countries." *Journal of Agricultural Economics*, 51(2): 289–302.

Ellis, Frank 2000b. *Rural livelihoods and diversity in developing countries.* Oxford: Oxford University Press.

Ellingson, Ter 1990. "Tibetan monastic constitutions: the bca'-yig." In Lawrence Epstein and Richard F. Sherburne (eds), *Reflections on Tibetan culture: essays in memory of Turrell V. Wylie*, pp. 205–29. Lewiston: The Edwin Mellen Press.

Emmer, Gerhard 2007. "dGa' ldan tshe dbang dpal bzang po and the Tibet-Ladakh-Mughal war of 1679–84." In Uradyn Bulag (ed), *The Mongolia-Tibet interface: opening new research terrains in Inner Asia.* Proceedings of the Tenth Seminar of the International Association for Tibetan Studies, Oxford 2003, pp. 81–107. Leiden: Brill.

Engelstad, Fredrik 1989. "The assignment of political office by lot." *Social Science Information*, 28(1): 23–50.

Fernandez, James 2003. "Emergence and convergence in some African sacred places." In Setha M. Low and Denise Lawrence-Zúñiga (eds), *The Anthropology of space and place: locating culture,* pp. 187–203. Oxford: Blackwell.

Fjeld, Heidi E. 2008. "Pollution and Social Networks in Contemporary Rural Tibet." In Robert Barnett and Ronald Schwartz (eds), *Tibetan Modernities: Notes from the Field on Cultural and Social Change.* Proceedings of the Tenth Seminar of the International Association for Tibetan Studies, Oxford 2003, pp. 113–138. Leiden: Brill.

Fjeld, Heidi E. 2022. *The return of polyandry: kinship and marriage in Central Tibet.* New York & Oxford: Berghahn.

Francke, A. H. 1999 [1914]. *Antiquities in Indian Tibet.* New Delhi: Low price publications.

Frechette, Anne. 1996. "Review of The Golden Yoke." *Himalayan Research Bulletin* 16(1–2), 54–57.

French, Rebecca R. 2002 [1995]. *The golden yoke: the legal cosmology of Buddhist Tibet.* Ithaca: Snow Lion Publications.

Fürer-Haimendorf, Christoph von 1988. *Himalayan traders.* New Delhi: Time Books International. [Original edition: Fürer-Haimendorf, Christoph von 1975. Himalayan traders. New York: St. Martin's Press.]

Gaerrang (Kabzung) 2011. "The alternative to development on the Tibetan plateau: preliminary research on the anti-slaughter movement." In Tim Myatt, Kalsang Norbu Gurung, Nicola Schneider, and Alice Travers (eds), *Revisiting Tibetan culture and history: proceedings of the second international seminar of young Tibetologists, Paris, 2009.* Revue d'Etudes Tibétaines, vol 21(October), pp 31–43.

Gayley, Holly 2011. "The ethics of cultural survival: a Buddhist vision of progress in mKhan po 'Jigs phun's *Heart advice to Tibetans for the 21st century.*" In Gray Tuttle (ed), *Mapping the modern in Tibet*, pp. 435–502. Halle: International Institute for Tibetan and Buddhist Studies GmbH.

Goldstein, Melvyn C. 1968. "An anthropological study of the Tibetan political system." Ph.D. thesis, University of Washington.

Goldstein, Melvyn C. 1971. "Taxation and the structure of a Tibetan village." *Central Asiatic Journal*. 15(3): 1–27.

Goldstein, Melvyn C. 1974. "Tibetan speaking agro-pastoralists of Limi: a cultural ecological overview of high altitude adaptation in the Northwest Himalaya." *Objets et Mondes* 14(4): 259–68.

Goldstein, Melvyn C. 1975. "Report on Limi panchayat, Humla district, Karnali zone." *Contributions to Nepalese Studies* 2(2), 89–101.

Goldstein, Melvyn C. 1976. "Fraternal polyandry and fertility in a high Himalayan valley in Northwest Nepal." In *Human Ecology* 4(3): 224–33.

Goldstein, Melvyn C. 1977. "Population, social structure and strategic behavior: an essay on polyandry, fertility and change in Limi Panchayat." *Contributions to Nepalese Studies* 4(2): 47–62.

Goldstein, Melvyn C. 1978. "Pahari and Tibetan Polyandry Revisited." *Ethnology*. 17(3): 325–337.

Goldstein, Melvyn C. 1981a. "The transformation of the social matrix of Tibetan populations in the high Himalaya." In *L'homme et son Environment à Haute Altitude*, pp. 101–105. Paris: Centre National de la Recherche Scientifique.

Goldstein, Melvyn C. 1981b. "High altitude Tibetan populations in the remote Himalaya: Social transformation and its demographic, economic and ecological consequences." *Research and Development*. 1(1): 5–18.

Goldstein, Melvyn C. 1981c. "New perspectives on Tibetan fertility and population decline." *American Ethnologist* 8(4) (November 1981): 721–38.

Goldstein, Melvyn C. 1998. "The Revival of Monastic Life in Drepung Monastery." In Melvyn C. Goldstein and Mathew T. Kapstein (eds), *Buddhism in Contemporary Tibet: Religious Revival and Cultural Identity*, pp. 15–52. Berkeley: University of California Press.

Goldstein, Melvyn C. 2010. "Tibetan Buddhism and mass monasticism." In Adeline Herrou and Gisele Krauskopff (eds), *Des moines et des moniales dans le monde. La vie monastique dans le miroir de la parenté*. Presses Universitaires de Toulouse le Mirail.

Goldstein, Melvyn and Paljor Tsarong 1985. "Tibetan Buddhist monasticism: social, psychological & cultural implications." *The Tibet Journal*. 10(1): 14–31.

Government of Nepal 2007. *The Public Procurement Act, 2063 (2007)*. Kathmandu: Government of Nepal.

Grimshaw, Anna 1983a. "Celibacy, religion and economic activity in a monastic community of Ladakh." In Dieter Kantowsky and Reinhard Sander (eds), *Recent research on Ladakh: history culture, sociology, ecology*, pp. 121–34. Munich: Weltforum Verlag.

Grimshaw, Anna 1983b. "Rizong: a monastic community in Ladakh." Unpublished PhD dissertation, University of Cambridge.

Grimshaw, Anna 1994 [1992]. *Servants of the Buddha: winter in a Himalayan convent.* Cleveland: The Pilgrim Press.

Gruber, Elmar R. 2010. *From the heart of Tibet: the biography of Drikung Chetsang Rinpoche, the holder of the Drikung Kagyu lineage.* Shambala, Boston and London.

Gurung, Harka 1980. *Vignettes of Nepal.* Kathmandu: Sajha Prakashan.

Gurung, Janita, Astrid Hovden, Paljor Tamang, Ishwari Bhattarai and Binaya Pasakala (forthcoming). "An indigenous system of resource management in Nepal's remote trans-Himalaya. Sourcing the capabilities of the Limi community to sustainably manage natural resources." Joint Policy brief by ICIMOD and HimalConnect.

Gutschow, Kim 2004. *Being a Buddhist nun: the struggle for enlightenment in the Himalayas.* Cambridge MA: Harvard University Press.

Gutschow, Niels 1990. "Chortens (mchod-rten) in Humla: Observations on the variation of a building type in north western Nepal." *Ancient Nepal.* 120: 10–21.

Haddix, Kimber A. and Jit Bahadur Gurung 1999. "'Excess women': non-marriage and reproduction in ethnic Tibetan communities of Humla, Nepal." *Himalayan Research Bulletin* 19(1): 57–62.

Hall, David D. (ed) 1997. *Lived religion in America: toward a history of practice.* Princeton: Princeton University Press.

Hammersley, Martyn, and Paul Atkinson 1995. *Ethnography: principles in practice.* London and New York: Routledge.

Hangen, Susan I. 2010. *The rise of ethnic politics in Nepal: democracy in the margins.* London: Routledge.

Havnevik, Hanna 1989. *Tibetan Buddhist nuns: history, cultural norms and social reality.* Oslo: Norwegian University Press.

Havnevik, Hanna 1996 [1994]. "The role of nuns in contemporary Tibet." In Robert Barnett and Shirin Akiner (eds), *Resistance and reform in Tibet*, pp. 259–66. New Dehli: Motilal Banarsidass.

Havnevik, Hanna 2011. "Bokkult i buddhismen. Buddhistiske teksters magiske og rituelle funksjoner i Tibet, Mongolia og Himalaya." In Bjarne Rogan and Saphinaz-Amal Naguib (eds), *Materiell kultur og kulturens materialitet.* pp. 233–55. Oslo: Novus forlag.

Havnevik, Hanna and Janet Gyatso (eds) 2005. *Women in Tibet.* London: Hurst and Company and New York: Columbia University Press.

Havnevik, Hanna, Astrid Hovden and Rinchen Loden (forthcoming). "Weather, water and work beyond borders. Gendered responses to climatic and socioeconomic changes in a high Himalayan valley in Nepal." In Riamsara Kuyakanon and Hanna Havnevik (eds), *Changing climate and communities in high places and icy spaces.* Cambridge, UK: Open Books Publishers.

Heckendorn Urscheler, Lukas 2012. "Innovation in a hybrid system: the example of Nepal." *Potchefstroom Electronic Law Journal* 15(3): 98–119.

Hervieu-Léger, Danièle 1997. '"What scripture tells me": spontaneity and regulation within the Catholic charismatic renewal.' In David D. Hall (ed), *Lived religion in America: Toward a History of Practice*, pp 22–40. Princeton: Princeton University Press.

Himalayan News Service 2020. "Humla linked to national road network." *The Himalayan Times* 14.12.20. https://thehimalayantimes.com/nepal/humla-linked-to-national-road-network, accessed 10.05.21.

Holmberg, David 2007. "Outcastes in an 'egalitarian' society: Tamang/blacksmith relations from Tamang perspective." In *Occasional papers in sociology and anthropology* 10: pp. 124–40.

Holler, David 2008. "The ritual of freeing lives." In Henk Blezer (ed), *Tibet, past and present*. Tibetan Studies I. PIATS 2000: Tibetan studies: proceedings of the ninth seminar of the International Association for Tibetan Studies, Leiden 2000. pp. 207–26. Leiden: Brill.

Hovden, Astrid 2006. "Ritual, place, and memory: maintenance of religious festival traditions in contemporary Lhasa." Unpublished Cand. Philol. thesis, University of Bergen.

Hovden, Astrid 2011. "If this is what a small flood can do—imagine a big one. *Nepali Times* no. 564 (29 July—04 Aug 2011). http://archive.nepalitimes.com/news.php?id=18418#.YKvC3I3itPY

Hovden, Astrid 2013. "Who were the sponsors? Reflections on recruitment and ritual economy in three Himalayan village monasteries." In Charles Ramble, Peter Schwieger, and Alice Travers (eds), *Tibetans who escaped the historian's net: studies in the social history of Tibetan-speaking societies*, pp. 209–30. Kathmandu: Vajra Publications.

Hovden, Astrid 2016. "Between village and monastery—a historical ethnography of a Tibetan Buddhist community in north-western Nepal." Unpublished PhD dissertation, University of Oslo.

Hovden, Astrid and Hanna Havnevik 2021. "Balancing the sacred landscape: environmental management in Limi North-Western Nepal." In Kuyakanon, Diemberger and Sneath (eds.) *Cosmopolitical Ecologies Across Asia: Places of Power in Changing Environments*, pp. 83–101. London: Routledge.

Huber, Toni 1998. "Foreigner at the judge's feet. Review of The Golden Yoke." *The Tibet Journal* 23(3), 78–91.

Huber, Toni 2003. "The chase and the Dharma. The legal protection of wild animals in premodern Tibet." In John Knight (ed), *Wildlife in Asia. Cultural perspectives*, pp- 36–55. London & New York: Routledge.

Huber, Toni and Tsepak Rigzin 1999. "A Tibetan guide for pilgrimage to Ti.se (Mount Kailas) and mTsho Ma- (Lake Manasarovar)." In Toni Huber (ed), *Sacred spaces and powerful places in Tibetan culture*, pp. 125–53. Dharamsala: Library of Tibetan Works and Archives.

ICIMOD 2011. "Kailash Sacred Landscape Conservation Initiative: Feasibility Assessment Report." Edited by Robert Zomer and Krishna Prasad Oli. Kathmandu: ICIMOD.

ICIMOD 2013. "Environmental Stratification of Kailash Sacred Landscape and Projected Climate Change Impacts on Ecosystems and Productivity: Working Paper 2013/1." By Robert J. Zomer, Antonio Trabucco, Marc Metzger, and Krishna P. Oli. Kathmandu: ICIMOD.

ICIMOD 2021. "Proceedings of the interaction workshop on Planning for sustainable tourism in Namkha Rural Municipality, Humla." https://lib.icimod.org/record/35202, accessed 07.06.21.

Inlogos 2009. "Assessment of village development committee governance and the use of block grants." Kathmandu: Ministry of local development and the United Nations Development Programme. <https://www.undp.org/sites/g/files/zskgke326/files/migration/np/UNDP_NP_Report-on-Assessment-of-Village-Development-Committee-Governance-and-the-Use-of-the-Block-Grants.pdf>, accessed 29.05.24.

Jahoda, Christian 2007. "Socio-economic organisation of village communities and monasteries in Spiti, H.P., India: the case of a religious administrative unit (chos gzhis)." In Amy Heller and Giacomella Orofino (eds), *Discoveries in Western Tibet and the Western Himalayas: essays on history, literature, archaeology and art*. Leiden/Boston: Brill.

Jahoda, Christian 2015. *Socio-economic organisation in a border area of Tibetan culture: Tabo—Spiti valley, Himachal Pradesh, India*. Vienna: Verlag der Österreichischen Akademie der Wissenschaften.

Jansen, Berthe 2013. "How to tame a wild monastic elephant: Drepung monastery according to the great Fifth." In Charles Ramble, Peter Schwieger, and Alice Travers (eds), *Tibetans who escaped the historian's net: studies in the social history of Tibetan-speaking societies*, pp. 111–39. Kathmandu: Vajra Publications.

Jansen, Berthe 2015. "The monastery rules: Buddhist monastic organization in pre-modern Tibet." Unpublished PhD dissertation, University of Leiden.

Jansen, Berthe 2023. "A Preliminary Investigation into Monk-tax: grwa khral / btsun khral / ban khral and its Meanings." In Alice Travers, Peter Schwieger and Charles Ramble (eds), *Taxation in Tibetan Societies: Rules, Practices and Discourses*, pp. 254–78. Leiden: Brill.

Jest, Corneille 1975. *Dolpo: Communautés de langue tibétaine du Népal*. Paris: Centre National del la Recherche Scientifique.

Kapstein, Matthew 1997. "Turning back gossip." In Donald S. Lopez (ed), *Religions of Tibet in practice*, pp. 527–537. Princeton NJ: Princeton University Press.

Kapstein, Matthew 2006. *The Tibetans*. Malden MA: Blackwelll Publishing.

Karmay, Samten G. 1988. *The great perfection (rdzogs chen): a philosophical and meditative teaching of Tibetan Buddhism*. Leiden: Brill.

Karmay, Samten G. 2003 [1980]. "The ordinance of lHa bla-ma Ye-shes-'od." Reprinted in Alex McKay (ed), *The history of Tibet, Volume II, the medieval Period: c. 850–1895, The development of Buddhist paramountcy*, pp. 134–46. London: RoutledgeCurzon.

Kelly, Thomas L and Carroll Dunham 1987. *The hidden Himalayas*. New York: Abbeville Press Publishers.

Key, Jeff 2003. "Nepal in crisis: democratization and the failure of local government." In Dhirendra K. Vajpeyi (ed), *Local democracy and politics in South Asia: towards internal decolonization?* pp. 93–113. Oplanden: Leske + Budrich.

Kohn, Richard J. 2001. *Lord of the Dance: The Mani Rimdu Festival in Tibet and Nepal*. Albany: State University of New York Press.

Konchok Pasang 2008. "The Drikung Kyabgon: 2008 Activities." Dehradun: The Private Office of H.H. Drikung Kyabgon Chetsang / Drikung Kagyu Institute.

Kramer, Karl-Heinz. (2003). "Nepal in 2002: Emergency and Resurrection of Royal Power." *Asian Survey* 43(1): 208–214.

Kropáček, Jan, Niklas Neckel, Bernd Tyrna, Nicolai Holzer, Astrid Hovden, Noel Gourmelen, Cristoph Schneider, Manfred Buchroithner, and Volker Hochschild 2015. "Periodic glacial lake outburst floods threatening the oldest Buddhist monastery in north-west Nepal." *Natural Hazards and Earth System Sciences*, VOL II, pp. 6937–71.

Kuijp, Leonard van der. 1999. "The yoke is on the reader: a recent study of Tibetan jurisprudence." *Central Asiatic Journal* 43(2), 266–92.

Kværne, Per 1977. "Continuity and change in Tibetan monasticism." In Chai-shin Yu (ed), *Korean and Asian religious tradition*, pp. 83–98. Toronto: Korean and Related Studies Press.

Kværne, Per 2001 [1995]. *The Bon religion of Tibet: the iconography of a living tradition*. Boston: Shambala.

Lama, Chhapal 2021. "Help extended to Humla residents facing shortage of rice." *The Kathmandu Post* 27.11.21. https://kathmandupost.com/karnali-province/2021/11/27/help-extended-to-humla-residents-facing-shortage-of-rice, accessed 31.05.24.

Lama, Tshewang 2012. *Kailash Mandala: a pilgrim's trekking guide*. 2nd edition. Kathmandu: Tshewang Lama/The Axis Mundi Foundation.

Lama, Tshewang. 1993. "Who cares for Humla." *Himal* 6(5):16–18.

Levine, Nancy E. 1976. The origins of sTod-pa: a Nyinba clan legend. *Contribution to Nepalese Studies*. 4(1):57–75.

Levine, Nancy E. 1987. "Caste, state and ethnic boundaries in Nepal." *The Journal of Asian Studies* 46 (1):71–88.

Levine, Nancy E. 1988a. *The dynamics of polyandry: kinship, domesticity, and population on the Tibetan border*. Chicago and London: The University of Chicago Press.

Levine, Nancy E. 1988b. "Webs of dependence in rural Nepal: debt, poverty and depopulation in the far Northwest." *Contributions to Nepalese Studies*, CNAS, Tribhuvan University 15(2): 213–45.

Levine, Nancy E. 1992. "Traditional taxation systems in Western Tibet: a comparative perspective." *China Tibetology*, (special issue) 322–45.

Limi Youth Society (n.d.). "*Limi: The Hidden Valley*." Kathmandu: Limi Youth Society.

Lo Bue, Erberto F. 2003. "Scholars, artists and feasts." In Françoise Pommaret (ed), *Lhasa in the seventeenth century: the capital of the Dalai Lamas*, pp. 179–98. Leiden: Brill.

Lochem, Monique J. van 2004. "Children of Sera Je: the life of children in a Tibetan Buddhist monastery and their opinion about that life." Unpublished MA thesis, Leiden University.

Luczanits, Christian 2004. *Buddhist Sculpture in Clay: Early Western Himalayan Art, late 10th to early 13th centuries*. Chicago: Serindia.

Manandhar, Sujata, Dietrich Schmidt—Vogt, Vishnu Prasad Pandey, and Futaba Kazama 2014. "Religion, indigenous knowledge and climate change in a mountain region: a case study of Thini village, Mustang, Nepal." In Robin Globus Veldman, Andrew Szaz and Randolph Haluza-DeLay (eds), *How the world's religions are responding to climate change: social scientific investigations*, pp. 37–46. London: Routledge.

Martin, Dan 1996. "Tables of contents (dkar chag)." In Roger Jackson and José Cabezón (eds), *Tibetan literature: studies in genre—Essays in honor of Geshe Lhundup Sopa*, pp. 500–514. Itacha: Snow Lion Publications.

Mathes, Klaus-Dieter 1999. "The Sacred Crystal Mountain in Dolpo—beliefs and pure visions of Himalayan pilgrims and yogins." *Journal of the Nepal Research Centre* 11: 61–90.

McKay, Alex (ed) 1998. *Pilgrimage in Tibet*. Richmond: Curzon Press.

McKay, Kimber H. 2003. "Challenges to health care access in Maoist Nepal." *Himalaya*, 22(2): 43–46.

Metcalf, Peter 1981. "Meaning and materialism: the ritual economy of death." *Man*. New Series 16(4): 563–78. Royal Anthropological Institute of Great Britain and Ireland.

Miller, Robert, J. 1961. "Buddhist monastic economy: the jisa mechanism." *Comparative Studies in Society and History* 3(4): 427–38.

Mills, Martin 2003. *Identity, ritual and state in Tibetan Buddhism: the foundations of authority in Gelugpa monasticism*. RoutledgeCurzon, London and New York.

Mullard, Saul 2013. "Recapturing runaways, or administration through contract: the 18830 covenant (gan rgya) on Kotapa tax exiles and Sikkimese border regions." In Charles Ramble, Peter Schwieger, and Alice Travers (eds), *Tibetans who escaped the historian's net: studies in the social history of Tibetan-speaking societies*, pp. 179–208. Kathmandu: Vajra Publications.

Nagoda, Sigrid de Barbentane and Siri E. H. Eriksen 2015. "The role of local power relations in household vulnerability to climate change in Humla, Nepal." In Tor Håkon Indreberg, Siri Eriksen, Karen O'Brien, and Linda Sygna (eds), *Climate change adaptation and development: transforming paradigms and practices*, pp. 200–18. New York: Routledge.

Namkha Rural Municipality and ICIMOD 2020. "Kailash confluence: reviving connections for a sustainable future." Photobook available at www.icimod.org/himaldoc, accessed 26.05.21.

Nebesky-Wojkowitz, René de 1996. *Oracles and demons of Tibet. The cult and iconography of the Tibetan protective deities.* Delhi: Book faith India.

Nepal Human Development Report 2014. "Beyond Geography, Unlocking Human Potential." Published by the National Planning Commission, the Government of Nepal.

Nepal Human Development Report 2020. "Beyond Graduation: Productive Transformation and Prosperity." Published by the National Planning Commission, the Government of Nepal.

Nornang, Ngawang L. 1990. "Monastic organisation and economy at Dwags-po bshad-grub-gling." In Lawrence Epstein and Richard .F. Sherburne (eds), *Reflections on Tibetan culture: essays in memory of Turrell V. Wylie*, pp. 249–69. Lewiston: The Edwin Mellen press.

Orsi, Robert A. 1997. "Everyday miracles: the study of lived religion." In David D. Hall (ed), *Lived religion in America: Toward a History of Practice*, pp. 3–21. Princeton: Princeton University Press.

Orsi, Robert A. 2002. "Is the study of lived religion irrelevant to the world we live in? Special presidential plenary address, Society for the scientific study of religion, Salt Lake City, November 2, 2002." *Journal for the scientific study of religion* 42(2): 169–74.

Pandey, Ram Niwas 1970a. "The ancient and medieval history of Western Nepal." *Ancient Nepal* 10: 53–62.

Pandey, Ram Niwas 1970b. "The ancient and medieval History of Western Nepal." *Ancient Nepal* 11: 45–60.

Pandey, Ram Niwas 1970c. "The Kallala dynasty of the Jumla valley." *Ancient Nepal* 12: 45–52.

Pandey, Ram Niwas 1971. "The history of the Kallala dynasty." *Ancient Nepal* 15: 39–61.

Petech, Luciano 1978. "The 'Bri-guṅ-pa sect in Western Tibet and Ladakh." In Louis Ligeti (ed), *Proceedings of the Csoma de Kőrös memorial symposium.* Budapest: Adadémiai Kiadó.

Petech, Luciano 1984. *Mediaeval history of Nepal (c. 750–1482).* Roma: IsMEO.

Petech, Luciano 1997. "Western Tibet: historical introduction." In Deborah Klimburg-Salter (ed), *Tabo, a lamp for the kingdom: Early Indo-Tibetan Buddhist Art in the Western Himalaya.* 229–55. Milan: Skira.

Petech, Luciano 2003 [1988]. "Ya-Ts'e, Gu-Ge, Pu-Rang: a new study." Reprinted in Alex McKay (ed), *The history of Tibet, Volume II, The medieval period: c. 850–1895, The development of Buddhist paramountcy*, pp. 33–52. London: RoutledgeCurzon.

Pirie, Fernanda 2005. "Tribe and state in Eastern Tibet: feuding, mediation and the negotiation of authority among the Amdo nomads." *Working paper no. 72*. Halle: Max Planck Institute for Social Anthropology.

Pirie, Fernanda 2007. *Peace and conflict in Ladakh: the constitution of a fragile web of order*. Leiden: Brill.

Pirie, Fernanda 2017. "Which 'Two Laws'? The concept of trimnyi (khrims gnyis) in medieval Tibet." *Cahiers d'Extrême Asie* 26: 41–60.

Pritzker, David 2000. "The treasures of Par and Kha-tse." *Orientations*, 31(7): 131–33.

Ramble, Charles 1984. "The lamas of Lubra: Tibetan Bonpo householder priests in Western Nepal." Unpublished PhD dissertation, University of Oxford.

Ramble, Charles 2002. "The victory song of Porong." In K. Buffetrille and H. Diemberger (eds), *Territory and Identity in Tibet and the Himalayas*, Tibetan Studies I. PIATS 2000: Tibetan Studies: Proceedings of the Ninth Seminar of the International Association for Tibetan Studies, Leiden 2000. pp 59–84. Leiden: Brill.

Ramble, Charles 2008a. *The navel of the demoness: Tibetan Buddhism and civil religion in Highland Nepal*. New York: Oxford University Press.

Ramble, Charles 2008b. "A nineteenth-century Bonpo pilgrim in Western Tibet and Nepal: episodes from the life of dKar ru grub dbang bsTan 'dzin rin chen." In Jean-Luc Achard (ed) *Tibetan Studies in Honour of Samten Karmay. Revue d'Études Tibétaines* 15(2), 481–502.

Ramble, Charles 2008c. *Tibetan sources for a social history of Mustang, Nepal. Volume 1: the archive of Te*. Halle: International Institute for Tibetan and Buddhist Studies.

Ramble, Charles 2012a. *Tibetan sources for a social history of Mustang, Nepal. Volume 2: the archives of the tantric priests of Tshognam*. Halle: International Institute for Tibetan and Buddhist Studies.

Ramble, Charles 2012b. *Tibetan sources for a social history of Mustang, Nepal. Volume 3: the archive of Baragaon*. Halle: International Institute for Tibetan and Buddhist Studies.

Ramble, Charles and Michael Vinding 1987. "The 'Bem-chag village record and the early history of Mustang District." *Kailash* 13(1–2): 5–48.

Rauber, Hanna 1980. "The Humli-Khyampas of far Western Nepal: a study in ethnogenesis." *Contributions to Nepalese Studies* 8(1): 57–80.

Rauber, Hanna 1982. "Humli-Khyampas and the Indian salt trade: changing economy of nomadic traders in Far West Nepal." In Philip Salzman (ed), *Contemporary nomadic and pastoral peoples: Asia and the North*. Studies in Third World Societies, 18, pp. 141–76. Williamsburg: College of William and Mary.

Regmi, Mahesh Chandra 1971. *Research papers vol 3*. Available at https://www.digitalhimalaya.com/collections/journals/regmi/, accessed 14.06.24.

Regmi, Mahesh Chandra 1978. *Land Tenure and Taxation in Nepal*. Kathmandu: Ratna Pustak Bhandar.

Regmi, Mahesh Chandra 1988. *Research papers vol 20*. Available at https://www.digitalhimalaya.com/collections/journals/regmi/, accessed 14.06.24.

Regmi, Mahesh Chandra 1999. *A study in Nepali economic history 1768–1846*. New Delhi: Androit Publishers.

Ricard, Matthieu 1994. *The life of Shabkar: autobiography of a Tibetan yogin*. Albany: State University of New York Press.

Rigzin, Tsepak 1984. "Rinchen Zangpo: the great Tibetan translator." *The Tibet Journal*, 9(3): 28–37.

Ronge, Veronika 1984. "Gedrecheselte Holzgefässe aus Tibet." *Sonderdrück aus Zentralasiatische Studien des Seminars für Sprach- und Kulturwissenschaft Zentralasiens der Universität Bonn*. 17 (1984), pp. 184–217. Wiesbaden: Otto Harrassowitz.

Ross, James L. 1983. "Adaptation to a changing salt trade: the view from Humla." *Contributions to Nepalese Studies*, 10(1–2): 43–49.

Roy, Rabindra 2010. "Contribution of NTFPS [Non-Timber Forest Products]

To livelihood in Upper Humla, Nepal." Unpublished PhD dissertation, the Asian Institute of Technology (AIT).

Samuel, Geoffrey 1993. *Civilized shamans: Buddhism in Tibetan societies*. Washington, D.C; London: Smithsonian Institution Press.

Sangyay, Thupten 1986. "Glossary of government, monastic and private taxation in Tibet." Translated by Tsepak Rigzin. *The Tibet Journal*. 11(1): 41–47.

Saville, Naomi M. 2001. "Practical strategies for pro-poor tourism: case study of pro-poor tourism and SNV in Humla District, West Nepal." PPT working paper no. 3. CRT, IIED and ODI.

Saxer, Martin 2013. "Between China and Nepal: trans-Himalayan Trade and the second life of development in Upper Humla." *Cross-Currents: East Asian History and Culture Review*. 8 (September): 31–52. https://cross-currents.berkeley.edu/e-journal/issue-8/saxer.

Saxer, Martin (2017). "New roads, old trades: neighbouring China in North-Western Nepal." In Martin Saxer and Zhang Juan (eds), *The art of neighbouring: making relations across China's borders. Asian borderlands*, Vol. 2. Amsterdam: Amsterdam University Press. pp. 73–92.

Schaik, Sam van 2011 (e-book). *Tibet: a history*. New Haven and London: Yale University Press.

Schneider, Hanna 2002. "Tibetan legal documents of South-West Tibet: structure and style." In Henk Blezer (ed), *Tibet, past and present*. Tibetan Studies I. PIATS 2000: Tibetan Studies: Proceedings of the Ninth Seminar of the International Association for Tibetan Studies, Leiden 2000. pp. 415–427. Leiden: Brill.

Schopen, Gregory 1997. *Bones, stones, and Buddhist Monks: collected papers on the archaeology, epigraphy, and texts of monastic Buddhism in India*. Honolulu: University of Hawai'i Press.

Schopen, Gregory 2004. *Buddhist monks and business matters—still more papers on monastic Buddhism in India.* Honolulu: University of Hawaii Press.

Schuh, Dieter 1981. *Grundlagen tibetischer Siegelkunde: eine Untersuchung über tibetische Siegelaufschriften in 'Phags-pa-Schrift.* St. Augustin: VGH-Wissenschaftsverlag.

Schuh, Dieter 1984. "Recht und Gesetz in Tibet." In L. Ligeti (ed), *Tibetan and Buddhist studies: commemorating the 200th anniversary of the birth of Alexander Csoma de Kőrös.* Budapest: Akadémiai Kiadó, 291–311.

Schuh, Dieter 1988. *Das Archiv des Klosters Bkra-šis-bsam-Gtan-Gliṅ von Skyid-Groṅ. Teil 1: Urkunden zur Klosterordnung, grundlegende Rechtsdokumente und demographisch bedeutsame Dokumente, Findbücher.* Bonn: VGH-Wissenschaftsverlag.

Schuh, Dieter 2000. "Srid ohne Chos? Reflektionen zum Verhältnis von Buddhismus und säkularer Herrschaft im tibetischen Kulturraum." In Christoph Cüppers (ed), *Religion and State (chos srid zung 'brel) in Traditional Tibet. Proceedings of a Seminar held in Lumbini, Nepal, March 2000*, pp. 291–298, Bhairahawa: Lumbini International Research Institute.

Schwieger, Peter 1997. "A note on the history of the cult of Padmasambhava on the 10th day of the month." In Helmut Krasser et al. (eds), *Tibetan studies. Proceedings of the 7th Seminar of the International Association for Tibetan Studies, Graz 1995.* VOL. II, pp. 851–57. Vienna: Verlag der Österreichischen Akademie der Wissenschaften.

Schwieger, Peter 2023. "The Tax System in Central and Far East Tibet Towards the End of the Ganden Phodrang Reign: An Outline of Its Structure and Terminology." In Alice Travers, Peter Schwieger and Charles Ramble (eds), *Taxation in Tibetan Societies: Rules, Practices and Discourses*, pp. 11–53. Leiden: Brill.

Scoones, Ian. 2009. "Livelihoods perspectives and rural development." *Journal of Peasant Studies* 36(1): 171–96.

Shahi, Raj Bahadur 2021. "Road track from Kalikot to Humla opens after seven years." *The Kathmandu Post* 27.11.21. https://kathmandupost.com/karnali-province/2021/02/28/road-track-from-kalikot-to-humla-opens-after-seven-years, accessed 28.02.21

Shakabpa, Tsepon Wangchuk Deden 2010. *One hundred thousand moons: an advanced political history of Tibet.* (2 vols). Leiden: Brill.

Shakya, Tsering, Tashi Rabgyas and John Crook 1994. "Monastic economics in Zangskar 1980." In John Crook and Henry Osmaston (eds), 1994. *Himalayan Buddhist villages: environment, resources, society and religious life in Zangskar, Ladakh*, pp. 601–630, Delhi: Motilal Banarsidass Publishers.

Sherring, Charles A. 1993 [1906]. *Western Tibet and the British borderland: the sacred country of Hindus and Buddhists with an account of the government, religion and customs of its peoples.* New Dehli: Asian Educational Services. [1st ed. London: Edward Arnold, Publisher to the India Office.]

Shneiderman, Sara 2015. "Regionalism, mobility, and 'the village' as a set of social relations: Himalayan reflections on a South Asian theme." *Critique of Anthropology* 35(3) 318–337.

Sinha, Ashish, Lowell Stott, Max Berkelhammer, Hai Cheng, R. Lawrence Edwards, Brendan Buckley, Mark Aldenderfer, and Manfred Mudelsee 2011. "A global context for megadroughts in monsoon Asia during the past millennium." *Quaternary Science Reviews* 30: 47–62.

Snellgrove, David L. 1967. *The Nine Ways of Bon: Excerpts from gZi-brjid.* Oxford: Oxford University Press.

Snellgrove, David L. 2004 [1987]. *Indo-Tibetan Buddhism: Indian Buddhists and their Tibetan successors.* Bangkok: Orchid Press.

Snellgrove, David L. and Tadeusz Skorupski with Phillip Denwood 1980. *The Cultural Heritage of Ladakh. Vol. 2: Zangskar and the Cave Temples of Ladakh.* Warminster: Aris and Phillips.

Snellinger, Amanda 2009. "Yuba, hamro pusta: youth and generational politics in Nepali political culture." *Studies in Nepali history and society* 14(1): 39–66.

Spiteri, Arian and Sanjay K. Nepal 2008. "Evaluating local benefits from conservation in Nepal's Annapurna Conservation Area". *Environmental Management,* 42(3): 391–401.

Stoddard, Heather 2004. "'Rekindling the flame': a note on royal patronage in tenth century Tibet." In Christoph Cüppers (ed), *The relationship between religion and state (chos srid zung 'brel) in traditional Tibet.* Lumbini: Lumbini International Research Institute.

Strøm, Axel K. 2001. "Continuity, adaptation and innovation: Tibetan monastic colleges in India." Unpublished PhD dissertation, University of Oslo.

Surkhang, Wangchen G. 1984. "The measurement of Lag 'don tax in Tibet." *The Tibet Journal* IX(1): 20–30.

Surkhang, Wangchen G. 1986. "Government, monastic and private taxation in Tibet." *The Tibet Journal* XI(1): 21–40.

Tenzin Namdak 1997. *sNga rabs Bod kyi byung ba brjod pa'i 'bel gtam lung gi snying po.* (*A study of the early history of Tibet according to Bon*). New Dehli: Paljor Publications.

Terrone, Antonio 2009. "Tibetan Buddhism beyond the Monastery: revelation and identity in rNying ma communities of present-day Kham." In Monica Esposito (ed), *Images of Tibet in the 19th and 20th centuries*, pp. 746–79. Paris: École Française d'Extrême-Orient (EFEO), Coll. "Études thématiques" (22.2).

Thargyal, Rinzin 2007. *Nomads of Eastern Tibet: social organization and economy of a pastral estate in the kingdom of Dege.* Edited by Toni Huber. Leiden, Brill.

Tournadre, Nicolas 2014. "The Tibetic languages and their classification." In Nathan W. Hill and Thomas Owen-Smith (eds), *Trans-Himalayan linguistics: historical and descriptive linguistics of the Himalayan area,* pp. 105–130. Berlin/Boston: Walter De Gruyter.

Travers, Alice 2023. "'When you count, everything is there, and when everything is there, everything vanishes": a criticism of tax collecting in Ngamring District (rdzong) during the first half of the 20th century.' In Alice Travers, Peter Schwieger and Charles Ramble (eds), *Taxation in Tibetan societies: rules, practices and discourses*, pp. 83–126. Leiden: Brill.

Travers, Alice, Peter Schwieger and Charles Ramble (eds) 2023. *Taxation in Tibetan societies: rules, practices and discourses*. Leiden: Brill.

Tsarong, Paljor 1987. "Economy and ideology on a Tibetan monastic estate in Ladakh: processes of production, reproduction and transformation." Unpublished PhD dissertation, University of Wisconsin-Madison.

Tsering Gyalpo 2006. (The religious history of Ngari in the land of snow, called the beautiful ornament) *mNga' ris chos 'byung gangs ljongs mdzes rgyan zhes bya ba*. Lhasa: Bod ljongs mi dmangs dpe skrun khang.

Tsering Gyalpo 2012. (A selection of festive songs from Ngari, Purang) *mNga' ris spu rangs kyi 'jig rten rtsa 'dzugs rten 'brel glu sna*. Beijing: Mi rigs dpe skrun khang.

Tsering Gyalpo, Christian Jahoda, Christiane Kalantari, and Patrick Sutherland, with contributions by Eva Allinger, Hubert Feiglstorfer and Kurt Tropper 2012. *Khorchag*. Lhasa: Bod ljongs bod yig dpe rnying dpe skrun khang [Old Tibetan Books Publishing House].

Tucci, Giuseppe 1956. Preliminary report on two scientific expeditions in Nepal. Roma: IsMEO.

Tucci, Giuseppe 1988. *Rin-chen-bzan-po and the Renaissance of Buddhism in Tibet around the Millenium*. New Delhi: Aditya Prakashan.

Tweed, Thomas A. 2015. "After the quotidian turn: interpretive categories and scholarly trajectories in the study of religion since the 1960s." *The Journal of Religion*, 95(3): 361–85.

Venturi, Federica 2013. "Creating sacred space: the religious geography of Sa skya, Tibet's medieval capital." Unpublished PhD dissertation, Indiana University.

Vitali, Roberto 1996. *The Kingdoms of Gu.ge Pu.hrang: According to mNga'.ris rgyal.rabs by Gu.ge mkhan.chen Ngag.dbang grags.pa*. Dharamsala: Tho.ling gtsug.lag.khang lo.gcig.stong 'khor.ba'i rjes.dran.mdzad sgo'i go.sgrig tshogs.chung.

Vitali, Roberto 1999. *Records of Tho.ling: a literary and historical reconstructin of the "mother monastery in Gu.ge*. Dharamsala: High Asia, Amnye Machen Institute.

Vitali, Roberto 2003. "A Chronology (*btsan rtsis*) of events in the history of mNga' ris skor gsum (Tenth-Fifteenth centuries)." In Alex McKay (ed), *The history of Tibet, Volume II, The medieval period: c. 850–1895, the development of Buddhist paramountcy*, pp. 53–89. London: Routledge Curzon.

Vitali, Roberto 2012. *A short history of Mustang (10th–15th century)*. McLeod Ganj: Amnye Machen Institute.

Wangdu, Pasang and Hildegard Diemberger 2000. *dBa' bzhed: The Royal Narrative Concerning the Bringing of Buddha's Doctrine to Tibet*. Vienna: Austrian Academy of Sciences Press.

Warren, Carol A. B. 1988. *Gender issues in field research*. Newbury Park: Sage Publications.

Warren, Carol A. B. 2001. "Gender and fieldwork relations." In Robert M. Emerson (ed), *Contemporary field research: perspectives and formulations*, pp. 203–23. Long Grove IL: Waveland Press.

Whelpton, John 2005. *A History of Nepal*. Cambridge: Cambridge University Press.

Wiebenga, Mariette and Tshewang Lama (in press). *Blue as Manasarovar, White as Kailash. Voices of a Vanishing World. Nyinba Valley in the Humla Himalaya of Northwest Nepal*. Kathmandu: Vajra Publications.

Wilde, Christopher Pekka 2001. Preliminary phonological analysis of the Limi dialect of Humla Bhotia. Unpublished M.A. thesis, University of Helsinki.

Wylie, Turrel 1959. "A standard system of Tibetan transcription." *Harvard Journal of Asiatic Studies*, 22:261–67.

Yeh, Emily T. 2021. "'The land belonged to Nepal but the people belonged to Tibet': Overlapping sovereignties and mobility in the Limi Valley Borderland." *Geopolitics*, 26(3): 919–945.

Documents from Limi

The Biography of Serta Rinpoche (alias Padma Lung rtogs rGya mtsho, 1891–1964) 1984. (Full title: *The biography of the siddha Pema Lungtog Gyatso, called the teaching on the path to enlightenment*, T. *Grub dbang padma lung rtogs rgya mtsho mchog gi rnam thar byang chub lam bstan zhes bya ba.*) Written by Tshe dbang rDo rje. 119 pages. Dalhousie: Damchoe Sangpo.

The Biography of Tshogkhang (*Tshogs khang*) *Rinpoche* (alias E ta rā dza or Pad ma bDe ba'i rGyal po, 1873–1933). (Full title: *Biography of the extraordinary life of Pema Dewa Gyalpo, called the ornament of the ocean of wisdom*, T. *mKhas sgrub rgya mtsho'i gtsug rgyan padma bde ba'i rgyal po'i rnam thar ngo mtshar mchog ldan zhes bya ba*). 53 pages.

Contract by the assembly of laity and monks 2011. (T. *lHa thog gnyis skya ser gnyis nas 'grig khrims kyi* [*khrim gi*] *gan rgya yin*). The document is a copy of the original contract from 2009.

Drigung dance manual (date unspecified). (Full title: *An introductory compendium to the 'cham dance called the lion's play*, T. *'Bri gung bka' brgyud kyi gar 'cham ngo sprod snying bsdus seng ge'i rnam rol zhes bya ba*). Dehradun: Drikung Kagyu Institute Jangchub Ling.

The *Drigung history of Kailash* 1896. (Full title: *The crystal mirror: an analysis which briefly explains the chronicle of past events at the great snow mountain Kailash together with the great lake Manasarovar*, T. *Gangs ri chen po ti se dang mtsho chen ma dros pa bcas kyi sngon byung gi lo rgyus mdor bsdus su brjod pa'i rab byed shel dkar me long*). The text is often referred to as *Ti se gnas bshad*, the short title printed on the folios. The text was composed by the thirty-third Drigung throne holder Tenzin Chökyi Lodrö.

The *Limi monastery regulations* 1806. (T. *Sle mi dgon gyi bca' yig*) The document was written by the twenty-ninth Drigung throne-holder, Tenzin Pema Gyaltsen.

The *Monastic recruitment contract* 1896. (Full title: *Contract [regarding] the obligation for each [household] with two sons in the three villages to [make] one son enter the monastery*, T. *Yul tsho gsum na bu gnyis byung phyin bu re chos sgor zhugs rgyu gan rgya*). Written during the visit of the thirty-third Drigung throne holder Tenzin Chökyi Lodrö.

The *Rinchen Ling dance manual* 1895. The untitled dance manual (*'cham yig*) was composed during the visit of the thirty-third Drigung throne holder Tenzin Chökyi Lodrö and consists of 48 lines written on cloth mounted on silk brocade.

The *Rinchen Ling list of ritual expenses* 1935(?) and 1995. (Full title: *Handbook of Rinchen Ling's offering expenses, the clear lamp*. T. *Rin chen gling gi mchod rgyun gtong gzhi'i [bzhi'i] len sprod [krod] lag khyer gsal ba'i sgron me*). The text exists in two copies: an older more detailed version and a more recent summary.

The *Rinchen Ling monastery inventory* 1870(?) [1690]. (Full title: *A summary of the great inventory of permanent [possessions of] the sacred Waltse Thubten Rinchen Ling temple, as an immaculate string of white lotuses*. T. *Chos 'khor dbal rtse'i gtsug lag khang thub bstan rin chen gling gi [gis] gtan deb [debs] chen mo don bsdus dri med padma dkar po'i 'phreng ba tshar du mngar ba*).

The *Rinchen Ling tax register* 1952(?). (Full title: *List of grain due as lease fee in the 8th month of the Water Dragon year*. T. *Chu 'brug zla 8 nang gi [kyi] bca' [ca] yong 'bab [bab] zhal 'bru [brus] tho bkod [bskod] pa la*).

The *Record of the resident lama's belongings*, 1949(?). (Full title: *Record of objects [belonging to] the lama's residence in Limi Rinchen Ling, the treasury of jewels*, T. *Sle mi rin chen gling gi bla brang sprod deb nor bu'i bang mdzod*).

Rinchen Ling monastery's old debt letters, (unnamed and undated).

The *Til Kundzom list of ritual expenses*, 1968(?). (Full title: *List of offerings to [Til Kundzom] Dongak Monastery*, T. *mDo sngags dgon [rgon] gyi mchod deb [debs]*).

Waltse tax register, ca 1950(?). Unnamed booklet consisting of two main documents referred to locally as the 'Book of the bca' tax' (*bCa' yig*) [1915] and the book of the *ban* tax' (*Ban yig*) [1888].

Other Literature in Tibetan

The *Biography of Chenga Lingpa* 2004. *sPyan snga 'bri gung gling pa'i rnam thar snyan pa'i 'brug sgra*. Composed by Rin chen phun tshogs chos kyi rgyal po (16th century). Printed in Lhasa. TBRC no. W00JW501203.

The *Catalogue of Khochar monastery* 1988. *Kho char dkar chag.* (Full title: *lHa bcas gro ba'i mchod sdong jo bo dngul sku mche gsum sngon byung gig tam rab brjod pa rin chen baidur sngon po'i pi wam.*) Composed by Ngag dbang bsod nams rgyal mtshan (1880). Dharamsala: Bod ljongs mnga' ris rig gzhung gces skyong khang.

The *Catalogue of the three silver brothers* 1996. *Jo bo rin po che ngul sku mched gsum rten dang brten pa bcas pa'i dkar chag rab dga'i glu dbyangs.* Composed by Nga dbang phrin las (Wa gindra karma, 16th century), introduction by Roberto Vitali. Dharamsala: Tho.ling gtsug.lag.khang lo.gcig.stong 'khor.ba'i rjes.dran.mdzad sgo'i go.sgrig tshogs.chung.

The *Collected biographical material* 1977. Collected biographical material about lo-chen rin-chen-bzań-po and his subsequent reembodiments: A reproduction of a collection of manuscripts from the library of Dkyil monastery in Spiti. Published by rDo rje Tshe brtan. Delhi: Laxmi Printing Works.

The *Collected biographical material* Text A: *Byang chub sems dpa' lo tsa+tsha ba rin chen bzang po'i khrungs rabs dka' spyad sgron ma rnam thar shel gyi phreng ba lu gu rgyud.* First composed by Gu ge khyi thang pa dpal ye shes in mTho gling. Pp. 51–128.

The *Collected biographical material* Text C: *bLa ma lo tsa+tsha ba chen po'i rnam par thar pa dri ma med pa shel gyi 'phreng ba zhes bya ba.* Based on the version composed by Gu ge khyi thang pa dpal ye shes in mTho gling. Pp. 230–278.

The *Great biography of the Kagyu masters* 1985. *bKa' brgyud kyi rnam thar chen mo rin po che'i gter mdzod dgos 'dod 'byung gnas.* A collection of lives of the successive masters in the transmission lineage of the 'Bri gung bKa' brgyud pa tradition in the Nepal-Tibet borderlands. Composed by rDo rje mdzes 'od/Don mo ri pa (13th century). Copy reproduced from a rare manuscript from Dzang Phelgye Ling in Limi. Published by D. Tsondu Senghe. Bir, Kangra H.P. TBRC no. 27600.

The *History of the three districts of Ngari* 1996. *sTod mnga' ris skor gsum gyi lo rgyus.* (Long title: *Bod ljongs stod mnga' ris skor gsum nye rabs chab srid kyi lo rgyus dang dgon sde khag zhig gsos grub pa'i gnas tshul/ spyi tshogs gsar pa'i 'phel shugs sogs rgyas par brjod pa'i 'bel gtam rin chen gter gyi phreng ba.*) Composed by mNga' ris srid gros rig gnas lo rgyus bsdu rub u yon lhan khang. Lhasa: Bod ljongs mi dmangs dpe skrun khang.

Internet Resources

Drikung website n.d. a) "A Brief History of the Drikung Kagyu Lineage of Tibetan Buddhism." http://www.drikung.org/drikung-kagyu-lineage#Chetsang, accessed 01.07.15.

Drikung website n.d. b) "His holiness the H.h. Drikung Kyabgon Chungtsang." http://www.drikung.org/their-holiness/hh-kyabgoen-chungtsang, accessed 12.07.15.

Drikung website n.d. c) "Drikung Kagyu Institute—history." https://www.drikung.org/drikung-kagyu-institute-history/, accessed 29.05.24.

Drikung website n.d. d) "Monasteries in the region of Purang." https://www.drikung.org/purang-and-limi/, accessed 07.06.24.

Drikung website n.d. e) "World wide centers." https://drikung.org/world-wide-centers, accessed 12.07.15.

Kailashzone website 2005. "Sustainable Solution for the monasteries and the monks of Limi." http://www.kailashzone.org/pages/project/limi.html, accessed 30.09.13.

Kailashzone website 2010. "Senge Tenzin Rinpoche." https://www.kailashzone.org/pages/senge_tenzin/tulku.php, accessed 29.05.24.

Limi Youth Society 2015. Facebook post about Senge Tenzin Relief Team. https://www.facebook.com/pages/Limi-youth-society/759595150739637?fref=ts, accessed 20.06.15.

The Social Welfare Council website 2019. "NGOs affiliated with Social Welfare Council (2034–2076 Asadh)." https://swc.org.np/sites/default/files/19/NGOs-affiliated-with-SWC-%20upto%20F.Y.%202075_76.pdf, accessed 10.06.24.

Teaching by Togden Rinpoche n.d. http://www.coreofculture.org/a-sacred-drikung-teaching-on-cham-by-his-eminence-togden-rinpoche-of-phyiang-monastery.html, accessed 18.07.15.

Index

Page references in **bold type** indicate a more in-depth treatment of the subject.

www.ingramcontent.com/pod-product-compliance
Lightning Source LLC
Chambersburg PA
CBHW071248230926
51849CB00001B/276
* 9 7 8 9 0 0 4 7 1 3 6 6 6 *